Mountaineering Tourism

In May 1993 the British Mountaineering Council met to discuss the future of high altitude tourism. Of concern to attendees were reports of queues on Everest and reference was made to mountaineer Peter Boardman calling Everest an 'amphitheater of the ego'. Issues raised included environmental and social responsibility and regulations to minimize impacts. In the years that have followed there has been a surge of interest in climbing Everest, with one day in 2012 seeing 234 climbers reach the summit. Participation in mountaineering tourism has surely escalated beyond the imagination of those who attended the meeting 20 years ago.

This book provides a critical and comprehensive analysis of all pertinent aspects and issues related to the development and the management of the growth area of mountaineering tourism. By doing so it explores the meaning of adventure and special reference to mountain-based adventure, the delivering of adventure experience, and adventure learning and education. It further introduces examples of settings (alpine environments) where a general management framework could be applied as a baseline approach in mountaineering tourism development. Along with this general management framework, the book draws evidence from case studies derived from various mountaineering tourism development contexts worldwide, to highlight the diversity and uniqueness of management approaches, policies and practices.

Written by leading academics from a range of disciplinary backgrounds, this insightful book will provide students, researchers and academics with a better understanding of the unique aspects of tourism management and development of this growing form of adventure tourism across the world.

Ghazali Musa is a Professor, a medical doctor and a PhD in tourism. He is the Head of the Services Research and Innovation Center and the Department of Strategy and Business Policy at the Faculty of Business and Accountancy, University of Malaya, Kuala Lumpur. He has a wide interest in tourism research which includes scuba diving tourism, mountaineering tourism, backpacking tourism, medical tourism and international second home.

James Higham is Professor of Tourism at the University of Otago (New Zealand) and Visiting Professor at the University of Stavanger (Norway). His research interests focus on tourism and environmental change at global, regional and local scales of analysis, with particular interests in climate change and sustainable mobility. He serves as co-editor of the *Journal of Sustainable Tourism*.

Anna Thompson-Carr is a Senior Lecturer at the Department of Tourism, University of Otago, New Zealand. She is on the editorial boards for *Tourism in Marine Environments* and the *Journal of Heritage Tourism*. Her research interests focus on the interdisciplinary aspects of sustainable ecotourism, adventure tourism, wilderness management and cultural landscapes. She is a founding Co-Director of the Centre for Recreation Research at the University of Otago. Prior to academia Anna was co-owner of two adventure tourism businesses and continues to be interested in industry issues related to guiding, interpretation, visitor safety and best practices.

Contemporary geographies of leisure, tourism and mobility

Series Editor: C. Michael Hall

Professor at the Department of Management, College of Business and Economics, University of Canterbury, Christchurch, New Zealand

The aim of this series is to explore and communicate the intersections and relationships between leisure, tourism and human mobility within the social sciences.

It will incorporate both traditional and new perspectives on leisure and tourism from contemporary geography, e.g. notions of identity, representation and culture, while also providing for perspectives from cognate areas such as anthropology, cultural studies, gastronomy and food studies, marketing, policy studies and political economy, regional and urban planning, and sociology, within the development of an integrated field of leisure and tourism studies.

Also, increasingly, tourism and leisure are regarded as steps in a continuum of human mobility. Inclusion of mobility in the series offers the prospect to examine the relationship between tourism and migration, the sojourner, educational travel, and second home and retirement travel phenomena.

The series comprises two strands:

Contemporary geographies of leisure, tourism and mobility aims to address the needs of students and academics, and the titles will be published in hardback and paperback. Titles include:

Routledge studies in contemporary geographies of leisure, tourism and mobility is a forum for innovative new research intended for research students and academics, and the titles will be available in hardback only. Titles include:

Mountaineering Tourism

**Edited by Ghazali Musa, James Higham
and Anna Thompson-Carr**

Routledge
Taylor & Francis Group

LONDON AND NEW YORK

First published 2015 by Routledge

2 Park Square, Milton Park, Abingdon, Oxon OX14 4RN
711 Third Avenue, New York, NY 10017, USA

Routledge is an imprint of the Taylor & Francis Group, an informa business

First issued in paperback 2017

British Library Cataloguing in Publication Data
A catalogue record for this book is available from the British Library

Library of Congress Cataloging in Publication Data
A catalog record for this book has been requested

ISBN: 978-1-138-78237-2 (hbk)
ISBN: 978-1-138-08393-6 (pbk)

Typeset in Times New Roman
by Wearset Ltd, Boldon, Tyne and Wear

This book is dedicated to the
memory of
Sir Dato' Dr Peter Mooney
(1923–2015)

Contents

Figures

Tables

Contributors

Agustina Barros is a Researcher at the Environmental Futures Research Institute at Griffith University in Australia. She has conducted her Masters and PhD examining the ecological impacts of tourism in alpine environments in the Andes region in South America. Her research interests include recreation ecology, alpine ecology and protected areas management and conservation.

Paul Beedie is currently a Principal Lecturer in the Sociology of Adventure and Sport at the University of Bedfordshire, UK. He is a dedicated outdoor activist and he teaches across a range of undergraduate and post-graduate courses. His research has been driven by an interest in adventure across its manifestations as education, recreation and tourism and is particularly focused on explorations of risk, identity and community.

Mike Boyes is an Associate Professor in outdoor education at the School of Physical Education, Sport and Exercise Science at the University of Otago, Dunedin, New Zealand. His research primarily focuses on outdoor education and outdoor recreation. He is particularly interested in teaching and learning in the outdoors, outdoor leadership and adventure engagement by older people.

Eric Brymer is a Principal Lecturer at Manchester Metropolitan University in the UK and currently holds an Adjunct Associate Professor position at Queensland University of Technology, Australia. He specializes in researching the psychological benefits of nature-based experiences with a particular interest in explicating psychological issues in nature-based extreme sports.

Carl Cater is a Senior Lecturer in Tourism at Aberystwyth University, Wales, and his research centres on the experiential turn in tourism and the subsequent growth of special interest sectors, particularly adventure tourism and ecotourism. He is a fellow of the Royal Geographical Society, a qualified pilot, diver, lifesaver, mountain and tropical forest leader, and maintains an interest in both the practice and pursuit of sustainable outdoor tourism activity.

Lee Davidson is Senior Lecturer in Museum and Heritage Studies at Victoria University of Wellington, New Zealand. Her research interests include the construction of meaning and identity through the experience of cultural and natural heritage. She is co-author, with R.A. Stebbins, of *Serious leisure and nature: Sustainable consumption in the outdoors* (Palgrave, 2011). She has also published on sustainable tourism and museum visiting. She is currently involved in a long-term transnational study of international touring exhibitions and their contribution to cultural diplomacy and intercultural understanding.

Adele Doran is a Lecturer of Tourism Management and a PhD student in the Sheffield Business School at Sheffield Hallam University. Her area of study is in the experiences of women participating in organized adventure tourism and the role of gender in mountaineering tourism.

Mahdi Esfahani is a Lecturer at Chabahar Maritime University in Iran and recently completely his PhD at the University of Malaya, Kuala Lumpur. He specializes in sport management and sport tourism. His current research focuses on mountaineering behaviour in Mt Kinabalu, Malaysia.

Alan Ewert PhD, is a Distinguished and Titled Professor at Indiana University. He is the holder of the Patricia and Joel Meier Endowed Chair in Outdoor Leadership, and serves as the Interim Chair for the Department of Environmental Health in Indiana University's School of Public Health. He has climbed and guided in North America, the Andes, Mexico and Central America, Europe and Nepal. His research interests include motivations for adventure recreation and the impacts of participation in adventure education programmes.

C. Michael Hall works at the Department of Management, Marketing and Entrepreneurship, University of Canterbury, New Zealand. At the time of writing he was undertaking research on World Heritage and high-altitude tourism in Finland and Mauritius, the geography of hummus in Occupied Palestine and green hotels in Merzhausen, Germany.

Guosheng Han is an Associate Professor at the Department of Tourism Management in the School of Business at Shandong University at Weihai, China. He received his PhD in tourism geography in the School of Geography of Nanjing University. His research focuses on community tourism development in mountainous areas.

James Higham is Professor of Tourism at the University of Otago, New Zealand, and Visiting Professor at the University of Stavanger, Norway. His research interests focus on tourism and environmental change at global, regional and local scales of analysis, with particular interests in climate change and sustainable mobility. He serves as co-editor of the *Journal of Sustainable Tourism*.

Charlie Hobbs is an internationally qualified (IFMGA/UIAGM) mountain and ski guide and runs several guiding companies at Aoraki Mt Cook. He has been on expeditions to remote areas, including Irian Jaya and Antarctica, where he made several first ascents. Charlie has contributed over 25 years of service to the NZ Mountain Safety Council.

Mary Hobbs is an NZ Registered Nurse and has accompanied Charlie on expeditions. After a career switch to writing and publishing, she published the award-winning *New Zealand Outside* magazine for ten years. She has written five books (several on mountain histories), with a sixth due out in 2015. Charlie and Mary own The Old Mountaineers' Cafe, Bar, Restaurant and Photographic Gallery at Aoraki Mt Cook (est. 2003).

Ming Feng Huang is an Assistant Professor in Tourism Management in the Global Institute of Management and Economics at Dongbei University of Finance and Economics, Dalian, China. He is a keen hiker and photographer of mountain environments.

Margaret E. Johnston lives in Thunder Bay, Ontario, and works for Lakehead University in the School of Outdoor Recreation, Parks and Tourism as a professor. She teaches in the areas of polar tourism, risk management and recreation programming. Her research examines the changes in and challenges of tourism in the Arctic and Antarctic, and she has recently completely a multiyear study on developments in cruise tourism in the Canadian Arctic within the context of climate change. Current research examines management of pleasure craft in the Canadian Arctic with a focus on safety and preparedness, interactions with the environment and community involvement in the pleasure craft sector.

Selina Khoo is a Senior Lecturer at the Sports Centre, University of Malaya. Her research focus on physical activity and sports for various populations including women and persons with disabilities. She is the current Vice President of the Asian Society for Adapted Physical Education and Exercise (ASAPE) and a member of the Commonwealth Advisory Body on Sport (CABOS).

Alan A. Lew is a Professor in the Department of Geography, Planning, and Recreation at Northern Arizona University where he teaches courses in geography, urban planning and tourism. He is the founding editor-in-chief of the journal *Tourism Geographies* and has published several books on geography and tourism, including *Tourism Geography*, 3rd edition, with Stephen Williams. His interests and writings focus on tourism across East and Southeast Asia.

Brent Lovelock is Associate Professor at the Department of Tourism, University of Otago, Dunedin, New Zealand. His research interests are guided by the principles of sustainable and ethical tourism. He has recently co-authored a book *The ethics of tourism* (Routledge, 2012). His recent work focuses on consumptive wildlife tourism, medical tourism, and tourism policy and planning. He also has an interest in nature-based recreation, as Co-Director of the Centre for Recreation Research at the University of Otago.

Susan Houge Mackenzie is an Assistant Professor in Recreation, Parks and Tourism Administration at California Polytechnic State University, San Luis Obispo. She received her BA in Psychology from Pomona College and her PhD from the University of Otago, New Zealand. She uses mixed-methods and positive psychology theories to investigate optimal experiences and psychological wellbeing amongst adventure participants and guides. Her research is published across tourism, leisure, psychology and education journals.

Kokel Melubo teaches at the College of African Wildlife Management-Mweka, Tanzania. He is currently undertaking PhD studies in tourism at the Otago Business School, University of Otago, New Zealand.

Erik Monasterio is a Consultant in Forensic Psychiatry, Deputy Clinical Director and Senior Clinical Lecturer, with the Canterbury District Health Boards Regional Forensic Service and the University of Otago. He is also an experienced mountaineer and explorer who has climbed and guided in most of the world's main mountain ranges. He has climbed more than 50 new routes, many on previously unclimbed mountains. His research interests include: personality factors associated with extreme sports, criminality and drug addiction; morbidity, mortality and physiological stress responses in extreme sports; inappropriate use of psychiatric medications; and impacts of trade law on health.

Yang (Sunny) Mu is a graduate student in Geography at the University of Waterloo. Her academic interests are on heritage tourism, mountain culture and sacred landscapes. Her research is focused on geography of sacred landscapes, with particular emphasis on local meanings and interpretations of cultural and spiritual landmarks, and their significance for tourism development in the Everest region of Nepal.

Ghazali Musa is a Professor, a medical doctor and a PhD in tourism. He is the Head of the Services Research and Innovation Center and the Department of Strategy and Business Policy at the Faculty of Business and Accountancy, University of Malaya, Kuala Lumpur. He has a wide interest in tourism research which includes scuba diving tourism, mountaineering tourism, backpacking tourism, medical tourism and international second homes.

Sanjay K. Nepal is Professor in the Department of Geography and Environmental Management, University of Waterloo, Canada. His speciality is in tourism and conservation geographies, primarily working in remote and peripheral locations including high mountains in the Nepalese Himalaya and the Canadian Rockies. He has a PhD in Geography from the University of Bern, Switzerland, and more than 20 years of research contributions in international conservation, and tourism.

Gyan P. Nyaupane is Associate Professor and Graduate Program Director in the School of Community Resources and Development at Arizona State University, USA, where he teaches graduate and undergraduate courses in sustainable tourism, critical issues in community development and tourism planning. He is also affiliated with the Julie Ann Wrigley Global Institute of Sustainability as a senior sustainably scientist. His research interests include tourism, conservation and livelihood linkages, heritage, community development and sustainability in South Asia, Africa and North America. Prior to academia, he worked for Mt Everest National Park.

Catherine Marina Pickering is Professor at the School of Environment, Griffith University, Gold Coast, Australia. She has over 200 publications including 100 refereed journal papers. Her research interests include recreation ecology, alpine plant ecology, climate change and protected areas management.

Gill Pomfret is a Senior Lecturer in Tourism at Sheffield Hallam University. She has published research papers about mountaineer tourists and adventure tourists, and she has co-authored a book on adventure tourism. Her current research interests focus on the motivations and emotional experiences of these tourists, and the role of gender in mountaineering tourism.

Zac Robinson is a historian and Assistant Professor in the Faculty of Physical Education and Recreation at the University of Alberta, where he teaches the history of parks, travel writing and tourism. An avid climber and skier, he is a principal member of the Canadian Mountain Studies Initiative and presently serves as the Vice-President of Mountain Culture for the Alpine Club Canada.

Robert A. Stebbins FRSC is Professor Emeritus at the University of Calgary. His most recent books include: *Careers in serious leisure: From dabbler to devotee in search of fulfillment* (Palgrave Macmillan, 2014) and (with Sam Elkington) *The serious leisure perspective: An introduction* (Routledge, 2014).

Stacy Taniguchi PhD, is an Associate Professor at Brigham Young University's Marriott School of Management in the Department of Recreation Management. His research focuses on experiential education as it relates to leadership skills and meaningful experiences. He has guided climbers in Alaska, the Andes, Europe, Africa and the Himalayas.

Thinaranjeney Thirumoorthi is a PhD candidate in the Department of Business Policy and Strategy, Faculty of Business and Accountancy, University of Malaya. She is interested in backpacking, scuba diving, homestay, medical and rural tourism research.

Anna Thompson-Carr is a Senior Lecturer at the Department of Tourism, University of Otago, New Zealand. She is on the editorial boards for *Tourism in Marine Environments* and the *Journal of Heritage Tourism*. Her research interests focus on the interdisciplinary aspects of sustainable ecotourism, adventure tourism, wilderness management and cultural landscapes. She is a founding Co-Director of the Centre for Recreation Research at the University of Otago. Prior to academia she was co-owner of two adventure tourism businesses and continues to be interested in industry issues related to guiding, interpretation, visitor safety and best practices.

Foreword

This book is a compilation of wide ranging chapters and case studies, written by recognized and emerging scholars worldwide, who research in different areas of mountaineering tourism and recreation. Our treatment of mountaineering tourism in this volume derives its structure from Weed and Bull's (2004) theorization of sport and tourism as a complex interplay of activity, people and place. In this context 'activity' relates to the geographical, historical and social development of mountaineering. 'People' focuses on those who (directly or indirectly) engage in the activity of mountaineering. 'Place' addresses unique destination contexts relating to the hosting of mountaineers to facilitate their climb, impacts on environment and host community, together with management practices. The book defines mountaineering tourism as the activities of mountaineering tourists, their interplay with members of the climbing community and all associated stakeholders, together with associated impacts and management at the environmental and local community level.

Employing this tripartite structure, the first part of the book addresses the activity of mountaineering tourism in terms of geography, history, the concept of wilderness experience and adventure mountaineering, guided mountaineering and the roles of alpine clubs. It is further illustrated by three case studies which address the early development of mountain recreation in New Zealand, mountaineering tourism in Taiwan and the commercial development of Southern Alps Guiding (New Zealand). The second part attends to 'people', exploring the narrative construction of self through a commitment to mountaineering, gender issues in mountaineering, mountaineering tourism experiences, mountaineers' personality and mountaineering risk. The part is further illustrated by two case studies which are mountaineering flow experience and mountaineers' responsible behaviour related to safety and security. Third, we deploy the concept of 'place' to examine the environmental impacts, mountaineering commodification and risk perception, ethical issues in mountaineering, health and safety issues and management perspectives of mountaineering tourism, as they exist in different spatial contexts. Four case studies included in this part are mountaineering and climate change, human waste management on Aconcagua, mountaineering on Mt Everest and working conditions of high altitude porters on Mt Kilimanjaro. In drawing together the insights provided by these chapters and case studies, we consider critical issues arising from the commercialization of mountaineering practices, and consider the future of mountaineering tourism and emerging research directions. Our overarching aim is a critical treatment of the possibilities and pitfalls of mountaineering tourism.

Reference

Weed, M. E. and Bull, C. J. (2004) *Sport tourism: Participants, policy and providers*, Oxford: Butterworth Heinemann.

Acknowledgements

The editing of this volume has been a collective effort and we have benefited greatly from the support of many people who were instrumental to the completion of this book. We are most grateful for the strong support of Philippa Mullins (Editorial Assistant) and Emma Travis (Commissioning Editor) at Routledge. Philippa's swift and supportive responses to our regular communications were critical to the completion of this book. We also enjoyed the energy and commitment of our chapter authors, who have contributed their theoretical and empirical research insights to this edited volume. This project would have been a completely different experience without the expert assistance of Thinaranjeney Thirumoorthi (Research Assistant and PhD Scholar at the University of Malaya) who was outstanding in providing administrative support for the editors. Her help greatly facilitated progress to completion of this volume. We also acknowledge the indexing of Sam Spector (University of Otago) with thanks. During the course of this book project Ghazali was supported by the University of Malaya with a period of sabbatical leave, for part of which he was hosted by the Department of Tourism, University of Otago (New Zealand). Along with the University of Stavanger, where James holds a Visiting Professorship, we are grateful to the support of our institutions.

Personally, Ghazali acknowledges the support of his father Sir Dato' Dr Peter Money for his valuable proofing and editing contributions and insightful discussions, and his daughter, Zara Ghazali, for keeping eyes on him when he deeply immersed into this book project at home.

Personally, James acknowledges the support of friends and members of the research community. He has benefited from the support of collaborators, family and friends including Polly and Charles Higham, Tom Higham, Katerina Douka, Emma Holt, Caroline Orchiston, Diana Evans, Jo O'Brien, Lars Bejder, Bill Bramwell, Colin Campbell-Hunt, Scott Cohen, Tara Duncan, Truls Engstrøm, Eke Eijgelaar, Sebastian Filep, Wiebke Finkler, Stefan Gössling, Åsa Grahn, C. Michael Hall, Jan Vidar Haukeland, Tom and Lorriane Hinch, Janet Hoek, Debbie Hopkins, Diana Kutzner, Bernard Lane, Francis Markham, Paul Peeters, Arianne Reis, Sabine Reim, Sam Spector, Sarah Tapp, Odd Inge Vistad, Trudie Walters, Ben Wooliscroft, Tianyu Ying and Martin Young.

Personally, Anna acknowledges the wonderful support of colleagues, friends and students at the Department of Tourism, University of Otago, especially

Brent Lovelock, Hazel Tucker, Stuart Grant, Sebastian Filep and Tara Duncan. Further afield the support of New Zealand Mountain Guides' Association members especially Charlie Hobbs, Mike Roberts, Guy Cotter, Pete Brailsford, Anne Palmer and John Entwistle. A special mention has to be made of climbers no longer here who encouraged Anna to love mountains – Andy Harris, Gary Ball, Rob Hall, Brede Arkless, Gottlieb Braun-Elwert and Anna's mother Relda. Mountain friends Gretchen Weeks, MaryAnn Geddes, Andy Thompson, Pip Walter, Simon Middlemass, Dave Bamford, Chas Tanner, Rob Mitchell, Shelagh Ferguson, Val Kerr, Maryrose Fowlie, Sandy Nelson, Chippy Wood, the Arkless family, Caryl, Baden and Dierdre.

Finally, our careers continue to be anchored by the love and support of our immediate families; Peter Money and Zara Ghazali; Ben Carr, Jessica Thompson-Carr and Rebecca Hobbs, Jason, Amelia and Oliver Neave; Linda Buxton, Ali, Katie and George Higham.

Ghazali Musa
Kuala Lumpur, Malaysia
James Higham
Dunedin, New Zealand
Anna Thompson-Carr
Dunedin, New Zealand

Abbreviations

ACA	Annapurna Conservation Area
ACAP	Annapurna Conservation Area Project
ACC	Accident Compensation Corporation
ACMG	Association of Canadian Mountain Guides
AMGA	American Mountain Guides Association
AMS	acute mountain sickness
BMC	British Mountaineering Council
BMGA	British Mountain Guides' Association
CBC	Canadian Broadcasting Corporation
CFA	Confirmatory Factor Analysis
cm	centimetres
CTAA	Chinese Taipei Alpine Association
DfID	UK Department for International Development
DOC	Department of Conservation
EBC	Everest Base Camp
EDT	Expectation Disconfirmation Theory
EFA	Exploratory Factor Analysis
ENSA	*Ecole Nationale de Ski et d'Alpinisme*
EOG	European Outdoor Group
ft	feet
g	gram
HAPE	high altitude pulmonary oedema
HAS	high altitude sickness
IAATO	International Association of Antarctic Tourism Operators
IFMGA	International Federation of Mountain Guides' Associations
IFMGA/UIAGM	International Federation of Mountain Guides' Associations or *Union Internationale des Associations de Guides de Montagnes*
IML	International Mountain Leader
in	inches
IPCC	Intergovernmental Panel on Climate Change
IUCN	International Union for the Conservation of Nature
IYM	International Year of Mountains

kg	kilogram
KINAPA	Kilimanjaro National Park
km	kilometre
KPAP	Kilimanjaro Porters Assistance Project
LMCs	lodge management committees
LS	life satisfaction
m	metres
mi	miles
MoTCA	Ministry of Tourism and Civil Aviation
MSL	mean sea level
Mt	Mount
NMA	Nepal Mountaineering Association
NOLS	National Outdoor Leadership School
NTNC	National Trust for Nature Conservation
NZMGA	New Zealand Mountain Guides' Association
PBC	perceived behavioural control
PNAs	protected natural areas
QNNP	Qomolangma National Nature Preserve
RSPB	Royal Society for Protection of Birds
SAR	search and rescue
SCARRA	Skilled Commercial Adventure Recreation in Remote Areas
SCD	sudden cardiac death
SEM	structural equation modelling
SLA	Sustainable Livelihoods Approach
SS	sensation seeking
SWB	subjective well-being
TCI	Temperament and Character Inventory
TPB	Theory of Planned Behaviour
TSP	transceiver, shovel and probe
UIAA	International Mountaineering and Climbing Federation
UNEP	United Nations Environment Programme
VDCs	village development committees
WDCs	women's development committees

1 Mountaineering tourism

Activity, people and place

*James Higham, Anna Thompson-Carr and
Ghazali Musa*

On 29 May 1953 two climbers in the ninth British Everest expedition, Sir
Edmund Hillary (New Zealand) and Sherpa Tenzing Norgay (Nepal), became
the first mountaineers to stand on the summit of Mt Everest. Four decades later,
in December 1993, Myra Shackley published an article in *Tourism Management*
entitled 'No room at the top?' in which she reported on a meeting about the
future of high-altitude tourism hosted by the British Mountaineering Council at
the Royal Geographical Society, London, in May of that year. Issues raised at
the meeting included the need to ensure reciprocity between expeditions, trekking agencies and local communities, environmental and social responsibility
and regulations to minimize impacts. The meeting attendees did not want to see
mountains as 'giant cash cows' (Shackley 1993: 485) and a member of the
United Nations Mountain Agenda group attending the meeting raised the issue
of the effects of climate change.

What was notable about the meeting was that climbers, adventure tourism
operators and international organizations addressed issues related to mountaineering tourism (commercial, guided and non-guided). Of concern to attendees at
the meeting were reports of queues on Everest and Shackley commented that
'On 12 May 1993, 38 mountaineers climbed Everest on the same day' (Shackley
1993: 483). Reference was made to British mountaineer Peter Boardman calling
Everest an 'amphitheater of the ego'. It is only possible to speculate on what the
British Mountaineering Council's invitees would have thought about the surge
of interest in climbing Everest (and the other Seven Summits) in the years that
have followed. Nepal and Mu (this volume) note in reference to Mt Everest that
'in 2012, a record 169 climbers reached the top on a single day from the Nepalese side' on a day in which a total of 234 climbers summited Mt Everest. In the
20 years since the British Mountaineering Council meeting, participation in
mountaineering tourism has surely escalated beyond the imagination of those
who attended that meeting. This book seeks to critically address the development of mountaineering tourism phenomena, exploring the role of people –
mountain tourists, mountaineers, porters, guides, support workers and local
communities – and the social and environmental impacts of mountaineering
tourism in doing so.

Defining mountains

Mountains are one of the major physical landforms on Earth. Defined primarily in terms of steepness and elevation, mountains are also now recognized by the United Nations as 'fragile environments' that are susceptible to human impact, subject to slow impact recovery rates and prone in fact to irreversible ecological damage (UNCED 1992). Mountains can be defined in physical terms that have been extensively measured and mapped, although the topography of the marine environment largely remains a mystery. The United National Environmental Programme provides various categorizations of mountains (Blyth *et al.* 2002) that capture the wide diversity of mountain environments in terms of topography and steepness, altitude and elevation, geology and geomorphology, ecology and biomass, and latitude and longitude.

Mountains are prominent on local and global agendas as places of relatively undisturbed nature and important natural resources (Goode *et al.* 2000). Most notably mountains are catchments of fresh water through rainfall or glacial storage and release. From upland mountain regions issue the great freshwater riverways of the world – the Yangtze, Mekong and Ganges, Nile and Euphrates (to name a few) being the birthplaces of human civilizations. Mountains may provide resources for agriculture, forestry, energy generation and extractive industries such as mining. Given the diversity of mountain environments, they are also places of species and genetic diversity, all of which may be considered to offer ecosystem services to human communities and intrinsic ecocentric value for past, present and future generations (Næss 1989).

Indigenous and western cultures have been observed to develop symbolic, emotional and ancestral links with landscapes. This is particularly apparent if successive generations have inhabited an area, and a 'sense of place' or 'inside-ness' for the landscape has been observed amongst members of non-indigenous cultures (Tuan 1974; Relph 1976, 1985; Bender 1993; Crang 1998). For many indigenous people around the world, mountains hold a special significance. Aoraki is held in the same regards by Māori as Uluru in Australia is significant for the Anangu Pitjintjara people or Sagarmatha for the Nepalese Sherpa and Buddhist communities in Nepal.

Managing the indigenous, often intangible, values of mountain landscapes is a challenging problem for resource managers (Shackley 2001; Carr 2004; Digance 2003). Mountains may have spiritual or culturally significant values and meanings for landscape, that may or may not be shared with 'outsiders' such as tourists (Relph 1976, 1985; Atkins *et al.* 1998). One notable impact of mountaineering has been the loss of traditional mountain place names that reflected specific associations with traditional lands, through the practice of renaming mountains upon first ascents, for instance McKinley (Denali), Everest (Saga-martha or Chomolongma) and Aoraki Mt Cook. Many indigenous peoples now work as porters, guides or area managers in mountaineering tourism destinations around the world. There are also many instances of indigenous peoples who are mountaineers and mountaineering tourists.

The relationship between humanity and mountains has a fascinating history (Glacken 1967). In classical times, mountains were places of worship that were associated with the deities. In Ancient Greece, sports were performed at Olympia where mountains offered immediate proximity to the Gods. Mountains remain places of religious or secular importance (Goode *et al.* 2000). Environmental philosophy explains that the sacredness of nature was undermined by the advent of agriculture and sedentism, the earliest evidence of which comes from the fertile crescent of the Tigris and Euphrates rivers, and was further eroded with the advent of industrialization (Oelschaeger 1991) and urbanization (Cronon 1995). Industrialization has greatly accelerated the humanizing of the Earth, transforming nature and reducing it to a human scale (Dubos 1972), or destroying nature altogether through largely unrestrained neoliberal capitalist 'development' (Harvey 2010).

One of the few major landforms that offered some resistance to this otherwise wholesale and continuing transformation was mountains. Viewed predominantly in the west as unproductive 'wastelands' (Hall 1992), most mountain regions were historically ignored in terms of agricultural development, and subject only to the least intensive forms of subsistence economy. European environmental philosophy at the time of colonization of North America in the seventeenth and eighteen centuries is informative. Wilderness areas survived in contemporary Europe at this time. Influenced by Judeo-Christian traditions (Oelschleager 1991) the colonists brought with them a value system based on survival to which untamed 'wild' nature was considered a threat. Morality and social order was considered to break down at the North American frontier, beyond which 'forests swarmed with demons and evil spirits' (Nash 1980). Mountain wilderness engendered feelings of insecurity and danger and were viewed as a 'cursed and chaotic wasteland' (Nash 1980) against which civilization was engaged in a ceaseless struggle.

Mountains were to the fore in the profound changes of modern environmental consciousness (Oelschlaeger 1991), inspired by the nineteenth century works of Henry David Thoreau and, some decades later, John Muir and Aldo Leopold (Oelschlaeger 1991; Grumbine 1994). Their works raised a consciousness of the complexity of the relationship between humanity and nature, drawing attention to concerns about the transformation of wilderness, nature conservation and sustainability (Dubos 1972). With the rise of European Romanticism, mountains came to be conceived as sublime nature – places of unimaginable beauty. Wilderness philosophy arose from the growing divinity of mountainous nature (Oelschlaeger 1991).

The influence of European Romanticism influenced the later colonization of New Zealand in the early nineteenth century. Initially wild nature was considered a threat to European settlement of New Zealand ('anti-Wilderness'). However, while lowland areas were systematically cleared for agricultural production (Hall and Higham 2000), early Europeans also marvelled at the sublime nature of the Southern Alps. Fiordland, with 'its girdle of high mountains and waterfalls is … an inspiration … to every beholder' (James McKerrow 1862, cited by Easdale 1988). Mountains were considered places of sublime nature; manifestations of the unimaginable beauty of nature. Hall (1992) charts the course of nature protection from 'wastelands to world heritage'; a philosophical transition that brought utility value to mountain conservation areas through recreation and tourism. Clearly mountains represent a complex interplay of physical and cultural dimensions (Cronon 1995).

In terms of this interplay, it is of little surprise that the cultural values associated with 'wild nature' are the subject of intense debate (Sarkar 2012). Fundamentally contrasting perspectives arise in the North and South, and between Europe and the new world (neo-Europe). The European context is one of historically cultural landscapes in which nature is tended and cultivated (Sarkar 2012). The relative abundance of wild nature in the new world, when colonized during the modern and Romantic periods (Glacken 1967; Oelschlaeger 1991) was associated with the deification of wild nature, commonly conceived in terms of the complete separation of nature and humanity. This required the ruthless and systematic removal of indigenous First Nation peoples from their land (Brown 1970). Human values associated with wild nature may be understood in many ways (Brennan and Lo 2010). Anthropocentrism ascribes human demand value to wild nature, which may be protected to provide ecosystem services (fresh water, hydro-electric power generation) and/or opportunities for recreation and tourism (Hall 1992). Biocentrism attributes intrinsic value to all living entities (human and non-human animals), while ecocentrism goes further to accommodate biological (living species) and non-biological nature (geological features, wild rivers) in ethical and moral deliberations (Sarkar 2012). The purist forms of ecocentrism (e.g. 'deep ecology') accommodate consideration of inter-generational equity and justice (Næss 1989).

Mountains, mountaineering and tourism

Mountains have been prominent in the post-war global tourism development (Britton 1991), which has brought anthropocentric values to the fore (Mowforth and Munt 2008). Tourism has been a driving force in what is described as capitalism's 'ecological phase' (O'Connor 1994), which has been implicated in the commodification of natural resources in regions around the globe (Bandy 1996; West and Carrier 2004). Accelerating since the 1980s due to expanding influence of neoliberal economic policies, nature-based tourism has rapidly developed into a mass-produced capitalist industry (Harvey 2010). Neoliberal capitalist systems are expressed through free market economic principles including deregulation of natural resource governance, marketization and privatization (Cater 2006; Castree 2008; Duffy 2010; Fletcher 2011). These principles have formed an underpinning to the systematic commodification of nature, and the transformation of nature in commodified tourism 'products' (Mowforth and Munt 2008; Neves 2004, 2010).

Nature-based tourism is understood by Fletcher (2011) to solve various capitalist contradictions, creating new forms of natural capital, and presenting a spatial fix by bringing new forms of development to regions of the world that had previously remained largely outside the reach of western capitalist development. While commonly justified on the grounds of nature conservation and regional development, nature-based tourism is a contentious form of contemporary economic development (Wheeller 1991). This development pathway has greatly expanded the hegemony of global capitalism (Cater 2006), extended the reach of neoliberal capitalist development to embrace a new range of biophysical resources, creating new consumer products including mountain tourism destinations (Goode *et al.* 2000).

This path of development has been driven by consumer demand. Naturebased tourism arises from the widespread sense of alienation from nature that is felt acutely by the expanding urban middle classes in post-industrial societies (Fletcher 2014). This alienation is also the product of the environmental destruction that accompanies capitalism (Žižek 2011). Nature-based tourism, including mountaineering tourism, which commonly takes place in association with protected natural areas (PNAs), such as national parks, affords the opportunity to portray tourism in association with both the development in disadvantaged regional economies, and the conservation of nature (Duffy 2008; Neves 2010).

With most of the population of the developed world living and working in urban areas, mountains have become places of 'excitement, stimulation and potential adventure' (Beedie and Hudson 2003: 625). Hence the emergence of mountain-based adventure tourism (Pomfret 2006, 2011; Hales 2006). However, the mountain regions that human communities depend on for critical ecosystem services and natural resources are susceptible to rapid change (Goode *et al.* 2000). In the process, boundaries and scales of analysis are being redefined (Hall 2007; Becken and Schellhorn 2007). While tourism may be associated with irreversible local environmental change (Pickering 2010), the causes of wholesale environmental change in mountain regions have expanded far beyond the local setting (Gössling and Hall 2006). So too have the consequences of global tourism (Hall 2007). Anthropogenic climate change, in which leisure travel is significantly and increasingly implicated (Peeters and Dubois 2010; Higham *et al.* 2013) has local public health consequences that now extend to the global population. The Tibetan icefields, for example, which provide fresh water for approximately 60 per cent of the global human population, are expected to disappear by the end of this century under current global warming modelling projections (IPCC 2013). These avenues of late-capitalist, nature-based tourism development, offer complexities that are worthy of close and critical analysis.

To many participants the connotations of the term 'mountaineering tourism' may seem a paradox and abhorrent (especially considering the philosophies expressed in a historically influential tradition of mountaineering literature that focuses on the personal escapism and freedom from the 'everyday'). Carr (2001) and Hales (2006) are amongst the few authors to explore the phenomenon of mountaineering adventure tourism, discussing the activities of commercial mountain guiding whilst acknowledging that such activities were the precursor of modern day adventure tourism. Hales refers to 'mountaineering adventure tourists', 'clients', 'commercial climbing clients', 'alpine tourists', 'climbers' and 'climbing tourists' in his chapter – all different terms used to describe mountaineering tourists. Pomfret (2006) discusses various motivational, personality and lifestyle factors to provide a framework that conceptualizes mountaineering adventure tourism, as opposed to recreation. Pomfret (2006: 122) concludes that it is yet to be determined whether 'fundamental differences between mountaineer adventure tourists and mountaineer adventure recreationists exist'.

Previous research on mountaineer recreationists has largely been confined to examining 'hard' mountaineers, resulting in only a limited understanding of 'soft' mountaineers. Research by Pomfret further considers the experiences of 'mountaineer tourists' (Pomfret 2011). A 2014 report by the University of Central Asia contextualized mountain tourism as 'tourism in, around or affecting mountain areas and the communities living in and around them' (Shokirov *et al.* 2014: 11). Further work is clearly needed to examine the spectrum of mountaineering tourism phenomena. In this volume reference is made to the term 'mountaineer tourists' and the concept of 'mountaineering tourism' in the 'hard' sense of the word – by focusing on the issues surrounding, and the people participating in, guided (commercial) or self-guided (private trip/expedition) alpine climbing and mountaineering.

Theoretical framework

For the purposes of this volume, we adopt a sports framework to give structure to the discussions of mountaineering tourism that follow. Sports may be defined as 'a structured, goal-oriented, competitive, contest-based, ludic physical activity' (McPherson *et al.* 1989: 15). Sporting activities can be differentiated in terms of power/performance (structured and organized team sports) and participation/pleasure (unstructured and individual subcultural sports). In accordance with this broad classification, sports may vary broadly in all aspects of definition. So, for example, technically sports are structured by rules that vary from the codified and strictly enforced (e.g. refereed) to the unwritten or unspoken (Coakley 2007). Subcultural sports such as surfing and mountaineering are associated with informal 'rules' of engagement that are developed by the individual through participation and socialization (Donnelly and Young 1988). Goal orientation may be understood in terms of inter-personal competition (winning and losing) but in sports such as mountaineering may equally describe the attainment of levels of personal achievement or competence. Goal orientation in mountaineering may be constantly redefined in relation to developing competence and physical and technical challenge.

There are inevitably differing views as to whether mountaineering could be classified as a sport. Mountaineering may also be conceived as an outdoor recreation or adventure activity – or a composite of all three. For some, mountaineering may be considered the antithesis of sport – an escape to the hills meaning freedom away from any organized or competitive constraints of society. Unlike sport, which is often undertaken as a continual uninterrupted activity for a limited time span, mountaineering tourism can take place over a period of days, weeks or months and thus aspects of rest (e.g. in communal accommodation such as mountain huts), socializing, meandering or slowing down, or simply disengaging completely from the activity can occur during the activity itself. The nature-based setting of mountaineering tourism also has similarities to ecotourism, and the high risk nature of mountaineering naturally situates mountaineering tourism as a subset of adventure tourism (as explored by Pomfret (2006) and in Hales' chapter on 'Mountaineering' in Buckley (2006)).

So can the tradition of mountaineering, in a commercialized tourism context, be conceptualized as a sport? Several contributors in this volume refer to mountaineering as a type of sport, be it an extreme or adventure sport (refer Chapters 4, 6, 8, 9, 10, 11, Case Study 1). Indeed Monasterio and Brymer (Chapter 11) define mountaineering as 'Mountaineering is the sport of climbing mountains, which often incorporates the skills of alpine rock and ice climbing.' Adventure sports in alpine settings, including mountaineering activities such as Everest expeditions and high altitude rock climbing, have been written about in the *Journal of Sport and Tourism*, *European Journal of Sport and Society*, *International Review of Sport Sociology*, *International Journal of Sport Psychology*, and *Journal of Applied Sport Psychology*. In many respects the commercialization of mountaineering and mountaineering tourism resembles similarities to developments in sport tourism, hence our adoption of a sport framework to structure this volume.

Since the first attempts by various national mountaineering expeditions to climb Mt Everest (and other specific peaks in different regions of the world) in the 1920s the activity of mountain climbing has displayed the competitive characteristics of sport, with nations racing to be first to ascend the highest and most technically demanding peaks and routes of various continents. Flag planting on iconic mountain summits has been seen to symbolize or 'claim' these unattainable heights, and as a way of politically asserting a nation's dominance or superiority over another (not to mention the claiming of geographical borders by early mountaineering expeditions where ascents were often undertaken alongside surveying teams). The International Climbing and Mountaineering Federation (UIAA) was founded in 1932, represents 2.5 million people involved in climbing, and separates mountaineering and climbing from sport climbing (UIAA 2014). However, several mountaineering-related activities have characteristics similar to sport including organized competitions, sport climbing on indoor wall routes and ice climbing competitions. The Swiss Alpine Club has promoted competitive climbing since 1994 (Swiss Alpine Club 2014). These sports are marketed as events with audiences, sponsors and television coverage, and many are available to audiences on a range of social media (e.g. www.iceclimbing-worldcup.org/).

Sport as a competitive, contest-based, ludic physical activity is defined in manifold ways (Coakley 2007). The competitive element of sport may pit participants against human opponents, but equally competition may arise from personal standards of performance (e.g. time), degrees of difficulty (e.g. technical challenge) and/or competition against the forces of nature (e.g. challenges of terrain, climate or other more or less natural phenomena). The contest-based nature of sport arises from the challenge of uncertain outcomes. Engagement in sporting competition tests the mettle of the participant in terms of the combination of physical prowess, strategy, skill, composure under pressure, critical decision making and, to a greater or lesser degree, chance (e.g. arising from the vagaries of the weather) (Higham and Hinch 2009). While any sport may present one of more of these aspects of contest, mountaineering, arguably, presents all of them in one form or another. The contest-based nature of mountaineering tests the physical, mental and technical prowess of participants, in terms that may include physical ability, concentration, endurance, stamina, strength and skill (Gibson 1998).

These criteria have defined sports since classical times (Coakley 2007) and they remain as relevant today as they were in ancient Greece, providing a framework for understanding contemporary mountaineering as a sport. However, technical definitions of sport have been critiqued on the grounds that they fail to accommodate or express the dynamic nature of sport phenomena, which vary considerably in space and time (Higham and Hinch 2009). Andrews (2006) provides an alternative approach that is informative in the context of this book. He argues that while all sports are physically based competitive activities, an interpretive approach to defining sports recognizes that different forms of sport and sport experiences are situated within their socio-historical context. Sports, like any socially constructed phenomena, are a reflection of their social and historical circumstances.

The socio-historical construction of mountaineering as a sport serves our purposes in this book well. This approach allows due recognition of the fact that mountaineering is dynamic. The ways in which mountaineering is practised and performed, and the values associated with mountaineering, vary between societies, and evolve over time. Sports such as mountaineering are constantly being adapted to reflect the changing face of the societies within which they are set (Keller 2001). Along with sports such as surfing, snowboarding and mountain biking, mountaineering is one of a new generation of *freestyle* sports that are individualized and unstructured (Thomson 2000). These sports are built upon strong and distinctive subcultural values (Heino 2000; Wheaton 2000, 2007). They may provide participants with a sense of personal or collective identity whereby performance is measured in terms of aesthetics and style, accommodating challenge and innovation, as well as success, however that is measured. The simply binary expression of success as winning or losing does not suit freestyle sports such as mountaineering, where competitive success may be measured in terms of personal achievement, team work, aesthetic or technical challenge, negotiating circumstances that change unpredictably and survival, not to mention summit success.

Participation and pleasure sports share close and unique associations with the tourism industry. Many, such as mountaineering, have originated and evolved from leisure/tourism practices which provide freedom from the sanctions of organizing bodies and rule-makers, and provide settings that are rich in freedom and autonomy. It is this autonomy that also provides a setting that is conducive to experimentation and innovation. However, alternative *freestyle* sports are no less subject to evolutionary processes than other social practices. Commercial interests, media, equipment, clothing manufacturers and the tourism industry all exert pressure on sports practices, including mountaineering, contributing to an inexorable shift from the alternative to the mainstream over time (Hoffer 1995; Heino 2000; Hinch and Higham 2005; Hales 2006). In recent decades tourism has for some become a search for serious leisure (Stebbins 1982), authentic experiences of place (MacCannell 1973; Wang 1999, 2000), a means of building personal or collective identity (Green 2001) or a search for self (Giddens 1991). Mountaineering provides a unique sporting setting for these forms of leisure engagement, but it has simultaneously evolved dynamically in response to increasing commercial tourist demands (Beedie and Hudson 2003; Hales 2006; Pomfret 2011).

Mountaineering tourism: activity, people and place

The theoretical framework that gives this book its structure is derived from Weed and Bull (2004) and Weed (2005) who conceptualize sport and tourism as a complex interplay of activity, people and place. As such, Weed and Bull (2004) would argue that mountaineering tourism must be understood as a complex phenomenon with many synergies that reach across the space/time spectrum, but also much more than a simple combination of particular sport practices performed in specific tourism contexts. Rather, the complex diversity of mountaineering tourism phenomena arises from mountaineering as the cultural experience of a physical sports activity and tourism as a cultural experience of place (Standeven and De Knop 1999).

Thus, mountaineering is a form of physical *activity* that may be understood to be competitive or recreational, structured or unstructured, goal orientated or participatory (Hinch and Higham 2004). The way in which the activity of mountaineering is performed differs between climbing locations and changes over time. In all of its diversity, mountaineering tourism involves engagements with *people* as fellow participants, team members, guides, porters, regulators, search and rescue (SAR) and host community residents. Even sports such as mountaineering, which may take place in hostile and remote environments, involve some forms of inter-personal interactions through which participation is referenced in relation to the subculture of the activity (Weed 2005). These forms of adventure may provide rich opportunities to experience inter-personal authenticity (Hinch and Higham 2005) through a sense of tourist 'communitas' (Turner 1974; Weed 2005). Tourism inevitably involves a spatial travel dimension (Dietvorst and Ashworth 1995) such that mountaineering tourism occurs within the unique context of *place*. Place may be understood as space that is infused with meanings that are constantly being reinterpreted and redefined (Higham and Hinch 2009). Place in some geographical contexts is defined in part based on unique historical associations with and cultural practices of sports such as mountaineering.

This conceptualization sits comfortably with the interpretive approach to defining sports. Weed (2005) has called for dedicated and critical consideration of sport tourism as conceptualized as the complex interplay of activity, people and place, and we seek to provide such a treatment of mountaineering tourism in this book (Figure 1.1). The first part of this book (Chapters 2–6) addresses the activity of mountaineering tourism initially by way of an analysis of the geography (Chapter 2, Lew and Han) and history (Chapter 3, Beedie) of mountaineering. Lew and Han explore the broad settings of the activity of mountaineering tourism with a focus on the geography of mountaineering tourism, while Beedie attends to the historical relationship between mountaineering and tourism. Among other things, these chapters make clear that the cultural practice of mountaineering is fundamentally anchored in environmental philosophy, which is further addressed in Chapter 4 (Boyes and Houge Mackenzie) in relation to areas of mountain wilderness. Boyes and Houge Mackenzie delve into the fascination of humankind with wild places and the pull of the sublime in the mountains.

One form of commodification, commercial guiding, is addressed in Chapter 5 (Thompson-Carr) and another, early alpine club culture and mountaineering literature, in Chapter 6 (Robinson). The discussions in Part I are illustrated with three case studies that address the early development of mountaineering in New

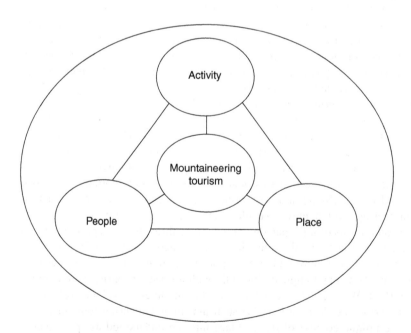

Figure 1.1 Mountaineering tourism theoretical framework (source: adapted from Weed and Bull 2004).

Zealand (Case Study 1, Johnston), mountaineering tourism in Taiwan (Case Study 2, Huang) and the commercialization of mountaineering (Case Study 3, Hobbs and Hobbs). The chapters by Beedie, Johnston, Thompson-Carr and Robinson illustrate the close relationships between activity, people and place. These chapters review histories of development and set the scene for contemporary mountaineering tourism by reviewing the commercialism of mountaineering but also the phenomena of clubs and guiding in facilitating mountaineering experiences.

Part II presents a series of chapters (Chapters 7–11) that address the *people* of mountaineering tourism. This part recognizes that personal values and identity are expressed through distinctive lifestyle and consumption patterns (Mowforth and Munt 2008) and that sport and tourism have emerged as important drivers of identity (Coakley 2007; Milne and Ateljevic 2004). The importance ascribed to mountaineering as a new form of identity construction has given rise to a flourishing field of social science research. Mountaineering may be conceived in terms of career stages that include pre-socialization, selection and recruitment, socialization, and acceptance or ostracism (Donnelly and Young 1988). Mountaineering has been examined by researchers through the lens of serious leisure which includes perseverance, leisure careers, significant effort based on special knowledge, training or skill, durable benefits, a unique ethos surrounding the activity and a strong personal identification with the pursuit (Stebbins 1982), each of which may be enhanced or embellished through engagement in tourism. Embellishing one's subcultural standing requires *perseverance* to learn technical skills and to attain the physical prowess required to achieve reputational enhancement. The durable benefits of serious leisure include self-actualization, self-enrichment, enhancement of self-image and a sense of belonging (Stebbins 1982).

Part II, Chapters 7–9, address the narrative construction of self through a commitment to mountaineering (Davidson), gender and mountaineering (Pomfret and Doran) and motivation and satisfaction (Ewert and Taniguchi) respectively. Chapters 10 and 11 then focus on mountaineering tourism experience and the protective frame (Susan Houge Mackenzie) and personality and risk (Monasterio and Brymer). The chapters in Part II are further illustrated by two case studies that address mountaineering flow experience (Case Study 4, Stebbins) and responsible behaviour related to and safety security among mountaineers (Case Study 5, Esfahani and Khoo).

Finally, Part III of this book presents five chapters that address *place* in terms of unique manifestations of mountaineering tourism environments and development. The environmental impacts of mountaineering tourism are comprehensively studied in Chapter 12 (Pickering and Barros), which is supported by two case studies that consider mountaineering in the context of climate change (Case Study 6, Hall) and human waste management in Aconcagua (Case Study 7, Barros and Pickering). Chapters 13–16 then present critical studies on mountaineering, commodification and risk perceptions in Nepal's Mt Everest region (Chapter 13, Nepal and Mu), mountaineering ethics in the context of Mt Kilimanjaro (Chapter 14, Lovelock), health and safety issues arising from mountaineering activity (Chapter

15, Musa and Thirumoorthi) and management perspectives of mountaineering tourism (Chapter 16, Cater). These chapters are further illustrated by Case Studies 8 and 9, which address mountaineering on Mt Everest from the perspective of evolution, economy, ecology and ethics mountaineering in the Everest region (Case Study 8, Nyaupane) and the working conditions of high altitude porters (Wagumu) on Mt Kilimanjaro (Case Study 9, Melubo).

Figure 1.1 highlights the close interplay of *activity*, *people* and *place* in the context of sport-related tourism, and this point is given emphasis in the final chapter (Chapter 17, Musa, Thompson-Carr and Higham). Collectively, these chapters draw attention to the complexity of mountaineering tourism phenomena, supported by case studies that specifically highlight and illustrate certain aspects of that complexity. The contributions that are brought together in this volume address the challenges of tourism as a form of development in the mountain regions of the world. We hope that they stimulate and inform ongoing critical debate concerning the possibilities and pitfalls of mountaineering tourism.

References

Andrews, D. (2006) *Sports – commerce – culture: Essays on sport in late capitalist America*, New York: Peter Lang.

Atkins, P., Simmons, I. and Roberts, B. (1998) *People, land and time*, London: Arnold.

Bandy, J. (1996) 'Managing the other of nature: Sustainability, spectacle, and global regimes of capital in ecotourism', *Public Culture*, 8: 539–566.

Becken, S. and Schellhorn, M. (2007) 'Ecotourism, energy use and the global climate: Widening the local perspective', in J. E. S. Higham (ed.) *Critical issues in Ecotourism: Understanding a complex tourism phenomenon*, Oxford: Elsevier Butterworth-Heinemann: 85–101.

Beedie, P. and Hudson, S. (2003) 'Emergence of mountain-based adventure tourism', *Annals of Tourism Research*, 30(3): 625–643.

Bender, B. (ed.) (1993) *Landscape: Politics and perspective*, Oxford: Berg Publishers.

Blyth, S., Groombridge, B., Lysenko, I., Miles, L. and Newton, A. (2002) *Mountain watch: Environmental change and sustainable developmental in mountains*, Cambridge: UNEP World Conservation Monitoring Centre.

Brennan, A. and Lo, Y. S. (2010) *Understanding environmental philosophy*, Durham: Acumen Publishing.

Britton, S. G. (1991) 'Tourism, capital, and place: Towards a critical geography of tourism', *Environment and Planning*, D9(4): 451–478.

Brown, D. (1970) *Bury my heart at Wounded Knee: An Indian history of the American west*, Swindon: Book Club Associates.

Buckley, R. (ed.) (2006) *Adventure tourism*, Wallingford: CAB International.

Carr, A. (2001) 'Alpine adventurers in the Pacific Rim', *Pacific Tourism Review*, 4(4): 161–170.

Carr, A. (2004) 'Mountain places, cultural spaces: Interpretation and sustainable visitor management of culturally significant landscapes: A case study of Aoraki/Mount Cook National Park', *Journal of Sustainable Tourism*, 12(5): 432–459.

Castree, N. (2008) 'Neoliberalising nature: The logics of deregulation and reregulation', *Environment and Planning*, A40(1): 131–152.

Cater, E. (2006) 'Ecotourism as a western construct', *Journal of Ecotourism*, 5(1–2): 23–39.

Coakley, J. (2007) *Sports in society: Issues and controversies*, Boston, MA: McGraw Hill.

Crang, M. (1998) *Cultural geography*, London: Routledge.

Cronon, W. (ed.) (1995) *Uncommon ground: Rethinking the human place in nature*, New York: W. W. Norton & Co.

Dietvorst, A. G. J. and Ashworth, G. J. (1995) 'Tourism transformations: An introduction', in G. J. Ashworth and A. G. J. Dietvorst (eds) *Tourism and spatial transformations: Implications for policy planning*, Wallingford: CAB International: 1–13.

Digance, J. (2003) 'Pilgrimage at contested sites' *Annals of Tourism Research*, 30(1): 143–159.

Donnelly, M. and Young, K. (1988) 'The construction and confirmation of identity in sport subcultures', *Sociology of Sport Journal*, 5(3): 223–240.

Dubos, R. (1972) *The god within*, New York: Charles Seribner's Sons.

Duffy, R. (2008) 'Neoliberalising nature: Global networks and ecotourism development in Madagascar', *Journal of Sustainable Tourism*, 16(3): 327–344.

Duffy, R. (2010) *Nature crime*, New Haven, CT: Yale University Press.

Easdale, N. (1988) *Kairuri, the measurer of the land*, Petone, New Zealand: Highgate/ Price Milburn.

Fletcher, R. (2011) 'Sustaining tourism, sustaining capitalism? The tourism industry's role in global capitalist expansion', *Tourism Geographies*, 13(3): 443–461.

Fletcher, R. (2014) *Romancing the wild: Cultural dimensions of ecotourism*, Durham, NC: Duke University Press.

Gibson, H. J. (1998) 'Sport tourism: A critical analysis of research', *Sport Management Review*, 1(1): 45–76.

Giddens, A. (1991) *Modernity and self-identity: Self and society in the late modern age*, Cambridge: Polity Press.

Glacken, C. J. (1967) *Traces on the Rhodian Shore: Nature and culture in western thought from ancient times to the end of the eighteenth century*, Berkeley, CA: University of California Press.

Goode, P. M., Price, M. F. and Zimmermann, F. M. (2000) *Tourism and development in mountain regions*, Wallingford: CAB International.

Gössling, S. and Hall, C. M. (eds) (2006) *Tourism and global environmental change: Ecological, social, economic and political interrelationships*, London: Routledge.

Green, B. C. (2001) 'Leveraging subculture and identity to promote sport events', *Sport Management Review*, 4(1): 1–19.

Grumbine, R. E. (1994) 'Wildness, wise use and sustainable development', *Environmental Ethics*, 16(3): 227–249.

Hales, R. (2006) 'Mountaineering', in R. Buckley (ed.) *Adventure tourism*, Wallingford: CAB International: 260–281.

Hall, C. M. (1992) *Wasteland to world heritage: Preserving Australia's wilderness*, Melbourne, Australia: Melbourne University Press.

Hall, C. M. (2007) 'Scaling ecotourism: The role of scale in understanding the impacts of ecotourism', in J. E. S. Higham (ed.) *Critical issues in ecotourism: Understanding a complex tourism phenomenon*, Oxford: Elsevier: 243–255.

Hall, C. M. and Higham, J. E. S. (2000) 'Wilderness management in the forests of New Zealand: Historical development and contemporary issues in environmental management', in X. Font and J. Tribe (eds) *Forest tourism and recreation: Case studies in environmental management*, Wallingford: CABI Publishing: 143–160.

Harvey, D. (2010) *The enigma of capital.* London: Profile Books.

Heino, R. (2000) 'What is so punk about snowboarding?' *Journal of Sport and Social Issues*, 24: 176–191.

Higham, J. E. S. and Hinch, T. D. (2009) *Sport and tourism: Globalization, mobility and identity*, Oxford: Elsevier.

Higham, J. E. S., Cohen, S. A., Peeters, P. and Gössling, S. (2013) 'Psychological and behavioural approaches to understanding and governing sustainable mobility', *Journal of Sustainable Tourism*, 21(7): 949–967.

Hinch, T. D. and Higham, J. E. S. (2004) *Sport tourism development*, Clevedon: Channel View Publications.

Hinch, T. D. and Higham, J. E. S. (2005) 'Sport, tourism and authenticity', *European Sports Management Quarterly*, 5(3): 245–258.

Hoffer, R. (1995) 'Down and out: On land, sea, air, facing questions about their sanity', *Sports Illustrated*, 83(1): 42–49.

IPCC (2013) *Climate change 2013: The physical science basis. Contribution of working group I to the fifth assessment report of the intergovernmental panel on climate change*, T. F. Stocker, D. Qin, G.-K. Plattner, M. Tignor, S. K. Allen, J. Boschung, A. Nauels, Y. Xia, V. Bex and P. M. Midgley (eds), Cambridge and New York: Cambridge University Press.

Keller, D. (2001) 'Sport and tourism: Introductory report', Paper presented at the World Conference on Sport and Tourism, Barcelona, February.

MacCannell, D. (1973) 'Staged authenticity: Arrangement of social space in tourist settings', *American Journal of Sociology*, 79(3): 589–603.

McPherson, B. D., Curtis, J. E. and Loy, J. W. (1989) *The social significance of sport: An introduction to the sociology of sport*, Champaign, IL: Human Kinetics Books.

Milne, S. and Ateljevic, I. (2004) 'Tourism economic development and the global–local nexus', in S. Williams (ed.) *Tourism: Critical concepts in the social sciences*, New York: Routledge: 81–103.

Mowforth, M. and Munt, I. (2008) *Tourism and sustainability: New tourism in the third world* (3rd edn), London: Routledge.

Nash, R. (1980) *Wilderness and the American mind* (3rd edn), New Haven, CT: Yale University Press.

Næss, A. (1989) *Ecology, community and lifestyle: Outline of an ecosophy*, Cambridge: Cambridge University Press.

Neves, K. (2004) 'Revisiting the tragedy of the commons: Whale watching in the Azores and its ecological dilemmas', *Human Organization*, 63(3): 289–300.

Neves, K. (2010) 'Critical business uncritical conservation: The invisibility of dissent in the world of marine ecotourism', *Current Conservation*, 3(3): 18–21.

O'Connor, J. (1994) 'Is sustainable capitalism possible?' in P. Allen (ed.) *Food for the future: Conditions and contradictions of sustainability*, New York: Wiley-Interscience: 125–137.

Oelschlaeger, M. (1991) *The idea of wilderness: From prehistory to the age of ecology*, New Haven, CT, and London: Yale University Press.

Peeters, P. M. and Dubois, G. (2010) 'Tourism travel under climate change mitigation constraints', *Journal of Transport Geography*, 18(4): 447–457.

Pickering, C. M. (2010) 'Ten factors that affect the severity of environmental impacts of visitors in protected areas', *Ambio*, 39(1): 70–77.

Pomfret, G. (2006) 'Mountaineering adventure tourists: A conceptual framework for research', *Tourism Management*, 27(3): 113–123.

Pomfret, G. (2011) 'Package mountaineer tourist holidaying in the French Alps: An evaluation of key influences encouraging their participation', *Tourism Management*, 32(3): 501–510.

Relph, E. (1976) *Place and placelessness*, London: Pion Ltd.

Relph, E. (1985) 'Geographical experiences and being-in-the-world: the phenomenological origins of geography', in D. Seamon and R. Mugerauer (eds) *Dwelling place and environment: Towards a phenomenology of person and world*, Dordrecht: Nijhoff Martinus Publishers: 15–23.

Sarkar, S. (2012) *Environmental philosophy: From theory to practice*, Chichester: Wiley-Blackwell.

Shackley, M. (1993) 'No room at the top?' *Tourism Management*, 14(6): 483–485.

Shackley, M. (2001) *Managing sacred sites*, London: Continuum.

Shokirov, Q., Abdykadyrova, A., Dear, C. and Nowrojee, S. (2014) 'Mountain tourism and sustainability in Kyrgyzstan and Tajikistan: A research review', Background paper No. 3, Mountain Societies Research Institute, University of Central Asia, July.

Standeven, J. and De Knop, P. (1999) *Sport tourism*, Champaign, IL: Human Kinetics.

Stebbins, R. A. (1982) 'Serious leisure: A conceptual statement', *Pacific Sociological Review*, 25: 251–272.

Swiss Alpine Club (2014) Online, available at: www.sac-cas.ch/index.php?id=1&L=3 (accessed 10 November 2014).

Thomson, R. (2000) 'Physical activity through sport and leisure: Traditional versus non-competitive activities', *Journal of Physical Education New Zealand*, 33: 34–39.

Tuan, Y. (1974) *Topophilia: A study of environmental perception, attitudes and values*, New York: Columbia University Press.

Turner, V. (1974) *Dramas, fields and metaphors*, New York: Cornell University Press.

UIAA (2014) 'Ice climbing world cup'. Online, available at: www.iceclimbingworldcup. org/ (accessed 28 November 2014).

UNECD (1992) The 'Earth Summit': United Nations Conference on Environment and Development (UNCED), Rio de Janeiro, Brazil, 2–14 June.

Wang, N. (1999) 'Rethinking authenticity in tourism experiences', *Annals of Tourism Research*, 26(2): 349–370.

Wang, N. (2000) *Tourism and modernity: A sociological analysis*, Amsterdam: Pergamon.

Weed, M. (2005) 'Sports tourism theory and method: Concepts, issues and epistemologies', *Sport Management Quarterly*, 5(3): 229–242.

Weed, M. E. and Bull, C. J. (2004) *Sport tourism: Participants, policy and providers*, Oxford: Butterworth Heinemann.

West, P. and Carrier, J. C. (2004) 'Ecotourism and authenticity: Getting away from it all?' *Current Anthropology*, 45(4): 483–498.

Wheaton, B. (2000) ' "Just do it": Consumption, commitment and identity in the windsurfing subculture', *Sociology of Sport Journal*, 17(3): 254–274.

Wheaton, B. (2007) 'After sport culture: Rethinking sport and post-subcultural theory', *Journal of Sport and Social Issues*, 31(3): 283–307.

Wheeller, B. (1991) 'Tourism's troubled times: responsible tourism is not the answer', *Tourism Management*, 12(2): 91–96.

Žižek, S. (2011) *Living in the end times*, London: Verso.

Part I

Activity

2 A world geography of mountain trekking

Alan A. Lew and Guosheng Han

Physical geography of mountains

Physical geography generally encompasses climate and weather, landforms and geology, and ecosystem biology. In mountain regions, especially, these three areas of study are intricately intertwined, shaping variations in the experience and attraction of mountains as trekking destinations. This is because climate conditions change rapidly with elevation, resulting in vegetation zones at different heights and in different micro-geographies. In lower latitudes (away from the north and south poles), the altitudinal zonation of a mountain with significant topographic prominence (elevation difference between its base and its peak), can vary from either deserts or tropical rainforest conditions at its base, through temperate deciduous and pine tree ecosystems in its middle elevations, then a thinning of vegetation leading to a treeless tundra at its peak.

Mauna Kea, on the island of Hawaii, offers an example of this, rising from sea level to 4,207 m (13,803 ft) in elevation. Tropical rainforests hug its lower northeast facing windward side, which receives consistent humid trade winds throughout most of the year. These winds rise up the slopes of Mauna Kea, forming clouds and up to 500 cm (200 in) of rain a year as the humid air encounters colder temperatures. Meanwhile, dry desert conditions (with less than 15 cm (5 in) of rain a year) are found on its western leeward slopes where descending air expands and dissipates its clouds by the time it reaches the popular Kona Coast resort area. These two extremes in the lower slopes give way to a more temperate grass and forest zone (up to the 3,000 m (9,800 ft) elevation), which turns to a shrub and treeless peak that is often covered with snow in winter and even shows evidence of past glaciation.

Altitudinal zonation patterns are especially prominent in tropical and subtropical environments where people seek out the cooler weather at higher elevations to escape the heat in the lowlands below. *Hill stations* became popular leisure and trekking destinations during the colonial era in humid South and Southeast Asia (Jutla 2000), while high mountain peaks in desert areas in Central Asia, the Middle East and the American southwest create islands of temperate ecosystems surrounded by a sea of aridity. In addition to cooler temperatures, the less populated and less industrialized mountain destinations and regions also offer cleaner air and an escape from urbanization.

Global climate change, however, is starting to have significant impacts in mountain environments, with high alpine ecosystems showing greater sensitivity to atmospheric fluctuations, especially shorter winter seasons and declining mean snow levels (Nyaupane and Chhetri 2009). Ski industry responses to warming conditions have included a significant increase in non-snow activities, including trekking, which can now be undertaken over a longer season (Steiger and Stötter 2013).

Geomorphology is the study of the Earth's surface, including continental drift (plate tectonics), mountain building processes and surface erosion processes. These geomorphological processes are slow, but consistent, as they reshape the surface of the planet, creating the spectacular mountain landforms that inspire hikers, trekkers and climbers.

Although the planet Earth seems to be a solid, it is actually more of a hot liquid ball, with only the outermost 1 per cent (5 to 50 km; 3 to 50 mi) comprising a solid crust that we can stand on. A constant churning of the molten inner core results in uplifts that cause the hard crust to crack and shake, which is felt as earthquakes. The lightest material in the Earth's crust has gradually come together to form the continents, which float on top of the heavier igneous rock that comprises most of the crust. The continents are pushed around by the churning core, resulting in continental drift. The major mountain chains of the world were pushed up when large chunks of the Earth's crust (consisting of both continents and ocean floor) collided in this drift process. As soon as they were pushed up, however, weathering processes (rain, snow, wind, rivers, waves and glaciers) began to erode them down, sometimes creating smaller hill and valley systems.

Most of the older mountains ranges of the world were formed about 360 million years ago when all of the continental land masses moved together to form the single land mass of Pangaea ('all lands'). Many large mountain chains were created from the colliding and coalescing continents. Approximately 200 million years ago, Pangaea started to break up into the separate continents that eventually became what we know today. The older mountains that were formed by Pangaea (including the Ural range in Russia, the Carpathian range in Eastern Europe, and the Appalachian range in the US, among others) stopped growing at that time and have been eroding ever since.

New mountain ranges, however, began to emerge from the breakup of Pangaea, and most of them are still rising today. The younger mountain ranges of the world are generally clustered into the the the *Alpide Belt* (extending from the Alps in Europe, through the Himalaya and Tibetan Plateau in Central and South Asia, and down to the islands of Indonesia in Southeast Asia) and the *Pacific Ring of Fire* (extending from the Andes in South America, up through the Rocky Moutains, Coast Mountains and Aleutian Islands of North America, then south to Japan, Taiwan, the Philippines and New Zealand). Each of these two global systems is broken down through a tree-like system from major mountain chains, to smaller ranges and individual mountain groups and peaks. Excluding under-water oceanic mountain systems, the Andes are considered the world's longest continuous mountain system at about 7,000 km (4,350 mi) in length.

A short history of mountain trekking

Mountains as sites that have special meaning and experiences for humans prob-ably originated early in human existence. Many cultures around the world attach special religious significance to mountains, which are revered as the homes of gods and destinations for spiritual pilgrims (Benbaum 2006). Among these are Mt Kailash in Tibet (the sacred centre of the world to Hindus, Buddhists, Jains and Bön), Mt Emei (Emei Shan) in southwest China (one of the four sacred Bud-dhist mountains of China), San Francisco Mountain in Arizona (sacred to most of the Indian tribes of the American southwest, but especially the Navajo and the Hopi), Uluru in central Australia (also known as Ayers Rock and sacred to the Aboriginal people of the region) and the Incan city of Machu Picchu in Peru, which was likely built on a mountain peak to honour the Incan Sun god. Most sacred peaks came to represent an *axis mundi*, connecting the physical and spir-itual realms of existence.

Spiritual pilgrimage treks to the sacred mountains were largely reserved for religious elites who were sufficiently pure to enter the sacred realm that the mountains embodied. For others, mountains served primarily as sources of extractive resources, but were otherwise not suitable for humans because they were wild, unknown and not safe (Rebuffat 1970; Tuan 1979; Honour 1981). This changed with the Age of Enlightenment and scientific rationalism in the eighteenth century. Modern science objectified and 'conquered' nature for utili-tarian and economic goals, the success of which resulted in the Industrial Revolution of the nineteenth century and unprecedented levels of environmental exploitation and degradation, along with urban squalor and pollution in Europe (Williams and Lew 2014). The Romantic movement rose in response to the increasing separation of nature from human experiences. In addition to the art and literature that they created, which idealized wilderness landscapes, European Romantics became the world's first recreational mountain trekkers and climbers (Davidson 2002).

The Alpine Club was founded in England in 1857 as the world's first moun-teering club, and marked the start of the 'Golden Age' of mountaineering in Europe (Lunn 1957). By the late 1800s, building on their experience in the Alps, Europeans began exploring new mountain destinations in colonial lands in other parts of the world (Temple 1969). They brought with them a particular attitude towards how to perform a trek and how to engage in a mountain experience. That model of trekking is the basis of modern international trekking as it is prac-tised in the most popular trekking destinations.

Other, non-western, cultures have also held long traditions related to how humans interact with mountains. Weaver (2002), for example, points out how the South Asian tradition is most compatible with the rugged mountaineering approach to trekking that emerged from nineteenth century Europe. The cultural traditions in East Asia, on the other hand, are more aligned with a mass tourism 'garden approach' towards mountain recreation, which appeals to the domestic markets in those countries and would probably be better defined as 'hikes' than 'treks'.

Through the twentieth century, international mountain trekkers in less developing economies were predominantly from more developed countries, especially Western Europe. More recently, however, domestic recreational mountain trekking (as opposed to hiking) has been increasing in the developing world, as Romanticism-like environmental awareness has taken hold in response to the introduction of global industrialization. China, for example, is the probably fastest growing market for trekking both within China and internationally today.

What is a mountain?

Mountains are one of the major geographical landforms that comprise our environment, along with hills, valleys, plains, plateaus, canyons, cliffs and peninsulas, among others. What distinguishes a mountain from other landforms is its prominence from the surrounding landscape. Prominence is mostly defined by elevation and steepness. In an attempt to define mountainous terrain on a global scale, the UN Environmental Program (Blyth *et al.* 2002) identified seven categories of mountainous terrain, including any land area over 2,500 m (8,200 ft; which they refer to as 'high mountains'), lower elevations with varying degrees of slope, and topographic prominence of over 300 m (980 ft) within a 7 km (4.3 mi) radius, among others. Topographic prominence is the elevation difference between a mountain peak and the lowest elevation contour line that fully encompasses or surrounds that peak.

Applying this definition to digital terrain models, UNEP determined that mountains comprised 27.5 per cent of the total land area of the Earth (including Antarctica) (Blyth *et al.* 2002) (Table 2.1). The Antarctic is clearly the most mountainous continent, with 47 per cent of its land area being mountains (and most of that being high mountains). However, because it is also relatively small, it only contains 15.6 per cent of the world's total mountainous terrain, almost all of which is inaccessible. Eurasia (Europe and Asia combined) has the majority of the world's mountainous terrain (44 per cent), with the Alpide Belt and the Pacific Ring of Fire (both described above), plus an extensive span of older mountains from Central Asia into eastern Siberia and China. Almost a third of North America is mountains due mostly to the broad Rocky Mountain cordillera that runs the west coast from Mexico to Alaska. South America has the narrow and tall Andes range (which is the world's longest single mountain range), but is only 19 per cent mountainous as the Brazilian Highlands are largely excluded from the UNEP definition of mountains.

The UNEP report also compares these regions based on 'high mountain' systems, which is defined as those with peaks consistently above 2,500 m (8,200 ft). By this measure, Antarctica has the majority of the world's tallest

Table 2.1 Mountainous land area by continental region

Continent/region/ earth	% of earth's total land area	% of earth's mountainous land area	% of continent/ region/earth that is mountainous
Antarctica	9.2	15.6	46.7
Eurasia*	32.7	44.4	37.3
North America*	16.5	17.5	29.0
South America	12.0	8.4	19.2
Africa	20.4	10.5	14.2
Australia and Southeast Asia	10.4	3.6	10.4
Earth	100.0	100.0	27.5

Source: calculated from Blyth *et al.* (2002).

Note
* Eurasia excludes Southeast Asia; North America includes Greenland.

mountains, with Eurasia lower in number and the other regions considerably lower still, although South America is third. China has more high mountain terrain, by far, than any other country, along with considerable lower mountains, as well. Russia, however, has the most lower elevation mountains.

These height calculations are based on mean sea level (MSL), which is based on a model of the Earth as an irregular shaped geoid. Based on MSL, the tallest mountain in the world is Mt Everest (*Sagarmatha* in Nepal, *Chomolungma* in Tibet) on the border of Nepal and China, which is 8,848 m (29,029 ft). An alternative way to measure the height of mountains is from the centre of the Earth, which results in Mt Chimborazo (6,268 m; 20,565 ft MSL) in Ecuador as being the tallest due to the Earth's bulge at the equator. Mt Everest is the fifth tallest peak measured from the centre of the Earth. A third way of measuring height is by topographic prominence, as defined above. The tallest mountain in the world by this measurement is Mauna Kea (4,207 m; 13,0802 ft MSL) on the island of Hawaii, which rises a total of 10,203 m (33,474 ft) from its base on the ocean floor to its peak.

Mountain trekking motivations

As interesting as the geographic definition and distribution of mountains may be, the use of elevation, steepness, prominence and similar metrics to define mountains and mountain systems are of mixed value when defining their importance from a human perspective. Nepal and Chipeniuk (2005) suggest that such a reductionist approach misses much of what make mountains distinct and valuable for economic and other purposes. They suggest that more important characteristics include:

- *Ecological Diversity* – through the altitudinal zonation of ecosystems and niche microclimate conditions.

- *Cultural Diversity* – due to geographic access challenges that result in isolation and marginality.
- *Fragility* – due to environmental hazards, remoteness and fragmented environmental and social systems.
- *Aesthetic Values* – mostly due to their dramatic natural diversity.

The idea of remoteness from major centres of human settlement runs through all four of these characteristics and provides the basis for most planning and management schemes for mountain regions. Borrowing from the Recreation Opportunity Spectrum (Clark and Stankey 1979), which is widely used in the management of National Parks in the US, Nepal and Chipeniuk (2005) suggest a transition from more intensely used mass tourism zones to less intensively used mountain areas:

- *Mountain Tourist Centres* – where large number of mass tourists have easy access to mountain environments – such as snow ski areas and mountain resort towns.
- *Frontcountry Regions* – where nature enthusiasts have relatively easy access to viewing landscapes and wildlife in small groups.
- *Backcountry Regions* – which are only accessible to small numbers of elite visitors who are either sufficiently healthy or skilled in hiking and trekking.

The *mountain backcountry* is the destination goal of mountain trekkers. The experiences they seek may sometimes sound similar to all tourists who visit natural attractions. However, the quality and intensity of that experience is usually much greater for the mountain trekker than the mass nature tourists. A summary, based on a qualitative review of several lists of trekking motivations (Holden and Sparrowhawk 2002; Fredman and Heberlein 2005; Nepal and Chipeniuk 2005; Nisbett and Hinton 2005; Pan and Ryan 2007; Saxena and Dey 2010; Hill *et al.* 2014; MacGregor 2013; Jaffe 2014), includes the following:

- *Physical Motivations* – including the embodied senses of movement, navigation, comfort and regulatory regimes to ensure appropriate physical exertion while also challenging or proving one's physical abilities, skills and 'toughness' – often by seeing the trek as a physical challenge or goal.
- *Mental Motivations* – including stress release (which often accompanies physical exertion) and escape from the workaday world, as well as experiences of existential authenticity, spirituality, contemplation, oneness with the environment and other sometimes unpredictable, but often memorable, experiences.
- *Intellectual Motivations* – including discovering and knowing more about one's personal boundaries of vulnerability and security, and building confidence and self-belief through learning and mastering new skills, technologies and knowledge about both trekking and trekking destinations.

- *Adventure Motivations* – including the sense of exploration, discovery and excitement, of having a fun and enjoyable experience, and of having occasional thrill, peak or flow experiences in nature, as well as the broader travel experience of new places, most of which is also safer (with less risk) due to modern technologies.
- *Social Motivations* – including camaraderie with other trekkers (who may be friends) and guides, a subjective sense of belonging and membership in a social group ('trekkers') and the role of past experiences, all of which contribute to one's social status, personal identity and commitments, and responsive performances and behaviours in mountain environments.
- *Nature Motivations* – including the attraction or pull of the aesthetic and sensory beauty and simplicity of mountain landscapes, their lack of urbanization, modernization and industrialization, and their concomitant lack of air, water, noise and visual pollution; much of this motivation forms the basis for the marketing of specific mountain destinations, with implied promises of meeting the other motivations on this list.

Interestingly, Pan and Ryan (2007) found that 'pull factors' (desirable characteristics of the destination) have a greater influence on the overall satisfaction of the mountain tourist than do 'push' motivations (such as the need to escape from an urban environment). Thus, the distinctive geographic aesthetic of a particular mountain destination (Nature Motivations, above), may be most important in enabling potential success in the other motivations.

The major barriers to participating in nature experiences in general, and mountain trekking in particular, are income and distance (Fredman and Heberlein 2005). Trekking, in particular, tends to require available time to visit mountain trekking destinations, as well as money to get there, to gain entrance (where required) and to purchase appropriate trekking supplies and possibly guide services. Most mountain trekkers, therefore, fall towards Nepal and Chipeniuk's (2005) far end of Elite and High Effort mountain tourists, as opposed to the Low Effort and Mass tourists found in Tourist Centres. In this way, modern trekking is somewhat similar to the traditional religious pilgrimage, for which some of the motivations also overlap.

Table 2.2 shows the average length and costs of trekking packages in several regions of the world from an international commercial mountain trekking company. South Asia treks tend to be the longest (over two weeks on average), which is required due to destinations that are often in some of the most remotely inaccessible mountainous regions of the world. Those in Western Europe and Africa are the shortest overall (8.5 days), which reflects them being in areas that are among the most accessible to modern transportation. The daily costs vary considerably between Africa at the low end (US$68) and South America as the most expensive (US$130). With the addition of airfare on top of those prices, clearly none of these trips is for lower income budget travellers.

Table 2.2 Average length and cost of mountain treks by continental regions

Continent	N	Mean number of days trekking	Mean total cost (US$)	Mean daily cost (US$)
South America	8	12.4	1,609	129.76
Central and Southwest Asia	6	11.0	1,204	109.45
South Asia	17	15.4	1,562	101.42
Eastern Europe and Russia	13	8.7	824	94.71
West Europe	39	8.4	756	90.00
Africa	15	8.5	581	68.35
Total	98	10.2	989	96.96

Source: compiled by authors from Walks Worldwide (2014).

Notes
Excludes travel to the destination. Insufficient samples were available for North America, East Asia, Oceania and Southeast Asia.

World trekking destinations

An assessment of the locations and relative significance of mountain treks around the world reflects a combination of (1) geographic location, including accessibility, (2) opinions of professional and advanced amateur mountain hikers and climbers, including mountaineering clubs and associations, and (3) popular media images of mountain destinations, including general news coverage and marketing efforts by government and private sector tourism interests. These three influences do not exist in isolation, as the renown of every trek is influenced by its location, accessibility and difficulty, its renown among prominent trekkers and trekking traditions, and its image and public popularity. Still, some trekking circuits are better known because of their geography, others are best known because they are for more skilled hikers only and still others are known because of their historical and cultural prominence.

One way to determine the most prominent trekking destinations in the world is to compare the contents in which treks are listed, and sometimes ranked, in various ways. This was done by the website, Wikiexplora (2014), which examined lists from nine trekking guidebooks. Table 2.3 shows the ranking of the top 29 treks (out of 142) based on the total number of books in which each trek was listed. (Table 2.3 differs from the Wikiexplora website, where the same list was weighted, with trek appearing on longer lists receiving lower values to determine the overall ranking.)

Not all of these treks are in mountains, such as the Grand Canyon's Kaibab Trail, although that depends on how a mountain is defined (see above). Most of the major mountain regions of the world are included at least once, and even more peripheral regions with fewer high mountains show up on the list, possibly reflecting a desire by the various authors to be inclusive on a global scale.

There is, however, a noticeable omission of treks in the three major mountain regions and countries of Antarctica, China and Russia. As mentioned before,

Table 2.3 The 29 most cited treks in nine trekking guidebooks

Rank and name of trek/hike/circuit	Rank and country	Citations*
1 Torres del Paine Trek, Patagonia	1 Chile	8
2 Haute Route, Alps	2 France/Italy/Switzerland	7
(tie) Inca Trail	3 Peru	7
(tie) Mt Kilimanjaro	4 Tanzania	7
5 Snow Lake/Biafo-Hispar/Lupke La Region	5 Pakistan	6
6 Everest Base Camp	6 Nepal	5
(tie) Routeburn Track, Fiordland, Mt Aspiring National Parks, South Island	7 New Zealand	5
8 Baltoro Glacier and K2	8 Pakistan	5
(tie) Kaibab Trail, Grand Canyon (Rim-to-Rim), Arizona	9 USA	5
(tie) Overland Track, Tasmania	10 Australia	5
(tie) Zanskar River, Ladakh	11 India	5
12 Annapurna Area: Annapurna Circuit, Kopra Ridge	12 Nepal	4
(tie) Milford Trek	13 New Zealand	4
(tie) Shackleton Crossing, South Georgia Island	14 UK (South Atlantic)	4
(tie) Tichka to Toubkal, Atlas Mountains	15 Morocco	4
(tie) West Coast Trail, British Columbia	16 Canada	4
17 Appalachian Trail, Georgia to Maine	17 USA	3
(tie) El Camino de Santiago	18 Spain	3
(tie) Grande Randonnee 20, Parc Naturel Regional de la Corse, Corsica	19 France	3
(tie) Horseshoe, North Pindos Mountains	20 Greece	3
(tie) Kalalau Trail, Kauai, Hawaii	21 USA	3
(tie) Kruger Wilderness Trails	22 South Africa	3
(tie) Larapinta Trail, West MacDonnell Range	23 Australia	3
(tie) Mont Blanc Tour, Alps	24 France/Italy/Switzerland	3
(tie) Northern Kungsleden, Lapland, Sweden	25 Sweden	3
(tie) West Highland Way, Scotland	26 UK	3
(tie) Northern Drakensberg, KwaZulu-Natal	27 South Africa	3
(tie) Semien Mountains, Semien National Park	28 Ethiopia	3
(tie) Tongariro Northern Circuit, Tongariro National Park	29 New Zealand	3

Sources: compiled by the authors from data published online at Wikiexplora (2014), based on the contents of Salvage and Markus (2011), Potterfield (2005), Razzetti (2001), Jackson (2003), Noland (2001), Witt (2008), Bain (2010, 2009), Birkett and McGrady (2000).

Note

* Number of references that cite each trek. Only the top 29 treks are shown, based on those cited in three or more of the referenced books.

although Antarctica has the most high mountainous land area in the world, almost all of it is inaccessible. China ranks second in terms of total mountainous land area, and second in high mountain mountains (over 2,500 m), while Russia is third in total mountainous land area (though with very few high mountains). Both China and Russia were closed for political reasons to international travel for a good part of the twentieth century, and although the situation is changing, they still today have significant restrictions on travel to most of their remote mountain regions (Cater 2000; Lew *et al.* 2003; Braden and Prudnikova 2008). Middle East and Central Asian mountains are also largely absent, again most likely because they are difficult to access due to political sensitivities.

The Wikiexplora website contains a comprehensive, though slightly dated, attempt to compile and rank treks on a global scale. However, data from other online sites with recommendations and opinions on trekking destinations provides a rich source for compiling an alternative list of trekking sites. The results of an examination of recommended treks from 25 websites is shown in Tables 2.4 and 2.5. Table 2.4 compares the regional distribution of treks from the nine guidebooks (Wikiexplora 2014) and the 25 websites. Both sources reflect potential biases, with the nine guidebooks giving greater emphasis to South Asia (Himalaya), South America (Andes) and Oceania (Australia and New Zealand). These three regions are possibly the most iconic international mountain trekking destinations in the world. For the large and wealthy European and North American trekking markets, they combine dramatic physical landforms in remote and distant locations (far from western urban culture). In addition, South Asia and South America have the added attraction of exotic cultures in emerging economies.

Table 2.4 Distribution of mountain treks by continental regions

Continents/regions	Number of total treks cited in nine books[1]	%	Number of total treks cited on 25 websites[2]	%
Western Europe	9	17	129	23.7
North America	10	18.9	91	16.7
Africa	7	13.2	77	14.1
South Asia	11	20.8	59	10.8
South America[3]	7	13.2	46	8.4
Oceania[3]	7	13.2	41	7.5
East Asia	1	1.9	37	6.8
Central and Southwest Asia	0	0	29	5.3
Eastern Europe and Russia	0	0	19	3.5
Southeast Asia	1	1.9	17	3.1
Total	53	100	545	100

Notes
1 Only including treks that appeared in two or more of the nine books. Source: compiled by authors based on Wikiexplora (2014).
2 Source: compiled by the authors from 25 websites (see references at end of chapter).
3 South American includes South Georgia Island. Oceania includes Australia, New Zealand, the South Pacific, Hawaii (USA), and Antarctica.

Table 2.5 The 43 most cited trekking sites in the world on 25 websites

Trek, hike, circuit name	Number of citations	Country(s)	Region
1 Tour du Mont Blanc, Alps	14	France, Italy and Switzerland	Western Europe
2 Everest Base Camp	13	Nepal	South Asia
3 Inca Trail	11	Peru	South America
(tie) High Atlas Mountains	11	Morocco	Africa
(tie) Mt Kilimanjaro	11	Tanzania	Africa
6 Annapurna Circuit	9	Nepal	South Asia
(tie) Camino de Santiago	9	Spain	Western Europe
(tie) Simien Mountains	9	Ethiopia	Africa
9 The Lycian Way	7	Turkey	Central and Southwest Asia
(tie) Toubkal Ascent	7	Morocco	Africa
11 Drakensberg	6	South Africa	Africa
(tie) Fitz Roy Trek, Patagonia	6	Argentina	South America
(tie) Grande Randonnee 20 (GR20), Corsica	6	France	Western Europe
14 El Caminito del Rey	5	Spain	Western Europe
(tie) Dachstein Alpine	5	Austria	Western Europe
(tie) Haute Route	5	France and Switzerland	Western Europe
(tie) Kalalau Trail, Kauai, Hawaii	5	United States	Oceania
(tie) Snowman Trek	5	Bhutan	South Asia
(tie) Tiger Leaping Gorge	5	China	East Asia
20 Grand Tour of the Carpathians	4	Romania	Eastern Europe
(tie) Central Tian Shan	4	Kyrgyzstan and Kazakhstan	Central and Southwest Asia
(tie) Chomolhari Trek	4	Bhutan	South Asia
(tie) Copper Canyon	4	Mexico	North America
(tie) Northern Hill Tribe Treks	4	Thailand	Southeast Asia
(tie) Huayna Picchu	4	Peru	South America
(tie) Mt Hua Shan, China	4	China	East Asia
(tie) John Muir Trail	4	United States	North America
(tie) Kokoda Track	4	Papua New Guinea	Oceania
(tie) Kungsleden (Kings Trail)	4	Sweden	Western Europe
(tie) Narrows, Zion National Park, Utah	4	United States	North America
(tie) Rwenzori Mountains	4	Uganda	Africa
(tie) Tongariro Northern Circuit, North Island	4	New Zealand	Oceania
33 Baltoro Glacier and K2	3	Pakistan	South Asia
(tie) Mt Elgon	3	Uganda and Kenya	Africa
(tie) Mt Kailas Circuit	3	China	East Asia
(tie) Mt Kenya	3	Kenya	Africa
(tie) Grand Canyon Kaibab Trail	3	United States	North America
(tie) Great Wall	3	China	East Asia
(tie) Huayhuash Circuit	3	Peru	South America
(tie) Israel National Trail	3	Israel	Central and Southwest Asia
(tie) Milford Trek	3	New Zealand	Oceania
(tie) Routeburn Track	3	New Zealand	Oceania
(tie) Shackleton's Crossing	3	South Georgia Island	South America

Source: compiled by the authors from 25 websites (see references at end of chapter).

The regional distribution of 25 websites seems to highlight all of the regions of the world underplayed by the nine guidebooks, except for North America, which is given about the same value in each of these lists. Most of the 25 websites for this list claim to be highlighting the best treks in the world. There were, however, four specialized lists that focused on Southeast Asia, China and Africa, and four lists that emphasized lesser known treks of the world. Quite a few of the websites were based in North America, giving a bias towards the subjective gaze of that trekking market, and also defining 'lesser known' and 'exotic' from a North America perspective. Most of the websites listed between six and 20 treks, with the exception of one list with 30 treks, one with 112 treks and the Wikiexplora (2014) site with 142 treks, hikes and circuits (see references for a list of all sites and the number of treks references on each).

While there may be some bias towards Southeast Asia, East Asia and Africa, this may be justified due to the gross under-representation of these regions (especially East Asia and Africa) in some of the trekking literature. In addition, the rapid growth of domestic tourism (and mountain trekking) in China, and its gradual opening up of more remote regions to international adventure tourists is leading to its emergence as an increasingly important mountaineering destination.

Table 2.5 shows the top 43 treks of the world, based on the number of times that they were listed in the 25 websites that were reviewed. The 25 websites listed 545 treks in total, and about 300 different treks around the world; the precise number is inexact due to overlapping treks. While it might be possible for a trek to be listed on all 25 websites, because some were specialized, as noted above, the practical maximum number of websites that might list the same trek is closer to 18. Therefore, the finding that the Tour du Mont Blanc and the Everest Base Camp Trek appears on 14 and 13 websites, respectively, clearly demonstrates the iconic symbolism of those world renowned experiences.

The diversity of worthwhile mountain treks around the world is demonstrated by the large number of some 300 different treks compiled from the 25 websites. The treks vary considerably in terms of length and challenge. Some websites give an indication of how challenging a trek is based on the amount of elevation per unit of distance, though most have no such information. A few, however, offer a more detailed interpretations of a trek's challenge that takes into account a greater diversity of environmental conditions, such as elevation, type of terrain covered, weather and snow conditions, physical fitness required, remoteness and total trip length (Walks Worldwide 2014). In general, the more challenging the trek, the more it will attract a narrowly defined elite trekking market, whereas 'easy' and 'accessible' trails will have a broader attraction and use (Hugo 1999). This is often referred to as the difference between 'hard' and 'soft' ecotourists (Sheena *et al.* 2015). In addition, for some destinations, it is not a single peak that is the goal of climbing, but rather a collection of them. This is known as 'peak bagging' and was first popularized in the UK in the 1800s with the 'Munros' (the 284 peaks in Scotland over 300 m, 914 ft) and today includes the state of Colorada's 'Fourteeners' (peaks over 14,000 ft, 4,267 m) (Kuby *et al.* 2001).

Comparing and ranking treks with these many different characteristics and markets is inherently difficult. Even among the best known and most recommended treks, only 16 of those in Table 2.5 also appear in Table 2.3, and the most cited trek in Table 2.3 does not even appear among the top 43 treks on Table 2.5. The top eight treks on Table 2.5, however, also appear on Table 2.3, indicating that these are among the best known mountain hiking destinations in the world. They cover most of the major international trekking mountain ranges, along with some of their best known mountain peaks, including Everest and Mont Blanc, as well as Mt Kilimanjaro in Tanzania and the Inca Trail in Peru. There are, however, some lesser known trekking destinations (at least among non-trekking enthusiasts) among the top eight trekking sites in Table 2.5, including the Camino de Santiago in Spain and the Simien Mountains in Ethiopia. This does not mean that they are less spectacular, but mostly that they have not been as widely imaged internationally as many of the other treks.

Further down the list in Table 2.5, all of the major regions of the world are represented, although Eastern Europe and Southeast Asia have only one trekking destination each, and both of those are more regional (the Carpathians and the Hill Tribes, respectively) than single destinations. China is fairly well represented, with four treks in the top 43 trekking sites in Table 2.5, whereas no East Asia treks appeared in Table 2.3. This may reflect that the websites are more recent and are showing the emergence of China as a trekking and adventure tourism destination.

Mountain climbing

Mountains provide a broad range of adventure challenges, from soft ecotourism hikes, to moderate exertion trekking, to highly skilled technical climbing. Technical climbing is limited to the most elite trekkers and usually involves a significant increase in time, cost, skill and equipment. For some trekkers, a technical summit up one of the more challenging mountains in the world is an adventure of a lifetime. For others, it is one of a bucket list of similar challenges around the globe.

While the elevation of a mountain is still significant, more important from a technical climbing perspective is its prominence (relative elevation) and steepness, which generally equates with difficulty. Table 2.6 shows a selection of some of the popular mountain climbing peaks around the world. Most are technical climbs, requiring specialized equipment and skilled climbers and guides, though a few are not. The most challenging peaks on this list are those of the greater Himalaya region in South Asia and in the southern Andes of South America.

Conclusions

Mountain trekking is an intensely embodied, physical and environmental experience that brings the participant into intimate contact with the space and time of

Table 2.6 Popular mountain climbing peaks

Mountain	Location	Elevation	Elevation of climb/ prominence	Year of first ascent	Popular route(s)	Notes: mean annual number of climbers or summits; mean annual deaths; typical cost of climb, where available
South Asia						
1 K2	Pakistan/China	8,612 m 28,253 ft	4,017 m 13,179 ft	1954	Abruzzi Spur	246 summits as of 2014, and 55 deaths, as of 2013 2nd highest peak in the world
2 Annapurna I	Nepal	8,091 m 26,545 ft	2,984 m 9,790 ft	1950	Jomson Trek; Annapurna Sanctuary Route; Annapurna Circuit	191 summits, 61 deaths, as of March 2012 10th highest peak in the world
3 Everest	Nepal/Tibet, China	8,848 m 29,029 ft	3,483 m 11,431 ft	1953	Southeast Ridge from Nepal North Ridge from Tibet	Nepal: 3,877 summits, 134 deaths, as of June 2012 Tibet: 2,331 summits, 106 deaths, as of June 2012 US$65,000 for 71 days from Kathmandu, Nepal Highest peak in the world
4 Lhotse	Nepal/Tibet, China	8,516 m 27,940 ft	5,250 m 17,224 ft	1956	Same as Everest until upper portions	243 summits, 11 deaths, as of October 2003 4th highest peak in the world, adjacent to Everest
5 Makalu	Nepal, Asia	8,462 m 27,765 ft	2,386 m 7,828 ft	1955	North Face and Northeast Ridge	19 summits, as of 2013 US$34,950 5th highest peak in the world
6 Baintha Brakk	Pakistan	7,285 m 23,901 ft	1,891 m 6,204 ft	1977	Southwest Spur to the West Ridge, and West Summit	3 summits as of 2004 87th highest peak in the world

North America

#	Name	Location	Elevation		Year	Route	Notes
7	Mt McKinley/Denali	Alaska, USA	6,194 m	20,320 ft	1913	West Buttress Route	Almost 500 summits annually US$4,800 for 22 days from Anchorage, Alaska
8	Citlatepeti and Itztaccihuatl	Puebla, Mexico	5,230 m	17,159 ft	1889	Iztaccihuatl, La Arista del Sol	
9	Mt Logan	Yukon, Canada	5,959 m	19,551 ft	1925	Hummingbird Ridge (South Ridge)	8 summits, as of 2013
10	Mt Elias	Alaska, USA/Yukon, Canada	5,489 m	18,008 ft	1897	Abruzzi Ridge, Livermore Ridge	2 summits, as of 2013
11	Long's Peak	Colorado, USA	4,346 m	14,259 ft	1868	Keyhole	53 summits, as of 2013

East Asia

#	Name	Location	Elevation		Year	Route	Notes
12	Mt Khuiten	Mongolia	4,374 m	14,350 ft	1963	Potanin Glacier	US$2,500 to $3,600 per person, depending group size
13	Melungtse	Tibet, China	7,181 m	23,560 ft	1992	Southeast Face	6 summits, as of 2013
14	Pomiu	Sichuan, China	5,413 m	17,759 ft	1982	Southwest Ridge	4 summits, as of 2013
15	Mt Fuji	Japan	3,776 m	12,388 ft	1868	Lake Kawaguchi, Subashiri, Gotemba and Fujinomiya Routes	Approximately 300,000 climb annually; not a technical climb

Europe

#	Name	Location	Elevation		Year	Route	Notes
16	Matterhorn	Switzerland	4,478 m	14,692 ft	1865	Hörnli Ridge	7 passes between 2,800 and 3,300 m must be crossed on a relatively difficult terrain
17	Eiger	Switzerland	3,970 m	13,020 ft	1858	West side Route	74 summits, as of 2013

continued

Table 2.6 Continued

	Mountain	Location	Elevation	Elevation of climb/prominence	Year of first ascent	Popular route(s)	Notes: mean annual number of climbers or summits; mean annual deaths; typical cost of climb, where available
18	Mont Blanc	France	4,810 m 15,780 ft	4,695 m 15,404 ft	1786	Voie Des Cristalliers, a.k.a. the Voie Royale	Average 20,000 mountaineer tourists annually
19	Dykh-Tau	Russia	5,205 m 17,076 ft	2,002 m 6,568 ft	1888	North Ridge	US$4,000
South America							
20	Fitz Roy/Cerri Chalten	Chile/Argentina	3,359 m 11,020 ft	1,951 m 6,401 ft	1952	Franco Argentina	About 1 summit annually
21	Ojos del Salado	Chile/Argentina	6,893 m 22,614 ft	3,688 m 12,100 ft	1937	Marcelo Camus	US$6,800
22	Cerro Torre	Patagonia, Argentina	3,128 m 10,262 ft	1,227 m 4,026 ft	1974	Compressor Route	US$4240 for 13 days
Central and Southwest Asia							
23	Mt Elbrus	Caucasus, Russia	5,642 m 18,510 ft	4,741 m 15,554 ft	1829	Elbrus Cableway	US$4,300 for 14 days from Moscow, Russia; €760 per person in a groups with fixed dates
24	Damanvand	Iran	5,670 m 18,600 ft	4,667 m 15,312 ft	1905	Southern Route	US$476
Africa							
25	Mt Kenya	Kenya, Africa	5,199 m 17,057 ft	3,825 m 12,549 ft	1899	North Face Standard Route	The park receives over 16,000 visitors per year

Antarctica

#	Name	Location			Year	Route	Notes
26	Mt Vinson	Antarctica	4,897 m 16,067 ft	4,892 m 16,050 ft	1966	Western side from Branscomb Glacier	1,500 summits, as of 2013 US$31,500 for 17 days from Puntas Arenas, Chile
27	Mt Tyree	Antarctica	4,852 m 15,919 ft	1,152 m 3,780 ft	1967	Corbet's Couloir	5 summits, 2012

Southeast Asia

#	Name	Location			Year	Route	Notes
28	Mt Kinabalu	Sabah, Borneo, Malaysia	4,095 m 13,435 ft	2,295 m 7,530 ft	1851	Low's Gully	3,000 or more climbers annually Not a technical climb About US$500
29	Puncak Jaya/ Carstensz Pyramid	Papua, Indonesia	4,884 m 16,024 ft	4,884 m 16,024 ft	1936	North Face	US$18,300 for 21 days from Bali, Indonesia

Oceania

#	Name	Location			Year	Route	Notes
30	Aoraki Mt Cook	New Zealand	3,724 m 12,218 ft	3,724 m 12,218 ft	1894	Hooker Valley routes, Linda Glacier	100 summits, as of 1955
31	Mt Townsend	NSW, Australia	2,209 m 7,247 ft	189 m 620 ft	1840	Dirty Face Ridge	Not a technical climb
32	Mt Kosciuszko	NSW, Australia	2,228 m 7,310 ft	2,228 m 7,310 ft	1840	Charlotte Pass	Over 100,000 people visit each summer Not a technical climb

the natural world (Williams and Lew 2014). In all of these ways, it is a geographical experience, and understanding the geography of mountains as landforms distributed in diverse and expansive ways across the planet, as well as the human relationship to them, provides insight into the nature of trekking as a touristic phenomenon. Every mountain, even if some of them they might consider more as a 'hill', holds the promise of bringing the hiker to a position above and beyond the humdrum of day-to-day life. The most majestic peaks of the world, which have inspired humans from time immemorial, are found on every continent. Their very names create a sense of awe at the wonders of the planet.

The geography of contemporary mountain trekking is a combination of the awesome grandeur of the world's most iconic peaks, from Machu Picchu to Denali and from the Matterhorn to Mt Kinabalu. But is it also a reflection of the history of mountain trekking, from the religious pilgrimages of South Asia to the Romantic emergence of hiking clubs in industrial Europe. However, one of the values of mountain trekking is that it is not necessarily only for the elite, with whom it is often associated, but is potentially accessible to anyone within range of an upward sloping incline. For the person who is in the right frame of mind to receive it, every trek, no matter its length or challenge, is a journey of discovery and wonder.

References

Bain, A. (2009) *1000 Ultimate experiences*, Melbourne: Lonely Planet.
Bain, A. (ed.) (2010) *A year of adventures: A guide to the world's most exciting experiences*, Melbourne: Lonely Planet.
Benbaum, E. (2006) 'Sacred mountains: Themes and teachings', *Mountain Research and Development*, 26(4): 304–309.
Birkett, B. and McGrady, C (eds) (2000) *Classic treks: The 30 most spectacular hikes in the world*, New York: Bulfinch.
Blyth, S., Groombridge, B., Lysenko, I., Miles, L. and Newton, A. (2002) *Mountain watch: Environmental change and sustainable developmental in mountains*, Cambridge: UNEP World Conservation Monitoring Centre.
Braden, K. and Prudnikova, N. (2008) 'The challenge of ecotourism development in the Altay region of Russia', *Tourism Geographies*, 10(1): 1–21.
Cater, E. A. (2000) 'Tourism in the Yunnan Great Rivers National Parks System Project: Prospects for sustainability', *Tourism Geographies*, 2(4): 472–489.
Clark, R. N. and Stankey, G. (1979) 'The recreation opportunity spectrum: A framework for planning, management, and research', General Technical Report PNW-GTR-98, Portland, OR: US Department of Agriculture, Forest Service, Pacific Northwest Research Station.
Cox, S. (2011) 'Seven of the world's most treacherous climbs: All that is interesting', Online, available at: http://all-that-is-interesting.com/seven-worlds-most-treacherous-climbs/4 (accessed 25 September 2014).
Davidson, L. (2002) 'The "spirit of the hills": Mountaineering in northwest Otago, New Zealand, 1882–1940', *Tourism Geographies*, 4(1): 44–61.
Fredman, P. and Heberlein, T. A. (2005) 'Visits to the Swedish mountains: Constraints and motivations', *Scandinavian Journal of Hospitality and Tourism*, 5(3): 177–192.

Hill, J., Curtin, S. and Gough, G. (2014) 'Understanding tourist encounters with nature: A thematic framework', *Tourism Geographies*, 16(1): 68–87.

Holden, A. and Sparrowhawk, J. (2002) 'Understanding the motivations of ecotourists: The case of trekkers in Annapurna, Nepal', *International Journal of Tourism Research*, 4(6): 435–446.

Honour, H. (1981) *Romanticism*, Harmondsworth, UK: Penguin.

Hugo, M. L. (1999) 'Energy equivalent as a measure of the difficulty rating of hiking trails', *Tourism Geographies*, 1(3): 358–373.

Jackson, J. (ed.) (2003) *The world's great adventure treks*, Capetown: New Holland.

Jaffe, M. (2014) '5 reasons why you should go hiking'. Online, available at: http://hiking. about.com/od/hiking-for-beginners/a/5-Reasons-Why-You-Should-Go-Hiking.htm (accessed 25 September 2014).

Jutla, R. S. (2000) 'Visual image of the city: Tourists' versus residents' perception of Simla, a hill station in northern India', *Tourism Geographies*, 2(4): 404–420.

Kuby, M. J., Wentz, E. A., Vogt, B. J. and Virden, R. (2001) 'Experiences in developing a tourism web site for hiking Arizona's highest summits and deepest canyons', *Tourism Geographies*, 3(4): 454–473.

Lew, A. A., Yu, L., Ap, J. and Zhang, G. (eds) (2003) *Tourism in China*, Binghamton, NY: Haworth Press.

Lunn, A. (1957) *A century of mountaineering 1857–1957*, London: Allen & Unwin.

MacGregor, T. (2013) '10 reasons why you love to go hiking'. Online, available at: www. egohiking.com/10-reasons-why-you-love-to-go-hiking/ (accessed 25 September 2014).

Nepal, S. K. and Chipeniuk, R. (2005) 'Mountain tourism: Toward a conceptual framework', *Tourism Geographies*, 7(3): 313–333.

Nisbett, N. and Hinton, J. (2005) 'On and off the trail: Experiences of individuals with specialized needs on the Appalachian Trail', *Tourism Review International*, 8(3): 221–237.

Noland, A. (ed.) (2001) *Outside adventure travel: Trekking* (Outside Destinations), New York: W. W. Norton.

Nyaupane, G. P. and Chhetri, N. (2009) 'Vulnerability to climate change of nature-based tourism in the Nepalese Himalayas', *Tourism Geographies*, 11(1): 95–119.

Pan, S. and Ryan, C. (2007) 'Mountain areas and visitor usage – motivations and determinants of satisfaction: The case of Pirongia Forest Park, New Zealand', *Journal of Sustainable Tourism*, 15(3): 288–308.

Potterfield, P. (2005) *Classic hikes of the world: 23 breathtaking treks with detailed routes and maps for expeditions on six continents*, New York: W. W. Norton.

Razzetti, S. (2001) *Top treks of the world*, Capetown: New Holland.

Rebuffat, G. (1970) *On ice and snow and rock*, London: Kaye & Ward.

Salvage, J. and Markus, K. (eds) (2011) *A journey along the world's great treks*, Philadelphia, PA: Walking Promotions.

Saxena, K. and Dey, A. K. (2010) 'Treks'n rapids: Identifying motivational factors for adventure sports', *American Journal of Economics and Business Administration*, 2(2): 172–178.

Sheena, B., Mariapan, M. and Aziz, A. (2015) 'Characteristics of Malaysian ecotourist segments in Kinabalu Park, Sabah', *Tourism Geographies*, 17(1): 1–18.

Steiger, R. and Stötter, J. (2013) 'Climate change impact assessment of ski tourism in Tyrol', *Tourism Geographies*, 15(4): 577–600.

Temple, P. (1969) *The world at their feet*, Christchurch: Whitcombe & Tombs.

Tuan, Y.-F. (1979) *Landscapes of fear*, New York: Pantheon.

Walks Worldwide (2014) 'Walks of the world online brochure'. Online, available at: www.walksworldwide.com/home.html (accessed 25 September 2014).

Weaver, D. (2002) 'Asian ecotourism: Patterns and themes', *Tourism Geographies*, 4(2): 153–172.

Wikiexplora (2014) 'Best treks and hikes of the world, top 100'. Online, available at: www.wikiexplora.com/index.php/Best_Treks_and_Hikes_of_the_World,_Top_100_ (Methodology) (accessed 25 September 2014).

Williams, S. and Lew, A. A. (2014) *Tourism geography* (3rd edn), Oxford: Routledge.

Witt, G. (2008) *Rough guide ultimate adventures*, London: Penguin.

Tables 2.4 and 2.5 references, with number of treks cited on each site

The 25 websites used for data in Tables 2.4 and 2.5, with number of treks cited on each site (all accessed 25 September 2014).

'10 best hiking trails in the world' (ten treks) www.bootsnall.com/articles/09-02/10-best-hiking-trails-world.html.

'10 top mountain treks in the world' (ten treks) www.itsnature.org/what-on-earth/10-top-mountain-treks-in-the-world/.

'20 world class walks' (20 treks) www.roughguides.com/gallery/epic-walks/#/0.

'7 of the most famous walking trails in the world' (seven treks) www.wildjunket.com/2011/05/27/7-of-the-most-famous-walking-trails-in-the-world/.

'Best treks/hikes of the world, top 100' (142 treks collected from nine trekking books, see Wikiexplora, 2014) www.wikiexplora.com/index.php/Best_Treks_/_Hikes_of_the_World,_top_100.

'Best treks in Africa' (20 treks) http://goafrica.about.com/od/adventuretravel/tp/besttreks.htm.

'Classic walking trails' (112 treks) www.walksworldwide.com/holidaySearch.html?keywords=classic_trail.

'Five great mountain walks' (five treks) www.theguardian.com/travel/2013/oct/25/five-unusual-mountain-hikes-walks-treks.

'Hiker's paradise: Seven essential walking trips' (seven treks) www.roughguides.com/article/the-ten-best-treks-in-southeast-asia/.

'National Geographic world's best hikes: 15 classic trails' (15 treks) http://adventure.nationalgeographic.com/adventure/trips/best-trails/world-hikes/.

'National Geographic world's best hikes: 20 epic trails' (20 treks) http://adventure.national-geographic.com/adventure/trips/best-trails/worlds-best-grail-trails/.

'National Geographic world's best hikes: thrilling trails' (19 treks) http://adventure.nationalgeographic.com/adventure/trips/best-trails/worlds-thrilling-hikes-trails/.

'Take a hike: 30 most spectacular hiking trails around the world' (30 treks) www.hellawella.com/take-hike-world%E2%80%99s-30-most-life-changing-treks.

'Ten of the world's best treks' (ten treks) www.telegraph.co.uk/travel/activityandadventure/739384/Ten-of-the-worlds-best-treks.html.

'The 10 best treks in the world' (ten treks) www.lonelyplanet.com/travel-tips-and-articles/76228.

'The 20 most dangerous hikes' (20 treks) www.bootsnall.com/articles/09-02/10-best-hiking-trails-world.html.

'The magnificent seven: The world's greatest treks' (seven treks) www.peregrineadventures.com/blog/13/10/2010/magnificent-seven-worlds-greatest-treks.

'The six best trekking routes around the world, from Everest to the Bungle Bungle' (six treks)   www.dailymail.co.uk/travel/article-2575785/The-six-best-treks-world-Everest-Bungle-Bungles-beyond.html.

'The ten best treks in Southeast Asia' (ten treks) www.roughguides.com/article/the-ten-best-treks-in-southeast-asia/.

'The top ten iconic treks' (ten treks) www.exodustravels.com/walking-holidays/top-ten-iconic-treks.

'The world's best unknown treks' (ten treks) www.backpacker.com/march_2009_worlds_best_unknown_treks/destinations/1277.

'The world's best walks: By the experts' (16 treks) www.theguardian.com/travel/2012/apr/27/worlds-best-walks-by-experts.

'Top 10 hiking trails in the world' (ten treks) www.placestoseeinyourlifetime.com/top-10-hiking-trails-in-the-world-2411/.

'Top 10 mountains for trekking: Top treks to do before you die' (ten treks) www.stylishandtrendy.com/travel/top-10-mountains-for-trekking-best-treks/.

'Top 10 trekking routes in China' (ten treks) www.chinatouristmaps.com/top-10s/trekking-routes.html.

3   A history of mountaineering tourism

Paul Beedie

Introduction

Tourism is the world's biggest industry. Although dominated by the mobility of people from developed countries, often travelling to less developed countries for extraordinary experiences, it remains a global phenomenon with a long history and a complex diversity of forms which represent a microcosm of contemporary life: 'often described as the democratisation of travel, tourism is, nevertheless, shaped and divided by wealth, gender, age, class, education and other social factors' (Sharpley 1994: 31–32). This chapter will focus upon one particular form, mountaineering tourism. Mountains are wild and dangerous places, surrounded in mythology that generate an attractiveness because of their essential 'otherness' – the antithesis of urban civilized life (Riffenburgh 1993). Mountaineering and tourism have evolved a symbiotic relationship, paradoxical and perverse in many respects given the ambition of modernity to control and even eliminate risk, but which nevertheless has created adventure tourism (Beedie and Hudson 2003). ATTA (2013) demonstrate this growth with research that shows 69 per cent of all international departures are from three key regions, Europe, North America and South America. Moreover, 42 per cent of these travellers reported an adventure activity as part of their last trip which values the adventure travel market at $263 billion. Not all of these adventure activities will be land based, but, for reasons that will be set out in what follows, mountains have become fascinating places (Macfarlane 2003).

This chapter will develop historical perspectives of mountaineering tourism with a view to illuminating how this relationship has emerged. The narrative will selectively draw upon key elements of this huge topic to first explain what tourism is, then what mountaineering is and finally what is created when the two elements come together. As the story unfolds it is a social and cultural perspective that will provide the analytical framework and several themes will operate as the glue that bonds the chapter together. These include the mechanisms of tourist consumption, the management of risk and processes of commodification. The story of mountain tourism fascinates precisely because: 'Three centuries ago, risking one's life to climb a mountain would have been considered tantamount to lunacy' (Macfarlane 2003: 14) yet today:

mountain-worship is a given to millions of people. The vertical, the ferocious, the icy – all these are now automatically venerated forms of landscape, images of which permeate an urbanised Western culture increasingly
hungry for even second-hand experiences of wildness and wilderness.

(Macfarlane 2003: 17)

Tourism

Tourism is, for those people not involved in delivering services, non-work activities that connect to the notion of holiday. Sharpley (1994) suggests tourism has
six characteristics: it is leisure offering short-term escape to extraordinary places;
it is socially determined; it is a fragmented and multi-faceted industry; it is
dependent upon the social and cultural attributes of the destination; it is commercial and brings together tourists and local communities; and, last, it reflects
trends and changes in tourist generating societies. This last characteristic is a
crucial point that is illustrated through the connectivity over time between
tourism as education, as enlightenment and as achievement or status. Sigaux
(1966) provides an analysis of tourism through the social and cultural perspectives embraced by Sharpley's typology. Tourism, he suggests, has existed for
millennia and has been created and then advanced by several key factors: (1) by
technical advances such as sea going ships which date from 3000 BC and wheeled
transport which has been traced back to 1600 BC; (2) an innate hedonism driven
by a desire for pleasant weather and a freedom from social and ethical constraint
to satisfy carnal desires and (3) fairs, ceremonies and other events characteristic
of social organization. The writings of the Greek explorer Herodotus demonstrate the capacity of even basic transport for travel and the Roman penchant for
coastal or hill resort villas and towns as escape locations from the heat and stric-
tures of Rome illustrate the first two points. However, whilst the ancient
Olympic Games, which date from 776 BC, illustrate the third point, Sigaux's
(1966: 10) analysis is insightful: tourism in ancient Greece 'was not so much a
voyage of adventure as a trip in accordance with tradition and ritual. The man
[*sic*] who travelled tightened his links rather than liberated himself from his
social background.' Ancient Greece was a distinctive class structured society
and the implications of reinforcement of status though adherence to a set of
socially defined criteria is an element of tourism that remains today – it was an
elite, rich in time, financial and other social resources that travelled, not the
under-class. Attendance at the Olympic Games, for example, was a point of *distinction* which sustained the social inclusivity of those who could afford to
travel.

The connection between travel, education and exclusivity was sustained in
Europe through the 'Grand Tour' (Buzard 1993). The Tour was an extended 'finishing school' for the aristocracy and was the archetypal form of tourism before
opportunities for travel, hedonism and social gathering became available to a
broader range of society from the middle of the nineteenth century. The Grand
Tour set out a template for travellers because it connected travel to education

and dictated the places where this education was to be found. As with the Greeks, the exclusivity of this Tour contributed to a class distinction. However, with the social changes catalysed by the new economic paradigm came a class battle. The tension between *travel* and *tourism* was thrown into full relief as part of the rapid economic changes commensurate with industrialization from 1750 onwards. The characteristics of the Grand Tour and those who participated in it changed over time.

Whereas *travel* had always existed, at least for an elite, Brendon (1991: 5) suggests the 'birth' of *tourism* occurred on 9 June 1841 when Thomas Cook addressed a public meeting in Leicester, England: 'His idea was to rally support for the temperance movement by organising a railway excursion, which would not only gain publicity but would provide a more attractive and wholesome form of recreation than the alehouse.' This example of Victorian paternalistic benevo- lence has some claim to be the start of popular tourism – railway excursions to the European Alps were to follow in the years ahead – but the 'tourism' of the 'Grand Tour' was the template. The evolution of the relevant descriptive terms is apposite: until the 1840s a 'tour-ist' was synonymous with 'traveller' and those that travelled did so for education via a loosely determined 'tour' of the great cultural foci of Europe such as Paris, Vienna, Florence and Berlin. Such people were rich and leisured and from the upper classes. Such an undertaking was considered as a rite-of-passage and it was an individual itinerary that required effort and the capacity not only to 'know' where the important places were (and how to appreciate these) but also to self-organize. Buzard (1993: 2) captures the essence:

> The traveller exhibits boldness and gritty endurance under all conditions (being true to the etymology of 'travel' in the word 'travail'); the tourist is the cautious, pampered unit of a leisure industry. Where tourists go, they go en masse, remaking whole regions in their homogenous image.

Tourism, then, has contained within its genesis a tension drawn from this class distinctiveness with an outcome that, with the emergence of popular or mass tourism: 'the aristocracy abandoned the traditional European tour in favour of more socially exclusive resorts or areas elsewhere in a pattern of behaviour that has been repeated throughout the development of tourism since the late eighteenth century' (Sharpley 1994: 41). Thus, the growth of 'mass' tourism began to have an effect on shaping the emergent tourism industry. It was not so much the development of tourism infrastructure (e.g. hotels and transport systems) and commodification (i.e. tourism as a 'package' in which the logistical details of the journey and/or activity are organized by an operator who can con- struct an attractive 'deal' by using economies of scale and also eliminate the time required to self organize for the client) but a desire to be *distinctive* by trav- ellers that shaped tourism patterns. One of the determinants of this pattern was Romanticism and mountains became an escape from mass tourism: 'people started for the first time to travel to mountains out of a spirit other than necessity, and a coherent sense began to develop of the splendour of mountainous land-scape' (Macfarlane 2003: 15).

The importance of the Romantic movement, and especially its hub in the English Lake District, is discussed in more detail later, but the key point here is that Romanticism re-calibrated the accepted understanding of wild mountain and moorland as inhospitable places best avoided, to a view of positive attraction. According to Riffenburgh (1993), this cultural shift can be traced back to the publication of Edmund Burke's *A Philosophical Enquiry into the Origin of Our Ideas of the Sublime and the Beautiful* in 1758. The sublime referred to the marvellous, the surprising and the awe inspiring. Sublimity was said to be present in natural landscapes such as 'perilous mountain peaks or abysses' (Riffenburgh 1993: 12) where the scale of the features and the extremes of nature could generate emotional responses, notably awe and terror. Burke's classification of the sublime: 'came to define nature, both in its actual state and as portrayed in art, architecture and literature' (Riffenburgh 1993: 120). Mountains, then, became sought after places to visit because of this potential to generate awe. Once the idea of mountains as attractive destinations took root and people became interested in this natural environment it became inevitable that these places would begin to change – tourists need the capacity to get there and places to stay when they arrive, and perhaps guidance into how and where to experience the excitement of the sublime.

So, although this 'escape' to wild places was driven by an artistic elite reacting against the mechanization and rationalization of urban life, in the same way that the aristocratic grand tour was populated by first professional middle classes and then mass tourism, so the Lake District became a sought after destination for a broader social demography. The attraction remains the wildness of its mountain landscape but, as Urry (1995: 193) explains, the authentic wildness is changed by the 'arrival' of tourism:

> Visiting the Lake District has not been undertaken simply because it exemplified nature. It was in some sense natural in the early eighteenth century but at that time hills and mountains represented 'unhospitable terror', rather than the kind of nature which drew people to it. The Lake District appears to be the very embodiment of nature, an area that naturally exists and requires no external factors to ensure its continued successful existence. But this is misleading. The area had to be discovered, then it had to be interpreted as appropriately aesthetic; and then it had to be transformed into the managed scenery suitable for millions of visitors. This particular leisure pattern has not been the inevitable consequence of the Lake District's 'natural' scenery.
>
> (Urry 1995: 193)

The social construction of landscape becomes an important theme in the narrative. As Macfarlane (2003: 18) explains:

> when we look at a landscape we do not see what is there, but largely what we think is there. We attribute qualities to a landscape that it does not

intrinsically possess – savageness, for example, or bleakness – and we value it accordingly.

Crucially, then, people read landscapes through their own experiences, but those experiences are shaped by the culture they live in. Such ethnocentricity adds to the complications in understanding mountain tourism but also is indicative of the dominance of certain ideologies. Here, for example, Macfarlane uses 'we' in an assumption that all cultures see or read mountains in the same way. This is not the case, but certain ideologies are more powerful than others, and the point can be illustrated through the example of Nepal.

Nepal is, economically, one of the poorest countries in the world. It is, however, rich in mountain resources because it contains eight of the 14 highest mountains in the world – those over 8,000 m – including Annapurna, Kangchenjunga and Mt Everest. Nepalese Sherpa were predominantly high altitude farmers and traders before 1950 when Nepal was 'opened up' to western influences, particularly exploratory mountaineers. Sherpa saw their mountains as the home of the gods and not as an environment of adventurous challenge steeped in symbolic capital. Today, however, many act as high altitude guides and porters for adventure tourists from the developed world which has created a 'career' for the best and a substantial boost to both local and the national economy. Sherpa might now 'read' their mountains in different ways, but as a place of 'work' it is still a different perspective from that of the tourists who want to trek in or climb these mountains. A western ideology of 'conquest' and the acquisition of symbolic capital through gazing upon, trekking through or ascending to the top of the highest mountains in the world has become dominant.

Tourism, then, both stimulates and responds to cultural changes. Of Thomas Cook (Sharpley 1994: 51), he: 'set standards of comfort and convenience that brought tourism to the masses but ... he could also be accused of diminishing the authentic travel experience and of creating, in the broader sense, the institutionalised mass tourist'. For example, the skiing holiday package was developed in Switzerland by Sir Henry Lunn in the 1880s; the first scheduled paying passenger air flight (London to Paris) was in August 1919 and flight–hotel packages became a common feature of the mid to late twentieth century. These structural and organizational changes contributed to the democratization of travel into tourism. The arrival of tourism stimulates changes to destinations so that nothing stays the same, but the patterns of growth are not linear or constant because there is both acceptance of and resistance to this change. Sharpley (1994) notes a move towards more individualized itineraries and self-catering activity-based holidays whilst ATTA (2013) – still utilizing the term 'traveller' – note a changing tourism demographic with a growth in younger adventure travellers and an increase in females in this category. Swarbrooke *et al.* (2003) suggest adventure tourism varies between countries and cultures in a number of ways and draw out three key factors that summarize this section of the narrative. (1) People need money, time and inclination to travel; adventure tourism is restricted to developed countries as a source of tourists; (2) the adventure tourism market is influenced by social, economic and political change; for example, the pilgrimage market in Europe peaked in the Middle Ages and has declined with the rise in secularization but pilgrimage is a growth market in places such as Indonesia and Nigeria where religious devotion is strong and incomes are rising; (3) the concept of adventure varies based on history, traditions and geography; for example, exploratory wilderness journeys that recreate those of the pioneers are popular in North America whereas spiritual enlightenment is important in Asian countries. However, one of the outcomes of a global tourism industry is that these culturally specific patterns get mixed up so that, for example, some Japanese are attracted to climbing in the Alaskan wilderness and some American youngsters seek out spiritual pathways in India and Thailand. The next section examines mountaineering and will develop the theme that mountains, as the domain of mountaineers, have a complex relationship with the growth of tourism.

Mountains and mountaineering

William Blake (1757–1827) wrote in his Gnomic Verses: 'Great things are done when men and mountains meet; this is not done by jostling in the street.' The act of conquest resides deep in the human psyche, and the motivation for such acts is located in the rewards that such a conquest might bring. The quote hints at the attractions of mountains, from a gendered (male) perspective and it separates quotidian life from being in the mountains. Such a fascination with mountains transcends time and is not culturally specific – the first recorded ascent was by the monk En no Shokaku of Mt Fuji (3,776m) in 633. However, the origins of mountaineering were not dominated by aesthetics and/or spiritual pursuits but by more mundane and economic issues such as crystal hunting, the search for minerals and the enhancement of scientific knowledge. For western explorers the utility of this ambition was not without its aesthetic dimension, as was the case with the nobleman and scientist Horace Benedict de Saussure who was a patron and supporter of the early attempts to climb Mont Blanc in the Alps (the highest mountain in the European Alps, but less photogenic than the better known Matterhorn) and who made the second ascent the year after Balmat and Paccard's success in 1786.

Mountains undoubtedly represent a harsh environment in which to live and, with the exception of places such as the Altiplano in Peru and Chile, and the Tibetan plateau few people live at high altitudes. This observation allowed Frison-Roche (1996: 10) to conclude: 'as mankind thought it was conquering mountains, the mountains were conquering mankind by obliging everything to adapt to its environment'. Mountaineers have always seen their activities as 'travail' and have had to adapt to survive during their visits to these extraordinary wild places: wool and then more sophisticated insulating clothing has been developed such as down-filled jackets and sleeping bags; technical equipment has been invented such as rucksacks, specialist boots, ice axes and crampons to aid progress up and across mountains and supplementary oxygen systems manufactured to assist in breathing in the rarefied air of high altitudes. Over time, these adaptations have become increasingly sophisticated by integrating technical advances made in other areas of industry to make clothing and equipment lighter, stronger and more comfortable, for example propane fuel stoves, light weight tents and breathable shell fabrics. It is easier to be more comfortable in the mountains today as some of the stoicism required by the early explorers – as in heavy load carrying and living off frugal rations – has been replaced by freeze dried food, warm functional clothing, satellite navigation systems, comprehensive mapping of remote regions and the adaptation of indigenous people to a 'new' economy (mountain guiding, provision of authentic food and accommodation and organizer of porters). That economy has facilitated adventure tourism and it indicates the in-roads tourism has made into mountaineering.

If Anderson (1970) and Mortlock (1984) are right, humans have an atavistic exploratory instinct that exists under a veneer of social conformity galvanized by the momentum of modernity towards a rationalized and risk averse world. A fascination with the sublime emerged in the developed world where the dislocations of modernity (Giddens 1990), that is the insulation from cold, hunger and other primal needs, have been most keenly experienced. This creates a paradox because the more sophisticated and safe life becomes the greater the desire of many people to experience thrills, excitement and otherness. In some respects this desire is an antidote to the ennui of city life in an industrialized, efficient and heavily bureaucratized world that positions productivity and the accumulation of capital above all else. It is no surprise that escape from this 'iron cage' (Varley 2013) is a constant aspiration for many, and it is tourism that provides this potential temporal and spatial escape.

Mountains are now attractive destinations because the dramatic landscape triggers an emotional response and raises the prospect of 'adventure'. However, the awe inspiring topography can only be intimately experienced by those with the knowledge, skills, equipment and physical capacity to climb. Walter (1982) explains this point with the example of the Matterhorn – arguably the archetypal mountain shape and an image famous the world over. This mountain can be viewed from the town of Zermatt and other locations by anyone and is therefore a 'material' good, but it can only be climbed by a relatively small number of people who could then claim such an ascent as a 'positional' good. This point of distinction supports the theme of exclusivity and captures an essential paradox within mountaineering tourism: to what extent can wild and undeveloped places which require visitors to adopt an adventurous and exploratory approach accommodate the infrastructure of the tourist industry without compromising the very qualities that make such destinations attractive in the first place? Mountaineers are attracted by the undeveloped wildness of mountains, and when this is compromised by incursions from tourism there is social resistance (Beedie 2014).

To understand how mountains have contributed to tourism development requires an understanding of what mountaineering is. Frison-Roche (1996: 8) provides this description:

What is generally called mountaineering can essentially be defined by the concept of danger and the techniques devised to parry that danger.... There are countless casual hikers, but only a very limited number of true mountain climbers ... only an elite few will deliberately risk their lives in the firm conviction that they can dominate danger thanks to their own expertise, intelligence, solid morale, quick reflexes and physical strength. On the other hand, whereas recreational trekkers are forever condemned to anonymity, a mountaineer can attain notoriety.

Mountains are not just attractive because they can inspire awe; here the implication is that they offer the possibilities of fame through the accumulation of measurable achievement. Mountains feature a lot in the promotion and undertaking of tourist activity. Wildness is an attractive other place that can add new visual dimensions to the tourist experience: this is why hotel views of mountains and cruise ship itineraries, for example, are often constructed around this safe proximity – the tourist experience is a vicarious thrill enjoyed from a position of relative comfort such as a balcony or a viewing deck. This distant, ocular consumption is, arguably, the commonest way that tourism and mountains meet. However, tourists are taking to the mountains more literally in increasing numbers (ATTA 2013). Many of these mountain tourists will be the hikers that Frison-Roche mentions above; people interested in being in the mountains, hiking up accessible mountains and enjoying panoramic views in an inspiring topography. But some – and the numbers are growing – want to be mountain climbers, that is, to ascend technical routes to the tops of the world's highest mountains.

Frison-Roche's implicit recognition of the potential notoriety of being a mountaineer is connected to the notion of risk. Risks are omnipresent in mountains and include physical threats such as volatile weather, unpredictable snow conditions, potential rock fall and social risks associated with human interaction and identity construction. Risks are understood in different ways by different people and are managed to reduce adverse consequences. In Burke's concept of the sublime the 'terror' has been ameliorated to 'thrill' over time, predominantly through these mechanisms of risk management. Walter (1984), in developing his argument about material and positional goods, continues to emphasize an essential difference between climbers and non-climbers. Jerome (1979: 41) concurs when he states: 'Non-climbers start calling climbers masochistic mystics with overweening death wishes; climbers maintain that non-climbers simply cannot understand.' A public outcry is often the outcome of spectacular deaths in mountaineering such as the 'ban' imposed by Queen Victoria following the deaths in descent among Whymper's group after the successful conquest of the Matterhorn in 1865. Such events invariably lead to a re-assessment of how risk is managed. However, such potential set-backs as emotive responses to death and injury in the mountains have not diminished the forward momentum of adventure tourism; paradoxically such 'distant' events fuel a general fascination with mountains and organizational responses within the industry appear to make visiting them safer.

One example is the professionalization of mountain guiding (Cousquer and Beames 2013: 186): 'guiding was a necessity of mountain life that became vocational rather than a vocation born of a passion for mountaineering. As such it clearly made use of everyday tacit knowledge acquired through living in the mountains.' Mountain guides have always existed but when the golden age of climbing in the European Alps was at its peak (through the 1850s up to the Matterhorn tragedy in 1865) guides were local people who through the economic practices of livestock farming, chamois hunting and/or crystal gathering had an intimate knowledge of 'their' mountains. When the upper classes (predominantly British) climbers came to the Alps in the nineteenth century their climbing expertise was added to this local knowledge to forge partnerships that were mutually beneficial: the guides got paid, could establish a reputation, develop their technical mountaineering skills and develop a 'career' to supplement their other relatively meagre income; the climbers gained the notoriety of making first ascents and thus a place in mountaineering history.

This collective ambition of a rich and educated relatively elite group buying local guiding services in the pursuit of personal glory has established a pattern that has spread to other parts of the world. As both the 'sport' of mountaineering and the most significant early ascents were made in the Alps a template was established for a system that could operate elsewhere. The example of Nepal as one location within the greater ranges (collectively the Himalaya–Karakoram chain in Asia, the Rockies in North America and the Andes in South America) has been introduced: the pattern is of a western driven expansionist agenda 'opening up' wild and remote mountain areas, often in relatively poorer countries. From this perspective it could be argued that mountain adventure tourism is a form of neo-colonialism. However, such a drive would not be possible without a risk management process. Cousquer and Beames (2013) explore the International Mountain Leaders (IML) accreditation scheme which illustrates one element of such a risk management process. Guiding as vocation required a wider skill set than technical climbing capacity – organizational and communication skills connected to a broadening range of services to meet the needs of a growing and diverse clientele led to an accredited, professional guiding training. In 1948 the French established the *Ecole Nationale de Ski et d'Alpinisme* (ENSA) to prepare mountain guides for the diploma that was now a legal requirement to take clients into the mountains. This development was concurrent to the operations of an international governing body for mountaineering, the *Union International des Associations d'Alpinisme* (UIAA) which emerged from 1932 (Beedie 2003). Mountain guides, however, find themselves positioned at the interface between two social worlds of mountaineering: those of the dedicated climbers who have experience, knowledge and technical skills and can operate independently in the mountains and adventure tourists who are wholly dependent upon being guided. As has been argued elsewhere (Beedie 2003), mountain guides might be trained in the Alps but they now operate in a global market that facilitates the flow of such training and accreditation schemes to other countries in the pursuit of risk management. The professionalization of

Nepalese Mountain Guides is an example: 'with the best local guides seeking recognition as professional alpinists so they transcend their image as mere auxiliaries' (Cousquer and Beames 2013: 187). In 2012 Nepal was accepted as a member of the *Union International des Associations de Guides de Montagne* that accredits the courses from 23 member countries.

The tourism industry response has been to build upon the credibility for mountaineering tourism generated by this and other elements of risk management to expand its interests (Beedie 2014). Thus we have arrived at a point where almost anyone who has enough time, a certain physical aptitude and, most importantly, enough money can pay to be guided to the top of the highest mountains in the world. There is still a significant body of people for whom a fascination with mountains is manifest through an ocular experience, preferably from a safe distance. For this group, the danger is lived vicariously and Walter (1984: 75) goes as far as to call this fascination a voyeuristic form of pornography based on a misconception of the climbing experience: 'awareness of death is not routinely in the forefront of the climber's mind. Risk-taking is part of what climbing is about; but for the outsider, risk is the sum total of what climbing is about.' It is these 'outsiders' that have become the biggest group of people interested in mountains, and for a growing number of these there is an aspiration to walk, climb and trek in mountains. The last section will, through an examination of mountaineering tourism, explore the tensions manifest through the contradictions created by the oxymoron of 'adventure tourism' in which adventure – defined as uncertainty of outcome – is connected to tourism, defined as the commercial infrastructure of (active) holiday provision. In essence, if Frison-Roche is right that only an athletic elite can be mountain climbers, how has it become possible for any person with time and money to buy into the (notorious) ongoing story that is mountain climbing in wild remote places such as the Himalayas, the Andes and the Rocky Mountains?

Mountaineering and tourism

In 1933 James Hilton published a book that became a best seller called *Lost Horizon*. It told a fictional story but it integrated an important element of western mythology – the search for Shangri-La. This place is a utopian paradise where people are happy and live perhaps hundreds of years; this ideal place of communal longevity and harmony is, crucially, found in remote mountains, surrounded and cut off from the rest of the world by an impenetrable orographic barrier. Shangri-La is a metaphor of escape to a better life and is a repeating motif in films and books throughout the twentieth century and beyond (Laing and Frost 2012). The theme of escape resonates with contemporary aspirations to leave work behind and go on holiday, the essence of tourism.

Part of the power of the metaphor of escape stems from the impact created by resistance to the pace and intensity of the social and economic processes catalysed by industrialization and is epitomized by the Romantic movement (see Urry 1995 on 'The Making of the English Lake District'). The philosophical origins of this movement are usually attributed to the work of Jean Jacques Rousseau who through his publications in the late eighteenth century – particularly 'The Noble Savage' set out the template for the movement. The Romantics were typically educated poets and artists who wrote about or painted the natural environment and promoted their view that the only authentic existence required one to stay in touch with Nature by living in, or at least visiting, those places untouched by industrial and commercial developments and by engaging directly in this environment by walking and in some cases living there. William Wordsworth is perhaps the most famous example; he lived at Grasmere in the English Lake District and drew inspiration for his poetry from long 'excursions' (walking tours, or hiking by today's terminology) through the Lakeland mountains. This was, and arguably still is, wild country of rocks, scree, high moorland and spiky summits – not the highest of mountains (around 1,000 m at the high points), but raw and windswept and remote, a place for real experiences and reflective contemplation. The Romantic movement became responsible for creating and then sustaining a set of ideas about discovery, exploration and the search for an authentic self that remain embedded in western culture and which have had important effects on the development of tourism (Laing and Frost 2012).

One of the key determinants of the traveller–tourist debate is the number of people a place can reasonably sustain. There are two elements to sustainability, the physical capacity of a place and the perceptual capacity – with this latter dimension aligned to differences in ideological emphasis. Walter (1982: 297) notes:

> It is the romantic notion with its emphasis upon solitude, privacy and getting away from it all that is positional and capable of only very low carrying capacities. This is because romanticism has to do with getting away from society ... one's real self, according to romanticism, can flourish only outside of the supposedly alienating structures of everyday life in modern industrial society.

Industrialization, the conditioning romantics wish to escape, brings with it rationalization, efficiency, manufacturing and productivity that shape all aspects of life. It is connected to an aspirational ideology that posits hard work will bring its rewards. To be successful requires a person to accumulate capital because this is what fuels the upward spiral of success. Marxist theory equates capital to money and wealth, but more interesting interpretations exist, notably that capital can take many forms. One of the key structural theorists to develop this idea was Bourdieu (1993), who extended the conceptualization to include such forms. For Bourdieu, capital is much more than money; it encompasses education, networks of contacts (social capital) and cultural capital. Cultural capital brings together what a person knows and how they have come to know it, and in this respect it is defining of social position and distinction. So, whereas people with money might need to demonstrate their status through the acquisition and display of conspicuous consumption in the form of material possessions (house, car(s), designer clothing etc.), Bourdieu's conceptualization allows for a value to be allocated to non-material 'possessions' or achievements, something expressed as symbolic capital. The amount of capital a person accumulates is definitive of the social standing achieved and, because the framework is socially determined, it needs constant maintenance.

There are, therefore, two important ideological strands contributing to an understanding of mountain adventure tourism and when they combine a number of tensions become evident which, over time, manifest themselves as ongoing social 'battlegrounds'. The first strand is escapism and the search for authenticity; the second strand is the accumulation of capital. In the first strand it is the pace, the complexity and the competition of contemporary western life that means many people yearn to get off the treadmill and escape to a slower, more organic, authentic and natural way of being. In the second – and in a demonstration of one of the paradoxes alluded to above – there is an extension of the status seeking, acquisitive, competitive drivers of contemporary life to the accumulation and display of the symbolic capital gained through experiences.

Johnston and Edwards (1994: 474) explore the relationship between the notion of adventure and the capacity to realize this in the mountains amidst the changing social, cultural and economic conditions today:

> Mountaineers are caught in a trap of their own making. To feed their own compulsion to climb, mountaineers have initiated and participated in various endeavours that attract an ever-growing number of people to mountain regions. Climbing motivations have become increasingly complex, with economic concerns playing a more central role. This has led to a loss of meaning and value in the experience as mountaineers confront at each step of their travels the adverse impacts of their presence.

This has implications for mountain-based adventure tourism, and is theorized through Varley's (2006) continuum which explains the relationship between risk in adventure activities and the capacity of such activities to be commodified as tourism products. The continuum has two axes, the vertical being the extent to which a guide or instructor is in control of the activity and the horizontal being the extent to which risk can be controlled and managed. At the left hand end of the scale are activities deemed 'shallow' in that adventure, if it is present at all when defined as uncertainty of outcome, is a veneer and the participants can experience thrills and excitement while 'knowing' they are reasonably safe. Safaris and balloon rides, and bungy jumps are examples of these controlled and managed activities, typically short lived and in which the clients do nothing off their own initiative and the guide assumes complete technical and organizational control of all decision making. At the other end of the scale is 'hard' adventure. In this domain the commercial possibilities are minimal or non-existent because the natural risks of operating through the activity in a specific environment are so great. Solo ascents of a major mountain would be an example, or a crossing of the Arctic icepack. Somewhere in between these two extremes lies a collective of activities that make some demands on the participant to be experienced and competent but in which the risks are managed to various degrees. The extent to which these activities are commodifiable will vary with different circumstances. For example, Jagged Globe (a business based in Sheffield but specializing in taking paying clientele on ascents of the highest mountains of all the continents, as well as many other ascents) insist on their clients having basic snow and ice climbing skills before coming on a big expedition, and even set up and run training courses in the Alps for this purpose. Over 60 per cent of its clients are the same people returning to the company year after year to continue to challenge themselves through progressive (tourist 'career') ascents. Thus the company manages risk to some extent by mostly working with clients who are known quantities with degrees of mountaineering competence that can be 'fitted' to the Jagged Globe system of technical difficulty (based on risk factors such as remoteness, expected weather, required climbing and altitude) across a range of its expedition packages. Mountaineering tourism, then, is difficult to typologize; as Jerome (1979: 118) says: 'Generalisations about mountain climbing are fated to fall flat on their faces.'

Conclusions

What is clear is that mountaineering tourism takes many different forms, and that to accommodate 'tourists' in mountaineering requires management of the risks they are exposed to: management and organizational systems operate to move activities leftwards on Varley's continuum so that active mountain tourism becomes viable when the activities are controlled – as they are in ski resorts – in ways that diminish the essential idea of adventure as uncertainty of outcome. For mountaineers, challenge and adventure are definitive of the experience and so, in the same way that the travellers who were the elite participants on the Grand Tour responded to the democratization of their social territory by moving to 'non-mainstream' exclusive locations, so mountaineers today belittle the incursion of tourists into their territory and 'move' towards ever wilder places to escape the changes generated by the arrival of tourism. For example, the term 'tourist route' (or the Yak Route on Mt Everest) is part of a complex discourse that has a purpose to sustain *distinction* in mountaineering.

There are, therefore, three important themes running through this historical narrative of mountain tourism. First there is the idea of social distinction: it is definitive of status, or even identity, when the symbolic capital of mountaineering is accumulated and translated into other forms of capital such as social and cultural. Second, there is the social construction of mountain landscapes that, despite considerable physical alteration and change through farming, sport (such as ski resort infrastructure) and transport development, retain the essential attractions of mountain destinations through a set of carefully projected images, words and ideas. Third is the operation of risk management which essentially mitigates the dangers of mountaineering in favour of the economic returns made possible by the huge surge of interest in adventure activity holidays. All three support and reinforce each other: mountains are made safe and accessible because paths are built, maps and guide books published, guides and instructors trained and people well equipped in footwear and clothing (risk management); certain mountains are demonstrably iconic and become desired objectives as they are invested in symbolic capital (social construction) and yet they remain 'positional' in that not everyone can climb them (status and identity). Meanwhile, the adventure tourism industry continues to 'work' to deliver its economic benefits whilst changing the social, political and cultural characteristics of all that it touches. Mountaineers, just like the ancient Greek travellers, use their positional experiences to 'tighten links to the social group' but tourism operates to 'liberate' such groupings to create a more fluid social demographic.

References

Anderson, J. (1970) *The ulysses factor: The exploring instinct in man*, London: Hodder & Stoughton.

ATTA (2013) *Adventure tourism market study August 2013*, Washington, DC: George Washington University.

Beedie, P. (2003) 'Mountain guiding and adventure tourism: Reflections on the choreography of the experience', *Leisure Studies*, 22(2): 147–167.

Beedie, P. (2014) 'Playing in the great outdoors: Risk and adventure activities in the twenty-first century', in S. Elkington and S. Gammon (eds) *Contemporary perspectives in leisure: Meanings, motives and life-long learning*, London: Routledge: 79–92.

Beedie, P. and Hudson, S. (2003) 'The emergence of mountain based adventure tourism', *Annals of Tourism Research*, 30(3): 625–643.

Bourdieu, P. (1993) *The field of cultural production*, Oxford: Polity Press.

Brendon, P. (1991) *Thomas Cook: 150 years of popular tourism*, London: Secker & Warburg.

Buzard, J. (1993) *The beaten track*, Oxford: Clarendon Press.

Cousquer, G. and Beames, S. (2013) 'Professionalism in mountain tourism and the claims to professional status of the international mountain leader', *Journal of Sport and Tourism*, 18(3): 185–216.

Frison-Roche, R. (1996) *A history of mountain climbing*, Paris: Flammarion.

Giddens, A. (1990) *The consequences of modernity*, Cambridge: Polity Press.

Hilton, J. (1933) *Lost horizon*, London: Macmillan.

Jerome, J. (1979) *On mountains*, London: Gollancz.

Johnston, B. and Edwards, T. (1994) 'The commodification of mountaineering', *Annals of Tourism Research*, 21(3): 459–478.

Laing, J. and Frost, W. (2012) *Books and travel: Inspiration, quests and transformation*, Bristol: Channel View Publications.

Macfarlane, R. (2003) *Mountains of the mind: A history of a fascination*, London: Granta.

Mortlock, C. (1984) *The adventure alternative*, Milnthorpe: Cicerone Press.

Riffenburgh, B. (1993) *The myth of the explorer: The press, sensationalism and geographical discovery*, London: Belhaven Press.

Sharpley, R. (1994) *Tourism, tourists and society*, Bury St Edmunds: Elm Publications.

Sigaux, G. (1966) *History of tourism*, London: Leisure Arts.

Swarbrooke, J., Beard, C., Leckie, S. and Pomfret, G. (2003) *Adventure tourism: The new frontier*, Oxford: Butterworth-Heinemann.

Urry, J. (1995) *Consuming places*, London: Routledge.

Varley, P. (2006) 'Confecting adventure and playing with meaning: The adventure commodification continuum', *Journal of Sport and Tourism*, 11(2): 173–194.

Varley, P. (2013) 'Max Weber: Rationalisation and new realms of the commodity', in E.
Pike and S. Beames (eds) *Outdoor adventure and social theory*, London: Routledge:
34–42.

Walter, J. (1982) 'Social limits to tourism', *Leisure Studies*, 1(3): 295–304.

Walter, J. (1984) 'Death as recreation: Armchair mountaineering', *Leisure Studies*, 3(1):
67–76.

Case study 1

Early development of mountain recreation in New Zealand and the place of risk

Margaret E. Johnston

In the years from 1880 to 1940, mountain recreation in New Zealand moved from localized and sporadic activity undertaken by small numbers of individuals to more extensive and varied activities that were supported by a strong subcultural framework of mountain clubs with the means to increase membership. Development took place within changing perspectives on the role of recreation and its benefits to the individual and society. Over time, views on risk have reflected those perspectives, leading to particular approaches to adventure and safety in mountain recreation. This case study describes the early development of mountain recreation, with a particular focus on approaches to risk and how they influenced the experience of mountain recreation.

Early travel in the mountain lands of New Zealand largely related to the search for resources, establishing territory, scientific study and exploration. Both Māori and Pakeha travellers had specific practical interests in the high country that largely pre-empted recreational activity (Langton 1996). Exceptions include tourist ascents of the volcanic peaks of the North Island beginning in 1839, day walking around settlements and some glacier walking (Johnston 1989; Langton 1996). Māori prohibitions on climbing the North Island peaks restricted activity by the settlers and tourists, but ascents were made sporadically, including the first Māori ascent of Taranaki in 1848 (Langton 1996). Recreational travel was localized, relying on a limited network of roads and tracks, until the 1880s when the activities of climbing, recreational hunting and walking for pleasure began to grow (Johnston 1992). Improvements in access and services encouraged both international and domestic visitors to participate in recreation at key sites farther afield such as Aoraki Mt Cook, where a guiding and transport service appeared in 1884 and the Hermitage hotel was built in 1885 (Pearce 1980). Wealthy, international visitors dominated the numbers at many of the well-known mountain destinations (Johnston and Pawson 1994). For example, about two-thirds of the 1,400 individuals who signed the visitor book at the Hermitage in its first ten years were international travellers (Pearce 1980) and the majority of the 200 walkers a year in the first ten years of the existence of the Milford track were from overseas (Owens and Fitzharris 1985).

Overseas interest in achieving a mountaineering first ascent spurred the advent of local climbing. The year 1882 is said to mark the start of New Zealand climbing when three climbers from Europe attempted the first ascent of Aoraki Mt Cook, the country's highest peak, and were nearly successful (Temple 1973; Logan 1984). When local climbers reached the summit of Aoraki Mt Cook on 25 December 1894, just days in advance of a second European attempt to make the first ascent, national pride and climbing intensity peaked (Molloy 1983; Johnston 1993). A small core of climbers had developed a climbing subculture largely modelled on the British approach, reflecting the broader international diffusion of sports and the cultural foundation of climbing through a subculture of science and exploration (Johnston 1993), tempered with ethics of athleticism (Robbins 1987) and romanticism (Nicholson 1959). The New Zealand Alpine Club was initiated in 1891 and in 1892 the club began to publish the *New Zealand Alpine Journal,* paying tribute to the formative influence of the Alpine Club in England (Johnston 1993). Early scientists/explorers and climbers in New Zealand wrote prolifically about their discoveries and experiences within this framework, with an emphasis on rational recreation – activities pursued to support individual development and nation building (Molloy 1983; Fitzharris and Kearsley 1987; Johnston 1993).

This strong link to the British tradition was also apparent in views about and approaches to risk. Qualifications were set for membership, likely restricting the growth of the club and also ensuring it was not seen as a place for beginners to learn how to climb (Johnston 1993); only those who had shown proficiency would be accepted as Members by the Membership Committee. The club began to establish and publicize its expectations about how climbing should occur and who should be able to do it. Early discussions examined whether mountain guides (professionals) could become members and this foreshadowed an ongoing conflict about the place of guided and unguided climbing. This restrictive approach of limiting numbers, emphasizing safety and controlling behaviour, represents a subcultural perspective on risk management that attempted to bring together the desire to ascent peaks with a belief that it must be done safely, not carelessly. Yet this early local enthusiasm for high climbing could not be sustained and the New Zealand Alpine Club fell into dormancy, related to a variety of organizational and personal challenges (Johnston 1989; Langton 1996).

Although many of the early climbers were unguided out of necessity, guided climbing became the norm, particularly at Aoraki Mt Cook with the formal guiding service at the Hermitage run by the New Zealand Tourist Department. This practice followed the Alpine Club's traditional approach to European climbing, even though unguided climbing had become more accepted in Europe in the preceding decades (Johnston 1993). The role of government in supporting climbing development through tourism was vital during the 'Golden Age' of climbing from 1908 to 1914, when the leading and teaching by guides resulted in an increase in standards and subsequent achievements by climbers. Until 1920 climbing activity was undertaken primarily by overseas climbers following the guided model, particularly at Aoraki Mt Cook (Johnston 1993; Langton 1996).

Hut and track development for both climbing and tramping (backpacking) continued up to the advent of war, alongside improvements in both road and rail access. The post-First World War revival of domestic climbing was accompanied by a broader surge in mountain recreation supported by further transportation improvements, the creation of mountain activity clubs and the growing provision of facilities (Johnston and Pawson 1994). Leisure grew in importance in post-war New Zealand (Henson 1982) and mountain recreation took on a greater role for individuals (Johnston 1989). Many of the new enthusiasts in climbing and the other activities were not wealthy. Private guiding and tourist facilities were beyond their reach. The work begun in the late nineteenth century to provide tracks and huts for access was continued by the state and the various clubs in the 1920s and 1930s, enabling larger numbers to participate at a manageable cost to the individual. Both downhill skiing and tramping grew considerably in the 1930s as these networks of tracks, huts and ski facilities added to those provided by the tourist hotels (Johnston and Pawson 1994).

Facing competition from regional climbing clubs, the New Zealand Alpine Club embraced change, beginning to provide climbing instruction, the inculcation of values and safety-first training through a club camp for the keen young people who were drawn to the mountains. Yet the camps, held in 1931, 1934 and 1939, were not able to resolve the ongoing clash in approaches to safety between the 'old guard' and the new enthusiasts (Johnston 1993). Considerable conflict surrounded the 'old guard' concern that unguided climbing was bringing the sport of mountain climbing into disrepute (Johnston 1989). The push for independent climbing was given a significant boost by the re-introduction of the use of crampons into climbing. Originally, crampons had been viewed as unsafe and used by 'foreigners'. In the 1920s, conflicting views remained about whether the use of crampons was ethical, safe and useful (Johnston 1989); however, a series of successful, fast climbs in the 1926–1927 season demonstrated that crampons could be used to advantage by unguided climbers, who would then have no need for the step-cutting labour of guides (Johnston 1989; Langton 1996). Crampons became an accepted and safe approach for competent, unguided climbers.

Tension about safety and acceptable behaviour occurred in other activities. For example, the Tararua Tramping Club experienced conflict between more experienced members, who advocated a safety-first, somewhat conservative approach, and the enthusiastic newcomers, who were interested in challenging themselves at a higher level, leading to prescriptions on behaviour and outright prohibitions on activities such as speed-tramping (Johnston 1989). The Tararua Tramping Club became something of a leader among clubs in providing club-sponsored trips affordable for the young members that enables the inculcation of safety values through graduated trips, and in the 1930s education and instruction through a variety of formats (Johnston 1989).

As mountain recreation became more accessible to New Zealanders, the developing model for introduction was through the mountain clubs. The role of guides subsided and the mountain clubs took on a large part of the safety framework through their activities to pass on knowledge and control behaviour. The growth in participation, combined with greater societal interest in the benefits of mountain recreation, set the stage for new approaches to risk and safety that were embodied in institutional arrangements. The mountain clubs provided substantial direction in the progression of the safety management framework through these arrangements, beginning with the instrumental role of the Tararua Tramping Club in the development of a national search and rescue organization, following its own experiences in organizing searches (Johnston 1989).

References

Fitzharris, B. and Kearsley, G. W. (1987) 'Appreciating our high country', in P. G. Holland and W. B. Johnston (eds) *Southern approaches: Geography in New Zealand*, Christchurch: New Zealand Geographical Society: 197–217.

Henson, D. (1982) 'The club, Federated Mountain Clubs, and the mountain world', in S. Woodham (ed.) *Christchurch tramping club 1932–1982*, Christchurch: Christchurch Tramping Club: 48–49.

Johnston, M. (1989) 'Peak experiences: Challenge and danger in mountain recreation in New Zealand', unpublished thesis, University of Canterbury.

Johnston, M. (1992) 'Facing the challenges: Adventure in the mountains of New Zealand', in B. Weiler and C. M. Hall (eds) *Special interest tourism*, London: Belhaven Press: 159–169.

Johnston, M. (1993) 'Diffusion and difference: The subcultural framework for mountain climbing in New Zealand', *Tourism Recreation Research*, 18(1): 38–44.

Johnston, M. and Pawson, E. (1994) 'Challenge and danger in the development of mountain recreation in New Zealand, 1890–1940', *Journal of Historical Geography*, 20(2): 175–186.

Langton, G. (1996) 'A history of mountain climbing in New Zealand to 1953', unpublished thesis, University of Canterbury.

Logan, H. (1984) 'Part one of a history of New Zealand alpinism', *Mountain*, 96: 16–23.

Molloy, L. (1983) 'Wilderness recreation: The New Zealand experience', in L. Molloy (ed.) *Wilderness recreation in New Zealand: Proceedings of the FMC 50th Jubilee Conference on Wilderness*, Wellington: Federated Mountain Clubs: 4–19.

Nicholson, M. H. (1959) *Mountain gloom and mountain glory*, New York: Cornell University Press.

Owens, I. F. and Fitzharris, B. B. (1985) *Avalanche atlas of the milford track and assessment of the hazard to walkers*, Wellington: NZ Mountain Safety Council.

Pearce, D. G. (1980) 'Tourist development at Aoraki Mount Cook since 1884', *New Zealand Geographer*, 36(2): 79–84.

Robbins, D. (1987) 'Sport, hegemony and the middle class: The Victorian mountaineers', *Theory, Culture and Society*, 4(3): 579–601.

Temple, P. (ed.) (1973) *Castles in the air: Men and mountains in New Zealand*, Dunedin: John McIndoe Limited.

Case study 2

Mountaineering tourism in Taiwan: hiking the '100 mountains'

Ming Feng Huang

Eastern cultures are no different from the west in revering mountain places, traditionally related to their inhospitable and inaccessible nature. In China, Kunlun Mountain, where many believe that the chief of gods lives on the Earth, has been revered from generations to generations. Geographically the area of Taiwan Island is 35,801 km² and two-thirds of the total area is covered by forested mountains. Taiwan has been generously equipped with forests and there are 258 mountain peaks over 3,000 m, with the highest peak, Yu Shan (Jade mountain), reaching 3,952 m, forced upward by the collision of the Eurasia Plate and the Philippine Sea Plate. Although barely acknowledged outside the country this mountainous spine does offer considerable potential for mountain recreation.

Despite the long history of mountain climbing in Europe, Taiwanese mountain hiking developed relatively late. Since the 1600s there has been significant immigration from mainland China, then under the control of the Ming dynasty. However, many of the mountainous areas of Taiwan were at this time occupied by aboriginals with a ferocious reputation. During the Qing Dynasty, from 1683 to 1895, a high proportion of new immigrants from the mainland chose to settle on reclaimed land or the plain nearby the ports or rivers. However, aboriginals who lived in the mountainous areas had a custom of head hunting those that intruded on to their territory. For this reason, the Qing Dynasty government set up several military bases as defence against the aboriginals, and also prohibited their citizens from entering the mountains.

However, around 1860, with increasing western influence in the region, a few Taiwanese ports were opened for trade. In particular the growth of the tea trade increased business activities and hence settlements in mountainous areas (Ling 2008). The Scottish tea merchant John Dodd went into the mountain areas several times in this period to discover new tea plants, and claimed to have reached the summit of 'Xue Shan', the second highest mountain during his stay in Taiwan (Lin 2002). Later, Dr George Leslie Mackay (1844–1901), a Scottish missionary, wrote in his diary of his ascents of, 'GuanYin Shan', and his failed attempt to climb Xue Shan in 1873 (Chen 1996a). During the period from 1860 to 1895, several mountains were explored by foreign traders, missionaries and government officers such as Robert Swinhoe, the first British consular representative.

Despite these few excursions in the late 1800s, most of the resident Han Chinese still stayed away from mountainous areas. In 1874, however, the Japanese government sent a number of students, photographers, scientists and geographers to study the wild/unsubjugated Taiwanese aboriginals in the Taiwan Expedition. Following the colonial annexation of Taiwan in 1895, the Japanese government launched a series of investigations and explorations in the mountain areas. In 1896 Japanese scholars surveyed the highest peak in Taiwan and named it 'New High Mountain' although they did not reach the summit. Four years later, in 1900, the Japanese anthropologist Torii Ryuzo attained the peak (Yiang 1996). In the first decade of Japanese rule, most of the activities that took place in the mountains were concerned with measurement and academic activities, surveying the country for maps, uncovering new species and investigating local indigenous communities. However, most of the team members involved in these activities were Japanese scholars, scientists, officers and policemen, not Taiwanese people. Indeed, an aboriginal resistance movement in the early years of colonization meant that mountain hiking as pleasure or sport was not encouraged until the Japanese army put down the rebellion. However, from around 1915, with the pacification of the indigenous population, the Japanese government started to encourage civilians to be involved in sports. Some Japanese officers further suggested that mountain hiking should be considered in off-campus teaching activities throughout primary school to university (Ling 2008). This led to the establishment of the Taiwanese mountaineering association (台灣山岳會) in 1926, which represented a milestone in Taiwanese mountaineering history. The association was housed in the highest administrative unit in Government House, and most of those involved in the committee were administrative officers. However, despite its name, the association was mostly for the Japanese, not the resident population because the latter were poor and restricted in their ability to partake in mountain hiking or mountaineering activities. This situation did not really improve until the end of the Second World War.

In the first two decades of Taiwanese self-rule, Taiwanese mountain hiking activities were more strictly controlled than under the Japanese colonial period. Due to the flight from the communist forces on the mainland, the KuoMinTang (KMT) used mountainous areas as military bases and controlled access to the mountains as a precaution against possible espionage. In addition, the mountainous areas were also those that were the least developed, lacking in infrastructure and access opportunities. However, a group of hikers did manage to walk through 60 mountains over 3,000 m in 32 days in 1970 under the auspices of Taiwan Provincial Mountain Sports Club Association (Chen 1996b). In order to encourage people's involvement in mountain hiking, the Taiwanese mountaineering association, which later renamed itself the Chinese Taipei Alpine Association (CTAA), planned the 'Five Mountain Club' and '100 Mountain Club' to motivate people through the objectives of specific peaks. The Five Mountain Club was introduced to the Taiwanese in 1966 by the CTAA which chose five mountains to represent the Taiwanese mountain environment. These are YuShan (3,952 m), XueShan (3,886 m), NanHuDaShan (3,740 m), BeiDaWuShan (3,092 m) and DaBaJianShan

(3,492 m). Following the publication of this list, over the next five years, there was a dramatic increase in the mountain hiking population, therefore, four members of the CTAA started to plan to list 100 mountains, finishing the list in 1972. This list can be seen as somewhat parallel to the establishment of the Munros which list all peaks over 3,000 ft in Scotland or the Nuttalls in Wales and England which are those mountains over 2,000 ft, and a popular focus of mountaineering tourism today.

However, the major difference is that the mountains used in the Taiwanese classification take emotive and historical aspects into their consideration in addition to relative or absolute height, which is the main aspect of western classifications. Rather, the selected standards included four conditions: first, the mountain should have a name on the map and triangulation point; second, a historical perspective, which comes from respect and beliefs about the mountain from historical records and ancestors' oral histories; third, the shape of the mountain, which is has its own specific shape and is different from other mountains; and fourth, the emotive characteristic, which will evoke the hikers' emotion during their walk because of the characteristics of the mountain itself. Thus these 100 mountains are divided further into 18 categories (Box CS 2.1).

Box CS 2.1 Descriptions of the Taiwanese 100 mountains

Five Mountain. These five mountains have a unique shape, have a very good uninhibited view from the summit and stand out from their surroundings.

Three Sharp. These are very tall and steep on the both sides like a pen's tip.

Ten Dangerous. These are dangerously steep, the rock cliff is sharp but the target is obvious.

Ten High. These mountains are high and huge with ups and downs, although the summit is wide and the slope is gentle.

Nine Lofty. Lofty indicates the mountain is like a tower standing out from other mountains and the shape is beautiful.

Nine Barrier. Barrier suggests that the peak looks like a wall blocking views.

Eight Beauty. Beauty is descriptive of the appearance of the mountain, the gradient is gentle without huge rocks.

Ten Smooth. Smooth indicates there are no rapid uphill or downhill slopes and the hiker does not need to climb rocks.

Ten Green. Green states the peaks have a dense covering of trees and plants so hikers have to shuttle back and forth through them.

Ten Rock. This means hikers have to climb the rocks to reach the summit.

Seven Precipitous. Precipitous represents that the slope is sharp and covered by scree.

Eight Cute. Cute refers to the summit being sharp with cliffs and a steep slope.

Eight Lean. Lean means the ridge of the mountain is narrow and long, and has a steep slope or cliff on both edges.

Nine Flat. The peak is wide and flat, there are no huge rocks or trees, with short grass and the hiker can walk easily.

Nine Secluded. Secluded means the mountain is located in a remote place which is apart from the main range.

Eight Hill. The summit can be ascended easily, with gentle slopes and can be visited on the way to a main mountain.

Six Easy. There are paths nearby and it is convenient to ascend.

Six Shoulder Edge. This describes peaks having their own name and shaped like a shoulder to an adjacent higher mountain.

Figure CS 2.1 Climbing Bei-Da-Wu Shan (3,090 m), one of the five mountains on the 100 mountain list.

Taiwanese mountaineers divide mountains in three categories, suburban area hills with an altitude less than 1,500 m; middle hills with a height between 1,500 m and 3,000 m and high mountains with a height over 3,000 m. Based on the different degrees of difficulty these 100 mountains are divided into six grades from one to six, one representing the most difficult and six the easiest (Republic of China Mountain Rescue Association 2010). Many of the higher mountains lie in protected areas. Lai *et al.* (2013) describe the establishment of national park infrastructure in Taiwan in the 1970s and 1980s. The National Park Law of 1972 led to the establishment of major protected areas in Taiwan, and there are currently eight national parks on the island, four of which protect mountain areas and are popular for mountain recreation, especially the Yushan National Park (with the highest peak) established in 1985. Here over 36,000 permits are issued to visitors of the Main Peak area every year, most of whom use the most popular route, the 21 km Jade Mountain peak trail. Capacity on this trail is set by the number of permits for a bed night at the Paiyun Lodge, the closest accommodation to the peak. The trail is open all year except for February and accounts for 77 per cent of the annual visits to the park's ecologically sensitive areas (Yushan National Park 2010).

Mountain regions in Taiwan have a stronger presence of indigenous populations, representing ethnic groups other than the Han Chinese majority who arrived in successive migrations from mainland China. As less favourable agricultural areas, indigenous populations were forced to upland and western areas. Christie *et al.* (2012: 75) note that 'in many indigenous communities, there may be strong cultural and/or spiritual values', and many of the mountains of Taiwan are sacred in indigenous mythology, for example Jade Peak (Yushan) (Lai *et al.* 2013). However, resource use of mountain areas between protected area managers and indigenous users has not always been without conflict. Chi and Wang (1996) note that in the case of Yushan National Park, the government representing the 'dominant ethnic group imposes its values and interests upon indigenous minorities'. This has contributed to continuing conflicts and a lack of trust between the park service and Bunun (indigenous) residents (Lai *et al.* 2013: 41). For example, checkpoints are still a feature in the entrances to many mountainous areas. The government has, however, generally relaxed access to mountain areas for recreation, which included removing an early requirement for having certified mountain guides to accompany recreation visits to areas that are 3,000 m above sea level. Further, 'the promotion of mountain tourism and ecotourism by different levels of government has further boosted the already popular mountain activities in a country dominated by mountain landscapes' (Lai *et al.* 2013: 38).

Following the publication of the lists, from the 1970s to 1990s, the atmosphere of attaining summits and reaching peaks meant that many local clubs were established within these two decades. However, observation suggests that Taiwanese mountain hikers/mountaineers are still in the stage akin to that of the 'pocket peak' in Alpine mountaineering, rather than improving mountaineering skills or knowledge discussed in the research field. According to the statistics from the Sports Affairs Council (2003), the population involved in mountain hiking (including the 100 mountains and 'picnic hills') was over five million people per year, which means one out of four Taiwanese is involved in mountain hiking activity annually. Clearly this represents a wide variety of skill levels, degrees of difficulty and rates of participation. However, in a recent survey mountain hiking activity was the second most mentioned activity that Taiwanese people would like to do on their vacation (Tourism Bureau 2002).

Research conducted with mountaineering groups by Huang (2014) investigated mountain hikers in Taiwan and their participation in the activity through dimensions of motivation, involvement and specialization. A particular feature of mountain recreation in Taiwan is the development of mountain hiking 'clubs', led by hiking agents who fulfil the role of guide, but also organize various social activities around mountain hiking. The mountaineering tourism market in Taiwan does seem to be relatively immature, as only about 19 per cent of respondents had climbed more than 50 of the peaks in the 100 mountains list. Further, a cluster analysis revealed that 32 per cent of mountain hikers were casual, 46 per cent were intermediate and 22 per cent were specialized. Nevertheless the study did uncover some important aspects to mountaineering tourism participation in Taiwan, notably the strength of aesthetic and health dimensions. The former was located within motivations, and involved a high preference for high altitude landscapes and participating in ancillary activities such as photography (Figure CS 2.2). Health was an important involvement element, and this

Figure CS 2.2 Taiwanese mountaineering photography exhibition.

echoes previous research by Buckley *et al.* (2008) which emphasizes the importance of health aspects in nature-based recreation in Chinese cultures.

References

Buckley, R., Cater, C., Zhong, L. and Chen, T. (2008) 'Shengtai Luyou: Cross-cultural comparison in ecotourism', *Annals of Tourism Research*, 35(4): 945–968.

Chen, H. W. (1996a) *Mackay's diaries: Original English version*, Tainan: RenGuang.

Chen, P. Z. (1996b) *Taiwanese mountain legend*, Taipei: Lian Jing.

Chi, C.-C. and Wang, J. C. S. (1996) 'Environmental justice: An analysis of the conflicts between aboriginal peoples and national parks in Taiwan'. Online, available at: http://wildmic.npust.edu.tw/sasala (accessed 18 February 2014).

Christie, M., Fazey, I., Cooper, R., Hyde, T. and Kenter, J. O. (2012) 'An evaluation of monetary and non-monetary techniques for assessing the importance of biodiversity and ecosystem services to people in countries with developing economies', *Ecological Economics*, 83(C): 67–78.

Huang, M. F. (2014) 'Hiking the 100 mountains in Taiwan, from beginner to specialist in mountain hiking activity', unpublished doctoral thesis, Aberystwyth University, UK.

Lai, P.-H., Hsu, Y.-C. and Nepal, S. K. (2013) 'Representing the landscape of Yushan national park', *Annals of Tourism Research*, 43: 37–57.

Lin, J. Y. (2002) *The leaf in the wing*, Taipei: Classic Press.

Ling, M. J. (2008) *Centenary history of Taiwan mountaineering*, Taipei: Taiwan Interminds.

Republic of China Mountain Rescue Association (2010) Online, available at: www.mtrescue.org.tw/main/index.php (accessed 23 January 2010).

Sports Affairs Council ROC (Taiwan) (2003) '2002 annual report'. Online, available at: www.sac.gov.tw/WebData/WebData.aspx?WDID=69&wmid=500 (accessed 2 March 2010).

Tourism Bureau ROC (Taiwan) (2002) '2001 annual report'. Online, available at: http://admin.taiwan.net.tw/public/public.aspx?no=317 (accessed 2 March 2010).

Yiang, N. J. (1996) *Explore Taiwan: Original Japanese version*, Taiwan: Yuan-Liou.

Yushan National Park (2010) 'Draft management plan'. Online, available at: www.ysnp.gov.tw/upload/documents/20101110_141659.42537.pdf (accessed 10 May 2013).

4 Concepts of the wilderness experience and adventure mountaineering tourism

Mike Boyes and Susan Houge Mackenzie

Mountains and wilderness areas are geographically and culturally interwoven. In New Zealand (NZ), most wilderness is located in national parks where mountains or ranges are cultural icons. For example, Mt Aspiring National Park and Aoraki Mt Cook National Park are named after their loftiest peaks. Although some wilderness areas lack an alpine peak, most have a high point on the horizon that is culturally significant. Mt Hikurangi, in the eastern North Island, is an example of a high point in a wilderness area with considerable spiritual, cultural and physical significance to local Māori and European people. Wilderness areas, with their unique ecosystems, are focal points of the touristic gaze and sites of mountain recreation. The natural assets of wilderness areas, coupled with increasing concern for conservation ethics globally, has made these places attractive for ecotourism, adventure tourism and mountaineering tourism.

Wilderness as a concept is contested, dynamic and malleable. A physical area of land complete with peaks, flora and fauna is the basis of widely different human perceptions. An alpine peak can be a Māori cultural god, a conservation site or a mountaineering objective. The notion of parallax describes the different interpretations that come from multiple perspectives (Timms 2008). Timms (p. 95) acknowledges the existence of: 'a complementary parallax of perspectives to address the human-nature dichotomy'. As society has developed from pre-industrialization to postmodernity, so too have perspectives of wilderness. The experience of wilderness has progressed from initially being a wild heathen place to avoid and fear, to a desirable asset that provides value to civilization. Nash (1963) identifies that value arguments are inherently anthropocentric and have promoted a separation of humans and nature. In contrast, an eco-centric perspective sees nature as inherently valuable in its own right. Hall and Page (2002) summarize a number of wilderness parallax values including: (a) experiential values that support recreation and tourism; (b) mental and restorative values for enhancing individuals; (c) scientific values of wilderness (e.g. genetic resources, ecological research); and (d) economic value that accrues from the commodification of wilderness and the resources and activities therein.

The postmodern tourism experience

The postmodern tourist experience reflects multiple perspectives of the past. Many forms of tourist experience have credibility and the tourist experience is complex, multifaceted and multidimensional (Sharpley and Stone 2012). Postmodern realities include the valorization of individualism and domination of consumerism where the consumption of goods and services delivered by neoliberal regimes is commonplace. Neoliberalism transforms nature into an expanding range of new commodities (Duffy 2014). For example, mountaineering tourism packages can range from a two-hour walk on a glacier to a multi-day expedition to climb a major peak. In these examples, wilderness has been captured, reconfigured and recreated to appeal to the consumer and create economic value and capitalist expansion.

In concert, the tourist experience reflects the social realities of modern life. Uriely (2005) summarizes these conceptual developments with four key aspects. First, the boundaries between tourism and everyday life have become blurred to a point of de-differentiation. The notion of tourism as an escape and contrast to everyday life has been transformed due to the abundance of destination media coverage and increasingly flexible and mobile employment options. Second, the plurality of tourist meanings and motivations are recognized through the postmodern principle of multiple realities. Third, tourists value the subjective negotiation of meanings that determine their individual understanding and value of an experience, especially with regard to perceived authenticity. Last, the wide range of relative and complementary interpretations of the tourist experience has moved from the absolute truths of modernity to the relative truths of postmodernity.

Driven by individualism, the postmodern tourist travels with a multiplicity of motivations, beliefs and values, although often subconsciously driven by consumerism. These lead to the desire for many different modes of tourist experience, by which an individual reveals their personal values, crafts social identity and creates social distinction (Beedie 2007; Sharpley and Stone 2012). Ideally, the tourist experience is sensory, experiential and evokes strong emotional elements linked to pleasure and excitement. The multidimensionality of tourism includes the good times and the bad times to invoke the complete experience. In effect, the individual tourist experience is co-created with the provider and other participants to reflect evolving meanings and modes of consumption. In postmodern tourism, the boundaries between producers and consumers have become blurred (Prat and Aspiunza 2012).

Grounded in the postmodern condition, this chapter explores the synergies between traditional and contemporary concepts of the wilderness experience and mountaineering tourism. To achieve this goal, wilderness concepts from a historical perspective are infused with mountaineering literature. The themes include: (1) wilderness as fear; (2) wilderness as the sublime; (3) wilderness as frontier; (4) wilderness as ecology; and (5) wilderness as recreation and tourism. Any influential ideology has a social history informed by the past.

Often there is disagreement about what the past was and uncertainty as to whether the past is over or still operative, albeit in different forms. Hence, early historical notions of wilderness may still be relevant, yet in transformed structures. This chapter will explore the relevance of historical wilderness concepts to today's postmodern world.

Wilderness as a fearful place

Light (1995) identifies an original classical view that, 'places wilderness as a place to be feared, an area of waste and desolation inhabited by wild animals, savages and ... supernatural evil'. Similarly in 1836, an American settler described the forest he was clearing as 'a savage wilderness resting in primeval solitude' (cited in Nash 1963: 4). Biblical references focus on arid, barren tracts lacking cultivation that reflect the geographical realities of those times and places (Hall and Page 2002). Distinctions are drawn between the uncivilized savage, wild nature, danger and fear on one hand and the civilized human, safety and prosperity on the other. In summary, Light (1995) characterizes classical wilderness as the separation of humans from untamed nature, the danger and savagery of the human and non-human inhabitants, and the superiority of civilization. These sentiments represent the origins of anthropocentrism.

Modern personifications of these wilderness portrayals include those who fear untamed and uncontrolled nature. For instance, some find the New Zealand rainforest as having a sinister quality, 'something that is not ours, something that has never belonged ... but has known centuries of undisturbed stillness' (Holcroft 1998: 152). Wilderness may appear enigmatic as ecologies do not obey human structure and provide glimpses of greater forces at play. People fear the unknown especially when the exact nature of hazards is obscured. In American wilderness, elements such as wild animals, snakes and spiders may contribute to these perceptions. Mountains in particular are inherently dangerous with hazards such as rock fall, swift water, avalanche weather and uneven ground, that may have unknown consequences (Powers 2009). Mountain lore is full of anonymous quotes that recognize the fear provoked by these wild areas. For instance: 'Mountain climbing is extended periods of intense boredom, interrupted by occasional moments of sheer terror.' Another example is: 'Anything I've ever done that ultimately was worthwhile, initially scared me to death.' In the modern context, fear and uncertainty of mountains forms the basis of strong emotional states that link these areas to the sublime.

Wilderness as the sublime

Beyond the power of words, wilderness landscapes contain elements of unspeakable beauty. Many an adventure tourist has been transfixed by the beauty of a sunset, a rock face or an alpine lake. Mountain peaks, glaciers, dramatic rock faces, pristine lakes and cascading waterfalls are unforgettable elements. Beauty is in the eye of the beholder and derives from the interaction of person, culture and environment. In 1915, Freda du Faur, one of the original guided mountain-eers who climbed Mt Cook in 1910, waxed eloquent about mountains:

> From the moment my eyes rested on the snow clad alps I worshipped their beauty and was filled with a passionate longing to touch those shining snows, to climb to the heights of silence and solitude, and feel myself one with the mighty forces around me.
>
> (du Faur 1998: 107)

She describes the beauty, images and sensations as being engraved indelibly on her memories.

The cultural interpretation of nature as sublime beauty represents a significant departure from notions of savage wilderness. Originating in Europe in the eight-eenth century, notions of the sublime drew upon aesthetic Romanticism that was linked to religious beliefs of God's presence on Earth. Dramatic environments of pristine wildness and beauty evoked emotions of awe, terror and exaltation (Nash 1963). These elements were, 'something irreducibly non-human, some-thing profoundly Other than yourself' (Cronon 1996: 8). Such powerful senti-ments were seen to parallel the religious experience of glimpsing God's face. Through nature, humans could draw closer to God and wilderness became a place of spiritual renewal. Similarly, Cronon (1996: 10) depicts the sublime as, 'found in powerful landscapes where one felt insignificant and reminded of one's own mortality'. Thoreau (cited in Cronon 1996), visualized mountains trans-muted into icons of the sublime and potent symbols of God's presence on Earth. The links between sacred wilderness and religion meant that some of the deepest core values of western civilization were being reproduced through interactions with wilderness.

The American Romantic movement (*c.*1770–1860) also reflected the change in attitude to wilderness with its emphasis away from the macabre to celebrating the aesthetic qualities of nature. This was particularly apparent through the work of artists, writers, philosophers and politicians of the day. For instance, Ralph Waldo Emerson (unknown date) wrote: 'Every particular in nature, a leaf, a drop, a crystal, a moment of time is related to the whole, and partakes of the perfection of the whole.'

Landscapes such as Niagara Falls, Uluru and Mitre Peak exemplify the spec-tacular and timeless natural beauty that Hall (2002) describes as monumental-ism. The aesthetic value of wilderness is upheld by the designation of National Parks, which were first established around outstanding natural features. The New Zealand national park mandate preserves in perpetuity, 'areas of New Zealand that contain scenery of such distinctive quality, ecological systems, or natural features so beautiful, unique, or scientifically important that their preservation is in the national interest' (*National Park Act 1980*, section 4(1)). All parks show-case the beauty of nature and have distinct iconic features. Shaping the sublime as a political construct enables legislated protection and the establishment of infrastructure to develop management strategies.

In a modern day context, what constitutes the sublime? It is relatively easy to describe the physical features that underpin the appreciation of scenic beauty, remoteness and peace in wilderness areas. When Shultis (2001) surveyed New Zealand residents on their images of wilderness, they identified native forest, peace and solitude, remoteness, wildlife, low human impact, rivers and waterfalls, and mountains and alpine areas as being important. Elements such as commercial mining, logging, high human impact, hydroelectric development, motorized travel and overcrowding were cited as intrusions into the purism of wilderness.

In contrast to physical attributes of the sublime, more complex understandings of this term originate from cultural and sociological understandings that influence human behaviour. Representations of the sublime reflect the culture from which the recognition emerges (Stranger 1999). Artists' and writers' elucidations are laden with cultural interpretations. From the 1800s, romantic artwork such as Bierstadt's (1868) *Among the Sierra Nevada Mountains*, the writings of Henry David Thoreau and Ralph Waldo Emerson, and Wordsworth's poem *The Prelude* are all examples of the aesthetic view of heavenly nature that prevailed at the time. Interestingly, present times have seen the return of romantic views of landscape that depict the sublime. A facet of postmodern landscape art is images that are hyper-real, with the sublime being enhanced by the artist's interpretation. Likewise, contemporary writers such as Brian Turner and Edward Abbey write romantically and emotionally of nature (see also Cowley 2008).

The need to accept gradations of the sublime highlights a key paradox of wilderness. Different ecosystems demonstrate differing degrees of 'naturalness' and human influence. Pure wilderness is a completely pristine state uncorrupted by human intervention (Light 1995). But in our modern world, finding a place that has not seen the footprint of humankind is difficult. As Cronon (1996: 17) noted, 'to believe that nature, to be true, must also be wild, then our very presence in nature represents its fall'. If an experience is to promote awe, terror and exaltation how pristine does the wilderness need to be? The participants in Shultis' (2001) study were prepared to accept some cultural artefacts in a landscape and still describe it as wilderness. These mostly included huts, tracks, bridges, campsites and road access. This led Shultis to describe a dualism in wilderness conceptions between a political construct (e.g. a national park) and wilderness as a state of mind. The notion of wilderness as a state of mind, rather than a description of nature, had been floated earlier by Tuan (1974). The application of parallax, promoted by Timms (2008), is also based on the dualism of a physical land area and a particular viewpoint. Timms believes landscapes can be viewed from multiple perspectives and different positions, which creates a complimentary parallax of perspectives that addresses the human–nature dichotomy.

Some, like Cronon (1996), argue that the sublime has been watered down from its original religious power and value. The transition from religious belief to postmodern, individual narcissism is profound and reflects a change in cultural values as civilization progresses. The dehumanizing rationalism of industrialization not only fuelled the seminal aesthetic reaction towards valuing nature, it also promoted the emergence of alpinism as a form of escape through embracing beauty and first hand experiences. As Marx contended, industrial rationalism leads to alienation wherein social conditions deaden the human spirit. Based on this premise, Lyng (2005: 5) explains current risk-taking as, 'a radical form of escape from the routines of contemporary life or a pure expression of cultural imperatives of the emerging social order'. The same could be said of wilderness. Experiencing the sublime is a form of escape that is culturally valued. Furthermore, mountaineering as a wilderness experience is a combination of embracing risk and the aesthetic experience of the sublime.

A present-day discussion of the sublime sees it positioned as a feature of neoliberal individualism. The seeking of sublime experiences is linked to the subjective construction of identity, concurrently influenced by and influencing broader social understandings. Stranger (1999) describes postmodern culture as involving an aesthetic of sensation, which gives primacy to sensual experience. The body and the physical experience enable the sensual and emotional experience of excitement and awe. The sublime is experienced first hand in union with a social appreciation of the sublime. Stranger also links the sublime to the experience of 'flow' where one becomes totally immersed in an activity, engaged in a transcendent, peak experience for personal development and pleasure.

For most people in the early Romantic period, wilderness and mountains were waiting in the distance to be visually consumed. Active mountaineers were few and far between. Urry's (2005: 78) romantic gaze was 'a solitudinous, personal, semi-spiritual relationship with place'. Pleasure flowed from emotions associated with the visual consumption of place; however, visual consumption is abstract and disembodied. Tourist mountaineering includes visual landscape aesthetics and a more genuine immersion in the locality through direct experience. As Mortlock (2001) recognized, there is a distinction between being in a wild place and looking at a view. The postmodern view envisages seeking the sublime through embodiment and physically being in wilderness.

Wilderness as a frontier

As European colonization progressed in the eighteenth and nineteenth centuries, new settlers cut down and burnt native hinterland to make way for pastoralism, exploitation of natural resources and European-style settlements. This progression occurred on multiple continents, along waterways in Canada, through relentless westward expansion in the USA and settlers moving inland from New Zealand and Australia's long coastlines. The forested wilderness regions at the edge of a newly settled area were known as 'frontier'. Mountains often form the last bastions of wilderness as they encompass unproductive pastoral land and provide natural frontiers beyond which it is not economically viable or welcoming to live. Thus the exploration of wilderness and mountains frontiers can be viewed as a form of boundary negotiation; the exploration of the edges of society.

Colonization saw European migrants moving to wild, unsettled frontier lands, where it was necessary to live off the land and lead simpler lifestyles. Cronon

(1996: 13) describes settlers as vigorous, independent, creative folk who had chosen to shed the trappings of civilization. The frontier offered unique opportunities to develop and shape their own properties, as well as an escape from the stifling structures of civilized life where, 'cities and factories were seen as confining, false and artificial'. The frontier was a rugged world where individualism, masculine values, physical prowess and independence were respected. Clearing the land was hard physical work and people had to create their own solutions to localized problems.

The realities of colonial life formed the basis of national identity stereotypes. Cronon (1996) believed that the wilderness was a sacred icon in American cultural traditions. This suggests that colonials were moulded by harsh frontier conditions where a simple life, adaptability and self-sufficiency were highly valued. These values form the basis of primitivism, a belief that 'the best antidote to the ills of an overly refined and civilized modern world was a return to simpler, more primitive living' (Cronon 1996: 13). This 'frontier myth' was embodied in wilderness and strengthened over the years by the mass media. For instance, twentieth century writers such as Crump, Leopold and Abbey portray the rugged outdoorsman as a central and desirable figure. Their heroes are at one with native forests, tolerate physical discomfort and enjoy primitive, simple living.

This image of the rugged outdoors person is alive and well today, with King (2003) noting that many New Zealand men still prefer to think of themselves as 'blokes from the backblocks' (ordinary men from the frontier regions). The primitive outdoor life is treasured by many New Zealanders who tramp, climb and ski in mountainous regions (Sport and Recreation New Zealand 2008). Tramping and climbing in particular require minimal (although specialized) equipment, necessitated partly by having to carry everything on one's back. Accommodation is a tent or mountain hut and food is basic and easily prepared. For their holidays, thousands of New Zealanders head to 'kiwi baches' (cabins) in remote wilderness areas where simple living prevails. Primitivism through wilderness has a powerful romantic attraction and is a popular choice for many adventure tourists (Yeo 2013).

As settlers cleared land, wilderness diminished and the traditional primitive lifestyle was compromised. For many it was a shock to realize that the frontier was vanishing (Nash 1963). People responded by recognizing the importance of preserving some wild landscapes in order to enjoy the frontier experience in perpetuity. This movement led to the establishment of national parks and wilderness areas. Wilderness as a frontier became not only a cultural artifact, but also a means of aesthetic and economic conservation (Hall 2002). In addition, national parks were a mechanism to present elements of the frontier for recreational and tourist consumption.

In today's context, the wilderness is still seen as a boundary between wild nature and civilization. As Hall and Boyd (2005: 7) identify, the wilderness is a moving boundary that symbolizes the dominance of humankind over nature. Hall proposes a wide frontier with a continuum from well-established settled land through to undeveloped land. Settled land offers decreasing remoteness and primitivism and no wilderness quality. On the other hand, undeveloped land presents increasing remoteness and primitivism with low, medium and high wilderness quality depending on proximity to settlements.

Wilderness is ecological

Wilderness and mountain areas are among the last bastions of original and minimally altered ecosystems. They embrace diverse wildlife populations, many of which are on the endangered species list, and vast assortments of flora with considerable genetic biodiversity. Wilderness areas are often managed by different agencies across a range of settings including national parks, wildlife refuges, national forests, other state lands and the public domain. For example, the first politically defined wilderness area (i.e. Yellowstone, USA in 1872) was protected through local National Forest administrative orders to preserve the sublime and the frontier in a broad sense (Cronon 1996). The first national parks in New Zealand were established for similar reasons, with the land area of Tongariro being gifted to the state by Māori chief Te Heuheu in 1887. National parks were first thought of as places for recreation and tourism and the New Zealand Alps were a popular playground for mountaineers, skiers and trampers. Deer and goats that destroyed natural flora were released into parks for sport hunting. In New Zealand, the hunting, shooting and fishing interest groups were powerful and drove early recreation and tourism trends. The notion that national parks should also protect native plants and animals came later in the twentieth century. Although the conservation ethic of *kaitiatikanga*[1] (environmental guardianship) was Te Heuheu's primary objective, European beliefs also held sway when national parks were first established.

In the late 1900s, greater primacy was given to the protection of ecological systems through mechanisms such as the *USA Wilderness Act of 1964*. In this act, wilderness was defined as: 'areas where the earth and its communities of life are left unchanged by people, where the primary forces of nature are in control, and where people themselves are visitors who do not remain' (Wilderness Institute 2014: 1). More recently, Timms (2008: 95) provided an ecologically friendly description of a national park: 'a bounded physical area of land protected from human habitation and exploitation for the conservation goals of biodiversity protection, continuation of ecological services and other more spiritual, intrinsic and aesthetic values'.

The Wilderness Act decreed that a wilderness area needed to comprise at least 5,000 acres, or be sufficiently large enough to make species preservation practical. Most species are vulnerable to external influences (e.g. the kiwi bird) and tolerate little human-engineered disturbance. Wilderness designation prevents direct economic exploitation of local resources, such as logging or mining, but promotes economic activity through visitors. Hence relatively harmless human activities are permitted within wilderness areas (Carafo 2001). Hall and Boyd's (2005) wilderness continuum expresses the relationships between wilderness quality and proximity and notes that as remoteness increases, so too does the likelihood of wilderness quality and effectiveness. A larger area also decreases the chances of interruption and helps preserve more intact ecosystems. In addition, a large wilderness area with a well-established infrastructure is more likely to be recognized by the public as an area of conservation significance, and therefore it may be more resistant to political interference.

One of the major goals of wilderness preservation is to provide undeveloped habitat for diverse fauna and flora. Even recognizing a wilderness preservation area expresses a belief in the rights of nature. Visiting a wilderness area involves being surrounded by plants, animals and physical landscapes, 'whose otherness commands our attention' (Cronon 1996: 23). Some fundamental conservation principles are learnt first hand in wilderness areas. Experiencing the impact of introduced predators, such as stoats and possums in New Zealand, and seeing the invasion of noxious weeds, like hierachium in the mountains, provides valuable lessons. Nash (2002: 42) believed that wilderness was an ideal place to learn environmental ethics and appreciate ecological limitations; 'Wilderness is the best environment in which to learn that humans are members in, and not masters of, the community of life.' Carafo (2001) also highlights the need to combat massive biodiversity loss and preserve habitat by cultivating better relationships with plants, animals and places.

To highlight the critical role wilderness can play in developing an environmental ethic, DeLancey (2012) proposes an ecological concept of wilderness. He conceptualizes wilderness from an ecocentric, rather than an anthropocentric, viewpoint that depicts humans as part of, rather than separate from, ecosystems. From this perspective, wilderness is an enduring ecosystem that it is optimally placed to maximize both the quantity and quality of organisms, relative to past historical conditions. This is achieved through the richness of ecosystems with their huge number and variety of organisms nested within a vast range of complex relationships. DeLancey documents how our present practice of unrestrained natural resource exploitation destroys existing organisms and lowers populations and species diversity to the point that the ecosystem is no longer a wilderness. In contrast, the anthropocentric view sees wilderness areas as stockpiles of genetic diversity, the loss of which could be considered an economic cost to humankind due to the potential loss of medically important genetic material (Hall and Page 2002).

Valuing wilderness includes consideration of both the integrated ecosystem as a whole and the moral value of the individual organisms (DeLancey 2012). Favouring one side of this duality poses philosophical problems. It is common practice to eliminate or control introduced species that are impacting on existing species (e.g. possum and stoat control in New Zealand). Rare species are moved to safer habitats or reintroduced into old habitats remade safe. Hence biodiversity preservation requires intrusive management by humans in the ecosystem. But as Carafo (2001: 8) points out, 'if biodiversity includes biological communities and ecosystems, their disappearance or "development" into something essentially different constitutes a loss of biodiversity'. Carafo (p. 11) recognizes that our understanding of wilderness as an unmanaged space has moved to, 'managing for the survival of particular species and biological communities'.

The preservation of wilderness for scientific study was specifically included in the *1964 Wilderness Act*. Hall and Page (2002) link the research function of wilderness to ecology and describe the scientific values of wilderness as: (1) genetic resources/biodiversity; (2) ecological research and biological monitoring; (3) determining environmental baselines; (4) the evolutionary continuum; and (5) long-term provision of conditions in which flora and fauna conservation can occur. Combinations of these activities form the basis of the ecotourism industry and flow into the activities of mountaineers.

The modern day role of national park administrators often centres on the dual roles of environmental conservation and visitor management, most of whom are recreationists or tourists. These dual administrative roles are sometimes in concert and often in conflict. Although visitors to wilderness and mountain areas often pose more environmental problems than solutions, there is growing awareness of visitors' ecological responsibilities. Mountaineers build special relationships with their places, despite lacking care in some cases (e.g. Everest Base Camp). The latest National Outdoor Leadership School's (NOLS) handbook on wilderness mountaineering emphasizes the importance of 'leave no trace' ethics on mountains. NOLS views protecting alpine environments as central to their mission and critical to preservation of mountaineering (Powers 2009). Concern for the alpine environment can be seen in trends such as packing out all human waste from peaks in the Aoraki Mt Cook National Park. Garrard (2005: 144) further articulates the necessary elements for preservation of alpine environments as, 'a proactive, integrated waste management response with minimum impact guidelines for mountaineers, carefully articulated to suit the alpine environment'.

In reality, mountaineers' environmental engagement in their special places embraces stewardship practices and social action that extend beyond 'leave no trace' ethics. There is growing recognition that in-depth relationships with natural environments are an essential and intrinsic component of extreme sport experiences (Brymer *et al.* 2009). Mountaineers have held this sentiment for years, as evidenced in early writing of John Muir describing the Sierra Nevadas or Freda du Faur's description of being in the Southern Alps. Houston (2006) describes the practice of climbing to be a kind of communion between nature and self. Similarly McCarthy (2002: 179) develops a theory of place in mountaineering where, 'tales of intense awareness and connection reveal a more fundamental integration between human subject and natural object than our culture has imagined'. The entwining of human and mountain defines identities. Each individual climber is shaped and defined by the mountains and becomes a component of that place. It is these intimate connections that also produce environmental sensitivity and the passion to be fine caretakers of the land.

Wilderness as recreation/tourism

During industrialization and modernity, recreation and tourism were seen as distinct entities that at times overlapped. With the multiple realities of postmodernity, the boundaries between the two concepts have become increasingly fragmented and blurred. To fully explore these relationships, wilderness as both recreation and tourism will be discussed. Initially the themes of fear, sublime, frontier and ecology are applied to human behaviour. Then we explore how the commodification of wilderness, mountains and mountaineering impacts individual experiences.

Earlier in the chapter it was established that, from the Romantic period, wilderness has been anthropocentrically valued and preserved for the recreational, spiritual and scenic values that it offers (Nash 1963). *The Wilderness Act (1964)* specifically identified recreation as one of the benefits of an enduring wilderness resource. McCloskey (1965–1966) noted that wilderness is regarded as the optimum setting for many high quality sports such as mountain climbing, fly fishing, trophy hunting, backpacking and cave exploration. The wilderness experience is primarily valued as an intense and highly personal encounter with natural wonder. Recreational activities are regarded as relatively harmless to the environment and are accommodated within wilderness policies and management strategies. In contemporary times, a key aim of the New Zealand Department of Conservation is to have more New Zealanders and international visitors enjoying nature-based recreational activities on conservation land (New Zealand Department of Conservation 2004).

In terms of participation, Tourism New Zealand (2012) data (see Yeo 2013) documents that one in two international holiday tourists engaged in an adventure activity and one in three in an extreme adventure. In 2012, $1.6 billion were spent on adventure tourism. Tourists rated landscape and scenery highest in terms of New Zealand brand attributes (84 per cent) with outdoor and adventure activities following as a close second (82 per cent). With regard to visitor satisfaction, mountain climbing was the highest rated activity, with an average rating of 9.1/10 (Yeo 2013). Outdoor recreation data from the NZ Department of Conservation (2013) identified that 70 per cent of New Zealanders had visited a national park for recreation more than once in the prior year (Binnie 2013). Day walks and multiday walks were the most common activities. Mountaineering data shows that in excess of 250,000 visits were made to Aoraki Mt Cook National Park in 2001. New Zealanders made about 30 per cent of these visits, with overseas tourists comprising the remaining 70 per cent. About 30 per cent of visitors were identified as climbers who explored the wider alpine areas, with alpine hut-based accommodation totalling about 7,000 bed-nights yearly (New Zealand Department of Conservation 2004).

As part of a risk management and safety review, the NZ Department of Labour (2010) specified activities that could be included in the adventure and outdoor commercial sectors domains. Tourism NZ further validated these in an adventure tourism insights publication (Yeo 2013). The activities include: abseiling, canoeing, caving, fishing, glacier walk, heli-skiing, jet boating, kayaking, mountain biking, mountain climbing, parachuting, rock climbing skiing, snowboarding, tramping and white-water rafting. Most of these rely on wilderness areas to provide the necessary environments in which to perform these activities.

In an extensive literature review, Manning (2011) identified that the interpretation of an outdoor recreation experience has evolved from an activity and settings approach, to a behavioural approach that also focuses on motivations and benefits gained from participation. Manning's study included both recreation and tourist data. The behavioural approach recognizes four levels of outdoor recreation: (1) activities; (2) settings – undertaken in a variety of environmental, social and managerial situations that represent different recreation opportunities; (3) multiple motives – aimed at meeting a need or providing satisfaction; and (4) benefits – these can be wide ranging and include personal, social, economic and environmental domains. Examples from Manning's taxonomies (2011: 179–185) are grouped in Table 4.1 alongside links to the wilderness themes.

Table 4.1 Possible motivations and benefits linked to wilderness themes

Theme	Domain	Item
Fear	Motivations	Excitement, autonomy, control, risk-taking/seeking, being with people of similar values, exploration and learning, introspection
	Benefits	Stress management, sense of control, adaptability, teamwork/cooperation, problem-solving, self-actualization, flow
Sublime	Motivations	Excitement, exploration, learning, enjoy nature, introspection, spirituality, escape, tranquility, environmental protection
	Benefits	Positive changes in mood and emotion, self-affirmation, value clarification, autonomy, aesthetic enhancement, spiritual growth, sense of freedom, self-actualization, flow, acceleration, stimulation, nature appreciation
Frontier	Motivations	Skill development, competence testing, independence, autonomy, control, family togetherness, learning, exploration, introspection, creativity, nostalgia, physical fitness, escape, tranquility, privacy
	Benefits	Sense of wellness, positive changes in mood and emotion, self-reliance, self-confidence, self-affirmation, learn new skills, independence, control, problem-solving, cultural appreciation, balanced living, sense of freedom, challenge, environmental stewardship, preservation of cultural sites
Ecology	Motivations	Learning, enjoy nature, introspection, escape, tranquility, stewardship
	Benefits	Environmental awareness, environmental stewardship, aesthetic appreciation, nature learning, identification with special places, husbandry, leave no trace, environmental ethics, involvement in environmental issues, environmental protection, ecosystem sustainability, preservation of natural sites, promotion of ecotourism

The commodification of the wilderness and mountaineering experience

Romantic traditions of mountaineering conceptualize wilderness areas as places of fear, sources of the sublime, the last frontier and valuable ecosystems. The need to explore and seek freedom came as an aesthetic reaction to the dehumanizing influences of industrialization. The rational imposition of order and control led climbers to seek their true selves in the mountains. Acknowledging Romanticism as a cultural context, Lester (2004) identifies seven main themes from the psychological research on climbers: sense of freedom, sense of power, energy and vitality, assertion of self, conquest of self, escape from self, contact with a higher power and a sense of unity/wholeness. Similarly, Beedie (2007: 25) recognized the formative components of mountaineering as: 'physical challenge, wilderness, solitude, contemplation, self-development, spirituality, mystery, authenticity and war in the face of sublime nature'.

The lives of mountaineers in the Romantic tradition have been explored by Houston's (2006) comparison of old school and new school climbers and Beedie's (2007) contrast of legislators and interpreters. We begin by exploring old school climbers and legislators before turning to new school climbers and interpreters in the following paragraphs. Houston's father was an old school, eminent mountaineer who saw a climb as a sacred and pure pilgrimage following those who had gone before. These climbers saw the wholeness of the experience as a communion with nature; they were in awe of the power of the mountain and revered the setting and the wilderness. To climb was seen as part of a bigger journey that was self-determined and self-propelled. Often the walk in and out would take much longer than the climb itself. On a serious climb, it was expected that there would be a brush with death and this immortalized the experience as something to be revered, remapped and mythologized. A strong *esprit de corps* existed between climbers who were committed to each other's welfare rather than achieving a summit at any cost. The process was seen as more important than the outcome and 'peak baggers' were treated with disdain. To achieve the skill and knowledge required for extreme mountaineering took years and was based in an informal apprenticeship-based system administered by alpine clubs.

Beedie (2007) bases his notion of legislators on the importance of a specific body of knowledge (rules) generated through first hand experiences. The systematic accumulation of knowledge such as climbing techniques, weather patterns and avalanche risk in many mountains provides a discourse that enables positions of power. These are played out not only in dominant and controlling mountaineering discourses, but also in the manners, style, customs and deportment of individuals. Controversial discussions of authenticity in mountaineering are influenced by such values. While notions of escape resisted capitalist discourse, some capitalist values, such as rational order and control, were embraced when they suited the ends of mountaineers. This introduced a tension between freedom and constraint in mountaineering that remains today. The Romantics were keen to measure mountain heights and establish scales that graded the difficulty of climbs and individual pitches. Discourses of safe practice were written into instruction manuals and instructor/guide certifications were established. Drawing on this knowledge, alpine guides are now able to exchange their enshrined knowledge for economic benefit. These developments demonstrate the continued Romantic influence in postmodern society, especially through increasing auditing, accreditation and risk management practices.

The commodification of mountaineering and other adventure activities sparked debates over the authenticity and sustainability of a paid experience. Tourists search for the authentic and the novel because their lives are dominated by inauthenticity and habitual rules (Henning 2012). For inexperienced participants, tourist experiences provide an ideal introduction to an activity in relatively benign settings. Risk levels are well managed, physical fitness expectations are lower and the locus of control is with a guide. As tourists' skill and knowledge levels are often low, experienced leaders teach progressively by 'scaffolding' experiences. Most providers also have rigorous gear checks and provide key items where necessary (e.g. crampons, ropes). These beginner tourist experiences have been described in the literature as 'soft adventure' (Ewert and Jamieson 2003; Hill 1995) or 'shallow adventure' (Varley 2006).

Varley believes shallow adventure has built-in comfort and convenience with the guide taking responsibility for a high quality, safe experience. This type of commodified soft adventure climbing could be considered a 'post-adventure' in the sense that, 'producers and consumers stage a theatrical performance which produces a visual representation of authentic experience transferable to a virtual witnessing audience' (McGillivray and Frew 2007: 54). While the expert sees soft adventures as inauthentic, the participant may not share this opinion. If state of mind is a measure of satisfaction, then a range of climbs and processes become legitimate. As skill levels and experience grows, challenges can incorporate higher risk levels and clients can be empowered to exercise more control. In these situations the boundaries between producers and consumers become blurred and the tourist is just as likely to become a colleague or a friend and part of the experience design process (Prat and Aspiunza 2012).

Varley (2006) identified a number of commodified outdoor adventure elements that incorporate the wilderness themes discussed above. These include removal from everyday life, individual responsibility through self-determination, engagement in risk uncertainty and transcendence through the ecstatic experience. Furthermore, Varley advocates for strong environmental attachments through multi-sensual engagement with nature, personally coping with the natural environment and developing a romantic attachment with the natural environment.

In contrast to soft skills and shallow adventure, 'hard adventures' and 'deep adventures' form the polar end of these continuums. Hard adventures involve high risk levels, intense commitment, advanced skills, advanced mental and physical fitness, and considerable previous experience. Varley (2006) suspected that some activities, such as BASE jumping or extreme alpinism, were too 'deep' to ever become a product. Mortlock (2001) also noted that tourism lacked the elements of original adventure, namely high risk levels with the possibility of death, personal responsibility for the welfare of self and colleagues, high levels of uncertainty and total personal commitment. However, as provider–client combinations undertake more audacious and extreme activities, the fragmentation of these defined positions continues.

In his discussion of 'interpreters', Beedie (2007) argues that rationalization and democratization of mountaineering has facilitated wider participation of nouveau mountaineers through increased access. These notions align with Houston's observation of 'new school' mountaineers. In contrast to the rule-bound legislators, interpreters are postmodern, self-determining, individualistic and engaged in contesting existing territory. The process of democratization is assisted by technological developments that make mountaineering safer and more accessible for wider swaths of the population. For instance, helicopters mean climbers can climb a number of peaks in a few days. New equipment and clothing is lighter, stronger and more fit-for-purpose. Maps are more detailed and accurate and supported by GPS location systems. In addition, participation is assisted by rationalized elements from the Romantics, such as instruction manuals and guidebooks.

Rationalization includes the ideas of control, mastery, organization and measurement played out through commodification. The free market provides trappings such as adventure clothing, navigational aids, equipment and packaged adventure activities for consumption. The NZ Department of Conservation has rationalized its resources to suit the consumer by providing tracks, huts, radios, rescue services and clear access. Visitors to high use areas, such as the Milford Track, are controlled and sustainably managed. Alpine guides use well worn routes and observe carefully crafted codes of practice. A key example of this trend is the rationalization of risk. We live in a globalized society where risk-taking is a key structural principle of postmodern life and an expected part of economic, political, cultural and leisure activity (Giddens 2009). For example, the state mandates the safety of tourists and students in educational programmes. On the other hand, it is expected that individuals will assume more responsibility for the risks they choose to take in their lives (Simon 2002). Extreme sports such as BASE jumping and climbing embrace an individualistic aesthetic sensibility and are forms of resistance to rational risk management (Stranger 1999).

Changing social constructions of wilderness and mountaineering are heavily influenced by representations and images communicated via social media. Mountaineering is discursively defined by words and images, with individual glory in wilderness and mountain areas as common as images of nature itself. Old and new school mountaineers co-construct the perspectives and contributions of each other through these mechanisms (Houston 2006). The marketing of adventure and recreational risk-taking with slogans like 'Live life on the edge' and 'Live the dream' promote certain stereotypes of adventure activities. As McGillivray and Frew (2007: 54) highlight, 'their gazing social network recognises and bestows value to displays of spectacle, style and show'. The undeveloped natural environment is an ever-present context. Depictions of people engaging in exciting risky activities, mountaineers experiencing the sublime and people living a simpler outdoor lifestyle, are now commonplace. These images inform a discourse that promotes and shapes tourism and recreation in wilderness places.

Conclusion

Concepts of wilderness and mountains are contestable social constructs that reflect the ideologies, dominant discourses and values of western civilizations over time. By examining the evolving meanings of wilderness, we can better understand the interconnectedness of humans and nature and the shape of these relationships in the present age of postmodernity. From the times of early settlement, civilization was carved out of the wilderness and the anthropocentric separation of humans and nature began. Wilderness as a heathen, fearful place needed to be tamed to produce an idealized conception of nature as having instrumental value.

The Romantics valorized the beauty and awe of the mountains initially as a religious experience, but also viewed them as places for exploration and journeys. Here humans could escape from the rigours of capitalist society and embrace freedom, excitement, authenticity and camaraderie in the sublime. With experience came rationalization, wherein knowledge and skills were codified into written forms that became a means of influence, ownership and control.

As wilderness was legislated into existence, the goals and purposes of reserves and national parks were debated. Tradition dictated that reserved wilderness areas and mountains should be sites of outdoor recreation, tourism, scientific exploration and ecological preservation. While nature conservation has always been an intention of wilderness, only in postmodern times has there been an increased focus on individual ecosystems, sustainability and eco-centrism. This shift in values has been hastened by pressing issues such as overpopulation, loss of biodiversity and global warming. Concurrently, there is growing recognition that strong environmental attachments are formed in the outdoors, and that engagement with these areas is accompanied by environmental responsibilities.

Neoliberalism, where the free market promotes the consumption of goods and services marketed to individuals with disposable incomes, is currently the dominant political ideology. Wilderness, mountains and mountaineering are commodified to fit this free market philosophy. Social media forms a key component of this trend by providing individualized interactive tools that promote choice, taste and style. The global risk society sees the mountains as sites of desirable risk-taking behaviour implemented in leisure domains. At the same time, the need to escape and define one's identity through aesthetic pleasure and individual expression has never been greater. This has led to leisure lifestyles marked by dynamic participation and enjoyment where identity is constructed by individual choice.

There are myriad ways to experience the wilderness underpinned by a wide range of individual motivations and benefits. Collectively, these lead to postmodern leisure experiences that are complex, multifaceted and multidimensional. The parallax of tourist meanings has led to ill-defined and fragmented boundaries between mountaineering-as-recreation and mountaineering-as-tourism, as well as blurred distinctions between hard and soft adventures.

Note

1 *Kaitiakitanga* is the Māori ethic of care and protection for waters, flora and fauna, forests, mountains, the Earth and the sky (Blundell 2006).

References

Beedie, P. (2007) 'Legislators and interpreters. An examination of changes in philosophical interpretations of "being a mountaineer"', in M. McNamee (ed.) *Philosophy, risk and adventure sports*, London: Routledge: 25–42.
Binnie, I. (2013) 'National survey of New Zealanders: Visitor and historic sites report', Department of Conservation, Wellington.
Blundell, S. (2006) '*Kaitiakitanga*: Sustaining our future', *Te Karaka: The Ngai Tahu Magazine*, 32: 49–53.
Brymer, E., Downey, G. and Gray, T. (2009) 'Extreme sports as a precursor to environmental sustainability', *Journal of Sport and Tourism*, 14(2–3): 193–204.
Carafo, P. (2001) 'For a grounded conception of wilderness and more wilderness on the ground', *Ethics and the Environment*, 6(1): 1–17.
Cowley, J. (ed.) (2008) *The new nature writing*, London: Granta Publications.
Cronon, W. (1996) 'The trouble with wilderness', *Environmental History*, 1(2): 7–28.
DeLancey, C. (2012) 'An ecological concept of wilderness', *Ethics and the Environment*, 17(1): 25–44.
du Faur, F. (1998) 'Reasons for mountaineering', in P. Temple (ed.) *Lake, mountain*, Wellington: Godwit: 107–108.
Duffy, R. (2014) 'Interactive elephants: Nature, tourism and neoliberalism', *Annals of Leisure Research*, 44(January): 88–101.
Emerson, R. W (unknown) Online, available at: www.brainyquote.com/quotes/quotes/r/ralphwaldo557664.html#gy7rVjAPwSowRojD.99 (accessed 24 August 2014).
Ewert, A. and Jamieson, L. (2003) 'Current status and future directions in the adventure tourism industry', in J. Wilks and S. J. Page (eds) *Managing tourist health and safety in the new millenium*, Boston, MA: Pergamon: 67–83.
Garrard, R. (2005) 'Alpine stewardship in Aotearoa/New Zealand: Towards zero-waste on mountaineering routes in Aoraki/Mount Cook national park', Paper presented at the 2005 Zero Waste Conference, Kaikoura, NZ, 5–8 April.
Giddens, A. (2009) *Sociology* (6th edn), Cambridge: Polity Press.
Hall, C. M. (2002) 'The changing cultural geography of the frontier: National parks and wilderness as frontier remnant', in S. Krakover and Y. Gradus (eds) *Tourism in frontier areas*, New York: Lexington Books: 283–298.
Hall, C. M. and Boyd, S. (2005) 'Nature-based tourism in peripheral areas: Introduction', in C. M. Hall and S. Boyd (eds) *Nature-based tourism in peripheral areas*, Bristol: Channel View Publications: 3–17.
Hall, C. M. and Page, S. J. (2002) 'Tourism and recreation in the pleasure periphery', in C. M. Hall and S. J. Page (eds) *The geography of tourism and recreation* (2nd edn), London: Routledge: 249–282.

Henning, G. K. (2012) 'The habit of tourism', in R. Sharpley and P. R. Stone (eds) *Contemporary tourist experience*, London: Routledge: 25–37.

Hill, B. J. (1995) 'A guide to adventure travel', *Parks and Recreation*, 30(9): 56–65.

Holcroft, M. (1998) 'The primeval shadow', in P. Temple (ed.) *Lake, mountain, tree*, Auckland, NZ: Godwit: 152–156.

Houston, D. L. R. (2006) 'Five miles out: Communion and commodification among the mountaineers', in L. A. Vivanco and R. J. Gordon (eds) *Tarzan was an eco-tourist … and other tales in the anthropology of adventure*, Oxford: Berghahn Books: 147–160.

King, M. (2003) *The Penguin history of New Zealand*, Auckland, NZ: Penguin.

Lester, J. (2004) 'Spirit, identity and self in mountaineering', *Journal of Humanistic Psychology*, 44(1): 86–100.

Light, A. (1995) 'From classical to urban wilderness', *Trumpeter*, 12(1): 19–21.

Lyng, S. (2005) 'Edgework and the risk-taking experience', in S. Lyng (ed.) *Edgework: The sociology of risk-taking*, London: Routledge: 3–14.

Manning, R. E. (2011) 'Motivations and benefits in outdoor recreation', in R. E. Manning (ed.) *Studies in outdoor recreation: Search and research for satisfaction* (3rd edn), Corvallis, OR: Oregan State University Press: 166–189.

McCarthy, J. (2002) 'A theory of place in North American mountaineering', *Philosophy and Geography*, 5(2): 179–194.

McCloskey, M. (1965–66) 'The Wilderness Act of 1964: Its background and meaning', *Oregon Law Review*, 45: 288–321.

McGillivray, D. and Frew, M. (2007) 'Capturing adventure: Trading experiences in the symbolic economy', *Annals of Leisure Research*, 10(1): 54–78.

Mortlock, C. (2001) *Beyond adventure*, Milnthorpe: Cicerone Press.

Nash, R. (1963) 'The American wilderness in historical perspective', *Forest History Newsletter*, 6(4): 2–13.

Nash, R. (2002) 'Power of the wild', *New Scientist*, 173(2336): 42–45.

New Zealand Department of Conservation (2004) 'Aoraki/Mount Cook National Park management plan'. Online, available at: www.doc.govt.nz/.../aoraki-mount-cook-np-management-plan-1.pdf (accessed 18 August 2014).

New Zealand Department of Labour (2010) 'Review of risk management and safety in the adventure and outdoor commercial sectors in New Zealand', Wellington, NZ.

Powers, P. (2009) *Wilderness mountaineering*, Mechanicsburg, PA: Stackpole Books.

Prat, A. G. and Aspiunza, A. R. (2012) 'Personal experience tourism: A postmodern understanding', in R. Sharpley and P. R. Stone (eds) *Contemporary tourist experience*, London: Routledge: 11–24.

Sharpley, R. and Stone, P. R. (2012) 'Experiencing tourism, experiencing happiness?' in R. Sharpley and P. R. Stone (eds) *Contemporary tourist experience*, London: Routledge: 1–18.

Shultis, J. (2001) 'The duality of wilderness', in G. Cessford (ed.) *The state of wilderness in New Zealand*, Wellington: Department of Conservation: 59–73.

Simon, J. (2002) 'Taking risks: Extreme sports and the embrace of risk in advanced liberal societies', in T. Baker and J. Simon (eds) *Embracing risk*, Chicago, IL: University of Chicago Press: 177–208.

Sport and Recreation New Zealand (2008) *Sport, recreation and physical activity participation among New Zealand adults*, Wellington: SPARC.

Stranger, M. (1999) 'The aesthetics of risk', *International Review for the Sociology of Sport*, 34(3): 265–276.

Timms, B. F. (2008) 'The parallax of landscape: Situating Celaque National Park, Honduras', in D. C. Knudsen, M. M. Metro-Roland, A. K. Soper and C. E. Greer (eds) *Landscape, tourism, and meaning*, Farnham, UK: Ashgate: 95–107.

Tuan, Y. (1974) *Topophilia: A study of environmental perception, attitudes and values*, Englewood Cliffs, NJ: Prentice Hall.

Uriely, N. (2005) 'The tourist experience', *Annals of Leisure Research*, 32(1): 199–216.

Urry, J. (2005) 'The place of emotions within place', in J. Davidson, L. Bondi and M. Smith (eds) *Emotional geographies*, Cornwall, UK: Ashgate: 77–83.

Varley, P. (2006) 'Confecting adventure and playing with meaning: The adventure commodification continuum', *Journal of Sport and Tourism*, 11(2): 173–194.

Wilderness Institute (2014) 'Wilderness: 50 years and counting'. Online, available at: www.wilderness50th.org (accessed 20 August 2014).

Yeo, P. (2013) 'The changing face of the adventure market', Paper presented at the Tourism Rendezvous New Zealand (TRENZ) Auckland, NZ, 10 May.

5 Guided mountaineering

Anna Thompson-Carr

Introduction

Guided mountaineering has a history dating back to the early nineteenth century where guiding was an alternative, but often necessary, activity that supplemented the income earnings of local people living in the European Alps. The professionalism of mountain guiding through the development of international guiding qualifications, increased demand from amateur or novice climbers and the global mobility of guiding businesses' activities have seen individuals' passion for mountaineering resulting in professional guiding careers. The commodification of mountaineering or the guided experience has been examined by researchers including Carr (2001), Beedie (2003, 2010, 2013), Beedie and Hudson (2003), Houge Mackenzie and Kerr (2013), Johnston and Edwards (1994), Martinoia (2013) and Pomfret (2011). Few studies to date have been conducted to examine specifically what motivates professional mountain guides to pursue their careers. Beedie (2010) observed in his research the role of guides 'choreographing' the experience of clients and noted the value of 'extensive mountaineering cultural capital' as a component critical to guides' identity and the guiding lifestyle. More academic research has explored the motivations of mountaineers in general and these motivations are often relevant to guides (Beedie 2010; Ewert 1985, 1994; Cronin 1991; Carr 2001; Cloutier 2003; Pomfret 2006, 2011). Rich mountaineering literature provides insights through autobiographies of guides where the pure necessity of employment was either secondary to, or accompanied by, a passion for alpine areas amongst early guides such as Peter Graham, Conrad Kain, Mick Bowie and Harry Ayres (Graham 1965; Bowie 1969; Kain 1979; Mahoney 1982). This passion for climbing and mountain environments is clearly a continual theme central both to guides' choice of profession and also for the non-professional climbers who have been referred to as 'mountaineering adventure tourists' (Pomfret 2006, 2011).

The chapter provides an overview of the development of professional mountain guiding with an initial focus on demand for guided experiences and then continues to explore the development of commercial guiding in New Zealand from the 1880s, with a predominant focus on international developments in the New Zealand guiding sector over the past 20 years. This chapter draws from mountaineering literature, academic research and the author's personal experiences and observations as a co-owner of a mountain guiding business in the 1980s and 1990s with several years as secretary/treasurer of the New Zealand Mountain Guides' Association (NZMGA).

Demand for mountaineering experiences

Mountaineering tourism would not exist without the demand from clients wishing to hire the services of mountain guides. As one of the earliest forms of adventure tourism activities there is evidence that many clients transition from another similar adventure activity towards guided mountaineering. A review of literature indicated that climbers making the transition from rock walls to the mountains, or developing their skills, recommend the positive learning and climbing experiences made possible by hiring a guide (Stevens 1997). Aukerman and Davison (1980) found that climbers acknowledged that the challenge of mountaineering satisfied their personal needs for esteem, self-actualization and achievement. Friendships and appreciation of mountain scenery were also important and mountaineers were seen as identifying strongly with wilderness ideals (Johnston 1989). Hiring a guide, or seeking their advice, has been a strategy commonly used by climbers in the Southern Alps to alleviate negative risks (Johnston 1989, 1992; Boekholt 1983). In a study by this chapter's author (Carr 1998) a survey of 67 guided mountaineering clients sought the reasons for hiring a guide. Respondents were 46 males and 21 females with a median age of 35–44 years; the majority of respondents were tertiary educated and held professional occupations. Thirty respondents (45 per cent) were participating in their first guided climbing trip. Twenty-six respondents (39 per cent) participated actively in guided mountaineering, making repeat visits on a regular basis. Eleven respondents (16 per cent) had participated in guided trips on one previous occasion. A variety of reasons for hiring a guide were given but the key attributes that influenced the respondents' decisions to hire a guide were relevant to the guides' experience and skills, including safety (management of risk), technical assistance in difficult conditions and learning new skills (refer Table 5.1).

Many guided climbers were experienced in related activities but sought the professional assistance to improve their abilities, for instance 'We did a ski tour with "A" – so we wanted to go with him again. We wanted to improve our mountaineering skills so we could climb more difficult peaks independently.' Others hired guides for organizational ease in an unfamiliar area – 'We had too little free time at home to figure out how to arrange lodging in the huts, helicopter transport, and all the other one million things we needed of which we had no local knowledge.'

Professional guides thus facilitate the adventure experience, judging the right level of challenge for each client so they can experience intrinsic benefits such as 'flow' safely. Similarly Beedie (2013: 28) noted clients may hire professional guides through adventure tourism companies in order to 'build skills and experience through participation that facilitates independent trips with friends who

Table 5.1 Important attributes when hiring a guide service

Rank	Mean*	Reason	% respondents
1	4.31	For increased safety, to reduce risk	91
2	4.22	The climbing experience of the guide	94
3	4.20	The guide's judgement/decision making	92
4	4.14	Assistance with conditions	91
5	4.11	Assistance with terrain	92
6	3.94	The guide's local knowledge	82
7	3.92	To learn skills from a professional	84
8	3.86	The company's reputation	92
9	3.81	The specific trip offered	82
10	3.70	The environment/setting	82
11	3.69	The guide's qualification	85
12	3.57	The instruction skills of the guide	80
13	3.33	Assistance to attain a personal goal	77
14	3.25	The guide's reputation	77
15	3.16	Value for money	76
16	3.08	Helpfulness of company staff	72
17	3.06	Assistance climbing a specific peak	60
18	2.76	Quality of pre-trip information	64
19	2.27	Rental equipment provided	40
20	2.05	Assistance with less able partners	31
21	2.02	No climbing partner available	33
22	1.95	Advertising of guiding services	34

Source: Carr (1998: 48).

Note
* '1' = not important to '5' = extremely important.

may or may not be members of a climbing club'. Beedie also observed that what makes mountaineering adventure tourism different from other forms of adventure tourism is 'the progression that is built into the activity' (2013: 28). Ewert (1987) argued that customer expectations of a commercial experience can be divided into three components – avoidances (i.e. unnecessary risks), antecedents (i.e. safety, professionalism) and benefits (enjoyment, personal growth, achievement). For the commercial operation to be successful these three components of participants' expectations need to be realized so that continued patronage of the operation occurs as satisfied clients spread their positive experiences by word of mouth. As noted by Beedie and Hudson (2003: 629) 'Companies tread a careful line between selling adventure as an idea and delivering the same as an experience.' Moreover individual mountain guides strive to offer their clients an experiential product in a challenging, alpine environment through the minimization of actual risk without taking the 'adventure' out of the experience. Guides' local knowledge regarding route finding, technical skills such as rope handling and informed decision making about navigation, weather and alpine conditions make the difference between a successful climbing holiday and potential adventure disaster. Since the early 1990s there has been a rise in the number of guiding companies (predominantly based in the Southern Alps), many of which now operate internationally. Similarly individual guides employed by these companies are increasingly mobile, pursuing international guiding careers when guiding clients in mountaineering pursuits including alpine snow and ice climbing, alpine rock climbing, heli-skiing and expeditions including meeting the demands of modern-day clients for climbing the 'Seven Summits'. This chapter will now discuss the development of guided mountaineering in the specific geographical context of New Zealand.

Early guided mountaineering in New Zealand

In 1882 the first professional mountain guides to work in New Zealand were Swiss guides Ulrich Kaufmann and Emil Boss, who were employed by Reverend William Spotswood Green, an Irishman from the English Alpine Club, to undertake the first ascent of Aoraki Mt Cook. The tradition of English Alpine Club members, such as Green, in employing European guides to achieve their objectives thus resulted in one of the first 'international' expeditions to a mountain range anywhere in the world. The subsequent attention of climbing in the region, and the 'race' for the first ascent of the mountain was a contributor the development of climbing infrastructure in what was at the time an extremely remote area, with the first Hermitage hotel being built at the present day Whitehorse Hill near Aoraki Mt Cook village in 1884 (McClure 2004: 67). Such infrastructure provided an important base for the development of commercial guiding but also enabled one of the first New Zealand guides, Jack Clarke, to gain experience in guiding techniques under the tutelage of Matthias Zurbriggen, a Swiss-Italian alpine guide. Zurbriggen had been employed by American mountaineer Edward FitzGerald in another attempt to be the first ascent of Aoraki Mt Cook in 1894 but the guided pair was unsuccessful as Clarke and two other young New Zealand climbers, George Graham and Tom Fyfe, ascended the mountain on Christmas Day 1894. Clarke then went on to climb in the European Alps, undoubtedly experiencing European guides in action as he travelled, returning to the Hermitage in 1903 to guide alongside Peter Graham, the latter becoming the Hermitage hotel's first Chief Guide (McClure 2004: 77).

Before the First World War the Hermitage dominated the provision of guided mountaineering experiences provided by New Zealand born guides who were employed by the Government Tourist Department. The 1900s to 1920s were the 'golden years' of guided mountaineering when well-to-do visitors would hire guides for an entire climbing season, waiting for perfect conditions to increase their likelihood of success (Logan 1987; McClure 2004: 78). Notable New Zealand guides of this era included Jock Richmond, Frank Milne, Darby Thomson, Tom Fyfe, Vic Williams and Peter Graham's brother Alex Graham. In 1914 tragedy struck the Hermitage hotel guiding community when the first alpine fatalities on Aoraki Mt Cook involved a guided group killed by an avalanche whilst crossing the Linda Glacier. Client Sydney King, who was a member of the English Alpine Club and Swiss Alpine Club, had employed senior guides Darby Thomson and Jock Richmond – all lost their lives. These fatalities occurred during the visit of notable Canadian guide Conrad Kain, who was guiding Otto Frind at the time. Kain was a central figure in the recovery of the victims and consequently his climbing skills (European, Canadian and New Zealand high alpine guiding) were noted by Peter Graham. As a result of the accident, and the loss of other young guides to First World War expeditionary forces, head guide Peter Graham urgently requested Kain's assistance with high peak climbing and as an instructor in a letter, dated 16 October 1914, to the manager of the Department of Tourist and Health Resorts. Consequently Kain was employed to 'teach the younger guides the finer points of high climbing' and 'do everything possible to train these men for high climbing as rapidly as circumstances will permit' (Wilson 1914). Kain went on to provide the first professional instruction courses (if they could be called courses at that time) to teach a new generation of guides alpine techniques, introducing technical rope and ice axe handling skills to the New Zealand guides.

After the First World War high guiding activities at the Hermitage began to wane during the Depression years as demand from clients decreased, and several guides had sustained serious injuries or died on the battlefields. Society was changing as recreational tramping and alpine clubs, including the New Zealand Alpine Club, began to provide instruction which offered the opportunity for amateur climbers to learn skills that meant they were no longer reliant on hiring guides (for more on this era see Johnston, this volume). One of the earliest attempts to regulate the industry resulted in the *Mountain Guides Act 1931* but this was never implemented, eventually being repealed in 1963 (Adcock 1970; Mahoney 1982). Throughout the 1930s skiing and tramping became popular activities for the general public, the 'club scene' flourished with increasing numbers of amateur climbers and the mountains were no longer the domain of the wealthy, leisured classes and their guides. The Second World War further interrupted the tradition of guided climbing in New Zealand and by the 1950s the combination of easier transport access to the outdoors, popularization of tramping and alpine clubs and the importation of technical climbing equipment from Europe by alpine personalities such as Oscar Coberger from Arthur's Pass, meant that the majority of alpine climbing trips in the New Zealand mountains were unguided – the adventure mountaineering tourist of the 1950s was now a self-guided recreationist.

It was not until the 1960s that guided mountaineering was to regain in popularity in the Mt Cook region. The next commercial phase of early adventure tourism mountain guiding experiences emerged when Alpine Instruction Ltd, the first independent commercial guiding company in New Zealand, was established in 1966 by a group of experienced climbers in Aoraki Mt Cook National Park. But it was with the adoption of an international qualification framework that professionalism in the guiding sector was to reach a new level of maturity.

By the 1970s the demand for, and availability of, suitably qualified guiding opportunities was in part facilitated by an internationally recognized training and certification scheme under the auspices of the IFMGA/UIAGM (International

Federation of Mountain Guides' Associations or *Union Internationale des Associations de Guides de Montagnes*). Risk is an inherent part of mountaineering tourism (Ewert 1994; Hales 2006) and mountaineering adventure tourists (the clients) need to be aware that even with a guide there will be an element of risk, often as a result of unforeseeable occurrences such as avalanches, extreme weather conditions, altitude sickness or equipment failure. However having a qualified guide as opposed to unqualified guide when pursuing such activities is even more critical when deciding which company to employ for mountaineering experiences. The next section of this chapter will thus explore the demand for such services and the role of the IFMGA/UIAGM and New Zealand Mountain Guides' Association (NZMGA) in meeting this demand.

The IFMGA/UIAGM

Mountain guides are uniquely placed in the world of adventure tourism because of the existence of an internationally recognized training and qualification system. The International Federation of Mountain Guides' Associations was formed in Italy in 1965 by guides from Austria, Italy, France, Switzerland and Germany (www.ivbv.info/en/ifmga/history.html). As of 2013 there were 24 member countries, including New Zealand. According to the IFMGA website (www.ivbv.info/en/ifmga/vision.html) some of the roles of the association include:

- administering standards of practice for consistency in the mountain guiding profession, including a code of professional ethics for mountain guides;
- facilitating information exchange amongst association members;
- overseeing mandatory training standards;
- promoting reciprocity of access to member associations' countries;
- representing the interests of members to national/international authorities and media.

Individual country's national mountain guides' associations need to apply for IFMGA membership before their country's guides can seek IFMGA/UIAGM qualifications. In order for a country's association to join the IFMGA there need to be at least 20 individual guide members and each country's government has to recognize the IFMGA/UIAGM qualification (www.ivbv.info/en/home.html).

Guides usually become qualified over a three to five year period through a series of climbing and ski mountaineering courses that are assessed during summer and winter months. They serve as trainee or aspirant guides whilst working on supervised guiding activities in the field before becoming fully qualified. Prior to starting the courses, guides need to have attained a set standard of technical competence in rock and ice climbing and skiing. Most will have completed several seasons of mountaineering, maintaining a log that details the number and level of difficulty of ascents as well as similar activities such as ski touring and rock climbing. Guides are also trained in skills related to search and rescue, weather and avalanche forecasting and alpine first aid (for detailed information about the training and certification programme, refer to the IFMGA website). Fully qualified IFMGA guides hold the carnet or badge of the IFMGA and can work internationally as climbing and ski guides. The global mountaineering tourism arena opens to these guides whose ability to work internationally is mentored through the collaborative efforts of the individual countries' guiding associations, for instance by lobbying governments to recognize the IFMGA qualification (see Table 5.2).

National guiding associations thus assist other members of the IFMGA by supporting their international colleagues in gaining legal access to mountains or employment in member countries, as noted by Johnson and Godwin (2006: 248) and Carr (1998). The role of guides' associations is also to support the skills development of members through administering the training and certification programme of the IFMGA, sharing the knowledge of fully qualified IFMGA guides with aspirant and trainee guides.

The ability of internationally qualified guides to perceive and manage risk at a more accurate level than their clients, alongside the increased mobility provided through air travel to enable extensive international climbing experiences for mountain guides, has in turn led to the globalization of guiding careers.

Table 5.2 Mountain guiding associations' websites

Country or region	Guiding association website
IFMGA (International Federation Mountain Guides)	www.ivbv.info/en/home.html
Aosta	www.guidealtamontagna.com
Argentina	www.aagm.com.ar
Austria	www.bergfuehrer.at
Bolivia	www.agmtb.org
Canada	www.acmg.ca
Czech Republic	www.horskyvudce.com
France	www.sngm.com
Germany	www.vdbs.de
Great Britain	www.bmg.org.uk
Italy	www.guidealpine.it
Japan	www.jfmga.com
Kyrgyzstan (Kandidat)	mguide.in.kg
Nepal	www.nnmga.org.np
New Zealand	www.nzmga.org.nz
Norway	www.nortind.no
Peru	www.agmp.pe
Poland	www.pspw.pl
Sweden	www.sbo.nu
Switzerland	www.4000plus.ch
Slovenia	www.zgvs.si
Slovakia	www.nahvsr.sk
Spain	www.aegm.org
Südtirol	www.bergfuehrer-suedtirol.it
USA	www.amga.com

Alongside the professionalism of guiding comes moral and ethical obligations to ensure the conduct of guided mountaineering tourism is undertaken in a socially and environmentally sustainable manner, whether in a domestic or international setting, however minimal attention has been paid by academic researchers on the ethical responsibilities or attitudes of guides apart from a work by Long *et al.* (2012).

The New Zealand Mountain Guides' Association

The New Zealand Mountain Guides' Association (NZMGA) was formed in 1975, but first mooted in 1974 when a group of 33 guides, instructors and park rangers met 'to establish the occupation of guiding on a firmly professional basis' (Johnston 1989: 153). The arrival from Germany of Gottlieb Braun-Elwert, an internationally qualified IFMGA/UIAGM mountain and ski guide, in 1978 no doubt helped the NZMGA to be admitted as the eighth member of the IFMGA/UIAGM in 1981. Gottlieb facilitated the discussions with the IFMGA and was to be an assessor on early NZMGA guiding courses. The international recognition of the NZMGA by the IFMGA coincided with Johnston's observation (1989) that by the 1980s commercial guiding businesses offered alternatives to traditional club-based climbing experiences. By the mid-1980s qualified NZMGA guides were providing instruction to alpine and mountaineering clubs (training their instructors and members) as well as providing professional instruction (including training and assessment of volunteer instructors) to organizations including the New Zealand Army, the New Zealand Mountain Safety Council and a range of tramping or climbing club members. Delivering instruction to club members, who could then self-guide themselves on their personal mountaineering trips, provided further security of income for many owner-operator guides.

Nowadays most guiding businesses are usually owned and operated by the guides themselves, as is the case with Alpine Guides at Aoraki Mt Cook National Park (owned by IFMGA guides Kevin Boekholt and Bryan Carter) and Southern Alps Guiding (owned by IFMGA guide Charlie Hobbs). The 1980s and 1990s had seen a transition in the national park concessions systems which had previously favoured the provision of all guiding services by one local company. Alpine Guides had held a monopoly until other IFMGA qualified guides applied for and were granted concessions to offer a choice of guiding businesses to clients (Carr 1998; Hobbs 2010). By 1987 there were three companies operating in the South Island with 22 fully qualified IFMGA guides and 21 trainee guides. By 1998 there were 32 fully qualified IFMGA guides, 37 trainee guides and 12 South Island based companies (NZMGA Directory 1998).

The NZMGA administers its own qualifications including the NZMGA Ski Guide, NZMGA Climbing Guide, NZMGA Hard Ice Guide and NZMGA Alpine Trekking Guide, enabling specialization in areas without full international qualification. There is a high uptake of the IFMGA qualification in New Zealand and there are, as of 2014, 50 fully qualified IFMGA guides as members of the

NZMGA. These fully qualified guides are specialists in their own right in areas such as avalanche forecasting, high altitude commercial filming, risk and hazards management, Antarctic field work and high alpine expedition climbing. Many of the IFMGA NZMGA members act as assessors on training courses for future guides, thus assisting with the development and implementation of IFMGA training and certification, member audits and continually reviewing safety standards. Like other individual country members of the IFMGA, the NZMGA is responsible for administering and implementing the IFMGA training programmes to enable guides to become fully qualified at a national and then the international (IFMGA/UIAGM) level.

For clients, hiring a guide is a substantial investment, not only in terms of the potential physical and mentally strenuous nature of the activity, but also from a financial perspective. The daily rate for hiring a guide can range from NZ$400–900 whilst an ascent of Aoraki Mt Cook, Mt Aspiring or Mt Tasman can range from NZ$4,600–6,500. The economic impact of mountain guiding has not been ascertained by research to date yet the policy setting for mountain guiding in New Zealand is complex, with an array of relevant legislation. The resulting management settings that govern the practice of most guided mountaineering means that guiding businesses are involved with administrative and practical aspects of their businesses. For example, Cater (2006) noted the influence of the *Resource Management Act 1991* and *Accident Compensation Act 2001* (administered by the Accident Compensation Corporation or ACC) on the adventure tourism sector in Queenstown (Cater 2006: 435–436). Whilst such Acts influence guiding businesses, clients would be assured that the operational environment is regulated (and should they have an accident the costs of evacuation and rehabilitation are covered by the ACC).

Even before guides can venture into the New Zealand mountains with paying clients they must be granted a concession by the Department of Conservation (DOC) so as to comply with management plans according to Part 3B of the *Conservation Act 1987*. Most commercial guiding operations occurring on the New Zealand conservation estate (particularly Aspiring, Fiordland, Westland and Aoraki Mt Cook National Parks) gain DOC approved concessions based on criteria including safety plans (fulfilling Department of Labour requirements) and Environmental Impact Assessments. More recently the *Health and Safety in Employment Act 1992* (Adventure Activities) Regulations 2011 (section 16) required all adventure tourism operators to register with WorkSafe New Zealand and mountain guiding businesses were amongst the first operations to register, thus complying with imposed regulations of the broader sector (www.dol.govt. nz/Tools/AAOAudit/Audit/Register). From a sustainability perspective several guiding companies ensure their websites refer to whether the company has a Code of Ethics, enact environmental plans and are members of organizations such as Outdoors Mark (Outdoors NZ's safety audit), LANDSAR or Leave No Trace. Companies may also have website information about cultural issues in the areas they operate, for instance guidelines about 'topuni' (Māori values) associated with mountains such as Aoraki Mt Cook.

Individual national park management plans administered by DOC require guiding concessionaires to be qualified members of the NZMGA and hold full IFMGA qualifications if working on glaciated or steep alpine terrain above a certain altitude. The Aoraki Mt Cook National Park Management Plan (2004) states that 'It is essential that alpine guides are appropriately qualified' and recommends the NZMGA qualifications (DOC 2004: 121). International guides visiting New Zealand who hold the IFMGA carnet are also required to apply for a one-off concession to guide in the New Zealand mountains. The management of guiding concessions by DOC has had minor issues over the years, for instance with the issuing of multiple guided heli-skiing concessions where concession-aires have concerns crowding issues can endanger client safety as a result of the potential for avalanches being triggered. Guiding companies who have developed systems and knowledge about particular alpine terrain can be wary of new concessionaires entering areas. In the past controversy has arisen over illegal guiding or the issuing of one-off concessions where visiting trekking and climbing guides did not have to provide safety plans or environmental impact assessments.

In 2014 there are 50 fully qualified IFMGA guides, NZMGA qualified guides specializing in ski guiding (23), climbing (four) alpine trekking (14), hard ice climbing in lower glacier areas (59) as well as a considerable number of trainee and assistant guides (NZMGA website). Companies offer a range of services aside from guided mountaineering including glacier skiing, glacier walks, heli-skiing, snow shoeing, cross-country skiing, Via Ferrata, international expeditions, professional development courses, ski touring, heli-hiking, trekking, glacier kayaking, search and rescue services, avalanche and weather forecasting services, guide training, film crew/filming services, charity fundraising expeditions and climbing equipment/clothing retail outlets. Eleven NZMGA guiding businesses are now associated with the IFMGA and the New Zealand guiding sector has made an impact overseas.

New Zealand mountain guiding on the international stage

In many regions of the world mountain guiding businesses are at the forefront of international, commercially significant, adventure tourism businesses (Beedie 2003; Beedie and Hudson 2003; Cloutier 2003). New Zealand guiding professionals have had an international impact through providing services overseas as individual guides who are IFMGA qualified can join one or more countries' mountain guides' associations. NZMGA members can join international counterparts, the most popular being the British Mountain Guides' Association (BMGA) and Association of Canadian Mountain Guides (ACMG). Consequently guides throughout the world are highly mobile and whilst based in one country they (or their businesses) can offer international expeditions or guiding programmes. Many New Zealand guides have opened climbing businesses with overseas bases, for instance Russell Brice employs over 25 guides for a programme of European and international mountaineering, based in Chamonix (www.chamex.com/) and Dave Begg established one of Canada's most well-known guiding companies, Yamnuska Mountain School and Guide Service, in 1977. The transition from small-scale New Zealand guiding business (typically provided by owner-operator guides employing staff as required) to world class company is exemplified by Adventure Consultants.

Based in Wanaka, Adventure Consultants was one of the first major mountain guiding businesses to provide commercialized expeditions to high altitude mountains on a truly international scale. Such businesses paved the way to a transition from international expeditions for competent or expert mountaineers to expeditions accessible to novice or amateur climbers with the financial means to benefit from guides' technical expertise in order to reach their aspirational summits. Adventure Consultants was founded by IFMGA guide Gary Ball and mountaineer Rob Hall in 1991. Gary Ball was to pass away on Dhaulagiri in late 1993, whilst Rob Hall and Andy Harris died on Mt Everest/ Sagamartha in 1996. Despite this very tragic period in the business's early history, Adventure Consultants now offers over 70 international expeditions including mountaineering trips to the seven continents' highest summits (Seven Summits), alongside more standard mountaineering experiences such as guided ascents and climbing instruction in Europe and New Zealand. Guy Cotter, an IFMGA guide who was employed in the early years of the business and mentored by both Hall and Ball, purchased the business shortly after the Everest tragedy and from his perspective 'the pleasure of the adventure business lies not in the financial rewards but rather in helping clients achieve their dreams' (Adventure Consultants 2014). The company employs 46 IFMGA or NZMGA qualified climbing and/or ski guides with seven based in Europe and 30 based in New Zealand. The guides instruct and guide clients on courses, ascents or expeditions in Europe, the Himalayas, the Americas, the Polar Regions, New Zealand and the ultimate motivation for many clients – the 'Seven Summits'.

What is notable about Adventure Consultants is the active acknowledgement of social and environmental responsibilities through its daily operations. Unlike many guiding companies where porters are incidental workers employed casually when needed, with no security of employment, Adventure Consultants acknowledge the role of Sherpa guides by including the Sherpa team on the company website, mentoring some Sherpa towards full IFMGA guiding qualifications. The business is registered with 'Leave No Trace'[TM] and supports the dZi Foundation. Expeditions, especially commercial mountaineering expeditions, do result in environmental impacts and perceptions of 'crowding' in remote or wilderness alpine areas (Kelly 2013, and see Barros and Pickering, Pickering and Barros in this volume).

Organized international expeditions and ascents managed by qualified guides continue to meet demand from clients wanting to access alpine climbing experiences in dangerous areas by operating in a socially and environmentally sustainable manner. However not all guiding companies operate with IFMGA qualified guides. As one guide observed in an interview conducted by the author.

A lot of people start up and the problem with international guiding is that people don't need to be qualified in many places you go to. So a lot of people who are actually starting businesses are people who their last five trips have been as clients and then they start their own expedition company. Now there's a difference between being guided and going on a commercially led expedition and buying services. So there's a whole lot of different levels of expeditions that are there ... we need to show that we as an industry were mature and that we [IFMGA guides] are self-regulating.

(IFMGA guide interview July 2007)

The guide further noted that many expedition companies go on to hire porters or Sherpa to do the actual guiding 'Which is way cheaper for the clients and yet the company is making more money per person than we can because we've got ratios (3 people for every guide)', thus the Sherpa or non-qualified guides are often exposed to risks but not remunerated accordingly. It is a case of 'clients' beware. Most guiding companies, predominantly those with IFMGA guides, will have base camp staff including doctors, communications officers and associated strategies and management plans should such events occur, managing the situation for the most positive outcome.

The irony of international mountain guiding companies accessing remote areas of the world through transportation that contributes to climate change and global warming undoubtedly concerns some mountaineering clients, and guides themselves; not to mention attracting media attention when base camps such as Everest Base Camp become polluted by expedition waste. Many commercial guiding companies have instigated waste management initiatives that they implement as an integral part of their expeditions or trips. Similarly the high cost, often in human lives, of mountaineering activities, can result in controversial and intense media attention even when positive outcomes are being reported (see Ibbotson 2012; Cotter 2012; Kelly 2013; Krakauer 2014). Guides and guiding companies become strategists in managing social and traditional media as they control the information surrounding commercial guiding businesses through updating webpages or blogs in real time whilst on expeditions, or through interviews when contacted by the press seeking guides' opinions as mountaineering experts. When the Everest climbing season of 2014 resulted in the loss of 16 Sherpa lives in the Khumbu Icefall on 18 April 2014 Guy Cotter was a spokesperson providing balanced views about the tragedy in the media. The company's response was to manage donations for the surviving family members of the three Sherpa employed by the 2014 Adventure Consultants Everest Expedition (AC Sherpa Future Fund), whilst also championing collaborative efforts to administer transparent financial trusts that care for the needs of the surviving families and communities of all 16 Sherpa who lost their lives, as well as workers in undeveloped countries affected by negative occurrences in the mountain adventure tourism sector, for example the Himalayan Trust (Adventure Consultants 2014). Of note, Nepal has only just recently been admitted as a member of the IFMGA and this has important ramifications for the international training and professional recognition of Sherpa guides and guiding on Everest/Sagamartha will increasingly require IFMGA qualifications. For further information on guiding in the Himalaya refer to the case study by Nyaupane and chapter by Nepal and Mu in this volume.

Conclusion

New Zealand's Southern Alps are held in awe by many, the scenic wilderness encountered there being one of the country's truly unique tourism attributes. Opportunities abound in the mountains for international and domestic visitors to pursue a variety of activities. Guided climbing can fulfil a variety of motivations for many people (both guides and clients) whether they seek extreme challenges, progression of their personal mountaineering skills or simply want to experience alpine environments as safely and conveniently as possible.

The activities of guided climbers, as a user group which values alpine environments, supports the conservation of New Zealand's wilderness. The personal benefits guided climbers seek ultimately create a social benefit as they provide guides with a livelihood and a lifestyle, whilst contributing to other sectors of the tourism industry via usage of transport and accommodation services. Amateur climbers from New Zealand and overseas, or experienced climbers who want organizational problems taken care of, are important markets for guiding operators. In 2014 the New Zealand Mountain Guides' Association will have experienced 40 years since its formation and the country had over a century of professional mountain guiding. Several issues affecting guiding concessionaires have arisen in the last two decades, for instance the impact of global warming has meant less snow resulting in difficult access across glaciers making some routes impassable. The impacts of climate change combined with the need to consider succession planning for guiding ventures can result in entrepreneurial activities as businesses adapt to changing alpine conditions. Guides respond to challenges, recognizing opportunities and acting to diversify businesses so they can continue to follow their passion for living in the mountains, with some New Zealand companies and individual guides travelling overseas to guide.

Finally, the NZMGA has led the way for other sectors of New Zealand's adventure tourism industry by adopting professional standards and being involved in developing global experiences. Mountain guiding is now a multi-million dollar industry in New Zealand with many clients returning annually to undertake activities indicating high satisfaction levels with their experiences. The Department of Conservation, through concession fees, and surrounding accommodation, hospitality, retail equipment and transport providers, also benefit from the socio-economic, flow-on, effects of the mountaineering tourism industry. Guides' passion for the mountains, alongside their expertise in managing the risks associated with mountaineering, are pivotal to their professional activities and their experience. The high skill levels and in-depth knowledge of alpine environments, as demonstrated by qualified guides achieving international IFMGA qualifications, will undoubtedly continue to be central to the sustainable management of guided mountaineering tourism. The continued global popularity of adventure activities means the members of the NZMGA, and other countries' guides' associations, can probably anticipate increased tourism demand for guiding services, despite future challenges that face the mountaineering tourism industry.

References

Adcock, D. (1970) 'A case for guides registration', unpublished essay, Victoria University, Wellington.

Aukerman, R. and Davison, J. (1980) 'The mountain land recreationist in New Zealand', Lincoln Papers in Resource Management, No. 6. Canterbury: Tussock Grasslands and Mountain Lands Institute, Lincoln College.

Adventure Consultants (2014) Online, available at: www.adventureconsultants.com/adventure/CompanyEthos (accessed 3 October 2014).

Beedie, P. (2003) 'Mountain guiding and adventure tourism: Reflections on the choreography of the experience', *Leisure Studies*, 22(2): 147–167.

Beedie, P. (2010) *Mountain based adventure tourism*, Saarbrucken: Lambert Academic Publishing.

Beedie, P. (2013) 'The adventure enigma: An analysis of mountain based adventure tourism in Britain', in S. Taylor, P. Varley and T. Johnston (eds) *Adventure tourism: Meanings, experience and learning, contemporary geographies of leisure tourism and mobility series*, London: Routledge: 22–33.

Beedie, P. and Hudson, S. (2003) 'The emergence of mountain based adventure tourism', *Annals of Tourism Research*, 30(3): 625–643.

Boekholt, K. (1983) 'The Copland track', unpublished diploma dissertation, Parks and Recreation, Lincoln College, Christchurch.

Bowie, N. (1969) *Mick Bowie the hermitage years*, Wellington: A. H. and A. W. Reed Publishers.

Carr, A. (1998) 'The motivations and experiences of guided mountaineering clients in New Zealand's Southern Alps', unpublished diploma dissertation, University of Otago, Dunedin.

Carr, A. (2001) 'Alpine adventurers in the Pacific Rim', *Pacific Tourism Review*, 4(4): 161–170.

Cater, C. (2006) 'World adventure capital', in R. Buckley (ed.) *Adventure tourism*, Oxfordshire: CAB International: 429–442.

Cloutier, R. (2003) 'The business of adventure tourism', in S. Hudson (ed.) *Sport and adventure tourism*, Binghamton, NY: Haworth Hospitality Press: 241–272.

Cotter, G. (2012) 'Guy Cotter responds to Everest criticism', *Otago Daily Times*, 6 August. Online, available at: www.odt.co.nz/opinion/your-say/220418/guy-cotter-responds-everest-criticism (accessed 3 October 2014).

Cronin, C. (1991) 'Sensation seeking among mountain climbers', *Personality and Individual Differences*, 12(6): 653–654.

Department of Conservation (2004) 'Aoraki Mt Cook National Park Management Plan', Department of Conservation, Christchurch.

Ewert, A. (1985) 'Why people climb: The relationship of participant motives and experience level to mountaineering', *Journal of Leisure Research*, 17(3): 241–250.

Ewert, A. (1987) 'Towards a theoretical understanding of commercialized outdoor recreation', *Trends*, 24(3): 5–9.

Ewert, A. (1994) 'Playing the edge: Motivation and risk-taking in a high altitude wilderness-like environment', *Environment and Behavior*, 26(1): 3–24.

Graham, P. (1914) 'Employment of temporary guide for Season 1915–16', letter dated 14 October 1914 to B. Wilson, General Manager, Department of Tourist and Health Resorts, Wellington. National Archives, Wellington (Hermitage – Guides and Ski Instructors' [Archives Reference: AECB 8615 Box 183/44/37 Part 1]).

Graham, P. (1965) *Peter Graham, mountain guide*, in H. B. Hewitt (ed.). Wellington: A. H. and A. W. Reed Publishers.

Hales, R. (2006) 'Mountaineering', in R. Buckley (ed.) *Adventure tourism*, Wallingford: CAB International: 260–281.

Hobbs, M. (2010) *The journey to Aoraki-Mount Cook*, Christchurch: Spirit Publishing.

Houge Mackenzie, S. and Kerr, J. (2013) 'Stress and emotions at work: Adventure tourism guiding experiences in South America', *Tourism Management*, 36(June): 3–14.

Ibbotson, L. (2012) 'Wanaka climber back in the hot seat', *Otago Daily Times*, 1 July. Online, available at: www.odt.co.nz/lifestyle/magazine/214967/wanaka-climber-back-hot-seat (accessed 12 October 2014).

International Federation of Mountain Guides' Associations (IFMGA) (2014) Online, available at: www.ivbv.info/en/home.html (accessed October to November 2014).

Johnson, J. and Godwin, I. (2006) 'Ice climbing', in R. Buckley (ed.) *Adventure tourism*, Wallingford: CAB International: 245–259.

Johnston, B. and Edwards, T. (1994) 'The commodification of mountaineering', *Annals of Tourism Research*, 21(3): 459–478.

Johnston, M. (1989) 'Peak experiences: Challenge and danger in mountain recreation in New Zealand', unpublished doctoral dissertation, University of Canterbury, Christchurch.

Johnston, M. (1992) 'Facing the challenges: Adventure in the mountains of New Zealand', in B. Weiler and C. Hall (eds) *Special interest tourism*, London: Belhaven Press: 159–169.

Kain, C. (1979) *Where the clouds can go*, Victoria: Rocky Mountain Books.

Kelly, J. (2013) 'Everest crowds: The world's highest traffic jam', *BBC News Magazine*. Online, available at: www.bbc.com/news/magazine-22680192 (accessed 12 October 2014).

Krakauer, J. (2014) 'Death and anger on Everest', *New Yorker*, 21. Online, available at: www.newyorker.com/news/news-desk/death-and-anger-on-everest (accessed 12 October 2014).

Logan, H. (1987) *The Mount Cook guide book* (2nd edn), Wellington: New Zealand Alpine Club.

Long, T., Bazin, D. and Massiéra, B. (2012) 'Mountain guides: Between ethics and socio-economic trends', *Journal of Moral Education*, 41(3): 369–388.

McClure, M. (2004) *The wonder country: Making New Zealand tourism*, Auckland: Auckland University Press.

Mahoney, M. (1982) *Harry Ayres: Mountain guide*, Christchurch: Whitcoulls Publishers.

Martinoia, R. (2013) 'Women's mountaineering and dissonances within the mountain guide profession: "Don't go thinking he was a guide for the ladies"', *Journal of Alpine Research*, 101–110.

New Zealand Mountain Guides' Association (NZMGA) (2014) Online, available at: www.nzmga.org.nz/ (accessed October to November 2014).

NZMGA Directory (1998) New Zealand Mountain Guides' Association brochure.

Pomfret, G. (2006) 'Mountaineering adventure tourists: A conceptual framework for research', *Tourism Management*, 27(3): 113–123.

Pomfret, G. (2011) 'Package mountaineer tourist holidaying in the French Alps: An evaluation of key influences encouraging their participation', *Tourism Management*, 32(3): 501–510.

Stevens, A. (1997) 'The learner's stand', *Climber*, Winter(21): 18.

Wilson, B. M. (1914) 'Letter date 23 October 1914 to Conrad Kain', Hermitage, National Archives, Wellington (Hermitage – Guides and Ski Instructors' [Archives Reference: AECB 8615 Box 183/44/37 Part 1]).

Worksafe NZ (2014) Online, available at: www.dol.govt.nz/Tools/AAOAudit/Audit/ Register (accessed 14 October 2014).

Case study 3

Southern Alps Guiding: a case study of guided mountaineering businesses in New Zealand

Mary Hobbs and Charlie Hobbs

This case study reflects on the history and diversification of an owner-operator business, 'Southern Alps Guiding', outlining the experience of becoming the second guiding business resident in the Southern Alps Aoraki Mt Cook National Park. Over the past 25 years their traditional guided climbing and skiing activities have expanded since seeking a concession for the development of The Old Mountaineer's Café, under a separate company.

Southern Alps Guiding was established in the late 1980s, by IFMGA qualified guide Charlie Hobbs. The idea of forming his own company came about as a result of his passion for the mountains, climbing and skiing. Working in this alpine environment skiing and guiding, in the Southern Alps in particular, and helping others gain skills in the mountains, seemed like the perfect job. By the early 1990s Southern Alps Guiding was offering guided ascents of peaks such as Aoraki Mt Cook and Mt Tasman, Tasman Glacier skiing and heli-skiing experiences in winter and a range of private instruction packages. There were challenges, chief of which, in Aoraki Mt Cook National Park, was that there had only ever been one resident guiding company. It took many years of jumping through bureaucratic hoops and dealing with the initial issues of the opposition to eventually attain a reasonable level playing field for Southern Alps Guiding, which has been established now for almost 25 years. The monopoly situation is not unusual in adventure tourism businesses. As noted by Beedie and Hudson (2003: 631) 'As with other industries, competition characterizes the adventure tourism market and big companies have a tendency to dominate.'

From the early years of the business a strong entrepreneurial personality and lifestyle preferences motivated Charlie Hobbs so that he could establish a business in the mountains he lived amongst. Charlie married Mary Hobbs, publisher of the award-winning *New Zealand Outside* magazine in 1995. They shared a love of the outdoors, adventure and the characteristics of a strong entrepreneurial personality and lifestyle preferences, which was of advantage to them, as it required both of them working together to secure and establish a base at Aoraki Mt Cook. These traits were found in other 'place' oriented New Zealand adventure tourism operators as noted by Ateljevic and Doorne (2000). To secure and establish a firm base for Southern Alps Guiding in an area like Aoraki Mt Cook, it was advantageous to build infrastructure and in the early

1990s the concept of building a restaurant and historic photographic gallery that saluted the rich history of mountain guiding in this area, and also provided the public with good, high quality, wholesome food, seemed like the perfect choice for several reasons.

First, it gave Southern Alps Guiding a 'home' in the village, where the public could learn about the different activities Southern Alps Guiding provided in a small village that, at that time, had a monopoly resident guiding company and a monopoly hotel. The public was not about to find out about Southern Alps Guiding activities at the hotel or at the competing guiding company's headquarters.

Second, the restaurant diversified the guiding business. It provided high quality, simple food, with a point of difference, which is that much of the food, meat and wine available are organic, fitting in natural alpine surroundings. The philosophy of choosing organic wherever possible is close to the heart of Charlie and Mary and is explained in the menu, along with a brief history on the restaurant, including the obstacles that had to be overcome to build and maintain the business in the park.

Finally, the architecture of the restaurant was reminiscent of the style of a mountain hut. Old photos, old skis, crampons and packs of a bygone era adorn the walls and bring alive the rich mountaineering history of the area. This fitted in perfectly with the guiding company's ethos. It further reinforced the genuine relationship between the restaurant, bar, historic gallery and the guiding business. The Old Mountaineer's Café, Restaurant, Bar and Historic Photographic Gallery was built in 2003, after an exhaustive and expensive concession process by the Department of Conservation that lasted for approximately ten years (*Matagouri and Other Pricks: The Journey to Aoraki/ Mount Cook*, Hobbs 2010). Once built the incumbent monopoly, and the Department of Conservation at that time, continued to do all they could to make it less than enticing to stay and the Commerce Commission and the Ombudsman became sufficiently interested to investigate and made clear recommendations that were helpful, enabling the company to strengthen (Hobbs 2010). In colder weather an open fire and a warm welcome greets customers. There is an old family piano in the restaurant, family photos, old family packs and crampons on the walls, and books for sale that Mary Hobbs has written on the history of guiding, their story of the battle to obtain permission to build and run the restaurant in the national park, the guiding business, Mary's publishing business, as well as an outline of many of their adventures and their family history. Old posters are available for sale, and t-shirts, with apt quotes, are also available for sale. This reinforces the authenticity of the relationship between all of these various elements that link together well, and revives stunning old posters that would otherwise have long been forgotten.

Other challenges facing the business have resulted in diversification of guiding services and products in a similar manner to the evolution of guiding companies in Canada and other overseas destinations (Cloutier 2003; Hales 2006). Weather is a constant issue for any guiding company seeking to carve out a viable living, as unpredictable weather patterns can see trips cancelled on frequent occasions. This was ameliorated by Southern Alps Guiding taking on commissions for other companies, in the New Zealand off-season, to remote international areas including Carstenz Pyramid and Antarctica where Charlie led search and rescue at Scott Base, or guided scientists to the summits of various unclimbed, remote Antarctic mountain peaks; Mary joining one expedition as camp manager.

Climate change has also had an impact but Southern Alps Guiding has responded entrepreneurially to the rapid increase in size of the Mueller and Tasman Glacier terminal lakes (from the warmer temperatures resulting in down wasting moraine and glacial melt) by developing guided sea kayaking on the glacier lake over the summer months. Espiner and Becken (2013) observed similar resilience and adaptations to climate change by vulnerable, mountain-based businesses in the Southern Alps region. For Southern Alps Guiding, other diversification occurred as opportunities such as snow-shoeing experiences on the valley floors of Aoraki Mt Cook National Park were offered during winter (an alternative for clients who oppose the potentially climate change effects associated with heli-skiing). The glacier kayaking business was established in the early 2000s with an eye to the future succession planning of the business. This was also initially met with opposition and is covered in the book by Mary Hobbs (2010). Guided ascents of mountain peaks are not always suitable once guides reach retirement years and glacier kayaking and snow shoeing are adventures in the park that can be guided within the confines of the concessions held, that don't require the guide to have knee replacements to do it!

Ironically the challenging access to the lower Tasman Glacier has meant the company still uses helicopter access to allow clients to access and experience how spectacular the World Heritage area of Aoraki Mt Cook National Park is. Helicopter access is a paradoxical, yet important, addition to the services offered by Southern Alps Guiding, owing to the increasing difficulty of access (due to the glacial recession on the west and east coast of the South Island) and low experience levels of many of the clients/visitors to the park in more recent years.

Other products enabling diversification of the guiding company include the writing and publication of local history and other various topics. Books, posters and cards about local history are all available for sale at the Old Mountaineers Restaurant, including *Matagouri and Other Pricks: The Journey to Aoraki/ Mount Cook* and *The Spirit of Mountaineering* (Hobbs 2010). Other books by Mary Hobbs are also available at the restaurant. The colour postcards for sale are all from photos by Mary Hobbs. Future plans for Southern Alps Guiding include a health spa and an inn to complement the Old Mountaineers' Café, Restaurant, Bar and Historic Gallery. Initial concession concept plans were submitted to the Department in 2004 and have just been signed in 2014.

In conclusion, the businesses work because we monitor and work in the businesses, we have respect for the environment, and do our utmost to ensure safety, professionalism, good customer service, and the providing of quality products that we love to create. Yet, in essence, what really makes the above combination of businesses work is a passion for, and a belief in, what we do. We are passionate about the environment here and we deeply respect it. We are also passionate about the spiritual nature of the land, and the activities that make up our various businesses, from ski-guiding to publishing, to the historic restaurant. We pour our heart and soul into what we do, and it seems that this is felt by those who arrive for anything from the purchase of a coffee, a poster, a postcard, a personally signed book, or a guided climb up a mountain or a ski-guiding expedition down a glacier.

References

Ateljevic, I. and Doorne, S. (2000) 'Staying within the fence: Lifestyle entrepreneurship in tourism', *Journal of Sustainable Tourism*, 8(5): 378–392.

Beedie, P. and Hudson, S. (2003) 'The emergence of mountain based adventure tourism', *Annals of Tourism Research*, 30(3): 625–643.

Cloutier, R. (2003) 'The business of adventure tourism', in S. Hudson (ed.) *Sport and adventure tourism*, Binghamton, NY: Haworth Hospitality Press: 241–272.

Espiner, S. and Becken, S. (2013) 'Tourist towns on the edge: Conceptualising vulnerability and resilience in a protected area tourism system', *Journal of Sustainable Tourism*, 22(4): 646–665.

Hales, R. (2006) 'Mountaineering', in R. Buckley (ed.) *Adventure tourism*, Wallingford: CAB International: 260–281.

Hobbs, M. (2007) *The spirit of mountaineering*, Christchurch: Spirit Ltd.

Hobbs, M. (2010) *Matagouri and other pricks: The journey to Aoraki-Mount Cook*, Christchurch: Spirit Publishing.

6 Early alpine club culture and mountaineering literature

Zac Robinson

Critics have called mountaineering 'the most literary of all sports' (Barcott 1996: 64). This may come as a surprise to anyone who regards climbing as nothing more than the driven antics of adrenalin addicts, kids with too much free time and too little good sense. Perhaps it would be equally surprising to the uninitiated to learn what Canadian climber and raconteur Sean Isaac pointed out not so long ago – that his country's second longest continuous running periodical (after *Maclean's*) is actually the Alpine Club of Canada's very own *Canadian Alpine Journal* (Isaac 2008: 5), first printed in 1907 with its green cover and size so conspicuously akin to that of England's older, revered *Alpine Journal*. Mountaineering today, globally, is the one sport that's most likely to have its own section in bookstores. Mountaineers often talk about their favourite climbing books with almost as much enthusiasm as they talk about their favourite climbing routes, and mountain book festivals – from Kendal to Banff – have become an annual highlight on many climbers' social calendar. And why not? Mountaineering has more than rested on its literary laurels since the mid-1800s. Indeed, the practice itself was predicated on the published word. It still is – and that is the subject of this chapter.

This inalienable relationship between mountaineering practice and mountaineering writing finds its roots in Victorian travelling culture and the emergence of alpine clubs. 'In the 1850s', Fergus Fleming writes, 'Britain was on a high. This was the decade of the Great Exhibition, the decade when British supremacy in almost every area was acknowledged around the world' (2000: 162). Certainly, Britain, at the time, was the most prosperous, the most technologically advanced, the most stable nation in Europe, having been spared in large measure the revolutions that swept across the continent in the late 1840s. With more than half its population living in towns, Britain was now the world's first urban, industrialized society. Energy was everywhere. The popular mood was expressed by Queen Victoria, herself, after a private visit to the Exhibition at Hyde Park: 'We are capable', she wrote on 29 April 1851, 'of doing anything' (Morris 1973: 196).

Behind Queen Victoria's happily chauvinistic observation was the further assumption that Britons *should* so act. More than any other imperial power, Britain took to itself the mission to make the difficult planet known – physically

sighted that is – and then measured, charted and mapped. The Royal Geographical Society, founded in 1830 'for the advancement of geographical science', had
set out with scholarly fury to reduce the world's remaining blank cartographic
spaces into measurable units. 'If there is talk of an unknown land into which no
Englishman has penetrated', declared a *Times* (London) editorial from 1854, 'he
must be the first to visit the place' (Macfarlane 2004: 178–179). Victorian publishing houses lionized heroes of all kinds – especially dead ones – but none
quite so much as the imperial explorers. Words like the following proliferated
through Victorian-age monograph titles: *Diaries, Gleanings, Glimpses, Impres-
sions, Narratives, Notes, Rambles, Sketches, Travels* and *Wanderings*. Victorian
exploration and travel writing attained and deployed another order of capability:
that of giving the imperial subject a sense of self-definition, of Englishness, and
of mission. Against this exploratory impulse to know, actual mountain spaces
could offer relatively little defence.

Mountains became a godsend to the lawyers, doctors, clergymen and others
who made up Britain's swelling upper middle and professional classes. Their
jobs prevented them from becoming fully fledged explorers. Few could afford,
as Robert Macfarlane put it, 'the year it might take to sail south to the Antarctic,
for example, or the many weeks battling north through ship-high waves and
ship-wide icebergs to the Arctic' (2004: 179). But they had money, and a good
six weeks' summer holiday. And *terra incognita* was to be found upwards in the
not-so-far-off Alps, buried in the heart of civilized Europe, previously concealed
by the veil of altitude. Developments in rail infrastructure meant that Mont Blanc
could be reached in 24 hours; the Swiss Alps a little more. Once there, in only a
day, with a pair of well-made boots and a rucksack, one could ascend from a
benevolent Swiss meadow to the Arctic severities of a high Alpine summit – and
be home not long after. Travellers brandishing alpenstocks were now to be seen
congregating on smoggy summer days at London Bridge station, for example,
chatting amongst themselves about their Alpine excursions, the Channel crossing or the benefits of the French rail system. And while climbing mountains was
already well established in scientific practices, and Romanticism and the Grand
Tour in Europe had long made mountain viewing fashionable, it was here, in the
middle decades of the 1800s, in London, that climbing mountains became institutionalized as a distinct and coherent activity.

Newcomers to the activity felt the need for a forum in which they could share
their ideas and experiences. And it took the shape of the quintessential Victorian
institution, the club. The idea was first floated in February 1857, by botanist
William Mathews to a climbing companion, Reverend Fenton John Anthony
Hort, a Fellow of Trinity College, asking him 'to consider whether it would be
possible to establish an Alpine Club' (Clark 1953: 79). The idea was later taken
up in August with E. S. Kennedy – another Cambridge man; an author of independent means – on an ascent of the highest mountain in the Bernese Alps of
Switzerland, the Finsteraarhorn. Ad-hoc meetings followed, and by December a
list of invitees had been drafted. So it was that on 22 December 1857, 'The
Alpine Club' was formally inaugurated at Astley's Hotel, Covent Garden, its

declared aim being 'the promotion of good fellowship among mountaineers, of mountain climbing and mountain exploration throughout the world, and of better knowledge of mountains through literature, science and art' (Clark 1953: 81). John Ball – the Irish politician and scientist (also a Cambridge man) – assumed the presidency, and a fourth-generation publisher, William Longman, was elected vice-president.

Initially, it was decided that all members should have ascended to a height of at least 13,000 ft; this was quickly toned down, however, and expanded to include those who had written about the Alps, performed 'mountain exploits' or simply had shown interest in the region. The height regulation meant, of course, that those without the wherewithal to climb on the continent were out. And the requirement that members had to write about the Alps – or otherwise show significant cultural/scientific engagement with them – secured the professional parameters. Whatever the case, new recruits had to be sponsored by existing members, those who Ball identified as a 'community of taste and feeling ... who have shared the same enjoyments, the same labours, and the same dangers, ... a bond of sympathy stronger than many of those by which men are drawn into ... mutual feeling' (Ball 1859: xi–xii). The club quickly swelled in stature and numbers. In its first year, 80 people joined; by 1861, there were 158 members; and two years later, the club's list contained 281 members, each of whom paid their annual fee of one guinea. Women – of whom there were several very successful climbers – were not permitted to join on account of their supposed physical and moral deficiencies in the matter of mountain climbing; they would have their own club – the Ladies' Alpine Club – but not until 1907. Continental climbers – of whom there were also several very successful individuals – were brushed aside as irritants. The Alps now belonged to a new breed of traveller, who practised a highly codified form of leisure: they were part of a consolidated, metropolitan, professional and mostly male community – 'mountaineers' (Slemon 2008: 236–237), who, as British climber Geoffrey Winthrop Young would later put it, each aspired to their 'own territory, ... [and] their own prophetic book of adventure' (1943: 62).

Three books – all written by founding members of the Alpine Club – appeared in 1856–1857 and whetted the appetite for the banquet of mountaineering literature that would follow: Alfred Will's *Wanderings among the high Alps* (1856), Thomas Hinchliff's *Summer months among the Alps* (1857) and *Where there's a will there's a way* by E. S. Kennedy and Charles Hudson. But it was a resolution adopted at an early club meeting – in November 1858 – that had the greatest effect: 'That members should be invited to send to the Honorary Secretary a written account of any of the principal expeditions, with a view to the collection of an interesting set of such documents for general information of the Club' (Irving 1955: 77). The following spring, *Peaks, passes and glaciers: A series of excursions by members of the Alpine Club* (1859), edited by Ball, was published by Longman. Its success was immediate. Four editions were printed before year's end. It contained a selection of thrilling narrative accounts outlining various ascents, which, all told, showed the Mont Blanc range, the Pennine Alps and the Bernese Oberland quite taken over as 'an unlimited field for adventure', a playground (Macfarlane 2004: 180). A second series of *Peaks, passes and glaciers*, in two volumes, followed in 1862, telling of the eastward extension of the Alpine playground, as well as drawing attention to the most attractive peaks in the Western Alps, which had hitherto been overlooked through concentration on their slightly higher neighbours.

The 1858 resolution to encourage writing among members shouldn't be too surprising given the club's self-fashioning as a 'learned society' (Robbins 1987: 586). Interest in geology, glaciology, botany and cartography motivated much of the early exploration of the European Alps – and the continuation of this tradition meant that a large number of Victorian mountaineers had a decidedly scientific bent. This was reflected in the early membership; indeed, some of the leading scientists of the day now scribbled the designation 'AC' alongside 'FRS' (Fellow of the Royal Society) or, say, 'FLS' (Fellow of the Linnean Society), after their names in hotel registers throughout the Alps. Back at home, members, just like in other learned forums, read their peer-reviewed articles at annual meetings, and these were subsequently printed – in *Peaks, passes, and glaciers*, or, by 1863, its predecessor as the club's official organ, the *Alpine Journal*, not inconsequentially sub-titled 'a record of mountain exploration *and scientific observation*' (my emphasis). Publication mattered. It established a mountaineer's claim to a particular summit achievement; for just as priority was a matter of intense concern and debate in science, so it was in mountaineering.

Publication served another necessary function. In the sciences, a shared ethos was elaborated and maintained through journals. The same can be said about mountaineering, which, unlike most other sports, had neither a formal 'rule book' nor a system of refereeing to enforce them. Mountaineering was characterized by a series of complex, tacit rules (or 'ethics'), which were articulated, sustained and debated in the journal and other literary products. Of course, not all Victorian mountaineers considered themselves scientists (some openly ridiculed science – a point to be discussed below), nor were they all writers. But that alpine club culture emerged at precisely the same time that mountaineering-as-sport evolved from an older tradition of mountain-exploration-as-science is, well, noteworthy.

The *Alpine Journal*'s first editor, a don at New College, Oxford, Hereford B. George, MA, FRGS (Fellow of the Royal Geographical Society), touted in his 'Introductory Address' that 'the amount of geographical and other information' annually acquired, and now published, was not only worthy of a wider audience, but that there was indeed a public appetite for such postings (George 1863: 1). The first volume of the journal set a fashion that was followed to a large extent: new ascents; exploration as distinct from climbing; science, such as a discussion on glacial theories; equipment, not only in terms of ropes and the development of the ice axe from the old alpenstock, but problems of camping out (tents, sleeping bags, cooking apparatus and so on), at a time when huts or cattle sheds were few and far between, also received attention (George 1863: 1–2).

The constituent sections of the journal nicely place on view that which quickly became the chief source of tension within the club's rank-and-file. As sociologist/climber David Robbins noted, Victorian mountaineering practices came into existence at an uneasy point of intersection between three very different and potentially conflicting discourses: scientism (climbing for geographical and geological information, which was embraced and encouraged by the scientific societies of London); Romanticism (ascending to sublime heights so to 'gain access to the fundamental truths touching on the human condition'); and, increasingly into the 1860s and thereafter, athleticism (mountaineering as purely sport, which virtues lay in the moral and physical improvement derived from the urban impulse to get back to manly nature) (Robbins 1987: 587–593). The existence of these three, seemingly incompatible, desires made Victorian mountaineering, to quote literary scholar Stephen Slemon, a 'deeply incoherent activity': 'one cannot, for example', writes Slemon, 'scientifically calculate altitude through boiling-point measurements for barometric pressure and at the same time experience Romantic awe in contemplation of the ineffable and mountainous Sublime' (2008: 238–239). To show how these various desires were articulated and debated within club culture – Robbins called their assemblage 'teeth gritting harmony' (1987: 581) – let's return to the membership, and their books. All three alternative ways of thinking and feeling about their practice were in play throughout the early years of the Alpine Club: each had its proselytizer, and each had its bible.

In November 1858 – at the same club meeting where the resolution to encourage literary submissions was adopted – two individuals, whose achievements were well known in fields other than mountaineering, were elected members: John Tyndall and Leslie Stephen. Both were keen, capable and active mountaineers. Tyndall – a teacher, an evangelist for the cause of science and an author of a dozen science books – was a prominent physicist, who did much to bring state-of-the-art experimental physics to a wider audience. Of the Alps, glacial motion was his specific interest, which he satisfied by climbing, and which resulted in his *The glaciers of the Alps: Being a narrative of excursions and ascents ...* (1860). Here, and on the mountain, Tyndall was always *the scientist*:

> My object now was to go as light as possible, and hence I left my coat and neckcloth behind me, trusting to the sun and my own motion to make good the calorific waste. After breakfast I poured what remained of my tea into a small glass bottle, and ordinary *demi-bouteille*, in fact; the waiter then provided me with a ham sandwich, and, with my scrip thus frugally finished, I thought the heights of Monte Rosa might be won. I had neither brandy nor wine, but I knew the amount of mechanical force represented by four ounces of bread and ham, and I therefore feared no failure from lack of nutrition.
>
> (Tyndall 1860: 151)

In contrast, Leslie Stephen – an essayist, and the editor of *Dictionary of national biography* (and the father of Virginia Woolf and Vanessa Bell) – was absolutely non-scientific. He was also a noted adherent of athleticism. Perhaps it was, in part, too, contemplation of the Weisshorn – a Swiss giant that had repelled

Stephen's best attempt in 1859, but yielded to Tyndall's in 1861 – which provoked Stephen to openly mock Tyndall's utilitarian value of mountaineering. In
a satirical paper read before the club in 1862, Stephen delivered what could have
only been a jaw-dropper:

> 'And what philosophical observations did you make?' will be the inquiry of
> one of those fanatics who, by a reasoning process to me utterly inscrutable,
> have somehow irrevocably associated alpine travelling with science. To
> them I answer, that the temperature was approximately (I had no thermome-
> ter) 212° (Fahrenheit) below freezing point. As for ozone, if any existed in
> the atmosphere, it was a greater fool than I take it for. As we had, unluckily,
> no barometer, I am unable to give the usual information as to the extent of
> our deviation from the correct altitude; but the Federal map fixes the height
> at 13,855 feet.
>
> (Robbins 1987: 590)

Tyndall was deeply offended, and resigned his membership in protest, despite
having just been made a vice-president. Science, it was increasingly felt among
some members, obscured the fact that mountaineering was simply sport and the
Alpine Club an association of sportsmen.

President of the Alpine Club (1865–1868). Editor of the *Alpine Journal*
(1868–1872). Leslie Stephen quickly spread his influence over the mountain
world not only by his energy, not only by the force of his character and the
doughtiness of his deeds, but also *by his ability to write*. *The playground of
Europe*, which was published in 1871 and recounted his most famous ascents,
was 'not merely the best-written book of Alpine climbing that had been published', estimated Ronald Clark, a noted biographer and alpine historian:

> It has one quality which all others ... notably lacked. It explained an attitude
> to life. It was, in the literal sense, literature, which the Oxford Dictionary
> defines as 'writing esteemed for beauty of form or emotional effect.' It had
> not only a lasting influence but a finish beside which almost all other Alpine
> books that men could then buy had the polish of a crusty loaf.
>
> (Clark 1953: 121)

One other book published in 1871 might well be the exception to Clark's claim.
In the same year that Stephen ascended to the club's highest office (1865),
another Englishman, a wood engraver from the south London borough of
Lambeth named Edward Whymper, was thrust into the limelight for the first
recorded ascent of the Matterhorn, a monolithic pyramid high above Zermatt
that, as the *last* unclimbed peak of its stature, had become the holy grail of
Alpine exploration. Although the Matterhorn brought Whymper fame – the
ascent is said to have crowned the great age of British mountaineering – the disastrous descent, during which a novice party member slipped into one of the
guides, a rope broke and four men perished, earned for him an accompanying

reputation that would stay with him for life: a reputation for intemperance, for reckless amateurism and for monumental self-privilege (Smith 2011: 11; Robinson and Slemon 2013: 20).

The disaster made news headlines around the world. It also stripped the Alpine Club's exploits of respectability. At home, a period of intense questioning began. 'Why', asked *The Times*,

> is the best blood of England to waste itself in scaling hitherto inaccessible peaks, in staining the eternal snows and reaching the unfathomable abyss never to return?... Well, this is magnificent. But is it life? Is it duty? Is it common sense? Is it allowable? Is it not wrong?
>
> (July 1865)

John Ruskin, the great shaper of a Victorian mountain aesthetic, and author of *Modern painters* (1843), publically denounced mountaineering as fatuous and irreverent: 'You have despised nature [and] all the deep and sacred sensations of natural scenery', he scolded members of the Alpine Club in 1865:

> The French revolutionists made stables of the cathedrals of France; you have made racecourses of the cathedrals of the earth.... The Alps themselves, which your own poets used to love so reverently, you look upon as soaped poles in bear gardens, which you set yourselves to climb and slide down with 'shrieks of delight'.
>
> (Ruskin 1893: 58)

The public backlash in the wake of the Matterhorn disaster was harsh and unprecedented; it had, writes Fergus Fleming, 'all the flavor of medievalism then so popular thanks to the novels of Walter Scott' (2000: 292). New admissions dropped, and stayed low for some time thereafter (Ruskin, despite his remarks above, was ironically one new recruit, 1869–1882). When Stephen visited a hotel in Berne, Switzerland, he now found that 'they think no more of an ex-president of the Alpine Club than of a crossing sweeper' (Bicknell 1996: 87).

The gloom persisted in 1871. In that year, Whymper – who, in life and prose, was fiercely competitive and entirely unromantic – published his *Scrambles amongst the Alps in the years 1860–69*, a 432-page door-stopper containing 90 of his own illustrations and relating his exploits in the Alps that culminated in him climbing the Matterhorn. It was received rapturously in some quarters. 'You can almost hear the tinkle of the bells on the Alps and by the chalet', noted *The Times* (Fleming 2000: 293). Leslie Stephen added:

> Those who have lived through the period which is just now closing – the period, that is, in which inaccessibility has been finally abolished – will probably admit, on reflection, that Mr. Whymper's book contains the most genuine utterance of the spirit in which victory has been won ... it is the congenial record of the most determined, the most systematic, and, on the

whole, the best planned series of assaults that were made on the High Alps during the period of which he speaks.

(1870–1872: 240)

Nostalgia helped. The contest for first ascents, having spread throughout the European ranges, had now exhausted the Alps in the minds of many climbers. 'The play is over', Whymper himself laconically wrote, 'the curtain is about to fall' (1871: 406). Faced with the disturbing prospects of the apparent lack of new challenges, Victorian mountaineers would now be forced abroad, beyond the confines of Europe, carrying with them British prejudices and standards into the mountain ranges of Asia, Africa, New Zealand and the Americas (they would also take with them their European guides). With the professionalization of science by the mid-to-late century, and the resulting decline of amateur science, athleticism would provide the dominant framework. And while Ruskin's Romanticism would always have a pervasive, though generally subordinate, influence, it was Stephen's and Whymper's athleticism – 'a discourse of rewards for hard and resolute effort, manliness, physical and moral fitness, competition and mastery over nature' (Robbins 1987: 591) – that prevailed.

Of course, the shift did not occur overnight, nor was it without conflict. Albert Fredrick Mummery – who distinguished himself from his climbing contemporaries in action and with pen by suggesting that 'the essence of the sport lies ... in struggling with and overcoming difficulties' (1895: 326) – was, for example, famously barred from admission to the Alpine Club in 1880. Fifteen years later, Mummery would write his own 'classic' text, *My climbs in the Alps and the Caucasus* (1895), and preface it by pointedly writing as follows:

I fear no contributions to science, or topography, or learning of any sort are to be found sandwiched between the story of crags and seracs, of driving storm and perfect weather. To tell the truth, I have only the vaguest ideas about theodolites, and as for plane tables, their very name is an abomination. To those who think with me, who regard mountaineering as unmixed play, these pages are alone addressed.

(p. vii)

And so Whymper's *Scrambles* (1871) proved itself to be not only the capstone document to what was now already being touted as 'the golden age' of mountaineering, but also a terrifying glimpse at mountaineering's turn into a post-heroic modernity'.[1] It's today considered an essential classic in the archive of mountaineering literature. It has never been out of print.

Although the immediate effect of the Matterhorn incident was to cast a cloud over mountaineers and mountaineering, Whymper's thrilling book, and others – now all insuperably roped to a virtual community of readers (from 'armchair mountaineers' to the curious) – did much to popularize the Alps. The Matterhorn, and even Whymper himself, who was always an awkward ambassador for Victorian mountaineering, became a *cause célèbre*. Having read the story, people wanted to visit the scene. Thomas Cook, the British temperance-worker-turned-entrepreneur, who had started his first conducted tours to Switzerland in 1863, soon had his ledgers full. By the early 1870s, the Alps were as busy as ever. And thus it's perhaps unsurprising that 'Alpine accidents' would soon become a standard feature in mountaineering's literature, as club members read with dismay (others with morbid fascination) letters from France or Switzerland in which survivors of accidents recounted their harrowing ordeals. In the language of triumphalism, stories about 'going down' were now part of the genre, too. Even Whymper's own gravesite in Chamonix – with its immense granite block for a gravestone, not dissimilar in shape from the Matterhorn – is today a modern site of pilgrimage for tourists and mountaineers alike (see Figure 6.1).

Figure 6.1 Edward Whymper's gravesite in Chamonix.

Scientism. Romanticism. Athleticism. However contested, whatever their relative positioning, each of Robbins' founding discourses demanded of Victorian mountaineering a wholesale dependency on print culture. With no immediate audience and no formalized 'rules of the game', mountaineering's literature gave the activity its stadium, its rules of engagement, its sense of priority, its pulpit. The subsequent outward spread of club culture and the further development of mountaineering practices thus gave rise to an immense body of literature. The Austrian Alpine Club formed in 1862; the Swiss and Italians followed suit a year later. Norway, Germany, France, Spain, Belgium and Sweden – they all had their own clubs by the mid-1880s. In the 1890s and 1900s, alpine clubs were formed in New Zealand, South Africa, Russia, the United States and Canada; in India and China in the 1930s and 1950s, respectively; and now exist in every place where money and interest conspire. Not inconsequentially, new 'Matterhorns' could suddenly be found in all the major ranges, as well. Ushba, for example, became 'the Matterhorn of the Caucasus'; Ama Dablam, 'the Matterhorn of the Himalayas'; the 'Matterhorn of India' was Shivling; Mt Assiniboine was 'the Matterhorn of North America'; and Mt Aspiring/Tititea in New Zealand became 'the Matterhorn of the South'.[2] All were new sites writ old, where climbers could recreate past glories – 'that fabulous age ... when the youth of England rushed to the conquest of the mountains' (Parker 1912: 126) – in the onward advance of mountaineering's self-globalization.

There is thus no single 'alpine club culture', not really. The clubs that followed the British example were, in some ways, very different in concept, some being large organizations open to all (irrespective of gender), others being organized into local sections and owning mountain huts, where their members could stay for a nominal fee.[3] Each would be inflected in different ways by nationalist politics (for instance, consider the German Alpine Club during the Third Reich); each would be tailored to their respective circumstances, geographies and histories. In other regards, though, Britain provided a model. The Alpine Club of Canada, for example, constituted itself in 1906 with, in the very first instance, an objective of science: 'The objects for the Club are: (1) the promotion of scientific study and the exploration of Canadian alpine and glacier regions' (Parker 1907: 3). The inaugural volume of its journal, the *Canadian Alpine Journal*, heralded the call both for book donations and a library. Its continental and slightly older cousin, the American Alpine Club, has what is today the largest library devoted to mountaineering in North America, the Henry S. Hall Jr. Library – it holds over 20,000 titles, and continues to grow. And then there's the Himalayan Club, an organization that so closely dovetailed with the British military presence in India, yet that region's famous librarian/archivist and eventual face is a woman, Elizabeth Hawley (McDonald 2005).

A final contingency of mountaineering's literary turn outwards from its origins in male-only, club-based, white privilege to something now even more ambiguously called 'the mountaineering community' is – and this is Stephen Slemon's finding (2008: 239–242) – the persistent disavowal of dependencies: technology, certainly, but also the laboured participation of women and Others.

The exemplary representation of this 'community' in Victorian times might well be the frontispiece to Whymper's *Scrambles* (1871), an engraving entitled 'The Club-Room of Zermatt, in 1864' (see Figure 6.2). The tableau neatly frames the whole cast of 'golden agers'.

At the centre, the Alpine Club's president, Alfred Wills, stands in a white climbing outfit next to Tyndall, who gestures towards John Ball, the past president with the rope and alpenstock in hand. Between them is William Matthews, while E. S. Kennedy and T. G. Bonney (a Cambridge geologist) look over his shoulder. The guide, a dark faced Ulrich Lauener, towers in the back. To the left, a future president, Leslie Stephen, casually props his leg on the bench, as Reginald Macdonald, a Colonial Office clerk, makes a point while straddling his chair. Behind Stephen are clustered a London barrister, a Cambridge banker, a Rugby schoolmaster, a Liverpool lead merchant and an India Office clerk. To the right, the mountain guides pose in front of the Monte Rosa Hotel: Peter Pernn is on the far right; then comes Peter Taugwalder, seated, facing forward on the bench; J. J. Maquignaz is leaning against the door post; and Franz Andermatten, seated, occupies the steps. In the doorway, the wife of the hotel proprietor turns towards the merchant's daughter.

Adding to this fanciful, wholly metropolitan scene – with all the constituent actors of London's upper middle and professional classes in easy camaraderie against a European touristic backdrop – Whymper introduces 'the strangely and wonderfully dressed *Messieurs*' as 'the most expert amateur mountaineers of the time': 'There is a frankness of manner about these strangley-apparelled and

THE CLUB-ROOM OF ZERMATT, IN 1864.

Figure 6.2 The Club-Room of Zermatt, in 1864.

queer-faced men', Whymper wrote, 'which does not remind one of drawing-room, or city life; and it is good to see – in this club-room of Zermatt – those cold bodies, our too-frigid countrymen, regale together when brought into contact' (1871: 262–263). In the margins, the local people – those who guided, cajoled or pushed and pulled climbers to the summits, and did all the additional physical labour (step cutting, carrying loads, cooking, etc.) – are cast only in their silent servitude:

> guides – good, bad, and indifferent; French, Swiss, and Italian – can com-monly been seen sitting on the wall on the front of the Monte Rosa hotel: waiting on their employers, and looking for employers; watching new arriv-als, and speculating on the number of francs which may be extracted from their pockets.
>
> (Whymper 1871: 262)

Further marginalized are the two unnamed women. The first is Katharina Seiler, who in *Scrambles* is only the hotel owner's 'excellent wife', excellent presum-ably for playing domestic host for rugged Londoners, now 'Zermatt men'. As for the other figure, that's Lucy Walker, the first woman to have climbed the Mat-terhorn, who faces the viewer head on.

Notes

1 The middle-class cultural producers of the club wasted little time in claiming the sport as their own. In 1887, Englishman C. D. Cunningham first offered up the foundational myth that placed the formation of the Alpine Club and its early members at the centre of what he called 'the Golden Age of Mountaineering'. See Cunningham and Abney (1887: 1). For critical commentary on the 'Golden Age' myth, see Hansen (2013: 180–181).
2 *Wikipedia* lists over 20 Matterhorns located in various countries and ranges around the world. See http://en.wikipedia.org/wiki/List_of_references_to_the_Matterhorn (accessed 24 February 2015).
3 By 1887, while the Alpine Club had 475 members, the Austro-German Club (they combined in 1873) could boast 18,020 members, the French 5,321, the Italians 3,669 and the Swiss 2,607. See Unsworth (1994: 383–384).

References

Ball, J. (ed.) (1859) *Peaks, passes, and glaciers: A series of excursions by members of the Alpine Club*, London: Longman, Green, & Roberts.
Barcott, B. (1996) 'Cliffhangers: The fatal descent of the mountain-climbing memoir', *Harper's Magazine*, 293(August): 64–68.
Bicknell, J. (ed.) (1996) *Selected letters of Leslie Stephen*, Vol. I, London: Macmillan.
Clark, R. (1953) *Victorian mountaineers*, London: B.T. Batsford.
Cunningham, C. D. and Abney, W. de W. (1887) *The pioneers of the Alps*, London: Sampson Low, Marston, Searle, & Rivington.
Fleming, F. (2000) *Killing dragons: The conquest of the Alps*, New York: Grove Press.
George, H. B. (1863) 'Introductory address', *Alpine Journal*, 1(1): 1.

Hansen, P. H. (2013) *The summits of modern man: Mountaineering after the enlightenment*, Cambridge, MA: Harvard University Press.

Irving, R. L. G. (1955) *A history of British mountaineering*, London: B.T. Batsford.

Isaac, S. (2008) 'Editorial: Taking the reins', *Canadian Alpine Journal*, 91: 5.

McDonald, B. (2005) *'I'll call you in Kathmandu': The Elizabeth Hawley story*, Seattle, WA: The Mountaineers.

Macfarlane, R. (2004) *Mountains of the mind: Adventures in reaching the summit*, New York: Vintage.

Morris, J. (1973) *Heaven's command: An imperial progress, Volume I of the Pax Britannica Trilogy*, London: Faber & Faber.

Mummery, A. F. (1895) *My climbs in the Alps and the Caucasus*, London: T Fisher Unwin.

Parker, E. (1907) 'The Alpine Club of Canada', *Canadian Alpine Journal*, 1(1): 3–8.

Parker, E. (1912) 'In memoriam: Edward Whymper', *Canadian Alpine Journal*, 5: 126.

Robbins, D. (1987) 'Sport, hegemony and the middle class: The Victorian mountaineers', *Theory, Culture and Society*, 4(3): 579–601.

Robinson, Z. and Slemon, S. (2013) 'After the Matterhorns', *Canadian Alpine Journal*, 96: 18–23.

Ruskin, J. (1893) *Sesame and lilies*, London: George Allen.

Slemon, S. (2008) 'The brotherhood of the rope: Commodification and contradiction in the "mountaineering community"', in D. Brydon and W. D. Coleman (eds) *Renegotiating community: Interdisciplinary perspectives, global contexts*, Vancouver: UBC Press: 234–245.

Smith, I. (2011) *Shadow of the matterhorn: The life of Edward Whymper*, Ross-on-Wye: Carreg.

Stephen, L. (1870–72) 'Review: Mr. Whymper's scrambles amongst the Alps', *Alpine Journal*, 5: 234–240.

Tyndall, J. (1860) *The glaciers of the alps: Being a narrative of excursions and ascents, an account of the origin and phenomena of glaciers and an exposition of the physical principles to which they are related*, London: John Murray.

Unsworth, W. (1994) *Hold the heights: The foundations of mountaineering*, Seattle, WA: The Mountaineers.

Whymper, E. (1871) *Scrambles amongst the Alps in the years 1860–69*, London: John Murray.

Young, G. W. (1943) 'John Norman Collie', *Alpine Journal*, 54: 62.

Part II
People

7 The narrative construction of self through a commitment to mountaineering

Lee Davidson

Introduction

Mountaineering is a demanding leisure activity that requires a high level of commitment. This chapter examines how this commitment is established and maintained, at a time when commitment and continuity are seen to be the exception rather than the rule. In doing so, it focuses on the narrative construction of self in the biographical narratives of committed mountaineers. Underpinning the questions explored in this chapter are social theories concerned with the problematic nature of self and identity in contemporary life.

The chapter draws on a broader study of the narrative construction of self and meaning by committed New Zealand mountaineers (Davidson 2006). The traditional New Zealand mountaineering experience and identity, rooted in the realities of a rugged and remote landscape, evolved an ethos of self-reliance and 'colonial ingenuity' in the late nineteenth century. This was strengthened as the sport gained wider popularity during the dislocation and hardship of the interwar period in the twentieth century (Davidson 2002). To be self-reliant and to go 'on nature's terms' implies a particular kind of experience that is central to the construction of self and identity in the narratives of New Zealand mountaineers. There are concerns, however, that this experience is threatened by the impact of commercialism and new technologies – both key aspects of the tourism industry (Davidson 2011).

The chapter begins by outlining the theoretical concerns about self and identity in contemporary social life, before identifying related themes in the literature on mountaineering and adventurous leisure. A brief overview of the study methodology introduces the discussion of how mountaineers construct a sense of self through their experiences in the mountains. The subsequent section considers the efficacy of a mountaineering self in the light of relevant theory, while the conclusion reflects on the implications of this analysis for mountaineering tourism.

Self-identity in liquid modernity: adventure as escape and the search for self

The processes of individualization which have accompanied modernity have transformed human identity 'from a "given" into a "task"' (Bauman 2001: 144) and the 'search for self in order to come to terms with oneself ... has become one of the fundamental themes of our modern culture' (Taylor 1989). According to Giddens (1991: 185) it is the reflexivity of modernity that has rendered a coherent narrative of self-identity if not impossible then 'inherently fragile'.

As Gergen (1991: 80) explains, 'the relatively coherent and unified sense of self inherent in a traditional culture gives way to manifold and competing potentials'. To compensate for a life devoid 'of firmly fixed and steady orientation points, of a predictable destination for the life itinerary', Bauman (2001: 43) argues, modern capitalist society offers an endless array of consumer goods that function as 'symbols of identity'. The convenience of these off-the-shelf identities is countered by their lack of permanence. They become 'successively worn masks' – 'continuously negotiated, adjusted, constructed without interruption and with no prospect of finality' (Bauman 1988: 41; 2001: 87). The implications of this for our leisure lives are described by Rojek (1993: 212–216):

> We shrink from deep commitments and cast our energies in leisure out toward reassuring, consumerist experience which requires passive involvement or transitory relationships which avoid putting ourselves on the line.... Dedicated leisure activity is quite rare, which is why the compulsive hill-walker, the serious amateur musician, or even the serious reader of fiction, stand out so starkly.... The ephemeral, the fugitive and the contingent describe our experience of leisure just as they are at the heart of the phenomenology of Modernity.

If these theorists are correct, then committed mountaineers are something of an anomaly. How do their identities and, by association, their commitment to a leisure activity, maintain an intensity and durability that elude others? Have they found for themselves some 'fixed points of orientation' from which they can navigate towards a 'predictable destination'? While the literature on mountaineering and other adventurous leisure activities is largely preoccupied with questions of motivations and risk-taking (see for example Creyer *et al.* 2003; Le Breton 2000, 2004; Olivier 2006; Palmer 2002; Pereira 2005), some theorists have considered its relationship with these wider social and cultural conditions. In particular, it has been seen as a response to an increasingly rationalized society, and as a vehicle for authentic and self-realizing action.

According to Vester (1987: 242), the comparative uncertainty of adventure gives it a 'liminal' flavour that functions to fulfil 'the romantic desire for a more fascinating state of being which is relatively independent of social structure'. The romanticism of adventure, Vester (pp. 245–246) argues, may be one of the last available opportunities in modern culture to experience 'an authentic state of being'; the possibility for 'true self-actualization, [as] opposed to the inauthentic ordinary everyday life'. Adventure, therefore, 'plays a significant part in providing an opportunity to compensate for the boredom and lack of authenticity felt in ordinary life' (Vester 1987: 238). But Vester (p. 245) warns that while adventure offers, for some, an opportunity to experience 'the essential sphere of existence and meaning', it may simultaneously contain a less attractive character which is routinized, standardized and ritualized. Indeed, its lasting effect may be to make one more acutely aware of the tedium of everyday life, and if adventure is commercialized and rationalized 'little room is left for risk, daring, and uncertainty' (Vester 1987: 246).

Similar themes appear in the work of Lyng, whose concept of 'edgework' views voluntary risk-taking, such as mountaineering, as a negotiation of the boundaries between chaos and order. Lyng (1990) argues that because of a lack of opportunities in contemporary western society for 'self-realizing action' people are increasingly seeking out skilful forms of play that involve an element of risk. Through these experiences, edgeworkers have 'the illusion of controlling the seemingly uncontrollable', and derive a sense of competence denied to them in other areas of their lives. He says:

> behavior in edgework appears to the individual as an innate response arising from sources deep within the individual, untouched by socializing influences. Thus edgeworkers experience this action as belonging to a residual, spontaneous self – the 'true self,' as it were.
>
> (Lyng 1990: 879)

Lester (2004: 87) identifies a number of themes relating to self within mountaineering literature 'which seem to work towards enhancing a sense of integration and diminishing a sense of fragmentation'. This leads him to suggest that 'mountaineering may have its strongest appeal to especially divided selves' (p. 97). In his sociological investigation of mountaineers in the US, Mitchell (1983) found that the meaning of mountaineering emerged from the 'reflective discussion and debate' and that through the successive recollections and anticipations of mountain adventures, experiences were blended together in such a way as to allow participants to develop 'new patterns of relationships' and self-images which were 'special and apart from conventional ones' (p. 77). Mountaineers, he argues, 'are seeking in their leisure a test of their limits in a gratifying no-compromise situation where their behavior is meaningful and outcomes depend upon their perceived capabilities' (Mitchell 1983: 224). In a 'rationalized world of amoral inconstancy' mountaineers infuse their chosen leisure activity with meaning, and hence create the purpose and direction that the world is lacking (Mitchell 1983: 214).

Similarly Macaloon and Csikszentmihalyi (1983: 377) examine the extent to which rock climbing can provide 'a base from which one can perceive culture more clearly'. They found that the stories rock climbers told were antistructural: in climbing they found a depth, meaning and morality which was lacking in 'real' life. A deeper understanding of intrinsically rewarding activities such as rock climbing, the authors argue, may be the solution to the alienation and meaninglessness of daily activities, and the key to making ordinary life more enjoyable.

However this is not possible, according to Mitchell (1983), in sports which have become too rationalized and institutionalized, or in commercialized adventure where the actions and abilities of the participants have little impact on the outcome. Indeed Kiewa (2002) and Heywood (1994), who both critically examine the notion of climbing as escape or resistance, find that rationalization encroaches even on the world of mountaineering through forms of regulation, commercialization and commodification.

Thus, a number of studies have concluded that issues of self or identity are related to participation, including the suggestion that the pursuit of adventure is growing because a lack of constancy and authenticity in contemporary society makes escape more necessary than ever before. However, an in-depth enquiry into the ways in which self is constructed within the lives of mountaineers, and the means by which it is sustained by those with an enduring and intense commitment, has thus far been lacking. This chapter examines the ways in which mountaineers integrate their experiences of the practice of climbing mountains into a 'narrative of self', and considers the conditions which underpin this process. Picking up on concerns in the literature that commercialism is a potential threat to the search for authenticity, I consider the implications of my findings for mountaineering tourism.

A narrative study of New Zealand mountaineers: constructing a mountaineering self

Narrative plays a prominent role in the construction of meaning and the process of self-making (Bruner 1990, 1996; Funkenstein 1993; Holstein and Gubrium 2000). We understand our lives, according to Taylor (1989: 47), as an unfolding story: in order to have an understanding of who we are we have to have a sense of 'how we have become, and of where we are going', and a coherent narrative provides such an understanding. Thus, a narrative methodology is particularly well-suited to investigations of the construction of self and meaning. This methodology treats interview material, not in the realist tradition, as directly mirroring a fixed, external reality, but as collections of stories and narratives that give access to the descriptions and explanations with which people make sense of their lives (Denzin 2001b; Elliott 2005; Roberts 2002; Spector-Mersel 2010). In addition to providing insights into lived experience (Clandinin and Connelly 2000; Denzin 2001a), biographical narrative interviews can provide access to the cultural repertoires of motivation (Jarvinen 2000), and the dynamics of the process by which they are utilized in an individual's search for self and meaning.

For this study, biographical narrative interviews were conducted with 22 New Zealand mountaineers whose level of dedication to their leisure fits Stebbins' (2005) definition of devotee hobbyists. Purposive and theoretical sampling (Strauss and Corbin 1998) were used to select interviewees that represented a range of ages, gender, length of climbing career and family/relationship situations. Potential participants were identified via the 'snowball technique', beginning with personal contacts in the New Zealand climbing community.

Fourteen interviewees were male and eight were female. Interviewees were selected according to three broad age/career stage categories: six were aged 20 to 35 years (early stage of mountaineering career); ten were aged 35 to 50 years (mid-career); and six were 50+ (late career). Thirteen of the interviewees were in long-term committed relationships (either married or de facto), and nine were single. Exactly half of the interviewees had children.

The interviews began with a single narrative prompting question (Wengraf 2001), asking participants to talk about their mountaineering experiences, beginning with when they first became interested in climbing and tracing its evolution from there. Once they finished telling their initial story I asked, if necessary, for clarification and elaboration, keeping to the original sequence in which themes were raised by the participant. Additional non-narrative questions were then used to prompt responses to specific issues of interest. To interpret the narratives, I first identified the problematic events or epiphanies that 'leave marks on people's lives' and which allow for the display of personal character and bring about the altering of 'fundamental meaning structures' (Denzin 1989: 70). Once these were identified, it was possible to interpret the basic features of the narrative.

The following analysis focuses primarily on an individual sense of meaning and 'self' centred on mountaineering. By identifying the commonalities that exist between the narratives in this regard, it highlights the aspects of mountaineering that facilitate a durable identity as a mountaineer and demonstrates how this sense of self is constructed through the biographical particulars of a mountaineering life. However these personal narratives are influenced by communal narratives and shared discourses within the social world of mountaineering, as well as broader historical and cultural contexts. Although there is not space to address these factors in depth in this chapter, further discussion can be found in Davidson (2002, 2006, 2008a, 2008b, 2011, 2012).

The discussion is divided into two main sections. The first examines stories about becoming a mountaineer, and the significance of these stories in terms of an emerging sense of being, or identifying as, a mountaineer. The second outlines the ways in which mountaineering facilitates the construction of a durable identity and a 'true' sense of self.

Emerging identities

Although most of the mountaineers did not start climbing mountains until their late teens or early twenties, their narratives about how they became mountaineers often begin with events or tendencies earlier in life which foretell or foreshadow their later desire to climb. There are variations to the story of an awakening identity as a mountaineer, but a number of important themes form the base ingredients: getting a 'mountain feeling'; entering the social world of mountaineering; and making choices.

Having considered the many available conceptualizations, Levin finds the most relevant meaning of self to be experience, a meaning which is associated with the idea of self as process: 'the central part of self is *felt*,... something directly experienced' (1992: 79). Self as feeling or experience is evident in the mountaineering narratives, particularly in stories about early mountain experiences. Dave[1] began his story with a reference to the first time he could remember being aware of the mountains: looking at them through a pair of binoculars, from the kitchen window of the house in the small town where he lived as a child. Then he recalled a critical moment on a hike in the foothills of his local mountains:

> I remember going off by myself ... and standing at the entrance to this valley ... and just getting this ... what I call, mountain feeling ... it's not something you can put into words ... it's quite emotional. You can stand at the entrance to a valley, or you can stand on a mountain and you get this wave of ... good feeling, or whatever, it's quite a euphoric sort of thing. I remember that feeling at ten or so.

Similarly, Jan's story begins with the exhilaration she has felt in the mountains from a very young age. She describes her first experience of becoming involved with climbing when she went on a family holiday:

> we went up to a little place in the foothills and my brother and sister were happy playing around in the little creek and all the rest of it. But I would always climb to the top of the hills and see what was over the other side ... my one ambition was to get to the top of the hill, to see what was on the other side.... So that was my initial spur was always to look over the mountain.

From her first experiences of hill walking and rock climbing at about eight or nine, Sue 'absolutely loved it' and from then on she always wanted to climb. When asked if she could imagine her life without mountaineering she said:

> I've never thought about it. Because it was always there. My oldest brother, tells me that when I was about four and we were travelling through this sort of hilly country to get to my Uncle's house that I looked up at the hills and said 'oh I wish I was up there' and like I have no recollection of that but I think that I must have always had this yearning to be on the heights. So it is strange isn't it?... I've never really questioned it, it was just me,... that was what I wanted to do.

These few examples illustrate a deeply felt personal response to the mountains, which both marks one's story as different from others' stories and aligns one with those who profess a similar feeling for the mountains. Entering the social world of mountaineering is the next key element in becoming a mountaineer. Most participants spoke of entering this world through connections with family and friends, which often leads to joining a club or taking a course. Through these networks young, aspiring mountaineers find like minds who nurture their development. Often, particular people have a pivotal influence and become role models as the mountaineers consolidate their identities.

Pete says he did not have any interest as a teenager in 'going into the hills or climbing or tramping, other than being dragged along with Dad every now and then'. But he starts his story there, with his parents exposing him to the outdoors at an early age. The turning point came when he started university and went on a tramping trip into an alpine area with a friend. Here they met a couple of experienced climbers who lent them their ice axes so that they could explore higher up. They

> got into a bit of crevasse country and poked around and had a good look around and I just came out of that and that's just what I wanted to do. I just wanted to get back into that country at every opportunity I could.

The older brother of one of Pete's friends was an active climber, one of the 'hard men' of a local group climbing new routes and 'pushing the boundaries' in New Zealand during the 1970s. Pete and his friends were taken 'under their wings' and he feels fortunate to have been exposed to good climbers at an early stage. He improved quickly, 'always aspiring to the stuff these guys were doing', and this was the focus of his life for the next 15 years. Almost without fail the mountaineers, like Pete, tell of formative experiences with various people in the early stages of being introduced to the outdoors and climbing. For Chris, it was the 'climber types' he met, 'all these bushy hairy guys'. Sue knew a 'climbing nun' who'd been on an expedition to the Hindu Kush.

The third narrative element of becoming a mountaineer is making choices that commit one to a mountaineering lifestyle. Making mountaineering the centre of one's life is often seen as the result of choices, and not always easy choices. Often it is narrated as a choice between doing what you love and being who you want to be on the one hand, and doing what is expected of you and being who other people want you to be on the other.

It took some time for Dan to reach the conclusion that climbing was not something that he was 'going to be happy doing on weekends':

> I guess it's something I've kind of always known but ... I've just been admitting it to myself really.... More of a confirmation within yourself of what you really want to do ... that it's alright to feel like this ... [it's] been a process over a couple of years of, experimentation really, trying different things, ways of living, different jobs and travelling.

For Kath it was a 'conscious decision' to 'put everything else aside' to climb mountains. She says: 'I decided I didn't want a career. I just wanted to be a climber.' It was an 'easy' decision to make, but that did not mean that it was necessarily an easy life she had chosen, and it certainly was not the life she was expected to have. While her friends from school were all at university 'going to parties' and 'meeting boys', she was living in 'dead end places' near the mountains and taking unskilled casual work.

In summary, the common narrative elements through which a sense of self as a mountaineer emerges in a personal history are: early experience which engenders (or illustrates) a strong emotional attachment to and sense of ease and exhilaration in the mountains; the intersection of the life story with others engaged in a similar process of self-making, their stories inspiring and nurturing their own; and making choices that lead them to 'follow their hearts' and climb mountains. In addition to these elements a durable and 'true' sense of self is constructed through a 'folk psychology' (Bruner 1990) of mountaineering, which emerges from the narratives as the mountaineers describe aspects of the activity that enhance and validate their sense of who they are.

The durability of mountaineering selves

> [W]ith true mountaineers, when you go into the mountains you are yourself, you aren't anybody else, . . . there's just those total moments of clarity. You know that, this is where you belong, . . . and it's weird because we weren't born there or whatever, . . . but you just feel so at home, you just feel grounded . . . mountaineering gives me so much that I wouldn't want to give it up. There's nothing else that I can conceivably think of doing that would give me as much as mountaineering has . . . if I couldn't go mountaineering then, you know, it's like gnawing my right arm off [laughs].
>
> (Dave)

To introduce this section and show how the themes discussed below are constructed in a full personal history, I focus on the story of Dave who, as mentioned above, stood at the entrance of a valley at the age of ten and fell in love with the mountains.

From being a self-described 'skinny, asthmatic, sickly and wouldn't-say-boo-to-a-fly' boy, Dave became a mountaineer who climbs technical and difficult routes. Also, he is now 'less polite', cares less about what people think of him and admits to being a little eccentric. But when he first started climbing he would often feel

> really scared and really sort of shaky and stuff, it was horrible . . . and wondering [laughs], . . . if I can actually go mountaineering. It can be quite scary because you know you love it and you know you want to do it, but it can be quite . . . a fearful thing.

To deal with these feelings Dave would 'just move on from them a little bit, or you relax about it and it comes right – the fear kind of goes away'. Sometime later he discovered that he could use his fear to 'tap into' an extremely focused state that allows him to succeed on difficult and dangerous solo climbs.

The evolution of Dave's sense of self through mountaineering emerges from a personal history that involves a detailed account of a mountaineering 'career path' with small steps of increasing difficulty as he gains more skills and courage to try harder things. This was largely self-taught, from reading books, and through trial and error. The goal of this 'natural progression' was to find the ultimate limit of his potential. It was a process of setting out to learn what he was capable of, both physically and emotionally, and attempting to expand this by pushing his limits through a series of challenges.

The difficulty with constantly climbing harder and harder, however, was recognizing when he had pushed his limits too far and should 'pull back'. Sometimes Dave makes mistakes and gets 'spanked', but that is part of the process of being self-taught – learning from experience. At the same time he has been driven on by the fear of ending up wondering 'what could have been':

> I don't want to end up a grizzly old 65–70 year old lamenting the loss of what I didn't do, or what I didn't achieve. I think I've pushed it as hard as my technical and mental abilities and physical ability. [But] there'll always be that little bit of doubt that, 'gosh maybe I could have pushed it that little bit harder', but, I'd probably be dead, I would imagine [laughs].

For Dave, any suffering endured due to the challenges of climbing are insignificant in relation to his love of and sense of commitment to being a mountaineer. He was once stranded for four nights in a crevasse – with a broken hip and nothing to eat – waiting to be rescued. At the time he was rescued, Dave does not think that he could have survived much longer. While he describes the experience as a hideous 'nightmare' at the time, of the aftermath he says:

> I had to deal with that little bit of, post traumatic stress syndrome or whatever. But, you … just move on and that's cool.... I don't have any lasting scars from that, you know sitting in the snow thinking badly about the mountains. I realise that, it's not the mountains it's me, you know.

Thus, despite fear and injury, mountaineering is for Dave both the expression of his 'true self' and the means by which he has found it:

> it's my individuality as, who I am, but, an honest benchmark is when … you know you're going to die, you know that's who you are and I've, I've seen that and I've felt it … it's a definite form of expression, mountaineering. I mean it does express my true, personality I think.... You've got to, know yourself pretty well to, to go away mountaineering.

Dave was a particularly engrossing and reflective story-teller, but the others told stories with a similar message: that certain characteristics of the mountain environment and mountaineering as an activity allow them to construct a 'true' sense of who they are. So much so that, as Pete says 'I just can't imagine not being in or around the mountains'. Terry felt there was no reason to ever give up 'because … it's a part of you, you see'. The desire to climb, and the sense that mountaineers are who they – irrepressibly – are, is so strong that it overrides bad experiences. As Dave says, 'I love it so much that, you just work through those things.'

The characteristics of mountaineering that aid the construction of a durable and 'true' sense of self are expressed in the narratives as a form of 'folk psychology';

that is, as stories containing certain beliefs about the way in which 'being in the mountains' is experienced, and how it *should* be experienced, particularly if one wants to stay alive. Bruner (1990: 35) describes folk psychology as 'a system by which people organize their experience in, knowledge about, and transactions with the social world'. As such, it is 'one of the most powerful constitutive instruments' of culture, comprising:

> a set of more or less connected, more or less normative descriptions about how human beings 'tick,' what our own and other minds are like, what one can expect situated action to be like, what are possible modes of life, how one commits oneself to them, and so on ... its organizing principle is nar-rative rather than conceptual.
>
> (Bruner 1990: 35)

There are three important dimensions in the construction of a durable sense of self. Mountaineering allows mountaineers, according to their 'folk psychology', to discover their capabilities and their limitations, through self-reliance and action in an environment which does not forgive inaccurate assessments of the self; to expand their sense of self by progressing through a series of ever-increasing challenges, and through experiencing committing situations in which they must, by necessity, 'tap into' resources they did not previously know that they possessed; and, finally, to express their individuality through the style in which they climb. These characteristics make mountaineering particularly con-ducive to the construction of a durable sense of self – a solid identity in a liquid world.

The remoteness and wildness of the mountains fosters an intense sense of self-reliance in mountaineers. By being 'left to one's own devices' mountaineers feel that they gain a sense of their true capabilities, as the 'unforgiving' nature of the mountain environment provides an 'honest test' of self, and of one's strengths and weaknesses. In light of this, the mountains should be approached, as Bob says, 'purely on nature's terms', then 'one can discover oneself ... on the real terms that are not contrived'.

> That whole business of being able to equip yourself and go and live out there. And experience what that means. And that's the guts of it. That's the raw guts of what it's about really. We live such cloistered lives.

Without 'crutches' or undue 'outside' assistance there is a sense of control in a demanding environment, and a sense that survival came down to one's own resources and skills. Steph says that her most satisfying mountaineering achieve-ments are:

> things that I've done by myself, which haven't been nearly as hard as things that I've done with other people ... but just doing things by yourself ... it's a way to sort of prove to yourself that, yeah, that you've done it all, been in

control … [and] it shows me how far I have come 'cause it's easy to, feel like, you're not really improving somehow. But if I go by myself and, I realise that I've got a whole new level of confidence than last time I went somewhere by myself, then that's really cool.

In addition to the sense of self-discovery through self-reliance, mountaineering provides the conditions for an 'honest test' or an 'honest benchmark' of 'who you are and what you're capable of'. As Pete says:

it puts you on edge and tests you really and I like being put in those situations … it's an honest test too. It's not sort of a contrived, thrill sport type of test where I mean sure you might fall off but everything's all protected … nothing's going to go wrong. So you're not really, out there on the edge … I think that test, that ultimate test of climbing's one of the big attractions and underneath it all.

Under these conditions, mountaineers must exercise precise judgement regarding their abilities. Tim says, it is important to know 'where you're at', so that he's not too 'pigheaded' to turn back when he has reached the limit at which he can climb safely. Also, if someone is climbing for the 'wrong' reasons – for fashion, to impress people, for fame and glory – their judgement may be compromised. Adam finds that 'you tend to come across a lot of people who like talking about themselves', but he thinks 'testosterone-charged climbing' can lead to mistakes.

In addition, mountaineering is not just about impressive feats of climbing, but also involves enduring hours in miserable conditions. It is by their behaviour in these circumstances that Steph judges her climbing companions:

I see them at times when it's, just miserable, we're really cold and we've run out of food and, we've lost the way or whatever, and you look over at your mate, they've got a big grin and make a joke or something, and so, you see people's true colours really.

So mountaineering is seen to provide ideal conditions for action through which one's 'true' qualities and abilities are revealed, and where artifice and an overestimation of one's abilities will be unmasked.

The expansion of one's sense of self through mountaineering occurs primarily in two ways in the narratives. First, mountaineers expand their climbing abilities by a series of progressively harder challenges, in an attempt to find the limits of these abilities. Second, as they age and the potential to expand their physical abilities wanes, there is a change of focus and expansion occurs at the level of judgement, self-assuredness and deepening enjoyment of the pleasures of mountaineering not related to physical challenge.

While it is important for mountaineers not to overestimate their abilities, if they underestimate their potential they risk never 'getting off the ground' at all, and never knowing what they might have been capable of, like Dave's grizzly old man lamenting the loss of what he did not do. So climbing is not only about knowing where their limits are, but trying to push them out a little bit and thereby to expand their sense of what is possible for them.

Tim sees himself as 'always trying to climb a bit harder', and 'wanting to see how far I can get'. He thinks that climbing lends itself well to this because it gives you 'immediate feedback of where your strength's at', and because it is 'very even between the physical and the mental', it 'contribute[s] to your understanding of yourself' more than other sports. Jess's most memorable trips are those in which she feels challenged but confident in her abilities:

> It's all about testing your limits and kind of getting an idea of where they are but not pushing them too hard you know what I mean. So it's not desperate but you kind of, you've seen how much further you can go which is further than you've been before which is quite neat.

As mountaineers grow older, they are generally not so able to have a sense of self-expansion through increasing their physical climbing abilities, and the mountaineering self expands and develops in different ways. Nearly all of the mountaineers, even some of those still in their twenties, spoke about how their focus had changed from their early days of climbing. It is seen to be part of the process of 'growing up' to ease back on the youthful enthusiasm for pushing the boundaries of one's strength and technical abilities, and instead to focus on enjoying the pleasures that come from the strong bonds formed with climbing companions, and 'just being there' in the mountains.

The third way in which the construction of self emerges from the folk psychology of the narratives is in terms of self-expression. The way in which someone climbs mountains is seen to reveal aspects of the self that can be read and interpreted by others. In this way, mountaineering is considered a medium for self-expression, and those I interviewed talk about styles of climbing and types of trips which they feel express their particular identity or style within the broad landscape of mountaineering. For example, Kath likes long technical ice routes, whereas Pip enjoys long solo journeys through the mountains, for the sense of isolation and the sense of moving through territory that she feels intuitively drawn to. As Thomas says 'the way you go to the mountains I think says a hell of a lot about people.... We do a thing in a particular way, and this says more about us.'

Mountaineering, authenticity and the spontaneous self

In a quote above, Dave says that if he could not go mountaineering, it would be 'like gnawing my right arm off'. That is, it would be like losing a part of himself in quite an unimaginable, self-inflicted way. A number of the mountaineers made similar comments about how unimaginable their lives would be if they did not climb. As discussed, conditions in contemporary western society are not considered to be conducive to establishing a consistent sense of self linked to a stable identity, as the traditional anchors for this have been undermined by prevailing economic, social and cultural forces. The best contingency under these conditions, it is argued, is a preparedness to change identities as situations dictate, and to shrink from seeing any one identity as fundamentally and inescapably synonymous with one's sense of self.

Nevertheless, in the narratives I collected a sense of self was constructed that *was* indeed synonymous with one's identity as a mountaineer, and consistently so. In the folk psychology of these mountaineers, climbing helps them to discover, expand and express their sense of who they are; and who they 'truly' are, is who they are when they are in the mountains. This is not to say that they are impervious to contemporary dilemmas of identity. Perhaps it is more accurate to say that their narratives represent a coherent alternative response to the identity challenge of current times. This conclusion is supported by Bruner's (2002: 28) argument that 'the impetus to narrative is expectation gone awry'. Stories then, are both coping mechanisms and a means of rectifying an untenable situation, of 'reassert[ing] a kind of conventional wisdom' (Bruner 2002: 31). If nothing has 'gone awry', there is no call for a story. So, stories about the durability and authenticity of one's sense of self suggest that while such a self is expected by conventional wisdom, it cannot, or can no longer, be considered a given. If who one is could be taken for granted, and is unlikely to change, there would be little need to talk about it.

According to Ricoeur (1992: 118) the 'entire problematic of personal identity [revolves] around this search for a relational invariant, giving it the strong signification of permanence in time'. It is narrative, he argues, which 'allows us to integrate with permanence in time what seems to be its contrary in the domain of sameness-identity, namely diversity, variability, discontinuity, and instability' (Ricoeur 1992: 140). In telling the story of a life, it is possible to reconcile change and contingency with a sense of permanence and self-constancy by correlating the development of character with the plot of the story. In Dave's narrative, for example, he changed considerably over time from a weak and timid child, to become a bold and aggressive solo climber. In his narrative, mountaineering was the vehicle or action required for this transformation, not as something that he chanced upon by accident, but as something he was irrevocably drawn to, despite fear and hardship. When he came to the end of telling me his personal history he said: 'So that's pretty much the end of the Dave Wood history of natural progression.' It is a story about the gradual realization, through mountaineering, of latent aspects of character: of the self that was always there, constant but hidden, authentic but not always manifest.

This sense of an innate self is important for creating a story of a continuous and unified self, as such stories are firmly rooted in the past. When they anticipate the future – as life narratives typically do – there is a strong feeling that this core self will not change, as this does not seem possible. Ricoeur (1992: 122) describes this process as the 'dialectic of innovation and sedimentation' which underlies the acquisition of habit:

> habit gives a history to character, but this is a history in which sedimenta-
> tion tends to cover over the innovation which preceded it, even to the point
> of abolishing the latter.... It is this sedimentation which confers on charac-
> ter ... [a sense of] permanence in time.
>
> (Ricoeur 1992: 121)

In similar ways to Dave, the other mountaineers tell narratives in which plot and character are mutually dependent. The dominant theme of these narratives is that certain characteristics of mountaineering enable them to understand and be their true selves, through a sense of self-reliance and an unforgiving environment which precludes the possibility of 'faking it'; through the potential to progress through successive challenges in order to learn where the limits of one's abilities are; through being able to change one's focus as one grows older and still to identify oneself as a mountaineer; and through being able to express one's individuality and fundamental values by the style in which one climbs.

Some of the previous research about mountaineering and adventurous leisure, discussed above, commented on its role as a vehicle for finding a 'true self'. However, this research overlooked the way in which this self is narratively constructed, often quite early on, and the resulting narrative anticipates future experiences of self which, when realized, in turn strengthen and confirm the narrative. The mountaineers in my study were not, I would argue, involved in an 'incessant search for self' (Lyng 1990). Nor were they especially 'divided selves' (Lester 2004). They already knew who they were. What they were engaged in was ensuring that their life experiences could be spun together into one continuous, unified self (Bruner 2002; Damasio 1999).

What is also striking about the recalled experiences of self is how closely they align with the psychologist Fromm's (1994: 259) 'moments of spontaneity'. Relating ourselves 'spontaneously to the world' is Fromm's 'healthy' solution to the 'inner contradictions' of human existence. Fromm describes *spontaneous* activity as 'free activity of the self'. He opposes it to activity undertaken compulsively or in order to be one of the crowd. Neither is it activity in the sense of 'doing something'. Rather, it is the 'quality of creative activity that can operate in one's emotional, intellectual, and sensuous experiences and in one's will as well' (1994: 257). Spontaneity and its accompanying 'moments of genuine happiness' can be experienced in a multitude of ways:

> the fresh and spontaneous perception of a landscape, or the dawning of some
> truth as the result of our thinking, or a sensuous pleasure that is not stereo-
> typed, or the welling up of love for another person – in these moments we all
> know what a spontaneous act is and may have some vision of what human life
> could be if these experiences were not such rare and uncultivated experiences.
>
> (Fromm 1994: 259)

Although Fromm considers *spontaneity* to be rare, the mountaineers in my study often experienced climbing mountains in this way. Associated with the expression of their 'true' selves, the resulting emotions were often hard to capture in words. For Dave it was 'euphoric', 'a wave of good feeling', and for Jan 'it feels like your soul's expanding'.

The relevance of *spontaneous* experiences for the construction of self is that through such activity, an individual 'embraces the world' while at the same time keeping the individual self intact. In this process the self, Fromm (1994: 260) argues, 'becomes stronger and more solidified. *For the self is as strong as it is active'.* 'Genuine happiness' is in 'the experience of the activity in the present moment' (Fromm 1994: 261): we have an awareness of our place in the world; our doubt concerning who we are and where we belong and what it all means, disappears.

Conclusion

A mountaineering self is underpinned by a strong sense of attachment to the mountains, membership of a social world of 'like-minded' mountaineers and a commitment to a lifestyle centred on the activity. This identity is further developed through self-reliance in an 'unforgiving' environment, which allows one to discover, expand and express an 'honest' or 'true' sense of self. In pursuing these types of experiences that develop and sustain their identity, committed mountaineers frequently travel to mountain ranges around the world seeking new challenges of higher altitude, varied terrain and conditions. In doing so they become 'mountaineering tourists'. At the same time they seek to limit the extent of the tourism services and products they consume so as to maintain a sense of going 'on nature's terms' and to safeguard the spontaneity of their experience. They also differentiate themselves from the more casual mountaineering or adventure tourist who they see as not being motivated by the same intensity of commitment and love of the mountains.

Commercial guiding, in particular, is seen as the antithesis of 'real adventures'. 'People want a package', says Pete, using guides and other 'aids' to streamline the experience and bring about a greater chance of success. Bob thinks that those who consume the products of the 'adventure industry' are 'people who want their creature comforts, and who aren't prepared to go on nature's terms': 'It probably won't have any ... major meaningful change or effect on their character, on their strength, on their self-reliance ... they haven't got a clue really about what it's *all* about.' This is sometimes construed as an elitist attitude, particularly in conflicts between the recreational and commercial use of popular mountain environments (see for example Davidson 2011). However in managing for mountaineering tourism, it is worth understanding the roots of these attitudes in the construction of the mountaineering self, and taking into consideration not only the commercial value of different types of mountaineering experience, but also their broader socio-cultural value and significance.

Note

1 Pseudonyms have been used to protect the anonymity of participants.

136   *L. Davidson*

References

Bauman, Z. (1988) *Freedom*, Milton Keynes; Philadelphia, PA: Open University Press.
Bauman, Z. (2001) *The individualized society*, Cambridge: Polity Press.
Bruner, J. (1990) *Acts of meaning*, Cambridge, MA; London: Harvard University Press.
Bruner, J. (1996) 'Frames for thinking: Ways of making meaning', in D. R. Olson and N. Torrance (eds) *Modes of thought: Explorations in culture and cognition*, Cambridge: Cambridge University Press: 93–105.
Bruner, J. (2002) *Making stories: Law, literature, life*, New York: Farrar, Straus & Giroux.
Clandinin, D. J. and Connelly, F. M. (2000) *Narrative inquiry: Experience and story in qualitative research*, San Francisco, CA: Jossey-Bass Publishers.
Creyer, E. H., Ross, W. T. and Evers, D. (2003) 'Risky recreation: An exploration of factors influencing the likelihood of participation and the effects of experience', *Leisure Studies*, 22(3): 239–253.
Damasio, A. (1999) *The feeling of what happens: Body and emotion in the making of consciousness*, London: Heinemann.
Davidson, L. (2002) 'The "spirit of the hills": Mountaineering in Northwest Otago, New Zealand 1882–1940', *Tourism Geographies*, 4(1): 44–61.
Davidson, L. (2006) 'A mountain feeling: The narrative construction of meaning and self through a commitment to mountaineering in Aotearoa/New Zealand', unpublished doctoral thesis, Monash University, Melbourne.
Davidson, L. (2008a) 'Tragedy in the adventure playground: Media representations of mountaineering accidents in New Zealand', *Leisure Studies*, 27(1): 3–19.
Davidson, L. (2008b) 'Travelling light in hostile country: Mountaineering, commitment and the leisure lifestyle', in J. Caudwell, S. Redhead and A. Tomlinson (eds) *Relocating the leisure society: Media, consumption and spaces*, Eastbourne, UK: LSA Publication No. 101: 77–95.
Davidson, L. (2011) 'On nature's terms: Preserving the practice of traditional backcountry recreation in New Zealand's National Parks', in E. Dorfman (ed.) *Intangible natural heritage: New perspectives on natural objects*, New York: Routledge: 105–124.
Davidson, L. (2012) 'The calculable and the incalculable: Narratives of safety and danger in the mountains', *Leisure Sciences*, 34: 298–313.
Denzin, N. K. (1989) *Interpretive biography*, Newbury Park: Sage.
Denzin, N. K. (2001a) *Interpretive interactionism* (2nd edn), Thousand Oaks, CA: Sage.
Denzin, N. K. (2001b) 'The reflexive interview and a performative social science', *Qualitative Research*, 1(1): 23–46.
Elliott, J. (2005) *Using narrative in social research: Qualitative and quantitative approaches*, London; Thousand Oaks, CA; New Delhi: Sage.
Fromm, E. (1994) *Escape from freedom*, New York: Henry Holt & Company.
Funkenstein, A. (1993) 'The incomprehensible catastrophe: Memory and narrative', in R. Josselson and A. Lieblich (eds) *The narrative study of lives* (Vol. 1), Newbury Park: Sage Publications: 21–29.
Gergen, K. J. (1991) *The saturated self: Dilemmas of identity in contemporary life*, New York: Basic Books.
Giddens, A. (1991) *Modernity and self-identity: Self and society in the late modern age*, Cambridge: Polity Press.
Heywood, I. (1994) 'Urgent dreams: Climbing, rationalization and ambivalence', *Leisure Studies*, 13(3): 179–194.

Holstein, J. A. and Gubrium, J. F. (2000) *The self we live by: Narrative identity in a post-modern world*, New York; Oxford: Oxford University Press.

Jarvinen, M. (2000) 'The biographical illusion: Constructing meaning in qualitative interviews', *Qualitative Inquiry*, 6(3): 370–391.

Kiewa, J. (2002) 'Traditional climbing: Metaphor of resistance or metanarrative of oppression?' *Leisure Studies*, 21: 145–161.

Le Breton, D. (2000) 'Playing symbolically with death in extreme sports', *Body and Society*, 6(1): 1–11.

Le Breton, D. (2004) 'The anthropology of adolescent risk-taking behaviours', *Body and Society*, 10(1): 1–15.

Lester, J. (2004) 'Spirit, identity, and self in mountaineering', *Journal of Humanistic Psychology*, 44(1): 86–100.

Levin, J. D. (1992) *Theories of the self*, Washington, DC: Taylor & Francis.

Lyng, S. (1990) 'Edgework: A social psychological analysis of voluntary risk taking', *American Journal of Sociology*, 95(4): 851–886.

Macaloon, J. and Csikszentmihalyi, M. (1983) 'Deep play and the flow experience in rock climbing', in J. C. Harris and R. J. Park (eds) *Play, games and sport in cultural contexts*, Champaign, IL: Human Kinetics Publishers: 361–384.

Mitchell, R. G. (1983) *Mountain experience: The psychology and sociology of adventure*, Chicago, IL; London: University of Chicago Press.

Olivier, S. (2006) 'Moral dilemmas of participation in dangerous leisure activities', *Leisure Studies*, 25(1): 95–109.

Palmer, C. (2002) '"Shit happens": The selling of risk in extreme sport', *Australian Journal of Anthropology*, 13(3): 323–336.

Pereira, A. L. (2005) 'The experience of risk in high-altitude climbing', *World Leisure*, 47(2): 38–49.

Ricoeur, P. (1992) *Oneself as another* (trans. K. Blamey), Chicago, IL: University of Chicago Press.

Roberts, B. (2002) *Biographical research*, Buckingham: Open University Press.

Rojek, C. (1993) *Ways of escape: Modern transformations in leisure and travel*, Basingstoke: Macmillan.

Spector-Mersel, G. (2010) 'Narrative research: Time for a paradigm', *Narrative Inquiry*, 20(1): 204–224.

Stebbins, R. A. (2005) *Challenging mountain nature: Risk, motive and lifestyle in three hobbyist sports*, Calgary: Detselig Enterprises Ltd.

Strauss, A. and Corbin, J. (1998) *Basics of qualitative research: Techniques and procedures for developing grounded theory*, Thousand Oaks, CA: Sage.

Taylor, C. (1989) *Sources of the self: The making of modern identity*, Cambridge, MA: Harvard University Press.

Vester, H.-G. (1987) 'Adventure as a form of leisure', *Leisure Studies*, 6(3): 237–249.

Wengraf, T. (2001) *Qualitative research interviewing: Biographical narrative and semi-structured methods*, London: Sage.

8 Gender and mountaineering tourism

Gill Pomfret and Adele Doran

Introduction

We live in gendered societies within which our identities are culturally developed and are categorized as either feminine or masculine (Humberstone 2000; Swain 1995). While femininity is associated with 'being emotional, passive, dependent, maternal, compassionate, and gentle', masculinity reflects 'strength, competitiveness, assertiveness, confidence, and independence' (Krane 2001: 117) and it embodies heterosexual characteristics (Messner 1992). The cultures within which we live value and reinforce masculinity, yet they devalue and undermine femininity (Wearing 1998). As gender is deeply ingrained within all aspects of society and it is central to explaining human behaviour (Humberstone 2000), it is inextricably linked to tourism development and tourism processes. It is argued, therefore, that 'tourism processes are gendered in their construction, presentation and consumption' (Rao 1995: 30). Gender shapes men and women's involvement in tourism in different ways. Gender divisions are most apparent in tourism employment, as women occupy most low-skilled, low-paid jobs, and in the commoditization of culture at tourist destinations, as women and men play different roles in selling their cultures (Kinniard and Hall 1994).

As gender is a societal construct which pervades all types of tourism, it is worthwhile exploring the role that it plays in mountaineering tourism. There is a lack of research on this topic and the discussion within this chapter highlights a dearth of studies which specifically focus on gender and mountaineering tourism. Ordinarily, mountaineering has strong associations with manliness, and its masculinity is reflected in mountaineers' personal narratives, media representations and people's experiences of mountaineering. The commodification of this adventure sport has resulted in the development of commercially organized, guided mountaineering holidays, fuelling the growth in demand for mountaineering tourism (Buckley 2010; Pomfret and Bramwell 2014). It has created more opportunities for more tourists to participate in a range of both soft and hard mountaineering activities while on holiday, meaning that 'tourists with relatively limited mountaineering experience can now attempt to scale impressively high peaks by booking a packaged mountaineering holiday' (Pomfret 2012: 145). For the purpose of this chapter, we have adopted a broad definition of mountaineering which includes various 'stand-alone' activities – such as rock climbing, ice climbing, scrambling and hill walking – and holidays which combine various activities – such as guided, skills-based mountaineering courses and high-altitude mountaineering expeditions.

Despite limited data on gender participation rates in mountaineering tourism and recreational mountaineering it is evident that men participate more than women. For instance, the UK mountaineering tour operator, Jagged Globe, reports that female demand for their skills-based courses in 2013 was only 23 per cent, for guided expeditions it was 27 per cent and for trekking trips it was 37 per cent (Jagged Globe 2014). In recreational mountaineering, men generate most of the demand, yet the most dramatic increase in participation currently is amongst women. Testament to this is that female membership of the British Mountaineering Council (BMC 2010, 2014) is on an upward trajectory – 16 per cent in 2002, 25 per cent in 2006 and almost 27 per cent in 2014. Women's participation in rock climbing has increased considerably, although accurate figures on the gender split are difficult to obtain. Additionally, the performance gap in climbing between genders is narrowing (Vodden-McKay and Schell 2010) with women increasingly performing as well as, or better than, men. Mountaineering participation rates amongst women also are rising in other countries. For instance, there has been a growth in demand by Japanese women partaking in pilgrimage mountaineering in Japan (Nakata and Momsen 2010). Nevertheless, this trend is not reflected in high-altitude mountaineering, in which women are markedly under-represented although, since the 1980s, there has been an increase in all-female teams summiting high mountain peaks (Vodden-McKay and Schell 2010).

It is worth noting that these changing trends in mountaineering participation also are reflected in the demand for adventure tourism generally, although there is a more equal gender split (57 per cent male and 43 per cent female) in the latter (Adventure Travel Trade Association 2013). Furthermore, there are no major differences between hard and soft adventure participation for men and women, although soft adventure remains slightly more appealing to women. In parallel with this, the supply of women-only adventure holidays such as mountain biking, snowboarding and skiing trips is growing (Mintel 2011), although perplexingly this growth is less apparent in mountaineering and climbing holiday provision.

Despite a substantial body of work on mountaineers (Buckley 2011), prior research has tended to neglect the role of gender, focusing instead on recreational mountaineers (see Delle Fave *et al.* 2003; Ewert *et al.* 2013; Lester 2004; Loewenstein 1999). Little is known about mountaineer tourists, with the exception of a small number of studies (Carr 1997, 2001; Pomfret 2006, 2011; Pomfret and Bramwell 2014). Hence, men and women's participation in mountaineering tourism merits fuller research attention so as to develop an appreciation of the role that gender plays.

Despite the lack of research on gender and mountaineer tourists, we can gain some insights from studies on recreational mountaineers. Mountaineering tourism and recreational mountaineering are inextricably linked as they share the same facilities and resources (Carr 2001), and they evoke similar psychological reactions from participants during mountaineering involvement (Pomfret 2006). Few studies on recreational mountaineers have examined the role of gender, and these tend to focus on masculinity. For instance, this is a prominent theme in studies on high-altitude mountaineers while 'feminist studies of women climbers and women-centred expeditions are still rare' (Rak 2007: 115) and a complete history of women climbers is lacking (Mazel 1994).

Similarly, as mountaineering tourism is a palpable type of adventure tourism (Swarbrooke *et al.* 2003), we can advance our understanding of gender's role in mountaineering tourism through considering other types of adventure tourism. Problematically, however, this also is an under-researched topic as most studies focus on recreational adventurers (Buckley 2011).

The lack of work which examines gender and mountaineering tourism reflects also the dearth of research on gender and tourism. Scholarly curiosity in gender and tourism gained prominence in the 1990s with the publication of several seminal texts (see Kinniard and Hall 1994; Sinclair 1997; Swain 1995) yet interest in this topic dwindled over time, although it recently has resurged (Pritchard *et al.* 2007). It is argued that mainstream tourism research mostly does not consider women's experiences and women's voices (Pritchard *et al.* 2007). This may, in part, be due to the prominent and traditional masculinization discourse typically associated with tourism, which provides an opportunity to escape from domestic environments and family commitments (Rojek and Urry 1997). This draws attention to the need for further investigations which explore the motives, behaviour and experiences of female tourists and how these differ from those of men (Harris and Wilson 2007; Timothy 2001).

The chapter is structured to encourage readers to appreciate the key issues around gender and mountaineering tourism, to consider the limited research that exists and to present opportunities for further investigations on this topic. It explores two key themes which feature most prominently within previous research related to gender and mountaineering tourism. The first theme examines representations of gender within mountaineering narratives and the media. This discussion introduces the notion of landscapes as socially constructed gendered spaces, and then it analyses masculine and feminine representations of these landscapes, both within mountaineering narratives and within different forms of media. The second theme appraises gendered experiences within mountaineering. It initially focuses on gendered motivations, then gendered expectations and identities within mountaineering, and finally gender and mountain guides. These two key themes are strongly linked by the long tradition of masculinity within mountaineering as the latter is represented and, consequently, perceived and experienced as an activity which epitomizes core hegemonic masculine features (Frohlick 2005; Ortner 1999). In the concluding section, suggestions for further research on the role that gender plays in mountaineering tourism are briefly outlined.

Gendered landscapes and their representation within mountaineering narratives and mountaineering media

Discussion now turns to the first theme which is concerned with gendered mountaineering landscapes and how these are represented both within mountaineering narratives and within mountaineering media. This section initially provides an overview of landscape characteristics, and gendered mountaineering and adventure tourism landscapes.

The word 'landscape' has many meanings, yet it is commonly viewed as a physical entity which is pictorially represented and understood 'in a single gaze' (Pritchard and Morgan 2010: 118). Aside from their physical features, landscapes are 'interpreted, narrated, perceived, felt, understood, and imagined' by us to give them meaning (Gieryn 2000: 465). As such, we experience landscapes subjectively and in different ways. Due to their socially constructed nature, and the significant role that gender plays in society, landscapes are gendered concepts.

Historically, mountaineering landscapes provided men with an opportunity to 'perform adventurous masculinities' (Stoddart 2010: 109), to journey far away from home and to escape domestic responsibilities for the purposes of exploration, conquest and adventure. The development of mountaineering was influenced by all-male institutions, particularly the army, which favoured male styles of interaction (Frohlick 1999, 2006; Logan 2006). At home, in the post-war years and with the onset of modernity, men felt that their manhood was threatened by more feminized landscapes within which life revolved around family matters and neighbourliness (Dummit 2004). Rak (2007) notes that from early in the nineteenth century until the golden age of high-altitude mountaineering in the 1950s – when all 8,000 m Himalayan peaks had been climbed – mountaineering came to be associated with 'masculine heroism', 'manly imperialism' and 'cultural superiority' (p. 114). The use of gendered language further reinforced the masculinization of mountaineering landscapes. For instance, Gaston Rébuffat, a mountaineer who climbed Annapurna in 1950, coined the term 'the brotherhood of the rope' (1999 cited in Rak 2007: 117) to describe the correct way to climb. This serves to emphasize the manliness of high-altitude mountaineering landscapes, through its associations with strength and leadership, while effectively disregarding women from participation. It is worth noting that femininity within mountaineering landscapes exists but only in metaphorical, subordinated forms. Mountains are referred to in a phallic way, using terms such as 'virgin peak' and 'virginal purity'. Their domination is eroticized, and mountaineering is played out as a ritualized competition for masculine supremacy (Charroin 2011; Logan 2006; Moraldo 2013).

Different types of landscape are apparent within mountaineering. While high-altitude, remote landscapes offer the most potential for participation in extremely challenging and 'hard' forms of mountaineering, tamer landscapes at lower altitude with supporting infrastructure – such as huts and cable cars – offer a broader range of hard and soft mountaineering activities. What is not fully understood is how these different mountaineering landscapes are interpreted and experienced by men and women, presenting another topic for further investigation. It is evident that masculinity still dominates present day mountaineering landscapes, despite women's increased participation and prominence in mountaineering over recent years. Many think that women are unable to cope with the demands of mountaineering, as they lack physical strength and mental endurance (Vodden-McKay and Schell 2010). However, the successes of renowned women mountaineers such as Wanda Rutkiewicz and Chantal Mauduit contradict this viewpoint and prove that women do indeed possess the fortitude to accomplish major peaks in mountaineering.

Adventure tourism landscapes, inclusive of mountaineering landscapes, offer tourists plentiful opportunities to participate in short, sharp fixes of adventure in which they can 'accelerate through increasingly compressed and hyper inscribed space' (Bell and Lyall 2002: 21) to enjoy adrenaline-fuelled experiences. While participation in such activities encourages adventure tourists to experience rather quickly these adventurous spaces, the longer length of time required for mountaineering allows for participants to immerse themselves more fully into the mountain landscape. Yet, while some mountaineering companies offer treks and expeditions which take place over long time periods, many provide much shorter skills-based courses, aimed at developing competence in mountaineering. As such, tourists on these skills-based holidays may, because of the more limited time spent in the mountains, also 'accelerate' through these sublime mountain landscapes. However, the pace and intensity at which tourists experience mountaineering within these landscapes, and whether there are differences in women and men's experiences, is unknown, highlighting the need for further investigation.

It is suggested that adventure landscapes are dominated by masculinity because men have prevailed as pioneers of unexplored, challenging landscapes, and they have developed codes of behaviour (Norwood 1988) which continue to be followed in the present day. Therefore, women experience men's interpretation of these landscapes and, while this may be a positive and enjoyable experience, they may prefer more 'gender-neutral' or feminized environments within which to participate in adventure activities (Humberstone and Collins 1998) or mountaineering tourism.

Consideration is now given to masculinity themes within mountaineering narratives and mountaineering-related research. Mountaineering is represented as a heroic and manly activity within mountaineering narratives, such as within guides and histories (Logan 2006). Early narratives convey hegemonic masculine features, such as bravery, risk-taking, competitiveness, physical strength, rationality, leadership, self-sacrifice, ruggedness and resourcefulness, and they describe the male body as dominating the natural environment (Frohlick 1999; Logan 2006; Moraldo 2013).

Mountaineers are considered to be the most highly literate group of individuals within all sports as they have written many personal narratives about their expeditions. Both past and present mountaineering narratives mostly have been written by men and they recount stories of physical hardship, referring often to themes of masculinity. However, because of this focus on masculinity, daily practices within mountaineering are often not mentioned within these narratives. These practices include everyday domestic acts (e.g. getting dressed, turning on the stove, melting water and erecting tents), the camaraderie which develops and the friendships which are formed. They are carried out by men and women alike, yet they are considered to be feminine acts and hence they get overlooked in narratives (Frohlick 1999). Therefore, it can be argued that our perception of mountaineering as masculine stems from what gets published in mountaineering narratives. This opens up mountaineering to new questions and new areas of research. Is mountaineering really a masculine activity? Are we assuming a hegemonic masculinity that all men are the same? Or, are there different types of masculinities within mountaineering? Within less institutionalized new sports, such as windsurfing, skateboarding and mountain biking, a number of different masculinities – many of which are more open to women – and femininities, are apparent (Wheaton 2000, 2004). As noted by Cornwall and Lindisfarne (1994: 20), 'Rarely, if ever, will there be only one hegemonic masculinity operating in any cultural setting.' Therefore it can be assumed that there are multiple masculinities and, equally, multiple femininities within mountaineering. Thus the prevailing view that masculinity dominates mountaineering can now be seen as more complex and multidimensional.

Like other mountaineering activities, rock climbing is a male-dominated activity with more males than females participating. Yet, there is a mix of both masculine and feminine characteristics in rock climbing. It involves high levels of risk and strength, which are often referred to as masculine features, but it also requires good technique, balance and grace, which are thought to be feminine characteristics. It is argued that climbing will continue to reinforce hegemonic masculinity unless the value of femininity is emphasized (Plate 2007). Therefore, studies on masculinities (see Robinson 2008; Wheaton 2000, 2004) and the role of gender (Kiewa 2001) should be supplemented with further research on women's experiences, their empowerment and expressions of femininity in a range of mountaineering activities. Additionally, focus needs to be directed towards the experiences of both men and women and the range of femininities and masculinities occurring within mountaineering tourism. In this way we can gain a fuller picture both of conformity and resistance to stereotypical gender characteristics within mountaineering.

The next topic to be appraised within this theme concerns how female mountaineers are perceived within gendered mountaineering landscapes. Very few mountaineering narratives have been written by women, reflecting their disproportionate number in mountaineering. Historically, women who participated in mountaineering and who wrote autobiographies were considered to be deviants (Moraldo 2013). This was especially the case for early mountaineers – mostly from the upper classes – who resisted gender norms both by being mountaineers and by having an unconventional social and family life within which they chose not to marry or to have children. These women were often labelled as masculine and sometime as lesbians, as Lopez-Marugan (2001: 15 cited in Moscoso-Sanchez 2008: 188) writes:

Venturing into the mountains was more than suspicious and to fasten them-selves to a rope in order to climb in the company of men was symptomatic of lesbianism. To those that succeeded in overcoming these prejudices, there remained a long road for them to travel, between the hounding of public opinion, the incomprehension of their families, and what was worse, the criticism of some climbers.

This criticism was still apparent in the 1970s when women were invited to join organized expeditions. For instance, Arlene Blum, an experienced climber, was not selected for an American-led expedition because the male leaders considered her to be insufficiently lady-like, and instead they chose women with less climb-ing experience. This implies that for women at that time, social skills were more important than climbing skills (Blum 2005).

While equality within mountaineering has since grown, in contrast to their pre-decessors, modern female mountaineers increasingly are adhering to gender norms (Moraldo 2013). Although they are considered to be deviant because they parti-cipate in mountaineering, female mountaineers are not seen as deviant in their daily lives if they choose to have a family while continuing with mountaineering. Nevertheless, this deviancy has not come without criticism. Within mountaineer-ing, motherhood provokes scrutiny and criticism in ways that fatherhood does not, with moral questions levelled at women but not at men (Frohlick 2006). This criti-cism comes not only from the media but also from the mountaineering community. Alison Hargreaves, a mother and professional mountaineer who died descending K2 in 1995, was accused publicly of 'acting like a man' in attempting to 'have it all' (Rose and Douglass 1999: 273). Hargreaves was regarded as a terrible and selfish mother because she chose to be away from her children and she was able to 'switch off' from being a mother to pursue her profession in mountaineering.

What a tenuous path fraught with obstacles mountaineering must have been for these women. Women were accepted within the mountaineering community, but only on the condition that they exuded femininity and hid any signs of mas-culinity. Yet, through displaying femininity they were considered to be inferior by their male peers. Furthermore, 'sacrificial motherhood' was, and possibly still is, assumed, whereby mountaineering mothers must forgo their adventure and give up their lives as mountaineers when they become mothers as they are expected only to be caregivers and to focus exclusively on their children (Frohlick 2006: 486). This perpetuates the male domination of mountaineering.

While it is clear that women have had to overcome a number of challenges imposed by male and societal attitudes towards their participation in mountain-eering, it is unknown if women are still experiencing such challenges today. With a growing number of women participating in mountaineering activities rec-reationally and when on holiday, men's attitudes towards increased female parti-cipation needs further analysis.

Attention is now directed towards media representations of gendered moun-taineering landscapes. It is evident from the above discussion that mountaineer-ing landscapes and narratives are dominated by themes of masculinity. Similarly, different media forms, such as magazines, holiday brochures and films fixate on the male gaze, depicting mountaineering landscapes as masculinized, sublime environments. However, previous research has neglected to examine media representations of masculinities and femininities within mountaineering landscapes.

As the media is influential in communicating the values and norms of different sport subcultures (Thorpe 2008), accurate representation of sports' participants – inclusive of mountaineer tourists – is important. The media influences 'understanding of who belongs in these places and which modes of interaction with these places are most highly valued' (Stoddart 2010: 114). It is argued that women are misrepresented, under-represented or they do not feature at all within mountaineering media, reflecting an untruth that their participation in mountain sports is remarkable rather than the norm (Stoddart 2010). As increasing numbers of women participate in mountaineering, it is important that they have a strong presence in the media and that they are represented correctly for their mountaineering accomplishments.

The growth and success of mountain film festivals in recent years has encouraged academic enquiry into the way in which mountaineering landscapes are represented through the media of film, and whether such festivals perpetuate perceptions of hegemonic masculinity within mountaineering through their emphasis on men's greatness and on their heroic adventure achievements. As Frohlick (2005: 178) notes, 'Mountain film festivals are spaces where contemporary versions of adventure are produced and imagined through "hypermasculinization"', and where traditional views of the heroic white male adventurer from colonial times are reinforced (Foster and Mills 2002). As such, these festivals are places within which women are considered to be 'gendered spectators' (p. 178), featuring only peripherally in the screened films as less significant 'others'. Women's position in mountaineering landscapes is, therefore, often displaced, leading viewers to assume that these women are part of the support team rather than part of the mountaineering team. Furthermore, women spectators are positioned at mountain film festivals as soft feminine adventurers, contrasting with 'hardcore' (p. 179) adventurers, who are usually men. These women are viewed as active consumers of soft adventure who are more likely to buy packaged adventure holidays. Such positioning does not take into account the narrowing gender split in mountaineering tourism participation, preferring instead to reinforce the masculinization and male-domination of recreational mountaineering.

Women mountaineers are represented within the media in a strongly feminized way, with attention focused more on their physical characteristics, particularly their feminine appeal, than on their athletic prowess in mountaineering. Furthermore, the media prioritizes women's private lives over their mountaineering accomplishments. Despite their importance to international climbing, women climbers continue to be represented in outdoor sports magazines as 'scantily-clad sexual objects' (Rak 2007: 132). Such portrayals can impact negatively on their social acceptance into the climbing community, generating feelings of disempowerment amongst women (Vodden-McKay and Schell 2010).

One study (Vodden-McKay and Schell 2010) analysed representations of women rock climbers in *Climbing* magazine – a leading specialist publication – between 1991 and 2004. Of the 421 articles assessed, only 3 per cent focused on women. While photographs showed women climbers participating in climbing, the most salient and homogeneous images were of 'young, white, able-bodied women with hair at least shoulder length' (p. 142). The magazine's narrative alluded to the maleness of climbing, mentioning characteristics such as power, strength, risk-taking and virility, and positioned women as 'real' women in spite of their participation in a male-dominated adventure activity. The magazine articles focused on women's heterosexuality, accentuating their involvement in romantic relationships, domesticity within their home lives and their roles as mothers. They highlighted women climbers' physical appearance, particularly their physique and their attractiveness, and they infantilized women, describing them as younger than their age and alluding to their childlike qualities. Such work shows the pressing need for the media to portray accurately women's climbing competence and accomplishments rather than depicting them in such a traditionally feminized way. By doing so, more women will be inspired to participate in climbing and other mountaineering activities through positive role models.

Gendered experiences within mountaineering tourism

The second key theme explores gendered experiences within mountaineering tourism. It focuses, firstly, on gendered motivations, secondly on gendered expectations, thirdly on gendered identities, then fourthly on gender and mountain guides.

Considerable previous research has examined the motivations of mountaineers. For instance, 14 out of 50 reviewed motive-based adventure activity studies investigated mountaineers (Buckley 2011), although a majority of these have focused on recreational mountaineers. Few studies (Carr 1997, 2001; Pomfret 2006, 2011; Pomfret and Bramwell 2014) specifically have examined the motives of mountaineer tourists. While there is some understanding of why people participate in mountaineering, there is a dearth of research about the role that gender plays in motivating mountaineers, and it is not possible to gain in-depth insights from the previous work as it has not specifically addressed gender. As mountaineering has higher participation rates for men than women, motivational comparisons according to gender are made more complex and this may explain, in part, why this topic has been neglected by researchers.

There is some uncertainty, therefore, about whether men and women are motivated differently or similarly to partake in mountaineering. Early work (Norwood 1988) on extreme female adventurers suggests that women and men want the same. Women want to prove to themselves that they are skilled and competent adventurers with the core psychological strength needed to help them to overcome their feelings of fear, risk and hardship. Whether such motivations are applicable to present day mountaineers and different types of mountaineers, from those on guided packaged mountaineering holidays to those on high-altitude unguided expeditions, is not fully known. More recent research on mountaineer tourists (Pomfret and Bramwell 2014) has looked briefly at gender's influence on motivations and found that challenge, developing mountaineering experience and socializing motivated both men and women, and while men were slightly more motivated by adventure, women were slightly more motivated by competence development. Other work (Plate 2007) concludes that women are strongly motivated to improve their climbing performance and they achieve this through climbing with other women, and through participation in women-only climbing events in which they can challenge themselves. They feel more inspired to climb harder when they climb with other women as they experience a supportive and less competitive environment within which 'there is less focus on partner dynamics and more energy going towards climbing itself' (p. 10). Men also appreciate climbing with women for the same reasons and they perceive strong women climbers as role models who provide inspiration.

In contrast to the aforementioned discussion on gendered motivations, research on male and female mountaineers generally has found that their expectations of one another, based on their past experiences, conform to stereotypical gender characteristics (Kiewa 2001; Moscoso-Sanchez 2008; Robinson 2008). Women expect men to be more focused on mountaineering, demonstrate greater involvement in clubs and associations, to be more physically capable, to have a greater pain tolerance and to be more concerned about their self-image. On the other hand, men expect women mountaineers to be masculine, yet they also expect them to be less capable, more focused on the social aspects of mountaineering, and less involved in clubs and associations. Furthermore, men expect women to have only a limited ability to self-sacrifice, and to prioritize family over mountaineering.

These gendered expectations play a part in shaping the behaviour of climbers, in that some male climbers would choose never to climb with women, as they expect women to hold them back and expect them to be less motivated (Kiewa 2001). Similarly, some female climbers choose not to climb with men as they find men hold them back. Women feel that men have low expectations of them, and men's enthusiasm to climb up a route quickly and complete as many routes in a day creates unwanted pressure and impacts negatively on their experience.

While these studies provide insights into the gendered expectations between men and women, they also adopt a binary approach. This approach assumes that men are strongly masculine whereas women are strongly feminine (Robinson 2008). However, the boundaries which have been conventionally associated with masculinity and femininity within mountaineering are becoming more blurred. Various studies (Kiewa 2001; Plate 2007; Robinson 2008) have reported that male and female climbers find no difference between climbing with men and climbing with women, and some male climbers regard women climbers as their equals. Some male and female climbers are equally focused on the activity, while others prioritize the spirituality and nature-based elements of the experience, or concentrate on the relationships that develop and enhance their climbing. Some male climbers avoid climbing with people who have a competitive attitude, while some female climbers choose to climb with men as they expect to be challenged and to be pushed by them.

What this demonstrates is the complexity of participants' expectations and, subsequently, their gendered experiences of mountaineering. As differences in expectations shape and sometimes limit engagement in mountaineering, further research needs to explore the gendered expectations of mountaineer tourists and how these influence the holiday experience. Rather than focusing on gender differences and how these restrict participation, the positive experiences which men and women enjoy during mountaineering participation with their gender opposites need to be explored. Taking this approach will provide a more stimulating way to think about how relationships between genders accentuate participants' experiences of mountaineering.

These clearly differentiated expectations of male and female mountaineers point towards a gendered identity within mountaineering. Moscoso-Sanchez (2008) believes that this identity develops through patriarchal domination and socialization processes, for instance through family, school, peer groups and mass media. It is thought that women are disadvantaged compared with men both within mountaineering and within society generally. Men exercise their influence, or dominance, over women, and women subconsciously accept their expected inferiority. For example, in mountaineering it is assumed that women will climb after men, and that they will organize the practical arrangements such as purchasing food for their mountaineering trip and booking mountain huts. Consequently, this limits women's opportunities to develop their mountaineering skills and constantly places them in second position. Similarly, when spouses or committed couples participate in mountaineering together, if the female mountaineer becomes pregnant and has children, she is expected to renounce or considerably alter her mountaineering participation habits. This reflects unequal gender roles and, more importantly, it reduces the opportunity for women to participate in mountaineering and pursue their mountaineering ambitions. Ultimately, it results in women having a less significant presence in mountaineering.

In addition to this gender identity, a mountaineering identity is also apparent (Moscoso-Sanchez 2008). Both men and women perceive this identity as an area (the mountain in its distinct forms) and as a sport (which comprises different activities and varied styles). Furthermore, it is seen as a subculture which unites all mountaineers by a common lifestyle based on values which reflect contact with nature, personal development, challenging experiences, expeditions and human relations. Rock climbing is particularly appealing to women, providing them with a space to 'fit in' and experience an empowering sense of belonging within this subculture. The more time that women are involved in climbing, the more that they cease to feel as if they belong to 'mainstream' culture and the more that they feel accepted within the climbing subculture. Therefore, some women climbers climb to differentiate themselves from traditional femininity and, by doing so, they construct their climbing and mountaineering identity (Dilley and Scraton 2010; Robinson 2008).

Packaged mountaineering tourism potentially offers women a more gender-neutral landscape within which they can play out their mountaineering identity, they can concentrate on developing their skills and they can achieve their ambitions. This is because gendered roles and differences may not be as prominent given that the tour operator's role is to arrange all the practicalities of their holidays. Within this landscape, the mountaineering identity gains prominence and it challenges stereotypical gender roles by encouraging women's empowerment.

The final topic to be considered within this gendered experiences theme is gender and mountain guides, as guides have considerable influence over the client's experience of packaged mountaineering tourism. Very few studies have specifically researched mountain guides (see Beedie 2003, 2008; Martinoia 2013) and to the authors' knowledge, there is no known research which focuses on mountain guiding from a gender perspective. However, Martinoia's (2013) study on the guide–client relationship provides a unique insight into the experiences of male mountain guides and it confirms gendered expectations and reinforces masculinity within male guiding. The study reveals that some male guides prefer women clients as generally they are more easily satisfied customers. These clients reduce risk-taking by being easier to coordinate. They underestimate their abilities and they prioritize seeking pleasure from their experiences rather than achieving high performance. However, the study found that guides did not share this preference for female clients with other guides, or with the public, as they feared being labelled as a 'guide for the ladies' and they did not want their professional mountaineering skills to be feminized.

It should be recognized that male mountain guides are under considerable pressure to maintain a mythical image of being masculine, highly responsible, physically irreproachable risk-takers. Since gender is hierarchical, signs of femininity in guiding – such as anxiety, refusal to take risks, managing the clients' emotions and 'mothering' the client – can lead to guides being downgraded by their peers, and this can impact negatively on their ability to secure employment (Martinoia 2013).

Female guides also face challenges within their profession. Similar to the under-representation of women in mountaineering, the guiding profession also sees few women qualifying. Since 2005, five women per year on average (3.7 per cent) have sat the entrance exam for the mountain guide training school in France (Martinoia 2013). Conversely, in Aconcagua (Argentina) 30 per cent of trainee mountain guides are women, yet few will become guides, or even assistant guides, within the Argentinean mountaineering tourism industry. This is because agencies are unwilling to place female guides in positions of authority over their male counterparts (Logan 2006).

Conclusion

This chapter has focused on two key themes concerning the role that gender plays in mountaineering tourism. First, it examined gendered landscapes and their representation within mountaineering narratives and within the media.

From this analysis, it can be concluded that mountaineering landscapes have evolved as, and remain, strongly masculinized concepts. Mountaineering narratives are rife with stories of heroic, masculine achievements because mountaineering has been, and still is, male dominated, despite more women participating in this adventure activity. These narratives employ sexualized terms to symbolize mountains in a strongly feminine way. In the same way that themes of masculinity pervade through mountaineering narratives, and in spite of limited research on media representations of mountaineering landscapes, it can be concluded that different media forms seem to positively emphasize the masculinity of mountaineering while negatively misrepresenting women mountaineers in an overly feminized way.

The second theme explored gendered experiences within mountaineering tourism. Discussion focused initially on the motivations of mountaineers, and it was apparent that very few researchers had adopted a gendered approach to explore this topic. Therefore, uncertainty exists about whether female and male mountaineers are motivated similarly or differently. Next, in considering the gendered expectations of mountaineers, it can be concluded that both men and women conform to gender stereotypes. Problematically, studies on gendered expectations adopt a binary approach despite the boundaries between femininity and masculinity becoming blurred and hegemonic masculinity within mountaineering being increasingly challenged. Following on from gendered expectations, the construction of gendered identities was appraised, and it was determined that men have a more prominent mountaineering identity than women. This is not the case, however, in rock climbing, in which women climbers develop strong climbing identities to distinguish themselves from mainstream feminine cultures. Finally, the expectations and experiences of male mountain guides, and how these reinforce masculinity within the guiding profession, and the challenges which female mountain guides face, were considered.

It is hoped that this chapter has encouraged readers to appreciate the key issues around gender and mountaineering tourism. The review of previous research presented highlights how little we know about the role that gender plays in mountaineering tourism. While the studies discussed reveal some insights into this topic, they also expose many gaps in our knowledge. In an attempt to address these gaps, we provide a number of suggestions for further research in Table 8.1. The themes presented in Table 8.1 – mountaineering landscapes, masculinity and femininity within mountaineering tourism, media representations of mountaineering landscapes, gendered experiences in mountaineering tourism, gendered motivations, expectations and identities in mountaineering tourism, and gender and mountain guides – are all important themes for further investigation if we are more fully to understand the role that gender plays in mountaineering tourism.

Table 8.1 Further research in gender and mountaineering tourism

Research theme	Suggestions for further research
Mountaineering landscapes	• How different types of 'hard' and 'soft' mountaineering landscapes are interpreted and experienced by men and women. • How female mountaineers interpret and experience strongly masculinized mountaineering landscapes. • The pace and intensity with which men and women experience different types of mountaineering tourism (e.g. skills-based holidays, guided expeditions) within mountaineering landscapes.
Masculinity and femininity within mountaineering tourism	• Move away from traditional research approaches which assume that a static dichotomy exists between male and female mountaineers, and that all male mountaineers are defined by their hegemonic masculinity. • The extent to which different types of masculinity and femininity exist within mountaineering tourism, as is the case in newer, less institutionalized adventure activities (e.g. windsurfing, mountain biking). • Women's experiences, feelings of empowerment and expressions of femininity in a range of different mountaineering tourism activities. • Men's attitudes towards increasing female participation in mountaineering tourism, and women mountaineers' perceptions of these attitudes.
Media representations of mountaineering landscapes	• Examination of feminist perspectives on mountaineering tourism to develop improved mountaineering experiences for women. • How men and women are represented in different types of mountaineering tourism media (e.g. travel guides, tour operator brochures). • The extent to which women mountaineer tourists are accurately represented, for their skills and accomplishments, within these different media forms.
Gendered experiences in mountaineering tourism	• Investigation into the experiences of different groups of mountaineers. For example, different abilities of mountaineer tourists participating in various mountaineering activities, comparative studies of single gender and mixed gender mountaineer groups, and experiences of recreational mountaineers and how they transfer their mountaineering skills to a tourism context.
Gendered motivations in mountaineering tourism	• Comparative analysis of the motivational similarities and differences which encourage male and female participation in mountaineering tourism. • Motivations which encourage each gender to participate in mountaineering tourism, to ascertain the extent to which different masculinities and femininities are motivated similarly or differently.
Gendered expectations in mountaineering tourism	• The expectations that male and female mountaineer tourists have of each other while mountaineering together on holiday, and how these expectations encourage a positive mountaineering holiday experience. • Exploration of how social relationships between men and women enhance rather than impair their mountaineering tourism experience.
Gendered identities in mountaineering tourism	• How participation in mountaineering tourism is used by men and women to differentiate themselves from traditional masculinities and femininities to construct a mountaineering identity. • Examination of how more gender-neutral, packaged mountaineering tourism landscapes facilitate opportunities for women to play out their mountaineering identities and to enjoy feelings of empowerment.
Gender and mountain guides	• Consider the challenges which guides face due to gender, and explore how gender influences the client–guide relationship and the overall holiday experience.

References

Adventure Travel Trade Association (ATTA) (2013) *Adventure tourism market study*, Seattle, WA: ATTA.

Beedie, P. (2003) 'Mountain guiding and adventure tourism: Reflections on the choreography of the experience', *Leisure Studies*, 222: 147–167.

Beedie, P. (2008) 'Mountain guiding and adventure tourism: Reflections on the choreography of the experience', in M. Weed (ed.) *Sport and tourism: A reader*, London: Routledge: 188–206.

Bell, C. and Lyall, J. (2002) 'The accelerated sublime: Thrill seeking adventure heroes in the commodified landscape', in S. Coleman and H. Crang (eds) *Tourism: between place and performance*, Oxford: Berghahn Books: 21–37.

Blum, A. (2005) *Breaking trail: A climbing life*, New York: A Lisa Drew Book/Scribner.

British Mountaineering Council (BMC) (2010) 'Popularity and economic benefit of mountaineering: Instant expert'. Online, available at www.thebmc.co.uk/participation-in-climbing-mountaineering (accessed 16 July 2014).

British Mountaineering Council (BMC) (2014) 'Male and female membership information for research purposes', e-mail, 16 July.

Buckley, R. C. (2010) *Adventure tourism management*, London: Butterworth-Heinemann.

Buckley, R. C. (2011) 'Rush as a key motivation in skilled adventure tourism', *Tourism Management*, 33(4): 961–970.

Carr, A. M. (1997) 'Guided mountaineering clients in New Zealand's Southern Alps', in J. Higham and G. W. Kearsley (eds), *Proceedings of trails, tourism and regional development*. Cromwell, New Zealand: Centre for Tourism and IGU, University of Otago: 23–32.

Carr, A. M. (2001) 'Alpine adventurers in the Pacific Rim: The motivations and experiences of guided mountaineering clients in New Zealand's Southern Alps', *Pacific Tourism Review*, 4(4): 161–170.

Charroin, P. (2011) 'Femmes et homes dans les sports de montagne: Au dela des differences (review)', *Journal of Sport History*, 38(1): 157–158.

Cornwall, A. and Lindisfarne, N. (1994) 'Dislocating masculinity: Gender, power and anthropology', in A. Cornwall and N. Lindisfarne (eds) *Dislocating masculinity: Comparative ethnographies*, London: Routledge: 11–47.

Delle Fave, A., Bassi, M. and Massimini, F. (2003) 'Quality of experience and risk perception in high-altitude rock climbing', *Journal of Applied Sport Psychology*, 15(1): 82–98.

Dilley, R. E. and Scraton, S. J. (2010) 'Women, climbing and serious leisure', *Leisure Studies*, 29(2): 124–141.

Dummitt, C. (2004) 'Risk on the rocks. Modernity, manhood, and mountaineering in postwar British Columbia', *BC Studies*, 141: 3–29.

Ewert, A. W., Gilbertson, K., Luo, Y. and Voight, A. (2013) 'Beyond "because it's there": Motivations for pursuing adventure recreational activities', *Journal of Leisure Research*, 45(1): 91–111.

Foster, S. and Mills, S. (2002) *An anthology of women's travel writing*, Manchester: Manchester University Press.

Frohlick, S. (1999) 'The "hypermasculine" landscape of high-altitude mountaineering', *Michigan Feminist Studies*, 14(1999–2000): 83–106.

Frohlick, S. (2005) '"That playfulness of white masculinity": Mediating masculinities and adventure at mountain festivals', *Tourist Studies*, 5(2): 175–193.

Frohlick, S. (2006) 'Wanting the children and wanting K2': The incommensurability of motherhood and mountaineering in Britain and North America in the late twentieth century', *Gender, Place and Culture: A Journal of Feminist Geography*, 13(5): 477–490.

Gieryn, T. F. (2000) 'A space for place in sociology', *Annual Review of Sociology*, 26: 463–496.

Harris, C. and Wilson, E. (2007) 'Travelling beyond the boundaries of constraint: Women, travel and empowerment', in A. Pritchard, N. Morgan, I. Ateljevic and C. Harris (eds) *Tourism and gender: Embodiment, sensuality and experience*, Wallingford: CAB International: 235–250.

Humberstone, B. (2000) 'The "outdoor industry" as social and educational phenomena: Gender and outdoor adventure/education', *Journal of Adventure Education and Outdoor Learning*, 1(1): 21–25.

Humberstone, B. and Collins, D. (1998) 'Ecofeminism, "risk" and women's experiences of landscape', in C. Aitchison and F. Jordan (eds) *Gender, space and identity*, Eastbourne: LSA Publication 63: 137–150.

Jagged Globe (2014) 'Client statistics', e-mail, 17 July.

Kiewa, J. (2001) ' "Stepping around things": Gender relationships in climbing', *Australian Journal of Outdoor Education*, 5(2): 4–12.

Kinniard, V. and Hall, D. (1994) 'Theorising gender in tourism research', *Tourism Recreation Research*, 25(1): 71–84.

Krane, V. (2001) 'We can be athletic and feminine, but do we want to? Challenging hegemonic femininity in women's sports', *Quest*, 53(1): 115–133.

Lester, L. (2004) 'Spirit, identity and self in mountaineering', *Journal of Humanistic Psychology*, 44(1): 86–100.

Loewenstein, G. (1999) 'Because it's there: The challenge of mountaineering ... for utility theory', *Kyklos*, 52(3): 315–343.

Logan, J. (2006) 'Crampons and cook pots: The democratization and feminisation of adventure on Aconcagua', in L. A. Vivanco and R. J. Gordon (eds) *Tarzan was an ecotourist ... and other tales in the anthropology of adventure*, Oxford: Berghahn Books: 161–178.

Mazel, D. (1994) *Mountaineering women: Stories by early climbers*, College Station, TX: Texas A&M University Press.

Martinoia, R. (2013) 'Women's mountaineering and dissonances within the mountain guide profession: "Don't go thinking he was a guide for the ladies" ', *Journal of Alpine Research*, 101-1: 2–10.

Messner, R. (1992) *Annapurna: 50 years of expeditions in the death zone* (trans. Tim Carruthers), Seattle, WA: The Mountaineers.

Mintel (2011) 'Adventure tourism in South Africa', *Mintel Marketing Intelligence*, September.

Moraldo, D. (2013) 'Gender relations in French and British mountaineering: A lens of autobiographies of female mountaineers, from d'Angeville (1794–1871) to Destivelle (1960)', *Journal of Alpine Research*, 101-1: 2–12.

Moscoso-Sanchez, D. (2008) 'The social construction of gender identity amongst mountaineers', *European Journal of Sport and Society*, 5(2): 183–190.

Nakata, M. and Momsen, J. D. (2010) 'Gender and tourism: Gender, age and mountain tourism in Japan', *Malaysian Journal of Society and Space*, 6(2): 63–71.

Norwood, V. (1988) 'Light, power, space, and sun: Women in landscapes of adventure', *Women's Studies International Forum*, 11(2): 155–165.

Ortner, S. (1999) *Life and death on Mount Everest: Sherpas and Himalayan mountaineering*, Princeton, NJ: Princeton University Press.

Plate, K. R. (2007) 'Rock climbing is a masculine sport? Understanding the complex gendered subculture of rock climbing', in V. Robinson (ed.) special issue for *Sheffield Online Papers in Social Research, Gender and Extreme Sports: The Case of Climbing*, August, 10: 1–14.

Pomfret, G. (2006) 'Mountaineering adventure tourists: A conceptual framework for research', *Tourism Management*, 27(3): 113–123.

Pomfret, G. (2011) 'Package mountaineer tourists holidaying in the French Alps: An evaluation of key influences encouraging their participation', *Tourism Management*, 32(3): 501–510.

Pomfret, G. (2012) 'Personal emotional experiences associated with packaged mountaineering holidays', *Tourism Management Perspectives*, 4: 145–154.

Pomfret, G. and Bramwell, B. (2014) 'The characteristics and motivational decisions of outdoor adventure tourists: A review and analysis', *Current Issues in Tourism*, DOI: 10.1080/13683500.2014.925430.

Pritchard, A. and Morgan, N. J. (2010) 'Constructing tourism landscapes: Gender, sexuality and space', *Tourism Geographies*, 2(2): 115–139.

Pritchard, A., Morgan, N., Ateljevic, I. and Harris, C. (2007) 'Editors' introduction: Tourism, gender, embodiment and experience', in A. Pritchard, N. J. Morgan, I. Ateljevic and C. Harris (eds) *Tourism and gender: Embodiment, sensuality and experience*, Wallingford: CABI Publishing: 1–12.

Rak, J. (2007) 'Social climbing on Annapurna: Gender in high-altitude mountaineering narratives', *ESC*, 33(1–2): 109–146.

Rao, N. (1995) 'Commoditisation and commercialisation of women in tourism: Symbols of victimhood', *Contours*, 7(1): 30.

Robinson, V. (2008) *Everyday masculinities and extreme sport: Male identity and rock climbing*, Oxford: Berg.

Rojek, C. and Urry, J. (1997) *Touring cultures: Transformations of travel and theory*, London: Routledge.

Rose, D. and Douglas, E. (1999) *Regions of the heart: The triumph and tragedy of Alison Hargreaves*, London: Michael Joseph.

Sinclair, M. T. (1997) *Gender, work and tourism*, London: Routledge.

Stoddart, M. C. J. (2010) 'Constructing masculinised sportscape: Skiing, gender and nature in British Columbia, Canada', *International Review for the Sociology of Sport*, 46(1): 108–124.

Swain, M. B. (1995) 'Gender in tourism', *Annals of Tourism Research*, 22(2): 247–266.

Swarbrooke, J., Beard, C., Leckie, S. and Pomfret, G. (2003) *Adventure tourism: The new frontier*, Oxford: Butterworth-Heinemann.

Thorpe, H. (2008) 'Foucault, technologies of self, and the media', *Journal of Sport and Social Issues*, 32(2): 199–229.

Timothy, D. J. (2001) 'Gender relations in tourism: Revisiting patriarchy and underdevelopment', in Y. Apostolopoulos, S. Sonmez and D. J. Timothy (eds) *Women as producers and consumers of tourism in developing regions*, Westport, CT: Praeger: 235–248.

Vodden-McKay, S. and Schell, L. A. (2010) 'Climbing high or falling flat? Representations of female rock climbers in climbing magazine (1991–2004)', *Journal of Research on Women and Gender*, March(2010): 136–151.

Wearing, B. (1998) *Leisure and feminist theory*, London: Sage Publications Ltd.

Wheaton, B. (2000) '"New Lads"? Masculinities and the "new sport" participant', *Men and Masculinities*, 2: 434–456.

Wheaton, B. (2004) '"New lads"? Competing masculinities in the windsurfing culture', in B. Wheaton (ed.) *Understanding lifestyle sports: Consumption, identity and difference*, Abingdon: Routledge: 131–153.

9 The motivations and satisfactions attendant to mountaineering

Alan Ewert and Stacy Taniguchi

> For the stone from the top for geologists,
> the knowledge of the limits of endurance for the doctors,
> but above all, for the spirit of adventure
> to keep alive the soul of man.
>
> (George Mallory 1923)

While best known for his immortal words, 'Because it is there', when asked why he wanted to climb Mt Everest, this quote by George Mallory perhaps best captures the transcendent yet driving force behind mountaineering. There is a connection between the human spirit and the experience of mountaineering, and it is this connection that impels individuals to visit inhospitable, dangerous and physically taxing mountainous terrain, often at great risk to themselves and their other teammates. Two of the components often associated with the human spirit are motivations and anticipated satisfactions, and this chapter addresses both of these constructs and how they are related to the mountaineering experience.

This chapter begins with an overview of the constructs of motivation and satisfaction, followed by a brief history of mountaineering with specific reference to motivations and satisfaction. This history is then expanded in past and current studies that have examined motivations and satisfactions associated with the mountaineering experience. We conclude this chapter with some implications and meanings related to current and future mountaineering endeavours and the motivations and satisfactions attendant to those experiences.

We fully recognize other forms of climbing, such as rock and ice, are related to the mountaineering experience, and, hence, there is much overlap and similarity between the various types of climbing. Despite this overlap, we have focused the majority of our writing and research on the mountaineering paradigm while fully recognizing a similar discussion could be made for other climbing activities.

Motivation as a construct

> You cannot stay on the summit forever; you have to come down again. So why bother in the first place?
>
> (*Mount Analogue* by Rene Daumal)

What is motivation and what role does it play in the mountaineering experience? To provide somewhat of a disciplinary framework, we paraphrase from Wiener (1992: 17) in describing motivation as a set of determinants of thought and action that direct why behaviour is initiated, persists, changes or stops, as well as what choices are made. Likewise, mountaineering evokes intense positive emotions, often dependent on the match between an individual's skills and consequential challenges, and in which the emotional processes that shape satisfaction are inherently intangible and not prone to rationality (Knowles *et al.* 1999; Pomfret 2006). From a more generalized perspective, motivation can be defined as a process that initiates, guides and helps maintain a goal-orientated behaviour. Moreover, three components comprise the motivation complex and include the activation of the specific motive, persistence of that motive and the intensity of that motive (Ewert and Sibthorp 2014).

Not surprisingly, motivations surrounding adventure activities, such as mountaineering, have a long history both within scholarship and actual practice. Beginning with such salient works as Wilfred Noyce's (1958) *Springs of adventure* and Samuel Klausner's (1968) *Why man takes chances*, a number of theories have been used to describe why people pursue recreational activities containing potential risk and danger. These theories have included instinctual drive (Klausner 1968; Noyce 1958), arousal seeking (Berlyne 1960), attributional constructs (Heider 1958), the peak experience (Maslow 1968) and expectancy valence theory (Atkinson 1964). Complementing these earlier theories has been the development of more contemporary perspectives regarding motivations for adventure recreation such as normative influences (Celsi *et al.* 1993), flow (Csikszentmihalyi and Csikszentmihalyi 1990), and edgework (Lyng 1990). Perhaps Charles Houston (1968: 57) best captured the connection between motivations and climbing in his statement:

> Climbing is one of the few human activities where the stress is clear, apparent, and freely sought. The goal is sharp and visible. There is no doubt when one has succeeded or failed. Mountaineering is more a quest for self-fulfillment than a victory over others or over nature.

Not surprisingly, a number of characteristics inherent in the climbing experience can play a role in the motivations for mountaineering. The physical characteristics such as weather, risk of falling, avalanche and rockfall, the often remote nature of the experience and the small group context from which mountaineering typically takes place often exert powerful influences on the activity. Other, more sociological- and psychological-based attributes are often more subtle yet just as important driving forces typically associated with mountaineering. Donnelly (2003) described two of these, and we see these characteristics throughout much of the history of mountaineering. The first includes the non-institutionalized and self-governing nature of the activity. That is, with some exceptions, such as the International Mountaineering and Climbing Federation (UIAA) and several country-based organizations, such as the Association of Canadian Mountain Guides (ACMG) and

American Mountain Guides Association (AMGA), there are no formal and global governing bodies that develop rules and enforce those rules for climbing and mountaineering through processes such as sanctions or negative assessments.

The other characteristic described by Donnelly (2003) addressed the continuous balance between the difficulty of the climbing route or making a specific 'move' in climbing that route and the risk involved. There is a relatively informal and socially constructed set of rules and guidelines that serve to govern climber behaviours and actions, and, essentially, those rules are focused on maintaining the 'difficulty' of a chosen climbing route while also being sensitive to the relative safety of the endeavour.

However, many routes can be made safer through the use of technology. The use of pitons, camming devices, fixed lines, ladders and even mountain huts or other types of permanent shelters, are all examples of how technology can serve to lessen the risks and dangers involved. And this is where the tension between the difficulty and the risk come into play with the question of how much technology and other contrivances one should bring into the mountaineering experience remaining primarily one of personal choice.

In sum, motivation can be thought of as a construct with many masters. Some would think of it in terms of intrinsic versus extrinsic rewards, that is, personally meaningful or externally located outside the individual's psychic (e.g. recognition by others). Other scholars would link motivation to goal setting and sense of achievement. There are expectations regarding the pursuit of a particular activity such as mountaineering, and these expectations have valence or strength; that is, the stronger the valence, the stronger the motivation (see Kyle *et al.* 2006). Others look at motivation as multiple dimensional, encompassing a wide-variety of components including social motives, escape from boredom and pushing personal boundaries (Kerr and Mackenzie 2012). In addition, Lewis (2003) points out not only are there expectations for certain behaviours among climbers to maintain a commonly agreed-to level of risk, but there is also a growing awareness of the ecological impacts of climbing that need to be attenuated, such as the ongoing clean-up effort now taking place at different locations on Mt Everest. The quest to understand the motivations for mountaineering has a long history with an understanding these motivations have changed from motives being concerned about religion, science or nationalism, to more contemporary issues such as personal fulfillment and adventure-seeking. The next section deals specifically with the connection between the construct of satisfaction and the mountaineering experience.

Satisfaction as a construct

> Somewhere between the bottom of the climb and the summit is the answer to the mystery why we climb.
>
> (Greg Child – accomplished mountaineer and adventure writer)

The word satisfaction implies an end goal or result, a consequence of action, or a perception of subjective well-being (SWB). This perception is an evaluative judgement arrived at by cognitive reflection and physiological responses to what is being done or what has been accomplished. As a contrast to motivation, satisfaction tends to describe the opposite end of the spectrum of an experience, but, in comparison, can qualify as a motivational rationale for future experiential endeavours.

Satisfaction is considered a positive emotion and lends itself to having positive affect on SWB (Andrews 1976; Arthaud-Day *et al*. 2005; Diener 1984). In recent research literature, satisfaction has usually been the focus of studies in Positive Psychology and correlated with the experience of happiness or SWB (Borrello 2005; Diener and Seligman 2004; Seligman and Csikszentmihalyi, 2000). Psychologists have regarded satisfaction as a personal positive judgement about experiences one has had, and this perception can come in a variety of forms, such as accomplishment, happiness, fulfillment, contentment, gratification and pleasure. All of these emotions contribute to the SWB perception a person may have about him- or herself. Psychologists, political scientists, employment specialists and consumer consultants use such judgements to predict future repeated behaviours and the consequences of those behaviours (Lévy-Garbous *et al.* 2007), thus pointing to the importance placed on satisfaction in our society. Understanding what satisfaction means and how we go about obtaining satisfaction has made this a construct of importance to be studied.

Research studies have shown goal attainment, or the lack thereof, is correlated to SWB (Harris *et al.* 2003; Lee and Ashforth 1996; Maslach and Jackson 1981). How one perceives his or her well-being appears to be related to the level of satisfaction a particular experience lends itself to the individual. Many factors contribute to such perceptions of satisfaction, but the construct lends itself to understanding why people engage in such challenging activities as mountaineering.

Adventure tourism has grown in popularity and been recognized as 'one of the newest and fastest growing sectors of the tourism industry' (Ewert and Jamieson 2003: 81). Emotions are vital to adventure tourism experiences (Carnicelli-Filho *et al.* 2009). 'Adventure tourism is characterized by its ability to provide the tourist with relatively high levels of sensory stimulation, usually achieved by including physically challenging experiential components' (Mueller and Cleaver 2000: 156). Consumption, especially intensive, experiential consumption, such as mountaineering, involves a variety of distinct and powerful emotional experiences. The growth of adventure tourism, especially with regard to mountaineering, is closely linked to strong emotional experiences because the activity lends itself to providing two components of intense experiential consumption, risk and fear (Pomfret 2006). Therefore, individuals seeking such intense perceptions, especially of the positive types, can usually find those emotions through experiences involving risks and fears.

The importance of understanding how such emotions influence a person's perception of satisfaction and, therefore, his subjective well-being have been emphasized by researchers (e.g. Beedie and Hudson 2003; Carnicelli-Filho *et al.* 2009; Pomfret 2006; Williams and Soutar 2009). As this understanding relates to both knowing why people gain satisfaction in their participation in mountaineering and providing such experiences to meet the desires of such intense experiences, investigators, seeking this understanding, must see satisfaction in measurable terms (Williams and Donnelly 1985).

Pomfret (2006) proposed joy and fear are core emotions evoked by mountaineering. Faullant *et al.* (2011) empirically confirmed mountaineers experience joy and fear, and both of these basic emotions are important to participants' experiences and to their resulting satisfaction. While joy increases satisfaction with a mountaineering experience, the opposite is true for fear. In Faullant *et al.*'s study, fear was clearly experienced as a negative emotional state, not a desired thrill. It has a negative impact on customer satisfaction. With respect to mountaineering, studies have shown mountaineers do not necessarily seek risk or danger, but diminishing it is part of the challenge they seek (Walter 1984, in Pomfret 2006). Therefore, the satisfaction they obtain from a mountaineering experience can be derived from overcoming the risk or danger they encounter. Nevertheless, mountaineering may be different from other forms of adventure experiences because the risks cannot be managed as effectively in mountaineering as they can be in other adventure sports activities; extreme elemental conditions such as the weather and loose rock, as well as the physical and mental condition of the participants, are crucial and often uncontrollable factors.

Fear has been identified as a *primary* consumption-related emotion. Faullant *et al.* (2011) suggested an instance of an 'emotions first, cognitions second' sequence in satisfaction formation. People who experienced fear (likely as an automatic response) attributed these negative feelings to the expectations (i.e. through cognitive appraisals), and in turn were less satisfied with their mountaineering experience. Thus, feelings of fear should be avoided as much as possible; this does not rule out the possibility a feeling of thrill and challenge might enhance overall satisfaction of mountaineering experiences. For mountaineering operators and guides, this means satisfaction can effectively be managed by mountain experiences providing feelings of joy, which is likely to occur when competence meets the corresponding level of challenge. Thus before starting a tour, the implication is mountaineering operators should invest time for a detailed discussion with their clients in order to get a thorough overview of the participants' mountaineering skill levels and to provide them with a realistic view of the challenges that will be encountered at the chosen tour. Feelings of fear can be avoided by providing a safe and well-managed tour preparation.

Thus, satisfaction is a construct that determines the perceptions of well-being and, in turn, can be a motivator for continued adventures in mountaineering. Obtaining a positive perception of overcoming the challenges and fears is a primary emotion and important to gaining a sense of satisfaction from the experience.

The history of motivation in mountaineering

The summit of Everest can deliver you from the prison of ambition.

(Peter Boardman, as cited in Coburn 1970)

The history of motivation in mountaineering has been dynamic, and this change is evident when one considers early indigenous mountain inhabitants feared and often despised the mountains. For many, the mountains represented a variety of manifestations of evil and death including the home of the devil, trolls, dragons and griffins (Breashers and Salkeld 1999). This is in stark contrast when many mountain landscapes are now virtually inundated with visitors of all types, some climbing, some hiking and some simply enjoying the scenery and mountain ambiance.

It is generally accepted mountains were first climbed for religion, nationalism and scientific research. For example, Scott (1974) reported Mont Blanc (France) was climbed in 1786 by Jacques Balmat and Michel-Gabriel Paccard with patriotism being the primary motivating force. Moving back in time, however, one of the first recorded ascents was made by Francesco Petarach and his brother, Gerardo, when they reached the top of Mont Ventoux in 1336 (Scott 1974). In a similar fashion, Conrad Gesner climbed Pilatus in 1555, ostensibly for 'exercise'.

It was not until around 1760 'serious' mountaineering began, at least in the Alps, with the ascent of the Wetterhorn in 1854 inaugurating the 'Golden Age' of mountaineering. Another milestone was the ascent of the infamous Matterhorn in 1865 by a party led by Edward Whymper. Upon descending from the successful climb, some of the climbers fell resulting in the death of four of the seven climbers, which lead to Whymper's now famous statement:

> Climb if you will, but remember that courage and strength are naught without prudence, and that a momentary negligence may destroy the happiness of a lifetime. Do nothing in haste; look well to each step; and from the beginning think what may be the end.
>
> (Whymper 1871)

By the 1890s, guidebooks began to appear, and by 1900 most of the major peaks in Europe had been climbed. Now the search for more difficult and challenging routes began in earnest. It is here we come back to the issue of motivation. For what began as a fear and loathing of mountainous landscapes transformed into something more intrinsic and of personal meaning. Perhaps, noted climber and medical doctor, Charles Houston, most eloquently captured this idea of mountaineering as being driven by motives that go far beyond simply getting to the top: 'Whom have we conquered? None but ourselves. Have we won a kingdom? No and yes. We have achieved an ultimate satisfaction, fulfilled a destiny. To struggle and to understand, never the last without the first' (cited in Klausner 1968: 58). Houston goes on to point out

> climbing is one of the few human endeavors where the goals and subsequent stress associated with getting there are clear, apparent, and voluntarily sought after. Moreover, mountaineering is more a quest for self-fulfillment than a victory over others or nature.
>
> (Klausner 1968: 57)

Thus, around the 1700–1800s, we start to see a change in the stated motivations for mountaineering moving from a more extrinsic focus (e.g. nationalism, science) to something concerned with more intrinsic reasons (e.g. personal testing, satisfaction). This intrinsic orientation for motivations is further exemplified by the search for new and more difficult routes, such as differing structural characteristics of climbs such as big wall climbing, alpine ascents and speed ascents. Admittedly, however, it is often difficult to parse out what constitutes an intrinsic motivation from a more extrinsic one. For example, Beedie (2013) noted, from a historical perspective, achieving a mountaineering 'first' often resulted in increased social status and concomitant enhanced influence and prestige. While there are still mountaineering 'firsts' being accomplished, this increased influence and social status now seems to be less applicable to the broader society and more relegated to mountaineering and climbing circles of people.

What about the issue of satisfaction? Has this variable moved in accordance with and similar to that of motivation, where satisfaction was more externally linked to achievement and later morphed into something more personal or intrinsic or they remained relatively stable over time? The next section deals with an historical overview of the construct of satisfaction in mountaineering.

The history of satisfaction in mountaineering

> I think I mainly climb mountains because I get a great deal of enjoyment out of it.... I think that all mountaineers do get a great deal of satisfaction out of overcoming some challenge which they think is very difficult for them, or which perhaps may be a little dangerous.
>
> (Sir Edmund Hillary – member of first documented Everest summit team 1953)

Over the last 250-plus years, mountaineering has evolved from generally an exploratory adventure, necessary to discover what lays beyond, to a sought after pastime necessary for some to feel the satisfaction of overcoming the challenges and fears mountains can bring. Over time, there has been a gradual taming of the wilderness where mountains usually exist, and as roads, huts, settlements and accessibility increase in these areas, the sense of adventure diminishes, but the satisfaction can still exist.

Surely the early mountaineers experienced exultation and joy when they safely climbed to their summit. Even while seeking out the easiest passage through the mountains or looking for the spiritual entity who supposedly lived on the mountain tops, there were still those who climbed for the satisfaction of getting a better view or to have the satisfaction of going where no one else had been.

In the early days of recorded mountaineering, such as the first ascent of Mont Blanc, the motivation and satisfaction of being the first and having your name recorded in the annuals of history, created a momentum for adventurers to seek that sense of recognition and well-being. As the first ascents became scarcer, new routes were sought after for the same reasons and more inaccessible peaks were ventured to in an attempt to obtain the first ascent or the new route. The exhilaration and satisfaction of 'conquering' the mountains became contagious and seemed to fulfil the desire of *man conquering nature*. When one did not have the level of knowledge and skill to curb the odds of danger in the mountains, professional guides were available for a price to supplement that deficiency and increase the chances of gaining the sense of satisfaction when standing on the top.

Most mountaineering historians will look to the European Alps as the birthplace of modern mountaineering. The reason why is probably due to the benefit of accessibility (Salkeld 1998). With the introduction of the railway systems in mainland Europe in the early 1800s, people began to have easy access closer to the high mountains of France, Austria, Switzerland and Italy. Daring builders constructed permanent huts in the mountains to accommodate the growing number of visitors and climbers. Eventually, cable cars and tramways were constructed in the early 1900s to make the approach times to the climbing quicker and the approaches safer. These modern accommodations attracted both experienced and inexperienced climbers from around the world to find their satisfaction in the European Alps.

Following the same pattern of development in North America, but in the late 1800s, the railroad development in Canada opened up the mountains of the Selkirks and Canadian Rockies. Yet, even with the opening of accessibility to these remote Canadian mountains, North American climbers found the European Alps were still more of the attraction due to the more numerous and widespread conveniences already established, therefore, increasing the chances of success.

As climbers continued to fulfil their restless need of satisfaction and well-being in the mountains, those who could afford the time and had the resources began to venture to far off exotic mountain ranges on other continents. During the early 1900s, the Himalayan mountains became a popular destination point for these individuals, mainly because the mountains were the highest in the world. The satisfaction of gaining the summit of these remote and high peaks took on not only individual satisfaction, but also national satisfaction for the countries represented by the summit climbers. When French climbers scaled the first of the 14 8,000 m peaks, Annapurna (8,091 m) in 1950, the gauntlet was thrown and countries like England, Switzerland, Austria, Germany and the United States all jumped into the fray to claim the other 13. The prize of course was Mt Everest, the highest one of all at 8,848 m. The English made several valiant attempts to be the first mounting large and expensive expeditions lasting up to five months. George Mallory, the famous British mountaineer, made three attempts to climb the mountain in 1921, 1922 and 1924 before succumbing to a fatal fall on his last attempt. His frozen body would not be discovered until 75 years later in 1999 still on the northern slopes of the mountain.

Although Mallory's reply to the question 'why climb?' is now considered an iconic answer, which has a tinge of flippancy to it, many climbers find they cannot explain the need to climb mountains any better than Mallory, so they borrow it as if it is their own. Some have even responded with his even more pretentious reply, 'If you have to ask why men climb, you wouldn't understand the answer.' Even though the motivation for climbing may vary, it is easy to see those who returned from their successful adventures had a common sense of satisfaction about their accomplishments and their well-being.

Studies related to motivation in mountaineering

> If the conquest of a great peak brings moments of exultation and bliss, which in the monotonous, materialistic existence of modern times nothing else can approach, it also presents great dangers.
> (Lionel Terray, French climber and author of *Conquistadors of the Useless*)

Within the confines of studying motivations for mountaineering, four questions serve to frame the discussion. First, what is the overall motivational structure often present in the mountaineering activity? Is the act of mountaineering primarily engaged in for excitement and thrill or are there other, perhaps more subtle but equally important aspects of participation? Second, does the type of mountaineering play a role in the motivations for engagement? For example, would the motives for doing a day climb up a relatively easy peak substantially differ from those related to be involved in a multi-week climbing expedition to a remote high-altitude mountain? Third, what roles do variables such as gender, age and experience play in understanding mountaineering motivations? Do motives for participating substantially differ between women and men? Are older or more experienced climbers significantly different in their motivations from those who are younger or less experienced? And, finally, have these motivations changed over time? Earlier in this chapter, it was discussed how motivations moved from a focus on religion or nationalism to more intrinsically important motives such as personal discovery, but are the many studies done on mountaineering motives essentially now showing similar results?

Attendant to these questions is a multitude of challenges in the study of motivations for mountaineering. For example, one challenge is the 'fluid nature' of motivations. In a previous work, Ewert (1994) reported motivations for participation in mountaineering were dynamic and subject to change depending on the outcome of the trip (i.e. did or did not accomplish the activity as anticipated). Thus, motivations often present a 'moving target' both in terms of their relationship to the outcomes of the experience as well as when the motivations are actually measured (Manfredo and Driver 1996).

A second challenge is understanding the influence the *level of experience* plays on motivational patterns. A growing body of research suggests experience can play an important role in the motivations for adventure recreation participation (Creyer *et al.* 2003; Todd *et al.* 2002). For example, Ewert (1994) reported consistent differences in the number and complexity of motivational factors when comparing the motivations of highly experienced mountaineers with those having less experience.

Highly experienced participants reported more complex sets of motivations. In addition, less experienced participants placed higher levels of importance on motivations related to technical skill development while more experienced participants placed greater importance on motives related to personal and aesthetic factors. Manning (2011) pointed out 'experience has been measured in a number of ways ranging from a single-item variable to composite indexes, and is linked to a variety of items such as attitude, preferences, and behaviors' (p. 253).

As previously alluded to, a third challenge involves the question of whether motivations vary across the variable of *type of climbing*. That is, do motivations for participation differ for those involved in climbing activities such as rock climbing, compared with those participating in ice climbing, expedition climbing or bouldering? To date, we did not uncover any research that specifically looked at this question.

A fourth challenge is in determining the influence *gender* plays in the motivations for participation. For example, some studies in adventure recreation suggest gender can play an important role in the motives deemed most important for participation, with males often indicating higher levels of motivation attached to items such as challenge and competition, while females placing more importance on social items (Cazenave *et al.* 2007; Estes and Ewert 1988; Jackson and Henderson 1995; Thapa *et al.* 2004). Few studies, however, have examined the interaction between gender, specific adventure activities and experience level with respect to the motivations for participation in mountaineering.

Finally, while motivations for mountaineering can be both dynamic and subject to change, they can also defy a precise understanding of the experience without an *experiential base* from which to draw upon. Lyng and Snow (1986) alluded to the same challenge of understanding motives for adventure recreation participation by suggesting, in order to understand the activity, a person has to actually 'do' the activity. Within the context of mountaineering, it can be difficult for a non-climber to understand the nuances often associated with the mountaineering situation, such as the 'pull' of the summit or the 'push away' from the routine of everyday life, or facing the challenge of what has sometimes been termed the mountain being an 'attractive enemy'.

While a great deal of literature has discussed the reasons for mountaineering (see Bonatti 1964, or Rebuffat 1981), one of the first and more formal research studies done on why people climb was done by Bratton *et al.* (1979). Using the responses from 266 members of the Alpine Club of Canada, Calgary Section, the results indicated a varying mosaic of motives for climbing including a social experience, health and fitness, excitement, relaxation, achievement, to be expressive and love of nature. They also found the variables of age, ability and sex served as important independent variables that were related to the motivations expressed by the climbers.

From the broader perspective of motivations in everyday life, George Loewenstein (1999), a behavioural economist, made the point there are many motivations in human behaviour that are not linked to consumption, of which mountaineering is one of this group. With this in mind, Loewenstein examined the mountaineering literature and developed these key insights regarding motivations for mountaineers. A partial list of these follows:

1   An empathy gap persists where mountaineers find it difficult to articulate the nature of their experience to others.
2   Despite being a prestigious activity in many social spheres, mountaineers generally shun overt publicity, thus they often couch their reasons for climbing as less related to image and personal achievement and more related to humanitarian or scientific reasons.
3   Mountaineers place a high value on the issues of goal completion and mastery. Both can be linked to control in one's environment, which is interesting in view of the often external possibilities such as rock fall where the climber can have little if any control.
4   Mountaineers often find deeper meanings from their mountaineering experience beyond simply reaching the top. In a sense, the characteristics of mountaineering often point out our mortality and hence, can deepen our interest in other aspects of our lives.

While based solely on the literature available at the time, Loewenstein provided some interesting insight in the human condition, and in what ways, motivations for mountaineering can contribute to our understanding of that condition.

Ewert (1985, 1994) looked at mountaineers from two different climbing sites, Mt Rainier, Washington State, USA and Mt McKinley, Alaska, USA, to identify motivations and whether these motivations changed as a result of a number of independent variables including age, sex and experience level. Using a composite of skill and ability to determine most likely actual climbing experience, he found five factors that describe 86 per cent of the variance, including Exhilaration, Social Aspects, Image, Aspects of Climbing and Catharsis/Escape. When examining the effect of experience level, Exhilaration and Image were common motivating factors for beginners/novices, intermediate and highly experienced skill level climbers. The factor, Image, was common to beginners and intermediate level climbers and Decision-Making was common to both the intermediate and highly experienced mountaineers. Likewise, females displayed a different motivational structure from males but no significant differences were detected as a result of age. In a more recent work, Ewert *et al.* (2013) found similar outcomes for rock climbers, white-water kayakers, sea kayakers and people canoeing, with both activity and sex serving as important mediating variables in the overall motivational structure.

Breivik (1996) investigated risk-taking behaviours, personality and sensation-seeking needs among members on the 1985 Norwegian Mt Everest expedition. In this study, other Norwegian climbers, sports students and military recruits were used as comparison groups. When comparing the four groups, the Everest climbers were more extreme in their drive factors, scored lower on avoidance factors such as worry and anxiety, and displayed more maturity and stability. In addition, they were generally more willing to take risks (political/military and physical but not in achievement-related, intellectual or social matters). Finally, they exhibited higher sensation-seeking scores than the other respondents. It was concluded the Mt Everest climbers demonstrated a high risk profile both in the personality and trait tests provided in the study.

Maher and Potter (2001) explored the cultural differences and motivations to climb for a group of elite, male mountaineers. Using a qualitative thematic analysis approach, common motivational themes identified by the five participants included the following: mountaineering because (a) of your level of skill, (b) to go places, (c) enjoying the hard work and physical difficulty, and (d) managing the risk. Cultural differences were not noted in this work, perhaps due to the similarity of the participants' background.

Buckley (2012) included mountaineering as part of an adventure tourism complex and identified at least 14 different motivations after examining approximately 50 previous studies. In this work, he categorized motivations into internal performance of the activity, internal/external, place in nature and external, social position. Representative motives from each category included thrill, fear, achievement and risk for internal performance, nature and internal/external place in nature, and friends, image and escape for external social position. In addition, Buckley argued, in the adventure tourism context, the experience of 'rush' or a simultaneous expression of flow and thrill is what provides the attraction in activities such as mountaineering.

In a similar fashion, when considering adventure sports, of which mountaineering was one, Kerr and Mackenzie (2012) found a range of motivations for participation. Like the Ewert *et al.* (2013) study, which used four different adventure activities, Kerr and Mackenzie included river surfing, mountain biking, kayaking, mountaineering and hang gliding as the activity base. Similar to what has been seen in a number of other studies, some of which are described here, the resultant motives were varied and multifaceted. A sampling of these motivations included goal achievement, risk-taking, social motivation, escape from boredom, pushing personal boundaries, overcoming fear and connecting with the natural environment.

In sum, while there are some differences in the motivations identified from these studies, there is also a great deal of commonality. For example, many of the motivations described from this past work have included reference to goal-achievement, taking or managing risks, for connections to either the natural environment or social structure of the climbing team, catharsis and excitement. A summary of the motives somewhat consistently reported in the literature is provided in Table 9.1. What seems increasingly clear is while there is a great deal of room in describing what motivates people to climb, there is a growing corpus of knowledge suggesting, while there might be many motivations to consider, there are some that are quite consistent and resilient. And while some of this consistently may reflect how the question is worded or being asked, measurement error does not explain the deep connection and congruence between what our early pioneering climbers said was their reasons for climbing and what our research has now begun to reaffirm.

Table 9.1 Often reported motivations

Reported motivations	Level of consistency[1]
Exhilaration/excitement	High
Self-image (e.g. to be known as a mountaineer)	Medium to high
Catharsis/escape/relaxation	Medium
Social aspects (e.g. to be part of a team)	High
Control over self	Medium
Using climbing skills	Medium
Personal testing/sense of achievement	Medium to high
Sensation-seeking	Medium
Overcoming fear	Low to medium
Risk-taking	Low

Note
1 Levels of consistency were based on presence in the literature and are arbitrarily determined by the authors.

Another interesting note is that of risk-taking. As Lockwood (2011) succinctly pointed out, and all mountaineers intuitively know, mountain climbing involves risk. Despite this obvious truism, risk-taking does not appear as a powerful motivating factor in many of the studies examined in this chapter. Two possible explanations emerge in the context of risk-taking. First, taking risks may simply not be a powerful motive in mountaineering. Even in considering other high risk recreational endeavours such as BASE jumping, actual risk-taking was reported by the jumpers as only a means to 'becoming positively transformed' (Allman *et al.* 2009). Thus, taking the risk was not the driving force but only the 'roadmap' to get somewhere else, namely, positive transformation that was essential to the quality of their lives.

The second explanation for the lack of importance placed on the construct of risk-taking may lie in the seeming paradox of having control. In this case, risk-taking may be less of a motivational issue because the participants feel they can control the risk and successfully deal with it. Far from being an out of control activity, Mitchell (1983) suggested risk recreation activities such as mountaineering, offer the individual opportunities to exert considerable influence over the outcome of a particular adventure by the virtue of their skills, strategies and perseverance. Martha and Laurendeau (2010) reported level of experience plays a role in whether participants in a high risk sport perceived themselves as being vulnerable to injury and able to manage the risk. Thus, it is not surprising the control-focused motivational theories, such as self-efficacy and locus of control (Eccles and Wigfield 2002), often serve as the theoretical framework in risk and adventure-based studies. Corroboration from other studies (Ewert 1994; Todd *et al.* 2002) also pointed to the issue of control as being a constant companion in the risk recreation setting. Palmer (2004) captured this idea in her statement about true aficionados of risk recreation activities engage in the activities, not for the risk, but because they 'provide a means of penetrating to realities not encountered in daily life' (p. 67). Thus, risk may not elicit a strong presence in the motivational structure for climbing because the individual, while recognizing its presence, assumes a sense of control through their actions and skills. The afore-mentioned, however, does not discount the often hidden role risk and risk-taking assume in the mountaineering experience, as elegantly articulated by Fred Beckey (2011):

> To reduce the chance of an accident, competent climbers develop a balanced relationship with fear, an awareness of danger, and turn their mental energy into positive means to overcome problems. Both instinct and acquired judg-ment are developed from experience.... It is important not to diminish the spirit of climbing and eliminate all risk. To reduce all commitment lessens the spirit and engagement of the adventure.
>
> (Fred Beckey's *100 Favorite North American Climbs*)

Thus, there appears to be a number of factors that can serve to influence the motivational structure inherent in the mountaineering experience. For example, levels of experience, sex or gender, type of mountaineering trip engaged in, the outcome or perceived success of the trip, the type of climbing group the indi-vidual is part of and the challenges associated with that particular climb, all appear to be able to influence the self-reported motivations of the climber (Ewert 1993). Thus, there is a substantial amount of 'flux' in the motivational system that can produce a wide range of motivations and, in turn, can cause a change in these motivations, even as the climb progresses. Can the same be said for the construct of satisfaction in mountaineering?

Studies related to satisfaction in mountaineering

> Great things are done when men and mountains meet.
> (William Blake – English eighteenth/nineteenth century poet)

Research studies focusing on the construct of satisfaction and mountaineering is minimal at best. Some studies have focused on the consumer satisfaction reported in the tourism field from a business perspective (Faullant *et al.* 2011; Pan and Ryan 2007) and some have studied satisfaction amongst mountaineers from the psychological perspective (Toros *et al.* 2010; Ward 2010). Another approach to studying satisfaction amongst climbers has been by focusing on their identity development and self-realization (Sparks *et al.* 2014; Taniguchi *et al.* 2005).

Faullant *et al.* (2011) studied consumption-related emotions and personality as operational indicators to design mountaineering experiences for adventure tourists and to assist in increasing the chances of consumer satisfaction. Consumption-related emotions, usually operationalized as broad, summary dimensions such as positive and negative emotions or, alternatively, pleasure and arousal, have been shown to be influenced by enduring personality traits and, in turn, to influence customer satisfaction. Experiential tourism activities, such as mountaineering, evoke powerful emotions that strongly influence tourist satisfaction. Although Zajonc (1980) proposed, and more recent neurophysio-logical evidence confirms, emotions, especially fear, can precede cognitions. Consumption-related emotions have heretofore been modelled as occurring con-currently with or consequent to cognitive appraisals. Results show two basic consumption-related emotions, fear and joy, are influenced respectively by neu-roticism and extraversion and, in turn, conjunctively with cognitive appraisals influence tourist satisfaction. Joy has direct effects on satisfaction not mediated by cognitions; fear's inverse effects on satisfaction are fully mediated by cogni-tions. These findings extend understandings of trait/basic-emotion relationships and of basic emotions' roles in satisfaction formation and also, importantly, demonstrate an instance of primary consumer emotions (Zajonc 1980).

Pan and Ryan (2007) reported on visitor motivations and satisfaction at Pirongia Forest Park, New Zealand. They noted a link between satisfaction and those attributes generating a sense of relaxation, namely the mountain scenery. The views from high up allowed for a sense of perspective and the vistas had a calming effect on those who climbed to the tops of the Park's peaks. This effect was the primary indicator of satisfaction expressed by the study's participants. The Park's management was encouraged to increase their efforts to make the peaks more accessible and doable for all visitors to their Park.

Toros *et al.* (2010) examined the relationship between task- and ego-oriented goals and life satisfaction in the people participating in mountaineering sports. Eighty-five sportsmen, who engage in mountaineering sports and whose average age was 25.15 years (±6.37 years), participated in this study. The goal orienta-tions of the mountaineers were determined by means of the *Task and Ego Orien-tation in Sport Questionnaire Scale* and *Life Satisfaction Scale*. The findings of the research showed there was no significant correlation between task-oriented goals and life satisfaction ($p=0.254$; $\alpha>0.05$). They also found no significant correlation between ego-oriented goals and life satisfaction ($p=0.352$; $\alpha>0.05$). Their results indicated the participants' life satisfaction was not related to doing the mountaineering activities or fulfilling their egocentric goals. Their conclu-sion was many other factors could affect the relationship between life satisfac-tion and mountaineering pursuits.

Ward (2010) looked at the balance of risk-taking in mountaineering and the benefits of climbing Mt Whitney (4,421 m) in the California Sierra Nevada Range, the highest peak in the contiguous 48 US states. Mountaineering does involve inherent aspects of risk; however, these individuals who participated in mountain type experiences did not perceive risk-taking as the objective, but merely a means to an end – to receive a benefit. Ward, utilizing a qualitative methodology approach, captured the subjective nature of perceptions of both the risks and benefits associated with climbing Mt Whitney in six themes ranging from social to physical and assessment to risk. Similar to previous research findings (Delle Fave *et al.* 2003; Ewert 1994; Slanger and Rudestam 1997), participants in this study were willing to accept risk as an inherent aspect of climbing to experience or maximize a beneficial outcome, usually the satisfaction of accomplishment. Ward's study provided a greater understanding of perceptions of risk and benefit of climbing Mt Whitney by utilizing the risk homeostasis framework.

Sparks *et al.* (2014) studied the solo climber's rationale for risking life and limb when rock climbing high cliffs at a challenging difficulty and height. Even though the study was focusing on motivation, the researchers learned the climbers gained a high level of satisfaction after their solo climbs. The results of their study seem to follow Hawkins and Weis's (1985) social development model of skill and opportunity accompanied by challenge leads to an experience that has the potential to assist the climber to learn things about him- or herself, which leads to a developing identity. That realization lends itself to not only a satisfaction of safely climbing the cliff without a rope, but the satisfaction of discovering things about oneself.

Taniguchi *et al.* (2005) wanted to identify the attributes of a meaningful learning experience. Their study was not looking at mountaineering, but outdoor recreational experiences involving challenge. What they discovered was similar to Sparks *et al.*'s (2014) findings specifically a person can re-discover who they really are behind the social façades he has layered on (e.g. position titles at work, academic degrees and/or certifications earned, wealth obtained) by facing risks and awkwardness, which helps to shed the social façade layers. What individuals can discover is what Immanuel Kant (1790) referred to as the *sublime nature* of a person. This is the discovery of weaknesses, strengths and potentials. In the end, there is a growth in the individual to come to a self-realization of who they really are.

The limited studies found on mountaineering satisfaction calls for this area to be studied more in a variety of circumstances. The important take away is that the research seems to suggest that the satisfaction found in mountaineering experiences can have an impact on enhancing self-realization and identity development.

Implications related to motivations and satisfactions

> Mountaineering involves putting up with extreme environmental conditions and the 'unrelenting misery' that comes with a very physical and dangerous activity…. This is not consistent with sensory pleasures or the benefit of wealth.
>
> (Neal Cole – nealcole.tumblr.com/post/4520227292/
> hidden-human-motivations)

As alluded to by Cole, the reasons for and outcomes from mountaineering now have increasingly little to do with wealth, nationalism or, even, sensory pleasures. And, as displayed in Table 9.1, the motivations for climbing can be thought to follow a fairly predictable pattern. This continuing effort to be able to articulate why people climb mountains remains at odds with the previous quotation from Mallory, where he states if you have to ask the question you will never know the answer. Certainly there is some truism in the preceding paragraph but beyond that, are some implications and meaning, perhaps elusive and ephemeral but nevertheless there, that can be attached to motivations and satisfactions related to the mountaineering endeavour. Quite clearly the constructs of motivation and satisfaction are similar but not identical. In one sense, motivations imply a driving force that impels or draws in an individual to engage in mountaineering. The construct of satisfaction, on the other hand, is often associated with either an ongoing or post-experience evaluation, which consists of am I or was I somehow fulfilled with the mountaineering trip? What specific implications and meanings can be derived from our understanding of both the constructs of motivation and satisfaction? The following section attempts to draw some conclusions about those potential applications and meanings.

Motivations and selected implications

In an earlier work, Ewert and Hollenhorst (1989) examined the concept of internal and external motivations within an adventure recreation context. Based on the Theory of Specialization (Bryan 1977), which provides a theoretical linkage between level of experience and attributes of a specific activity such as social orientation, type of environment, etc., the Adventure Recreation Model (Ewert and Hollenhorst 1989; Todd *et al.* 2002) depicts a relationship between the level of engagement in a particular adventure-based activity, and suggests that as the level of engagement increases, there will be a corresponding increase in skill, frequency of participation, internalized locus of control and preferred level of risk (see Figure 9.1).

Both Buckley (2012) and Ewert and Hollenhorst (1989) hypothesized as individuals become more engaged in a particular adventure recreation activity, motivations for participation will become more aligned with internal motivations such as challenge, achievement, control and risk-taking, as opposed to external motivations such as feeling pressured by friends or family to participate. In the Ewert and Hollenhorst study, internal motivations were defined as motives originating directly within the individual, while external motives were more likely to be other-directed, that is, emerging from factors outside the individual, such as other people. Thus, there appears to be a strong link between the motivating forces driving or impelling an individual and the types of attributes they seek out within a given activity. In turn, Ewert and Sibthorp (2014: 45) reported these motivations and subsequent actions can be tempered by four questions often inherently asked by the climber:

- How much interest and time is necessary to learn the prerequisite skills to successfully engage in this mountaineering trip?
- What knowledge of the equipment and material is needed for this trip?
- Will I need additional instruction and practice to prepare for this engagement? Do I need a guide or instructor?
- What will be the relative need for physical strength and personal abilities for this trip?

The above questions also have some implications to the management and regulation of the mountaineering experiences. The previously described research suggests mountaineers look for climbs that are 'tailored' to match their motivations. If true,

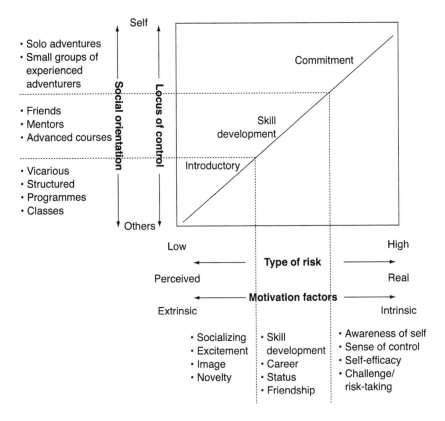

Figure 9.1 The adventure model.

this fact alone has numerous implications for the resource provider and mountain manager. For example, should the level of risk be reduced, accentuated or restricted? Are some mountain landscapes simply too hazardous to allow climbing? Are there ethical issues involved that are specific to mountaineering? For example, the recent 2014 spring season tragedy on Mt Everest, where 16 Sherpa lost their lives in an ice avalanche, speaks to the issue of who is getting the benefits from climbing, and who is really taking the risks? Swarbrooke *et al.* (2003) pointed out risk-taking can be a multifaceted construct involving risk to the individual, group leaders, environment, rescuers, as well as other entities. Thus, an individual's motivations for mountaineering can often have implications to numerous other people and organizations.

Satisfaction and selected implications

The perception of satisfaction from a mountaineering experience can be one of those few truly intrinsic valued experiences. Although not always a consequence of participating in a mountaineering activity, heightened self-awareness and self-actualization (Maslow 1968) gained through a flow experience (Csziksentmiyalhi 1975) have been discovered to be common consequences of facing the challenges and risks associated with mountaineering and surviving them (Ewert 1985). Whether such consequences were originally sought after as motivating factors, this sense of a better understanding of oneself and deriving satisfaction from such enlightenment provides a good example of mountaineering's intrinsic value.

Faullant *et al.* (2011) made the case for an understanding of the power of satisfaction and how that understanding can be used to promote adventure tourism. They suggested the two most basic consumption-related emotions experienced in mountaineering are joy and fear. 'Joy has direct effects on satisfaction' (Faullant *et al.* 2011: 1423), while fear can have an adverse effect on satisfaction. Which of these two emotions rises to the forefront of an experience is correlated to not just the experience but also the personality traits one possesses. Two affective traits identified as having such a relationship are extraversion (positively related to joy) and neuroticism (positively related to fear). George Mallory said:

> People ask me, 'What is the use of climbing Mt Everest?' and my answer must at once be, 'It is of no use.' There is not the slightest prospect of any gain whatsoever. Oh, we may learn a little about the behavior of the human body at high altitudes, and possibly medical men may turn our observation to some account for the purposes of aviation. But otherwise nothing will come of it. We shall not bring back a single bit of gold or silver, not a gem, nor any coal or iron.... If you cannot understand that, there is something in man which responds to the challenge of this mountain and goes out to meet it, that the struggle is the struggle of life itself upward and forever upward, then you won't see why we go. What we get from this adventure is just sheer joy. And joy is, after all, the end of life
>
> (Mallory and Gillman 2010: 196)

Having an understanding of such relationships can help programmers for adventure tourism, especially mountaineering experiences, to design such experiences to include challenges and risks appropriate for the personality type of clients served.

There also appears to be a positive relationship with the satisfaction one gets from mountaineering and other outdoor adventure activities and one's life satisfaction (LS) levels (Ardahan and Turgut 2012). This implies consideration should be given to promoting such activities for the well-being of the citizenry. The results of this study were clear that participating in any outdoor activities affect LS level of participants positively. From this perspective, in order to increase LS of persons and society, local, private, commercial and governmental solutions must be organized to enhance that opportunity. Plans, such as adding outdoor activities in curricula at all levels of the educational process from primary school to university or later and promoting and supporting outdoor activities by job providers to their employees, should be considered. Municipalities, educational institutions, youth centres, nonprofit organizations, private and public sector must take responsibility and provide leadership to organize and deliver outdoor activities. Some activities must be organized for different parts of society especially for the disadvantaged groups like the elderly, the disabled and their families, those with chronic illnesses, the homeless and the young people in dormitories. Some activities must be done free of charge or with low costs to increase the number of participants.

Satisfaction derived from climbing mountains appears to contribute to a physical and mental state of well-being. The physical abilities needed to achieve a sense of accomplishment in mountaineering requires a higher level of fitness than most people have and are often translated into better overall health. The perception of well-being has been interpreted to mean a positive psychological state leading to a better quality of life (Seligman 2002). The experiential nature of mountaineering has been shown to have positive potential for those seeking a better quality of life.

Concluding comments

The mountains are calling and I must go.

(John Muir)

There are those who see mountaineering as a selfish, egocentric and foolish activity, where participants risk life and limb to the pursuit of self-gratification and aggrandizement (Krakauer 1997), but the research is also clear there are positive influences for those who find satisfaction in such participation. Mountaineering also has its own social connections to those who share the enthusiasm for climbing mountains, especially those who participate repeatedly. The camaraderie brings a sense of connectedness to others who understand the motivation and satisfaction derived from the mountains. The mountains can become the gathering places for seeing friends and meeting new ones. Such connections can spill over into other areas of life, including business, family and spirituality.

Mountaineering also opens the world to those who pursue the mountains in their remote ranges. The pursuit of facing the challenges and risks of mountaineering can take a person to the far corners of the world, especially when such pursuits include the highest mountains on each of the seven continents. The places and people one can meet expand the knowledge of cultures and lifestyles of a variety of people and can connect people from different points on the planet with each other. The world becomes a smaller place where cultural appreciation can flourish.

Moreover, a number of data sources suggest adventure challenge activities, such as rock climbing and mountaineering, will increase in popularity, despite the growing concern over the effect of climate change on mountain landscapes (Bürki *et al.* 2003). Nevertheless, even adjusting for increased warming paradigms, mountain climbing and rock climbing are expecting to increase from 16–22 per cent in the northern United States alone (Bowker and Askew 2013).

In addition, this continued growth is reflected in market-level data. For example, the European outdoor industry has matured and now enjoys a globally significant status in terms of size, and, increasingly, profile. It continues to be resilient despite wider economic challenges and this is evident when reviewing the latest State of Trade report, the annual market study conducted by the European Outdoor Group (EOG) on behalf of the industry. Now in its third year and tracking a five-year trend in the outdoor market, the State of Trade study reports the wholesale sell-in figures for outdoor products across 22 European countries. Based on these wholesale data supplied for the report, the EOG makes a conservative estimate the annual industry turnover at retail exceeded €10 billion in 2012, with expenditures for climbing equipment accounting for over 3 per cent of that investment.

There are, however, many things science cannot and will not fully explain or measure relative to the mountaineering experience. Issues such as 'peak experiences', 'authentic experiences', 'enduring involvement', 'extraordinary experiences' (Beedie and Hudson 2003) do not always lend themselves to empirical-based or even qualitative-based research. Complex and ethereal constructs such as perceived competence, a sense of connection with the mountain environment, the unconscious self-assurance mentioned by Ewert and Hollenhorst (1994), the notion of the French term, *jouissance*, or the climber's ability to make sense out of the symbols, images and reality of the mountaineering experience (Allman *et al.* 2009), and the sense of achievement one gets from reaching the summit or at least attempting to, are difficult to measure or even often articulate by the climbers themselves. Thus, and perhaps rightly so, the motives and satisfactions we experience as mountaineers, while somewhat permeable to the cold objectivity of science, will remain, for the most part, ours alone to understand and feel. Sir Edmund Hillary perhaps said it best and most succinctly in his statement, 'Nobody climbs mountains for scientific reasons. Science is used to raise money for the expeditions, but you really climb for the hell of it.'

References

Allman, T. L., Mittelstaedt, R. D., Martin, B. and Goldenberg, M. (2009) 'Exploring the motivations of BASE jumpers: Extreme sport enthusiast', *Journal of Sport and Tourism*, 14(4): 229–247.

Andrews, F. M. (1976) *Social indicators of well-being: Americans' perceptions of life quality*, New York: Plenum Press.

Ardahan, F. and Turgut, T. (2012) 'Effect of outdoor activities on the life satisfaction: Turkey case', *Online Journal of Recreation and Sport*, 2(2): 11–18.

Arthaud-Day, M. L., Rode, J. C., Mooney, C. H. and Near, J. P. (2005) 'The subjective well-being construct: A test of its convergent, discriminant, and factorial validity', *Social Indicators Research*, 74(3): 445–476.

Atkinson, J. W. (1964) *An introduction to motivation*, New York: Van Nostrand.

Beckey, F. (2011) *Fred Beckey's 100 favorite North American climbs*, New York: Patagonia Books.

Beedie, P. (2013) 'Anthony Giddens: Structuration theory and mountaineering', in E. C. J. Pike and S. Beames (eds) *Outdoor adventure and social theory*, London: Routledge: 89–980.

Beedie, P. and Hudson, S. (2003) 'Emergence of mountain-based adventure tourism', *Annals of Tourism Research*, 30(3): 625–643.

Berlyne, D. E. (1960) *Conflict, arousal and curiosity*, New York: McGraw-Hill.

Bonatti, W. (1964) *On the heights*, London: Rupert Hart Davis.

Borrello, M. E. (2005) 'The rise, fall and resurrection of group selection', *Endeavor*, 29(1): 43–47.

Bowker, J. M. and Askew, A. E. (2013) 'Outlook for outdoor recreation in the northern United States: A technical document supporting the Northern Forest Futures Project with projections through 2016 (*Gen. Tech. Rep. NRS-120*)', Newtown Square, PA: U.S. Department of Agriculture, Forest Service, Northern Research Station: 62 p.

Bratton, R. D., Kinnear, G. and Koroluk, G. (1979) 'Why man climbs mountains', *International Review of Sport Sociology*, 14(2): 23–36.

Breashers, D. and Salkeld, A. (1999) *Last climb: The legendary Everest expeditions of George Mallory*, Washington, DC: National Geographic.

Breivik, G. (1996) 'Personality, sensation-seeking and risk-taking among Everest climbers', *International Journal of Sport Psychology*, 27(3): 308–320.

Bryan, H. (1977) 'Leisure value systems and recreational specialization: The case of trout fishermen', *Journal of Leisure Research*, 9(3): 174–187.

Buckley, R. (2012) 'Rush as a key motivation in skilled adventure tourism: Resolving the risk recreation paradox', *Tourism Management*, 33(4): 961–970.

Bürki, R., Elsasser, H. and Abegg, B. (2003) 'Climate change-impacts on the tourism industry in mountain areas', Paper presented at 1st International Conference on Climate Change and Tourism, Dierba, 2003.

Carnicelli-Filho, S., Schwartz, G. M. and Tahara, A. K. (2009) 'Fear and adventure tourism in Brazil', *Tourism Management*, 31(6): 953–956.

Cazenave, N., Le Scanff, C. and Woodman, T. (2007) 'Psychological profiles and emotional regulation characteristics of women engaged in risk-taking sports', *Anxiety, Stress, and Coping*, 20(4): 421–435.

Celsi, R. L., Rose, R. L. and Leigh, T. W. (1993) 'Exploration of high-risk leisure consumption through skydiving', *Journal of Consumer Research*, 20(1): 1–21.

Coburn, B. (1970) *Everest: Mountain without mercy*, Washington, DC: National Geographic.

Creyer, E. H., Ross, W. T. and Evers, D. (2003) 'Risky recreation: An exploration of factors influencing the likelihood of participation and the effects of experience', *Leisure Studies*, 22(3): 239–253.

Csikszentmiyalhi, M. (1975) *Beyond boredom and anxiety*, San Francisco, CA: Jossey-Bass.

Csikszentmihalyi, M. and Csikszentmihalyi, I. S. (1990) 'Adventure and the flow experience', in J. C. Miles and S. Priest (eds) *Adventure education*, State College, PA: Venture: 149–156.

Daumal, R. (1952) *Mount analogue: A novel of symbolically authentic non-euclidean adventures in mountain climbing*, Paris: Stuart.

Delle Fave, A., Bassi, M. and Massimini, F. (2003) 'Quality of experience and risk perception in high-altitude rock climbing', *Journal of Applied Sport Psychology*, 15(1), 82–98.

Diener, E. (1984) 'Subjective well-being', *Psychological Bulletin*, 95(3), 542–575.

Diener, E. and Seligman, M. E. P. (2004) 'Beyond money: Toward an economy of well-being', *Psychological Science in the Public Interest*, 5(1): 1–31.

Donnelly, P. (2003) 'The great divide: Sport climbing vs. adventure climbing', in R. E. Rinehart and S. Syndor (eds) *To the extreme: Alternative sports, inside and out*, Albany, NY: State University of New York Press: 291–304.

Eccles, J. and Wigfield, A. (2002) 'Motivational beliefs, values, and goals', *Annual Review of Psychology*, 53(1): 109–132.

Estes, C. and Ewert, A. (1988) 'Enhancing mixed-gender programming: Considerations for experiential educators', *Bradford Papers Annual*, 3: 34–43.

Ewert, A. (1985) 'Why people climb: The relationship of participant motives and experience levels to mountaineering', *Journal of Leisure Research*, 17(3): 241–250.

Ewert, A. (1993) 'Differences in the level of motive importance based on trip outcome, experience level and group type', *Journal of Leisure Research*, 25(4): 335–349.

Ewert, A. (1994) 'Playing the edge: Motivation and risk-taking in a high altitude wilderness-like environment', *Environment and Behavior*, 26(1): 3–24.

Ewert, A. and Hollenhorst, S. (1989) 'Testing the adventure model: Empirical support for a model of risk recreation participation', *Journal of Leisure Research*, 21(2): 124–139.

Ewert, A. and Hollenhorst, S. (1994) 'Individual and setting attributes of the adventure recreation experience', *Leisure Sciences*, 16(3): 177–191.

Ewert, A. W. and Jamieson, L. (2003) 'Current status and future directions in the adventure tourism industry', in J. Wilks and S. J. Page (eds) *Managing tourist health and safety in the new millennium*, Oxford: Pergamon: 67–84.

Ewert, A. and Sibthorp, J. (2014) *Outdoor adventure education: Foundations, theory, and research*, Champaign, IL: Human Kinetics.

Ewert, A., Gilbertson, K., Luo, Y.-C. and Voight, A. (2013) 'Beyond "because it's there": Motivations for pursuing adventure recreational activities', *Journal of Leisure Research*, 44(1): 91–111.

Faullant, R., Matzler, K. and Mooradian, T. A. (2011) 'Personality, basic emotions, and satisfaction: Primary emotions in the mountaineering experience', *Tourism Management*, 32(6): 1423–1430.

Harris, C., Daniels, K. and Briner, R. B. (2003) 'A daily diary study of goals and affective well-being at work', *Journal of Occupational and Organizational Psychology*, 76(3): 401–410.

Hawkins, D. J. and Weis, J. G. (1985) 'The social development model: An integrated approach to delinquency prevention', *Journal of Primary Prevention*, 6(2): 73–97.

Heider, F. (1958) *The psychology of interpersonal relations*, New York: Wiley.

Houston, C. (1968) 'The last blue mountain', in S. Z. Klauner (ed.) *Why man takes changes: Studies in stress-seeking*, Garden City, NY: Double Day Books: 49–58.

Jackson, E. and Henderson, K. A. (1995) 'Gender-based analysis of leisure constraints', *Leisure Sciences*, 17(1): 31–51.

Kant, I. (1790) *Kant's kritik of judgment* (trans. J. H. Bernard), London: Macmillan.

Kerr, J. H. and Mackenzie, S. H. (2012) 'Multiple motives for participating in adventure sports', *Psychology of Sport and Exercise*, 13(5): 649–657.

Klausner, S. (ed.) (1968) *Why man takes chances: Studies in stress-seeking*, New York: Anchor Books.

Knowles, P. A., Grove, S. J. and Pickett, G. M. (1999) 'Mood versus service quality effects on customers' responses to service organizations and service encounters', *Journal of Service Research*, 2(2): 187–199.

Krakauer, J. (1997) *Into thin air*, New York: Anchor Books.

Kyle, G. T., Absher, J. D., Hammitt, W. E. and Cavin, J. (2006) 'An examination of the motivation–involvement relationship', *Leisure Sciences*, 28(5): 467–485.

Lee, R. T. and Ashforth, B. E. (1996) 'A meta-analytic examination of the correlates of the three dimensions of job burnout', *Journal of Applied Psychology*, 81(2): 123–133.

Lévy-Garboua, L., Montmarquette, C. and Simonnet, V. (2007) 'Job satisfaction and quits', *Labour Economics*, 14(2): 251–268.

Lewis, N. (2003) 'Sustainable adventure: Embodied experiences and ecological practices within British climbing', in B. Wheaton (ed.) *Understanding lifestyle sports: Consumption, identity, and difference*, London: Routledge: 70–93.

Lockwood, N. C. (2011) 'Motivations for mountain climbing: The role of risk', unpublished doctoral thesis, University of Sussex.

Loewenstein, G. (1999) 'Because it is there: The challenge of mountaineering … for utility theory', *Kyklos*, 52(3): 315–343.

Lyng, S. (1990) 'Edgework: A social psychological analysis of voluntary risk taking', *American Journal of Sociology*, 95(4): 851–886.

Lyng, S. G. and Snow, D. (1986) 'Vocabularies of motive and high risk behavior: The case of skydiving', in E. J. Lawler (ed.) *Advances in group processes vol. 3*, Greenwich, CT: JAI: 157–159.

Maher, P. T. and Potter, T. G. (2001) 'A life to risk: Cultural differences in motivations to climb among elite male mountaineers', in G. Kyle (comp.) *Proceedings of the 2000 northeastern recreation research symposium: Gen. Tech. Rep. NE-276*. Newtown Square, PA: U.S. Department of Agriculture, Forest Service, Northeastern Research Station: 155–158.

Mallory, G. and Gillman, P. (eds) (2010) *Climbing Everest: The complete writings of George Mallory*, London: Gibson Square.

Manfredo, M. and Driver, B. (1996) 'Measuring leisure motivation: A meta-analysis of the recreation experience preference scales', *Journal of Leisure Research*, 28(3): 188–213.

Manning, R. E. (2011) *Studies in outdoor recreation* (3rd edn), Corvallis, OR: Oregon State University Press.

Martha, C. and Laurendeau, J. (2010) 'Are perceived comparative risks realistic among high-risk sports participants?' *International Journal of Sport and Exercise*, 8(2): 129–146.

Maslach, C. and Jackson, S. E. (1981) 'The measurement of experienced burnout', *Journal of Occupational Behaviour*, 2(2): 99–113.

Maslow, A. (1968) *Toward a psychology of being*, Princeton, NJ: D. Van Nostrand Company Inc.

Mitchell, R. G. (1983) *Mountain experience: The psychology and sociology of adventure*, Chicago, IL: University of Chicago Press.

Mueller, T. E. and Cleaver, M. (2000) 'Targeting the CANZUS baby boomer explorer and adventurer segments', *Journal of Vacation Marketing*, 6(2): 154–169.

Noyce, W. (1958) *The springs of adventure*, New York: World Publishing Company.

Palmer, C. (2004) 'Death, danger and the selling of risk in adventure sports', in B. Wheaton (ed.) *Understanding lifestyle sports: Consumption, identity and difference*, London: Routledge: 55–69.

Pan, S. and Ryan, C. (2007) 'Mountain areas and visitor usage: Motivations and determinants of satisfaction: The case of Pirongia Forest Park, New Zealand', *Journal of Sustainable Tourism*, 15(3): 288–308.

Pomfret, G. (2006) 'Mountaineering adventure tourists: A conceptual framework for research', *Tourism Management*, 27(1): 113–123.

Rubuffat, G. (1981) *On ice and snow and rock*, Hereford: Addyman Books.

Salkeld, A. (1998) 'Introduction', in A. Salkeld (ed.) *World mountaineering*, London: Bulfinch: 12–19.

Scott, M. B. (1974) *Big wall climbing*, New York: Oxford University Press.

Seligman, M. E. P. (2002) *Authentic happiness: Using the new positive psychology to realize your potential for lasting fulfillment*, New York: Free Press.

Seligman, M. E. P. and Csikszentmihalyi, M. (2000) 'Positive psychology: An introduction', *American Psychologist*, 55(1): 5–14.

Slanger, E. and Rudestam, K. E. (1997) 'Motivation and disinhibition in high risk sports: Sensation seeking and self-efficacy', *Journal of Research in Personality*, 31(3): 355–374.

Sparks, J., Taniguchi, S. and Arnesgard, J. (2014) 'Extreme sports participation: A study of free solo rock climbers', unpublished masters thesis, Brigham Young University.

Swarbrooke, J., Beard, C., Leckie, S. and Pomfret, G. (2003) *Adventure tourism: The new frontier*, Burlington, MA: Butterworth-Heinemann/Elsevier Science.

Taniguchi, S. T., Freeman, P. A. and Richards, A. L. (2005) 'Attributes of meaningful learning experiences in an outdoor education program', *Journal of Adventure Education and Outdoor Learning*, 5(2): 131–144.

Terray, L. (1963) *Conquistadors of the useless: From the Alps to Annapurna*, London: Gollancz.

Thapa, B., Confer, J. J. and Mendelson, J. (2004) 'Trip motivations among water-based recreationists'. Online, available at: www.metla.fi/julkaisut/workingpapers/2004/mwp002-30.pdf (accessed 11 January 2014).

Todd, S. L., Anderson, L., Young, A. and Anderson, D. (2002) 'The relationship of motivation factors to level of development in outdoor adventure recreationists', *Research in Outdoor Education*, 6: 124–138.

Toros, T., Akyuz, U., Bayansalduz, M. and Soyer, F. (2010) 'Examining the relationship between task- and ego-oriented goals and life satisfaction: A study of people doing mountaineering sports', *International Journal of Human Sciences*, 7(2): 10–39.

Ward, W. (2010) 'Perceived risks and benefits of climbing Mt. Whitney: A qualitative application of risk homeostasis theory', *Journal of Outdoor Recreation, Education, and Leadership*, 2(2): 186–190.

Weiner, B. (1992) *Human motivation: Metaphors, theories, and research*, Newbury Park, CA: Sage Publications.

Whymper, E. (1871; reprinted 1981) *Scrambles amongst the Alps: In the years 1860–1869*, Ten Berkeley, CA: Speed Press.

Williams, T. and Donnelly, P. (1985) 'Subcultural production, reproduction, and transformation in climbing', *International Review for Sociology of Sport*, 20(1/2): 3–15.

Williams, P. and Soutar, G. N. (2009) 'Value, satisfaction and behavioral intentions in an adventure tourism context', *Annals of Tourism Research*, 36(3): 413–438.

Zajonc, R. B. (1980) 'Feeling and thinking: Preferences need no inferences', *American Psychologist*, 35(2): 151–175.

Case study 4

The mountaineering flow experience

Robert A. Stebbins

Flow is a cherished experience wherever it can be found in work and leisure. Csikszentmihalyi (1990: 48–67) set out eight components of this experience, which must be present when maintaining that someone is in flow:

1   sense of competence in executing the activity;
2   requirement of concentration;
3   clarity of goals of the activity;
4   immediate feedback from the activity;
5   sense of deep, focused involvement in the activity;
6   sense of control in completing the activity;
7   loss of self-consciousness during the activity;
8   sense of time is truncated during the activity.

These components are self-explanatory, except possibly for the first and the sixth. With reference to the first, flow fails to develop when the activity is either too easy or too difficult; to experience flow the participant must feel capable of performing at least a moderately challenging activity. The sixth component refers to the perceived degree of control the participant has over execution of the activity. Csikszentmihalyi (1990: 59) says this is, more precisely, a matter of 'lacking the sense of worry about losing control'. It is the sense of participants in flow that they can successfully handle any usual condition that comes along in their activity. On page 61 he further observes that 'what people enjoy is not the sense of *being* in control, but the sense of *exercising* control in difficult situations'.

Furthermore, components 1 and 6 are intricately intertwined: feeling competent in doing an activity generates a sense of being able to exercise control, especially in difficult situations. It follows that, to qualify as productive of flow, an activity must be seen by its participants as allowing for situations where control may be a challenge. They are aware of these situations, even though they are uncommon. Indeed, most of the time the activity presents the usual challenges, though stiff enough to generate flow. In such conditions participants execute the activity, while feeling that they can handle anything unusual that comes along. Additionally Elkington (2006, 2008) found in his research that trust in the other participants in the activity being pursued at the time is often an important condition for feeling that one has control.

These eight components are necessary conditions of flow; they must all be present for the participant to experience this state. If one or more of them are absent, the leisure experience at the time cannot be qualified as flow based. This is an important criterion. For example a person can be deeply involved (component 5) in a film or a roller coaster ride without having to be competent at doing the activity or feel a sense of control or both. If we adhere strictly to the eight components, these two activities cannot be described as flow based (they are casual leisure). On the other hand, if we avoid strict adherence, the two might then be regarded as flow based.

Indeed loose adherence to the eight components would expand immensely the list of flow-based activities. But this approach would also force an unwanted imprecision on the idea, making it scientifically less useful. Therefore it is best to stay with the strict version, labelling as flow those activities to which it applies and developing other concepts for those activities that are characterized by some but not all eight of the components (Stebbins 2010).

Flow in serious leisure

Given the criteria that distinguish serious, casual and project-based leisure – three main forms of leisure (see Stebbins 2007) – flow can only occur in the first. Serious leisure is the systematic pursuit of an amateur, hobbyist or volunteer activity sufficiently substantial, interesting and fulfilling for the participant to find a (leisure) career there acquiring and expressing a combination of its special skills, knowledge and experience. It is the skill, knowledge and experience in serious leisure that harmonize especially well with components 1, 2 and 6 in flow. That said, empirical evidence for this proposition is still thin (for a review see Stebbins 2010).

Casual leisure is immediately, intrinsically rewarding, relatively short-lived pleasurable activity, requiring little or no special training to enjoy it. According to this definition, which revolves around activity requiring little or no special training to enjoy it, casual leisure lacks the first component of flow. Some of the casual leisure activities, especially the sensory stimulation type, look as though they offer flow-based experiences. But application of the eight components contradicts this impression.

Project-based leisure, the third form comprising the serious leisure perspective, is a short-term, reasonably complicated, one-shot or occasional, though infrequent, creative undertaking carried out in free time, or time free of disagreeable obligation (Stebbins 2007). Flow is certainly possible in projects where some skill, knowledge or both are needed to complete them. It appears, however, that most for most leisure projects the needed skill and knowledge are fairly minimal, as in kit assembly, family history and one-off volunteer involvements.

In those serious pursuits qualified as flow based we would expect to find flow in their core activities, either all the time (as in basketball, alpine skiing, hang gliding and ice hockey) or a significant part of it (as in acting, bird watching, fishing ('when they're biting'), and mountain cycling).[1] Activities like these require physical skill commonly enacted with mental acuity and relevant knowledge. The twin components of competence and control are also obvious here. More generally, all the amateur activities and physically active hobbies would seem to generate full or partial flow.

Mountaineering

Mountaineering has been analysed as a hobby (Stebbins 2005). Using the following classification of mountain climbing, it can be shown that this leisure activity by no means always generates flow in its participants. The classification is a truncated version of the six-class Sierra Club rating system published in Mitchell's study (1983: 89–90). The intent here is to give an idea what the core activity of mountaineering actually looks like, and not to provide a technical description for climbers. Such would require much more detail, including addition of the many subdivisions within the more advanced classes.

The mountain climbing in which flow is most liked to be experienced is found in Classes 4 through 6, though to reach the approach (starting point of the planned ascent), climbing of the sort described in Classes 1 through 3 may also be required.

Class 1
Cross-country hiking. Hands not needed.

Class 2
Scrambling, using hands for balance. Rope not usually necessary or desired.

Class 3
Easy climbing.... Rope may be desired and important for safety of less experienced climbers.... Handholds and footholds are necessary.

Class 4
Roped climbing with belaying. Ropes will be used by almost all party members.

Class 5
Roped climbing with protection. The leader's progress is safeguarded by the placement of intermediate points of anchorage to the mountain between the belayer and the next belay point.

Class 6
Direct aid. Climbing with belaying. Upward progress is made by using chocks, pitons, slings and other devices as handholds and footholds.

In general, flow is felt more frequently as the class of mountaineering gets higher. Scrambling (Class 2) typically requires no equipment, for the climber needs only to use hands, feet and perhaps knees to mount successfully low vertical or nearly vertical surfaces. Nonetheless, this activity does concentrate the mind – generate flow – since scramblers must search for secure environmental features (e.g. rocks, roots, trees) for support and then, without falling, climb the surface. Commonly, scrambling at this level is required for one or a few brief periods during what is otherwise a Class 1 hike to a mountain summit or ridge top.

Class 3 mountaineering involves much longer and higher sessions of scrambling, wherein upward progress depends on finding the aforementioned environmental features. For seasoned participants the angle of ascent is not so severe that they need rope. Nonetheless, they experience flow, doing so much more frequently than in Class 2 activity.

Classes 4, 5 and 6 rank mountain climbing that is vertical or very close to it. It requires great concentration, simultaneously giving the participant a vertiginous view of the surrounding environment above, below, in back and to the sides. Flow is more or less continuous here. It is experienced while moving up the face being climbed, and is experienced through the panoramic views taken in while resting.

> At the most challenging levels, people actually report a *transcendence* of self, caused by the unusually high involvement with a system of action so much more complex than what one usually encounters in everyday life. The climber feels at one with the mountain, the clouds, the rays of the sun, and the tiny bugs moving in and out of the shadow of the fingers holding to the rock.
>
> (Csikszentmihalyi 1988: 33)

Yet, mountaineering fails to generate flow from start to finish, as do basketball, alpine skiing and hang gliding, for example. Most of the time climbers have to hike to the place where they can start climbing. That hike, often through forest and along a creek or river, may well be enjoyable (it can be long, too), but at the same time it is unlikely to lead to flow.

Conclusions

The desire to experience flow in leisure, in general, and mountaineering, in particular, is highly motivating, and the concept is clearly a major theoretic breakthrough for the study of leisure activities of great variety. That said, we cannot explain the appeal of all leisure using this idea. Even mountaineering at Class 6 generates flow only while ascending and descending a massive rock face. The comparatively dull part of the outing consisting mainly of the trek through the forest must be explained otherwise, such as by the need to persevere in serious leisure through its less agreeable aspects.

Note

1 A core activity is the distinctive set of interrelated actions or steps that must be followed to achieve the outcome or product the participant finds attractive (e.g. enjoyable, satisfying, fulfilling) (Stebbins 2007).

References

Csikszentmihalyi, M. (1988) 'The flow experience and its significance for human psychology', in M. Csikszentmihalyi and I. S. Csikszentmihalyi (eds) *Optimal experience: Psychological studies of flow in consciousness*, New York: Cambridge University Press: 15–35.

Csikszentmihalyi, M. (1990) *Flow: The psychology of optimal experience*, New York: Harper & Row.

Elkington, S. (2006) 'Exploring the nature of pre and post flow in serious leisure', in S. Elkington, I. Jones and L. Lawrence (eds) *Serious leisure: Extensions and applications*, LSA publication No. 95, Eastbourne: Leisure Studies Association: 145–159.

Elkington, S. (2008) 'The need for theoretical originality when taking the flow of leisure seriously', in P. Gilchrist and B. Wheaton (eds) *Whatever happened to the leisure society? Theory, debate and policy*, LSA publication No. 102, Eastbourne,: Leisure Studies Association: 135–164.

Mitchell, R. (1983) *Mountain experience: The psychology and sociology of adventure*, Chicago, IL: University of Chicago Press.

Stebbins, R. A. (2005) *Challenging mountain nature: Risk, motive, and lifestyle in three hobbyist sports*, Calgary, AB: Detselig (also online, available at: www.seriousleisure. net/Digital Library).

Stebbins, R. A. (2007) *Serious leisure: A perspective for our time*, New Brunswick, NJ: Transaction.

Stebbins, R. A. (2010) 'Flow in serious leisure: Nature and prevalence', *Leisure Studies Association Newsletter*, 87(November): 21–23 (also online, available at: www.seriousleisure.net/Digital Library 'Leisure reflections', no. 25).

10 Mountaineering tourism experience and the protective frame

A reversal theory perspective[1]

Susan Houge Mackenzie

Introduction

Mountaineering, along with a range of traditional adventure activities, has become increasingly commodified as a product of the growing adventure tourism industry. In order to better understand these unique mountain-based tourism experiences, researchers may benefit from moving beyond traditional quantitative, market segmentation approaches. Employing psychological approaches, such as those examined in Chapter 9, may help illuminate how mountaineering tourism experiences can vary both from traditional consumer experiences, as well as from mountaineering recreation experiences. To this end, this chapter proposes alternative psychological concepts and evaluates them in the context of an autoethnographical case study of mountaineering tourism in Bolivia. It is hoped that this perspective may illuminate new ways of conceptualizing mountaineering tourism experiences. Specifically, the psychological framework of 'reversal theory' is used to explain: (a) paradoxical desires for risk and safety in adventure and mountaineer tourism and (b) emotional and motivational fluctuations experienced by mountaineer tourists. The importance of creating a 'protective frame' to ensure enjoyable experiences is explored, along with key factors that can influence this frame. Theoretical and practical implications for adventure and mountaineering tourism researchers and practitioners are discussed, as well as the potential for psychological frameworks and autoethnography to enhance tourism discourses.

Mountaineering tourism versus adventure recreation

Research has generally treated adventure tourism, and by extension mountaineering tourism, as a form of adventure recreation. This research has also focused primarily on 'external' views of preconceived market segments and the physical risks inherent in adventure tourism (Weber 2001). Due to the commercial nature of adventure tourism, there may be a number of inherent differences between mountaineering recreationalists versus mountaineering tourists. Research has yet to establish whether recreational models of experience and motivation apply to adventure tourism. In adventure recreation, positive outcomes appear to result from increased opportunities to develop personal skills, exercise personal control over risk, experience autonomy and overcome high challenges. In mountaineering tourism, these opportunities may be constrained by commercial expediency or management approaches. Thus, psychological models applied in adventure recreation studies may require modification for mountaineering tourism contexts.

Reversal theory and mountaineering tourism

Adventure and mountaineering tourism are characterized not only by physical risks (e.g. injury or death), but also social (e.g. humiliation) and emotional (e.g. fear, anxiety) risks. While the physical risks inherent in mountaineering tourism are presumably 'managed' by responsible operators, there are additional risks (e.g. psychological) that may be (mis)managed, or overlooked entirely, by operators. Adventure tourists' paradoxical desires for risk *and* safety (e.g. Arnould *et al.* 1999; Holyfield 1999; Holyfield *et al.* 2005) requires that operators 'hide' one of two key elements from participants (Fletcher 2010). Providers can either increase risk perceptions while minimizing 'actual' risk (Holyfield *et al.* 2005) or, conversely, minimize risk perceptions in activities with relatively high levels of 'actual' risk (Palmer 2004), such as mountaineering. Research indicates that adventure tourists only seek risk to the extent that they feel simultaneously protected from various forms of risk by operators (e.g. Cloke and Perkins 2002). Thus mountaineering tourism requires a framework that can account for this paradox. Reversal theory (e.g. Apter 1982, 2001) is a general psychological model that describes the structure of subjective experiences and offers a theoretical basis from which to understand seemingly paradoxical states and emotional fluctuations (e.g. relaxation, excitement, anxiety) in mountaineering tourism.

Reversal theory posits that seemingly paradoxical behaviours (such as the voluntary risk-taking inherent in mountaineering) can be explained by predictable underlying structures (i.e. motivational states or 'frames of mind') that dictate these behaviours and cognitions (Apter 1992). Reversal theory proposes four pairs of motivational states that account for subjective experiences and emotions. Psychologically healthy individuals are able to alternatively satisfy opposing needs via regular *reversals* amongst the states in Table 10.1 (Frey 1999).

Table 10.1 Motivational state pairs in reversal theory

Telic: serious, outcome oriented, arousal avoidant	Paratelic: playful, process oriented, arousal seeking
Conformist: rule abiding	Negativistic: rebellious
Mastery: domination oriented	Sympathy: relationship oriented
Autic: self-focused, concern for self	Alloic: other focused, concern for others

The protective frame and positive mountaineering tourism experiences

Of perhaps greatest relevance to mountaineering tourism is the *protective frame* concept. This concept developed from a diverse range of case studies that refuted traditional optimal arousal models by showing that high arousal could be interpreted as anxiety *or* excitement (Apter 1992; Kerr 1999). A 'protective frame' provides feelings of protection from risk or danger and is generally operationalized as confidence in oneself, others and/or equipment (Apter 1993). When the protective frame is active, heightened arousal and challenges associated with risk are experienced as exciting; thus the presence of a protective frame characterizes a playful (paratelic) state. When the protective frame is lacking, a serious (telic) state ensues wherein heightened arousal is experienced as anxiety.

A useful metaphor for this is viewing a tiger in a cage, a generally exciting experience as the danger (tiger) is coupled with an element of protection (the cage) (Apter 1992). Conversely, the absence of a tiger (i.e. danger) would likely be boring, just as the absence of a cage (protection) would incite fear. Thus excitement (pleasant heightened arousal) is only possible when risk is coupled with some form of protection. Reversal theorists postulate that a strong, resilient protective frame is fundamental to exciting, playful (paratelic) experiences (Apter 1993). Without protection, the risk-taking inherent in mountaineering tourism will likely be experienced as anxiety and fear, whereas within this 'psychological bubble' it is predicted to feel exciting. Successful adventure operators are able to reduce actual risk while 'effectively commodifying the thrills within' (Cater 2006: 317). Thus the protective frame may be an essential element of mountaineering tourism satisfaction, as explored in the previous chapter.

Autoethnographical case study: mountaineering tourism in Bolivia

Recent tourism research reflects the emergence of more interpretative and critical forms of inquiry. Participatory research and experimental writing are being embraced and narrative methods increasingly emphasize reflexivity and personal voices, including those of researchers themselves. Autoethnography is an important part of this methodological shift that Denzin and Lincoln (1994) identified as the fifth moment in the history of qualitative research. A central distinction between autoethnography and traditional methodologies is that researcher biases and reflexivity are openly acknowledged and discussed in autoethnography. In contrast to ethnography, in which the researcher attempts to become an insider, the researcher in autoethnographical inquiry *is* the insider who provides unique insights into personal and emotional lifeworlds (Ateljevic *et al.* 2007). Critical literature regarding situated methodologies supports the use of emergent methods such as autoethnography to enhance tourism research (e.g. Hall 2004).

Autoethnography has been cited as a methodology with 'considerable untapped opportunity' to explain leisure activities (Anderson and Austin 2012:

131). This approach has been used successfully to describe a range of sport and tourism experiences, including mountain guiding (Beedie 2003). The current case study used *analytical* autoethnography to capture a mountaineering tourism experience as it unfolded and employed a reversal theory framework to conceptually analyse data. Analytical autoethnography is more aligned with traditional social science epistemologies and theoretical analyses than *evocative* autoethnography (Snow *et al.* 2003). However, evocative autoethnography techniques are used when presenting data as this allows readers to empathize (Anderson and Austin 2012) and, hopefully, gain a fuller understanding of the author's experiences as they relate to theoretical explanations. This study was guided by Anderson's (2006) five key autoethnographic features: complete member status of researcher; analytic reflexivity; narrative visibility of the researcher's self; dialogue with informants beyond the self; and commitment to theoretical analysis.

Autoethnographical data was collected when I, the author, embarked on my first mountaineering tourism experience in Bolivia. During a three-day guided climb of Huayna Potosi, I collected detailed qualitative data on the psychological aspects of my experience throughout each day, as well as supplemental data from my fellow mountaineer tourists. Although Huayna Potosi rises just shy of 20,000 feet, it is considered 'the easiest "6,000[metre]er" in the world' (*Refugio Huayna Potosí* n.d.). As such, it attracts novice tourists, such as myself, with little or no mountaineering experience. My climbing group consisted of: Scott, the author's best friend; Sally and Fred, recent acquaintances; Mike, an independent traveller; and the guides Juan, Oscar and Pedro.[2]

Data consisted of diary entries, experiential diagrams, emails and field notes. The 'experiential diagrams' visually charted my current mental state (e.g. 'high' ascending lines=positive mood; 'low' descending lines=negative mood) coupled with field notes. Textual analysis of these data was conducted by identifying key themes relating to influences on emotional states. Raw quotes associated with a particular part of the trip (e.g. Day 2, evening) were grouped together within the experiential diagram and perused for distinct themes. Repetitious themes were identified in each data source along with themes related to reversal theory constructs (e.g. motivational states, reversals, protective frames). The metamotivational state coding schedule was also used to guide data coding (O'Connell *et al.* 1991). Multiple data sources were used to triangulate and verify the consistency of interpretations, while integration of data within a visual diagram clarified how this experience unfolded in relation to state changes (positive or negative) and pertinent reversal theory constructs. Finally, an audit trail was conducted by an external auditor with methodological and subject matter expertise. The auditor did not identify inconsistencies in the data analyses.

Results and discussion

Data analysis suggested four key elements that appeared to influence the protective frame, motivational states, emotions (positive or negative) and overall satisfaction during this mountaineering tourism experience. These factors were the guides, the equipment, other participants and the environment. Each factor is discussed below in relation to practical and theoretical implications.

Guides. Interpersonal interactions with our guides emerged as the single most influential factor in determining overall experience quality and satisfaction. The guides' apparent lack of concern, organization and effective communication damaged my confidence in their ability to protect us. While these perceptions may have resulted from my Euro-centric background and expectations of guided tours, the guides' nonchalant approach greatly diminished my protective frame and activated a serious, arousal-avoidant (*telic*) motivational state characterized by concern for myself over others (*autic* and *mastery* states) during the majority of our climb. This was demonstrated particularly on the first day during gear fitting when our guides either did not have appropriate equipment or gave us broken or ill-fitted gear, and the last day on the final ascent when they did not communicate hazards or climbing instructions. The quotes below illustrate these issues:

> While driving through traffic into middle of La Paz the driver seemed clueless – no idea where our hostel was. We had to make two separate gear stops ... it seemed disorganised and unnecessary. The guides/owner didn't care that the gear didn't fit right or was broken. No communication between the owner/staff and clients – no one seemed to know what was going on.
>
> The first day ... the owner ... took us to different sites to get our gear, all of which seemed to be broken or in some state of disrepair. Jackets did not have zippers; the pants were too small, etc.... After much trying on of different gear and swapping around and fixing things, we got very frustrated.
>
> Pedro didn't seem too concerned with safety in general – he even questioned my 'unnecessary' decision to wear a helmet. I frequently asked him whether the ice was stable, only to be asked: how much to you both weigh? And then told we were 'heavy'.... This did not bode well with me. He also neglected to alert us when we were crossing many of the crevasses which littered the walk up to the summit and only spoke to us to complain at how slowly we were walking, even though Scott's crampons didn't fit and kept falling off. Pedro then asked why we had these crampons as they were too 'technical' for us.... It was his company that gave us this equipment ... Scott's helmet broke half way up and that, combined with his poor headlight, no Spanish, and altitude sickness, meant he was ... getting dragged up the mountain behind me with [no] idea what lay ahead.

Conversely, during social 'down time' with guides, I became more personally acquainted with them and felt affectionate, sociable and interested in their personal histories. '[Over dinner we had] some nice interactions with the hut staff and local [guides] – we learned about them and their history.' These segments of the trip were characterized by reversals to the *alloic* (concern for others) and *sympathy* (relationship-oriented) motivational states.

My interpretations of guide behaviours largely determined whether I experienced the adventure as pleasant excitement (within a protective frame) or unpleasant anxiety (without a protective frame), and thereby overall satisfaction levels. While there were episodes in which I felt excited (*paratelic* motivational state; e.g. afternoon of Day 1), the majority of the experience was characterized by unpleasant anxiety (telic motivational state) due to low satisfaction with guide–client interactions. It is also noteworthy to consider at this point how the secondary factors discussed below (i.e. equipment, environment) may have been mitigated or transformed into positive experiences through different guiding approaches. For example, the guides may have been able to instigate reversals in clients' motivational states through effective comunication and framing of hazards.

Equipment. A related, but distinct, factor that influenced my experience was the type and quality of equipment provided. As detailed in the quotes above, poor equipment negatively influenced the mountaineering experience daily and almost prevented my climbing partner (to whom I was roped) from ascending on the final day as his crampons were falling off. The poor quality, or absence, of equipment, was apparent from the start of the trip and led to negative emotions and low satisfaction throughout the group. For example, helmets were not provided until we insisted on them, at which point they were borrowed from another group descending the mountain. 'When we questioned the wisdom of not distributing helmets for ice climbing, we were greeted with laughs and told that our guides were professionals ... [As though this meant we couldn't get hurt].' These events further eroded my protective frame, through lack of trust in the equipment and the guides who distributed it, and fostered unpleasant anxiety throughout the trip.

Other participants. Fellow clients played a lesser role than the guides in influencing my motivational and emotional states; however there were instances in which peers elicited strong emotions. For instance, feelings of playfulness and camaraderie developed during training (e.g. while practising 'walking like ducks' and self-arresting) and evening socializing on the first day (e.g. while caring for a fellow tourist, Fred, with a stomach ailment).

> Much improved attitudes in whole group in the second half of training and on the way down from training. Great meal; nice warm fire. People were happy, sharing stories, socialising, feeling well fed and relaxed – except for Fred [who was] sick. I wanted to look after him...
>
> Good team spirit in group – we all wanted to help out and encourage Fred. Excited to go up.

While ascending the mountain, however, Fred's sluggish pace became annoying as I selfishly preferred to walk faster without feeling 'stuck' behind someone (telic, mastery motivational states). I also felt anxious and frustrated by peers' slow progress when we were roped together in unstable ice and snow conditions. '[Fred and Mike] were really struggling. It was annoying to keep waiting for them.' Depending on my motivational state and protective frame (or lack thereof), other clients elicited feelings ranging from concern, caring and affection to anxiety, frustration and anger. Thus the impact of clients' diverse motivations and skill levels on emotions and satisfaction in mountaineering tourism groups is worthy of consideration.

Environmental conditions. The physical environment also influenced my motivational and emotional states and satisfaction. Feeling warm, well-fed and physically comfortable (e.g. evening of Day 1, morning of Day 2), facilitated playful (paratelic), other-focused (alloic) and relationship-oriented (sympathy) motivational states. However, the novel and unstable natural environment also diminished my sense of protection from danger (paratelic protective frame) while climbing. This was particularly evident on the final assent when ice was cracking continuously under our feet and we travelled in darkness over crevasses without warning.

> My trouble was the sheer terror I felt at being stuck on what appeared to be unstable ice and snow, roped up to a … guide who [did not seem to care about] our safety, or instructing us on what to do in the event that we fell down a wall, there was an avalanche, or a crevasse opened up beneath us.
>
> As we stopped to watch the sun rise over Bolivia … Scott heard the sound of a train roaring down the mountain, which turned out to be an avalanche! He told us to get to the side, while our guides started laughing. They said it was too far up to reach us. How reassuring. Now all I wanted to do was get the hell off that mountain and spent the next few hours trying to put one crampon in front of the other and quelling the rising panic I felt every time we jumped a crevasse or the ice popped. At two points Sally slid down sheer ice faces and we had to dig in to break her fall.

I realized that ice was shifting due to warmer conditions and that many groups were using the same trail, which crossed obscured crevasses; however my status as a tourist with limited technical knowledge precluded a reasoned, accurate risk assessment and diminished my protective frame. These conditions, coupled with my mountaineering ignorance and witnessing two avalanches, further contributed to my serious (telic), self-focused (autic) motivational state.

Reversal theory posits that, despite these environmental trepidations, either (a) instigating motivational state reversals or (b) lowering felt arousal levels may have positively transformed my experience. For example, if the guides reframed hazards or setbacks as exciting and adventurous, this may have instigated a reversal to a playful (paratelic) state in which environmental challenges were relished (e.g. excitement due to a paratelic protective frame). Alternatively, providing more information regarding hazards and how to safely negotiate hazards may have sufficiently lowered my arousal levels and instigated pleasant telic emotions. These psychological changes may have helped us to overcome the 'crux' of the climb, and thereby achieve a key expectation of most mountaineering tourists: reaching the summit. As many mountaineer tourists, perhaps unrealistically, expect to summit, fostering positive psychological states that give them the best chance of achieving this goal, or more realistic goals and expectations, may markedly increased overall satisfaction with a mountaineering trip. By using techniques such as overtly demonstrating their expertise, using more frequent and informative communication, discussing hazards and safety techniques and/or outwardly displaying genuine, caring behaviours towards their clients, guides may instil greater client confidence (protective frame) and facilitate an exciting and enjoyable climb in the face of obvious environmental dangers.

In summary, this mountaineering tourism experience was primarily characterized by the absence of a protective frame due to guiding styles, equipment, and the natural environment. The motivational states most commonly identified were the telic (serious, outcome-oriented, arousal-avoidant), autic (self-focused) and mastery (domination-oriented) states. Reversals to other-focused (alloic) and relationship-oriented (sympathy) states were primarily experienced while resting or during 'down time' when I could converse and share my experience with others, or assist struggling group members.

Implications for theory and practice

This case has a range of practical and theoretical implications. It emphasizes the crucial role of guides in fostering and maintaining a 'protective frame' for clients, as conceptualized within reversal theory. It also identifies potential motivational differences in mountaineering tourists versus mountain recreationalists, and reinforces the importance of ensuring that client expectations of mountaineering tourism match their experiences. Furthermore, data highlights potentially overlooked psychosocial risks involved in mountaineering tourism, in addition to physical risks. Analysis suggests that psychological constructs such as reversal theory's motivational states and the protective frame may be useful tools for improving management strategies and understanding mountaineering tourists' experiences.

Potential differences amongst mountaineer tourists and recreationists in terms of their background and expectations (e.g. comfort, protection, fun for mountaineer adventure tourists versus hardship and personal challenge for mountaineer adventure recreationists) may contribute to these findings. These differences could lead to poor outcomes for both tourists and operators if, as is generally the case, mountaineering recreationists become mountaineering guides and continue to maintain 'recreational' expectations and notions of adventure in an mountaineering tourism setting. While positive mountaineering recreation experiences result from opportunities to exercise personal control over risks, feelings of competence gained through experience, and matching challenges with personal skills (e.g. Ewert and Hollenhorst 1989), this case suggests that different elements may facilitate optimal mountaineering tourism experiences. While true risk, danger and uncertainty may optimize mountaineering recreation experiences, mountaineering tourists may respond negatively to these perceptions. These findings are somewhat incongruent with research suggesting that adventure tourists are motivated by fear and thrills (Cater 2006). Rather, the mountaineering tourists in this case sought a 'protective frame' in which they felt sufficiently protected from the physical risks to enjoy a challenging, yet 'safe' experience. Reversal theory helps to explain this 'adventure paradox' sought by mountaineering tourists. The paradoxical desire for perceived risk and security in mountaineering tourism may not be paradoxical when understood in the context of the protective frame and motivational state changes. In this case, the tourists were not seeking risk, but rather a 'secure' environment in which to successfully complete an activity beyond personal skill levels. Thus, the adventure paradox may result from motivational state fluctuations and the presence of a protective frame during mountaineering tourism. Understanding the telic and paratelic states, accompanying emotions and identifying clients' dynamic motivational reversals may allow operators to react more effectively.

There are a number of strategies that guides could utilize to influence clients' motivational states, attentional focus and emotional responses. For example, in the telic (serious) state, high arousal is experienced as anxiety. One way to reduce this unpleasant emotion is for guides to help lower clients' arousal levels using relaxation techniques, such as breathing or concentration exercises, offering alternative options, or providing more detailed instructions and information in difficult sections. Alternatively, guides may develop strategies to help clients' reverse to the paratelic (playful) state in which high arousal is pleasantly experienced as excitement. Strategies to induce this reversal might include the use of humour, increasing clients' focus on process and the present moment (rather than future outcomes) and reframing perceived risks as exciting challenges. Guides might also seek to induce a reversal to the telic (serious) state if clients are insufficiently focused on risks and key safety information. For example, guides could discuss previous accidents or potential hazards at key points if they wish to induce the telic state. These are just a few examples of how managers can teach guides to identify clients' motivational states and react effectively to maximize safey and satisfaction.

This case also suggested that operators could adjust their mountaineering products to suit true novices. Although Beedie and Hudson (2003: 627) claim 'there exists something of a paradox whereby the more detailed, planned and logistically smooth an itinerary becomes the more removed the experience is from the notion of adventure', this case recommends that providing a detailed and logistically well-organized itinerary may be highly desirable for some mountaineering tourists. Ensuring a trip is systematically planned and managed may (a) allow guides to focus their attention on providing skill instruction, safety information and building client trust, rather than becoming distracted by logistics and (b) foster the protective frame necessary for clients to experience positive emotions associated with adventure.

Key factors that may influence mountaineer tourists' protective frames and risk perceptions were identified in the data: guides, equipment, environment and other clients. Although operators have less control over the latter two elements, all of these aspects can be managed to an extent. In terms of guides and equipment, managers should consider broadening their training focus beyond physical risks to include enhancing cross-cultural communication skills and empathy-building strategies with clients. Pre-trip meetings should also include activities that allow guides to gain a clear understanding of clients' diverse abilities, backgrounds, expectations and concerns prior to the trip, while building trust and relationships amongst guides and the group. Management should also select appropriate routes for the group to ensure that challenges can be met or exceeded by clients' skill levels. In addition, at least two viable contingency options should be available to ensure that (a) guides feel no pressure to complete an unsafe intinerary and (b) clients' expectations are still met despite potential changes. During the trip, guides should be trained to provide continual skill training and safety information and frequently monitor clients' psychological states. Management should also focus on overtly displaying quality equipment and well-organized logistics from the outset, as this will further foster clients' protective frame in the initial trip stages.

Conclusion

At a theoretical level, reversal theory is a paradigm that may account for the 'paradoxical' nature of mountaineering tourism and emotional fluctuations during these experiences. By fostering a salient protective frame for clients (e.g. via developing personal skills and confidence in guides and equipment) operators may potentially reduce psychological risks, and allow physical risks to be experienced as simultaneously exciting and secure. As this has been proposed as the penultimate goal of successful adventure tourism experiences (e.g. Cater 2006; Fletcher 2010), it is important to develop a robust theoretical rationale of how this experience can be facilitated and why it does (or does not) occur in mountaineering tourism. This case study suggests that guides, equipment, the environment and the social group can all contribute to or detract from positive mountaineering tourism experiences. Managers should therefore closely examine guide training programmes, equipment purchasing and maintenance protocols, pre-trip activities and trip protocols to ensure the clients' protective frame is reinforced at each point. Guide training in motivational state recognition and strategies to successfully induce reversals or affect arousal levels may also help maximize client satisfaction. Furthermore, psychological concepts, such as the protective frame and the telic and paratelic states, can help tourism managers identify ways to improve mountaineering tourists' experiences and overall satisfaction.

Notes

1 Please note that this chapter is informed by a larger research study conducted on adventure tourism in South America. Expanded information regarding this case study and the project can be found in the following articles:

196 S. Houge Mackenzie

Houge Mackenzie, S. and Kerr, J. H. (2012) 'A (mis)guided adventure tourism experience: An autoethnographic analysis of mountaineering in Bolivia', *Journal of Sport and Tourism*, 17(2): 125–144.

Houge Mackenzie, S. and Kerr, J. H. (2013) 'Stress and emotions at work: Adventure tourism guiding experiences in South America', *Tourism Management*, 36: 3–14.

Houge Mackenzie, S. and Kerr, J. H. (2013) 'Can't we all just get along? Emotions and the team guiding experience in adventure tourism', Special edition of *Journal of Destination Marketing and Management*, 2(2): 85–93.

2 All names are pseudonyms.

References

Anderson, L. (2006) 'Analytic autoethnography', *Journal of Contemporary Ethnography*, 35(4): 373–394.

Anderson, L. and Austin, M. (2012) 'Auto-ethnography in leisure studies', *Leisure Studies*, 31(2): 131–146.

Apter, M. J. (1982) *The experience of motivation: The theory of psychological reversals*, London: Academic Press.

Apter, M. J. (1992) *The dangerous edge: The psychology of excitement*, New York: Free Press.

Apter, M. J. (1993) 'Phenomenological frames and the paradoxes of experience', in J. H. Kerr, S. J. Murgatroyd and M. J. Apter (eds) *Advances in reversal theory*, Amsterdam: Swets & Zeitlinger: 27–39.

Apter, M. J. (ed.) (2001) *Motivational styles in everyday life: A guide to reversal theory*, Washington, DC: American Psychological Association.

Arnould, E., Price, L. and Otnes, C. (1999) 'Making magic consumption: A study of white-water river rafting', *Journal of Contemporary Ethnography*, 28(1): 33–68.

Ateljevic, I., Pritchard, A. and Morgan, N. (2007) *The critical turn in tourism studies: Innovative research methods*, Oxford: Elsevier.

Beedie, P. (2003) 'Mountain guiding and adventure tourism: Reflections on the choreography of the experience', *Leisure Studies*, 22(2): 147–167.

Beedie, P. and Hudson, S. (2003) 'Emergence of mountain-based adventure tourism', *Annals of Tourism Research*, 30(3): 625–643.

Cater, C. I. (2006) 'Playing with risk? Participant perceptions of risk and management implications in adventure tourism', *Tourism Management*, 27(2): 317–325.

Cloke, P. and Perkins, H. C. (2002) 'Commodification and adventure in New Zealand tourism', *Current Issues in Tourism*, 5(6): 521–549.

Denzin, N. K. and Lincoln, Y. S. (eds) (1994) *Handbook of qualitative research*, Thousand Oaks, CA: Sage.

Ewert, A. and Hollenhorst, S. (1989) 'Testing the adventure model: Empirical support for a model of risk recreation participation', *Journal of Leisure Research*, 21(2): 124–139.

Fletcher, R. (2010) 'The emperor's new adventure: Public secrecy and the paradox of adventure tourism', *Journal of Contemporary Ethnography*, 39(1): 6–33.

Frey, K. P. (1999) 'Reversal theory: Basic concepts', in J. H. Kerr (ed.) *Experiencing sport: Reversal theory*, New York: John Wiley & Sons: 3–17.

Hall, M. (2004) 'Reflexivity and tourism research', in J. Phillimore and L. Goodson (eds) *Qualitative research in tourism*, London: Routledge: 137–155.

Holyfield, L. (1999) 'Manufacturing adventure: The buying and selling of emotions', *Journal of Contemporary Ethnography*, 28(1): 3–32.

Holyfield, L., Jonas, L. and Zajicek, A. (2005) 'Adventure without risk is like Disney-land', in S. Lyng (ed.) *Edgework: The sociology of risk-taking*, New York: Routledge: 173–185.

Kerr, J. H. (ed.) (1999) *Experiencing sport: Reversal theory*, New York: John Wiley & Sons.

O'Connell, K. A., Potocky, M., Cook, M. R. and Gerkovich, M. M. (1991) *Metamotivational state interview and coding schedule instruction manual*, Kansas City, MO: Midwest Research Institute.

Palmer, C. (2004) 'Death, danger, and the selling of risk in adventure sport', in B. Wheaton (ed.) *Understanding lifestyle sports*, New York: Routledge: 55–69.

Refugio Huayna Potosí (n.d.) 'Huayna Potosí'. Online, available at: www.huayna-potosi.com/mountaineering.html#huayna (accessed 12 April 2012).

Snow, D., Morrill, C. and Anderson, L. (2003) 'Elaborating analytical ethnography: Linking fieldwork and theory', *Ethnography*, 4(2): 181–200.

SummitPost.org (n.d.) 'Huayna Potosi'. Online, available at: www.summitpost.org/huayna-potosi/150675 (accessed 12 April 2012).

Weber, K. (2001) 'Outdoor adventure tourism: A review of research approaches', *Annals of Tourism Research*, 28(2): 360–377.

11 Mountaineering personality and risk

Erik Monasterio and Eric Brymer

Mountaineering challenges

Torres Del Paron – Peru

The granite friction on the sloping belly of the Paron Towers was good, deceptively good. With my brother Grigota, we were climbing 2,000 m above the serpentine road that wound its way into the Paron Valley of the Cordillera Blanca, in Peru. With a dominant 'El Niño' weather pattern it had been a difficult climbing season; it was hot and humid with mosquitoes buzzing above 5,000 m, and heavy rainstorms by mid-afternoon. Grigota belayed from a scoop on the enormous slab face. Over the years constant rain had polished the granite wall featureless. The only protection we could find, in a shallow crack by the belay station was useless, but the climbing was straightforward. Grigota kept paying the rope out ... and the friction holding me to the wall was good ... so I kept moving. As I climbed there were no cracks or fissures on the rock, so no protection, but the friction was, oh ... so good. With feet spaced well apart, maximizing the contact of the rubber soles with the granite wall and flat hands pushing up the slope, I kept moving. Twenty metres out of the belay station, there was still no protection. The gentle angle had become deceptively steep. 'Any pro, bro?' Hmm, nothing, so I stopped moving to have a good look around. When I stopped, the balance no longer felt so good.

Above me I spotted a thin hairline crack, a subtle wrinkle on the youthful rock. To reach that crack I would have to step high and rock over a mantle. I hesitated for a moment; this was an irreversible move. The simplicity of stepping over something that cannot be reversed embodies the spirit of adventure and exploration. By making that single move we would cross a threshold where success on the pitch was measured against certain death. The finer the balance between difficulty and ability, the better the adventure and the sweeter the taste of the summit. I took the step and crossed the threshold where great adventure and tragedy lies in wait! I reached up to the crack; it was the thinnest of lines and choked up with dirt, but there was nothing else. With hands and feet spread apart and pushing into the wall, the balance was still OK. But I needed to free my hands to clean the crack. I pushed down hard on to the balls of my feet, rested my elbows on the rock and with one free hand started cleaning the crack – it wasn't much of a crack. From my harness I unclipped a piton and scraped away, revealing a margin so thin it was almost useless. The tension through my flexed ankles caused increasing calf strain. I leaned into the slab and shifted the weight on to my elbows. I shook each foot, one at a time, trying to ease the strain, but the pain increased. I cleaned some more. I repeated the motion through my feet, but each time the recovery was less effective. Despite the urgent cleaning it looked like the crack would be too thin to take the piton. I looked down past my brother, past the 100 m of climbing we had just completed, and straight down the 600 m ravine we had climbed the day before. The Paron River water foamed into a cavalcade of white caps, I was stuck and this was serious!

The aching and cramping in my legs disproportionally intensified with the realization of the situation. Trying to steady myself I again leaned on to the rock, rested my left elbow and with my left hand held the thin piton to the crack. I hammered gently and the piton danced refusing to bite. Mosquitoes swarmed my arms and face. The sweat of fear and exhaustion burned my eyes and dripped steadily on to the rock. I persevered with gentle hammer blows until finally the piton held. With each blow it crept in deeper. Then in desperation I gave a solid blow. The piton jumped out of the crack, bounced and disappeared down the precipice.

The fear of falling intensified with waves of calf cramp and panic. The belay had no chance of holding a fall and so I yelled to Grigota to take himself off the rope. He could still down climb to safety. Shaking his head he emphatically refused. I insisted, but he would have none of it – 'work it out, I am with you bro…' My legs shook uncontrollably. I was fighting for both our lives. I unclipped the last (knife-blade) piton from my harness, placed it in the crack and again gingerly hammered. It held. The thin blade slid in a couple of centimetres. As it crept in some more the hammering sounds became reassuringly duller. The pain through my legs was excruciating. I hit harder and then again the piton jumped out, somersaulting and bouncing, heading straight for Grigota. As the piton bounced away the passage of time froze – we were doomed! The only piton that had a chance of biting into the crack was falling away. Everything stopped, the image in my mind frozen in a still-life frame. It was trance-like. The spell was finally broken when Grigota reached out and caught the flying piton! 'This time, use a sling and secure the piton to the rope, bro.' The third attempt succeeded and the piton slid far enough into the crack to clip the rope and rest.

As I hung the pent-up pressure just drained away allowing me to recover. I could then climb on and eventually reach a safe balcony of rock. Not realizing that behind us a thick chariot of clouds was moving up the valley we committed further up the face, swapping leads. Undeterred Grigota ran out the next pitch over poorly protected ground. Absorbed, we just kept moving, driven for the summit. Then in an instant the valley fell asleep, the mosquitoes disappeared and the sky blackened. The flaming filaments of lightning heralded the first roar of thunder. There were no abseil points or escape routes, and so as the first drops of rain built to streams of water we began down-climbing. When there are no choices, decisions are quite simple – we descended. The tropical rain didn't dampen the feverish pitch. The water gushed down and we pushed hard into the rock. The friction was gone and blindly we groped. The water seemed possessed, committed to washing us away. It ran up my arms, into my face, punched my chest and bounced off my shoes. I remembered what a Spanish philosopher once said summarizing the human condition, 'The best a man can do is hope', and against all odds that is all we did – hoped. And that was enough to keep us moving. Lower down Grigota managed to secure himself sufficiently to protect me over the difficult, final descent to the balcony. Then in a surreal display of controlled desperation, he free-climbed to my side. We fixed the rope and retreated back to high camp.

Introduction

The anecdote of an alpine climb by one of the authors (E. M.) is included to portray the type of experience encountered and courted by mountaineers. This type of experience is not rare in high performance and exploratory mountaineering. The description highlights many important characteristics associated with high performance mountaineering, which will be the focus of this chapter. Informed from the basis of personal experience and research interest we argue that mountaineers are not only driven and influenced by innate personality characteristics, but also seek out a range of experiences associated with mountaineering, which includes but is not limited to; a search for mastery in challenging and unstable environments, confrontation with varying degrees of risk and risk-taking, the search for freedom and the transcendence of fear, physically and mentally demanding challenges, and the unique camaraderie found in situations of mutual reliance in isolated, stressful and dangerous situations.

We will summarize findings from two main areas of research; quantitative data from personality models exploring the influence of personality factors on mountaineers and qualitative data from phenomenological studies exploring the meaning of mountaineering through first person experiences.

Mountaineering

Mountaineering is the sport of climbing mountains, which often incorporates the skills of alpine rock and ice climbing. Mountaineering has for a long time been regarded as a high risk sport that can lead to severe physical injuries and fatalities (Malcolm 2001; Monasterio 2005; Pollard and Clarke 1988). Paradoxically, the popularity of mountaineering has continued to increase in the past 20 years and it is now one of the fastest growing outdoor sporting activities, despite the significant risks (Castanier *et al.* 2010). Dramatically publicized disasters such as the 1996 and 2004 Everest tragedies in which a total of eight climbers (five from two commercial expeditions) and six climbers died respectively, appear to have done little to dissuade climbers. The number of commercial guiding companies continues to grow and the list of paying clients increases, with many adventure-climbing companies offering novices guided ascents of the world's highest peaks, such as Mt Everest for a fee of $40,000 to $50,000 (Alavrez *et al.* 2011).

Personality characteristics

Sensation seeking

A number of studies have investigated the relationship between personality traits and participation in high risk physical sports, such as mountaineering. Sensation seeking is by far the most consistently studied personality factor in the literature (Castanier *et al.* 2010; Cronin 1991; Diehm and Armatas 2004; Freixanet 1991; Jack and Ronan 1998; Zuckerman 1983). Zuckerman (1979) defined sensation seeking as 'the need for varied, novel, and complex sensations and experiences and the willingness to take physical and social risks for the sake of such experience' (p. 10). Most studies have found that high risk sports participants, including mountaineers tend to score higher on Zuckerman's Sensation Seeking (SS) Scale compared to low risk sports participants and control groups (Cronin 1991; Freixanet 1991; Jack and Ronan 1998; Zuckerman 1983; Fowler *et al.* 1980). The sensation-seeking model has to some extent dominated the traditional view that mountaineers are driven by an instinctive need for new or novel experiences and intense sensations, attracting the pejorative label of 'adrenaline junkies'. The type T theory follows a similar logic and explains mountaineering experiences as the realization of a deviant personality trait, characterized by the need for uncertainty, novelty, ambiguity, variety and unpredictability (Self *et al.* 2007).

Neuroticism and extraversion

A smaller number of studies have also considered other personality variables, such as neuroticism, extraversion and conscientiousness (Castanier *et al.* 2010; Freixanet 1991). Freixanet (1991) investigated the personality traits of high-physical risk sports participants, including 97 alpine climbers and mountaineers, and found that extraversion was positively correlated, while neuroticism was negatively correlated to high risk climbing. They found that there was no difference in personality traits between alpine climbers (who had participated in several expeditions to the Himalayas at altitudes greater than 8,000 m) and mountaineers (mountain climbers and mountain skiers). They determined that alpine and mountain climbers generally presented with a personality profile characterized by extraversion, emotional stability, conformity to social norms, and seeking thrill and experience by socialized means. More recently, Castanier *et al.* (2010) found individuals with personality types demonstrating a combination of low conscientiousness, high extraversion and/or high neuroticism were greater risk-takers in a population of 302 men involved in high risk sports (e.g. downhill skiing, mountaineering, rock climbing, paragliding and skydiving), of which 50 per cent were mountaineers.

Cloninger's Temperament and Character Inventory (TCI)

Monasterio *et al.* (2012, 2014) have extended the scope of the personality research literature, which as argued above has focused almost exclusively on the relationship between a particular personality trait, sensation seeking, and participation in mountaineering. Monasterio *et al.* have utilized a comprehensive assessment model of personality, the Temperament and Character Inventory (TCI) (Cloninger *et al.* 1994) to determine to what extent particular personality factors contribute to participation in extreme sports (mountaineering and BASE jumping) and to determine whether these personality variables are associated with a higher risk of accidents (Monasterio *et al.* 2012, 2014).

The TCI postulates that personality consists of four temperament and three character dimensions, each of which can be measured using the TCI. *Temperament* refers to the automatic emotional responses that are thought to be moderately heritable, independent, genetically homogeneous and stable over time. The temperamental traits are called novelty seeking (NS), harm avoidance (HA), reward dependence (RD) and persistence (P). NS captures the responsiveness to potential rewards (curious, monotony avoiding, impulsive), HA the responsiveness to potential punishment (cautious, fearful, pessimistic) and RD to social dependency (tender hearted, warm, sensitive). *Character* refers to self-concepts and individual differences in goals and values that can be influenced by social factors, learning and the process of maturation. The character traits are self-directedness (SD), cooperativeness (C) and self-transcendence (ST). SD refers to an individual's self-determination, personal integrity, maturity and willpower; C to social acceptance and identification with other people; ST to spiritual acceptance and identification with a wider world (Cloninger *et al.* 1994).

Forty-seven mountaineers with a high level of skill and experience were included in the study; they had UIAA median climbing grade scores of 8– and V+ for alpine rock climbing and mountaineering, a median of 15 years' participation in mountaineering and all participants had climbed more than once in situations of high risk (FRC score of 3) (Schofflet *et al.* 2011). High risk was defined as climbing over dangerous terrain, in dangerous weather conditions or in situations where the climber did not feel fully confident in his or her abilities and where a mistake would lead to significant risk of serious injury or death; this level of risk is inherent in high performance mountaineering. The study findings are therefore only generalizable to experienced mountaineers who have reached the level of technical proficiency required to climb in the major mountain ranges in the world.

Morbidity and mortality associated with mountaineering in this group was high, evidenced by a high climbing-related injury rate involving 50 per cent of the participants and an 8.5 per cent death rate at four-year follow-up (Monasterio 2005).

Scores for temperament and character dimensions of the TCI were higher for mountaineers on NS and SD and lower on HA and ST, compared to an age matched normative population. However, the mountaineers' scores did not differ significantly from the normative population on RD, P or C (see Table 11.1).

Table 11.1 Climber (*n*=47) and normative population (*n*=181) TCI-235 score means (and SD)

	NS*	HA**	RD	P	SD*	C	ST**
Climbers	21.36	9.1	14.1	5.0	35.5	34.1	11.2
	(5.2)	(4.8)	(4.4)	(1.5)	(5.1)	(4.6)	(6.8)
Population	19.0	12.4	15.6	5.7	32.0	33.6	18.7
	(5.8)	(6.9)	(4.3)	(2.1)	(7.0)	(6.7)	(6.3)

Notes
*=$p<0.05$; **=$p<0.001$.
NS – novelty seeking, HA – harm avoidance, RD – reward dependence, P – persistence, SD – self-directedness, C – cooperativeness, ST – self-transcendence.

As there is a high correlation between Zuckerman's SS and Cloninger's NS scales (Zuckerman and Cloninger 1996), the finding of high novelty seeking (NS) supports the notion that in part mountaineers seek out novel experiences and intense sensations and avoid monotony and predictability through mountaineering. Harm avoidance (HA) consists of a heritable bias in the inhibition or cessation of behaviours and is positively correlated with pessimistic worry in anticipation of future problems, passive avoidant behaviours such as fear of uncertainty and shyness of strangers, and rapid fatigability. The finding of low HA in mountaineers is not surprising because individuals with low scores on this dimension are carefree, relaxed, daring, courageous, composed and optimistic, even in situations that worry most people; their energy levels tend to be high and they impress others as dynamic, lively and vigorous. Mountaineering is an activity that by its very intensity, uncertainty and adventurousness is likely to engage individuals with low HA. The advantage of low HA is confidence and stimulation in the face of danger and uncertainty, leading to optimistic and energetic efforts with little or no distress. The disadvantages of low HA are related to unresponsiveness to danger, which can lead to foolhardy optimism (Cloninger *et al.* 1994).

Previous research has shown that a combination of high NS and low HA increases the risk of drug use and antisocial behaviours, including criminality (Gunnarsdottir *et al.* 2000; Wills *et al.* 1994). This temperament configuration therefore predisposes to disorganized personality development associated with antisocial risk-taking. However, as self-directedness (SD) refers to self-determination and maturity, or the ability of an individual to control, regulate and adapt behaviour to fit the situation in accordance with individually chosen goals and values, it is unsurprising that mountaineers scored high on this measure. It is likely that due to their high SD mountaineers are able to channel their instincts for risk-taking, and confidence at times of uncertainty, into mountain climbing and adventure sports. High SD with an emphasis on discipline and skill acquisition may also help to explain why mountaineers are able to acquire the required skills and experience, through repeated practice, to develop the proficiency and expertise in order to organize expeditions and climb in the challenging environment of the mountain. SD is also likely to provide the focus and persistence to achieve mastery in an activity of high risk. It also helps to explain why mountaineers engage in risk-taking behaviours by normative rather than impulsive/disorganized antisocial means (such as drug use and criminal behaviour).

Self-transcendence (ST) is a character trait that in general denotes a propensity to religious and transpersonal experience, and a tendency to self-forgetfulness. Self-transcendent individuals are spiritual, unpretentious, humble and fulfilled. Mountaineers often report transcendental and spiritual experiences in the mountains, and mountaineering literature often highlights spiritual values and mysticism associated with mountaineering. The finding of low ST therefore is counterintuitive and unexpected. However, as mountaineering is a physically demanding sport that is pursued in unstable environments and often in unpleasant weather conditions, mountaineers need to have a capacity to focus and pay close attention to detail over prolonged periods of time, and in situations of pronounced physical and psychological stress. High ST is associated with self-forgetfulness and openness to transpersonal experience. In the climbing environment this is likely to be disadvantageous because it may lead to impaired focus and attention by factors not directly related to the climbing process; this may help to explain the very low ST scores amongst mountaineers. Moreover, people who are low in ST are described as practical, self-conscious, materialistic and controlling. They don't accept failure with equanimity. This suggests that high performance mountaineers may not principally seek spiritual or mystical experiences through mountaineering. Reaching the summit or the achievement of the climbing goal is likely to be a stronger motivator. Taken to an extreme this may help to explain some of the disturbing reports of callousness and selfishness from mountaineering expeditions, particularly those reported in the Himalayas. For example on Everest in 2006 over 40 ascending climbers, most with significant team back-up and radio contact to base camp, walked past a dying English mountaineer, David Sharp, only one hour away from advanced base camp. Subsequent reports reveal that film footage of the unfortunate climber was gratuitously taken and despite David's poor health he was able to speak to the climbers. Tragically and incredulously despite the teams being well equipped with modern equipment, oxygen and medicine no rescue attempts were made. Ambitious mountaineers walked around David and left him to die, choosing instead to direct their energy to the summit. They appear to have given more value to the summit than to the life of a fellow mountaineer. The climbers once again stumbled past the moribund David on their way down and still offered no help. Other similar regrettable episodes are depicted in the investigative journalist and mountaineer M. Kodas's book *High crimes* (2008).

Qualitative perspective

In addition to the many quantitative perspectives, the mountaineering experience has been explored from a variety of qualitative frameworks and findings from these studies have provided a different perspective on the essence of mountaineering. Qualitative studies have elicited a range of possible motivations and descriptions of the experience that suggest a move away from mountaineering as the epitome of sensation seeking, risk-taking, competition and the need to test oneself against the elements (Brymer 2010; Brymer and Gray 2010; Kerr and Houge Mackenzie 2012). That is not to say that for some mountaineers these experiences are not essential motivators, but that these factors may not be relevant for all mountaineers. For example, Kerr and Houge Mackenzie (2012) undertook a qualitative study into a range of adventure sports, including mountaineering, and found that as well as goal achievement, social motivations, risk-taking and the need to escape from boredom, participants also spoke about testing personal abilities, overcoming fear and connecting with the natural environment. They also found that participants described pleasurable bodily sensations and a feeling of unselfconsciousness. In the following sections, we explore mountaineering through the interpretation of first-hand accounts of high performance mountaineers.

Reframing risk and fear

The idea that adventure sports, including mountaineering, are all about risk and risk-taking has been questioned before (Brymer 2010). For many mountaineers risk is not something that is actively pursued as if attempting to make up for a deficit in another part of a participant's life. Instead, everyday life activities, such as driving a car are often described as riskier than mountaineering. Mountaineers accept that dangers are part of the experience in the same way that many of us would accept the risks involved with driving are part of the experience of driving. For example, Jim suggests that everyday life has many risks that are taken for granted and that in his experience mountaineering might actually be safer than many mundane activities.

> Well you know risk is a funny thing, most people label people like myself as thrill seekers or risk takers and the person who is labelling me that, you know, the newspaper journalist or whoever, is kind of way off course in a sense. I mean life is risk, you know we are at risk of dying from before we are even born. Life is a risky thing we do and everybody takes risks with their life every day. We do things that threaten our lives and even if we're not actually doing things that threaten our lives, you know if we're sitting in a steel box eating the healthiest possible thing, you know our life is still at risk from outside influences. Life is risk. You know some of the biggest risks I face are on the roads because really you know the most dangerous thing I encounter are people. They are the most unpredictable animals on the planet. So risk is a part of our daily lives and I don't feel, although I acknowledge the risk when I go on an adventure I don't feel like I'm putting my life in any greater danger going on an adventure whether it's climbing Mt Everest or walking across the desert. But I do when I get out on the road. So we face risks in our lives every day and I don't really draw a big distinction. I do feel safer when I'm in the natural world, in the Himalaya than I do out in the home environment when I'm driving around.

This is not to suggest that mountaineers do not understand the dangers involved, but as Jim makes clear in the quote above the experience of mountaineering is coupled with knowledge of the environment that means the mountaineer might feel safer moving through the natural environment than the urban environment. In fact, Jim went on to explain that mountaineering has, on occasion, 'brought out the deepest fears in me'. However, fear is not considered something to hide away from, rather fear is seen as something to be embraced. According to Jim mountaineering allows the mountaineer to feel fear in its raw sense, as human beings were meant to feel fear, where fear is essential information required for survival (Brymer and Schweitzer 2013):

> I think fear is probably the most important single facet in survival. Yeah I think it's a good healthy emotion, fear. People are afraid of fear I think and I get the feeling that most people see fear as a negative thing; you know I was really afraid and that means it's terrible. I don't know, fear is what keeps you alive, you know, it's your fear that stops you from standing right on the very edge; you know fear is the most important thing in survival; the most important thing.

Beyond this, the experience of fear has not only been described in terms of its importance for mountaineering, but also that the mountaineering experience and its relationship to fear allows a participant to experience moving through fear and making decisions despite a fear.

> You have to actually face your fears, which is an exciting bit too because I think that once you've done enough of what you're doing, in this case mountaineering, your experience gets you out of any difficult situation. But even when you're experienced and you look at something and it's scary because it should be scary, that's the way it is. Although you know you'll be able to deal with it hopefully. But there's still that overwhelming feeling of crikey what the hell am I doing here? And then you start it, you know, you start it.
>
> (Brenda)

Paradoxically, fear might actually be the emotion that enables a mountaineer to undertake their chosen activity in the safest manner possible.

> I've always said people who say that they have no fear, either they are liars or they are dead or they will be dead soon. It's a safety valve and it's like everything else and that's what fascinated me when I started climbing.
>
> (Ernie)

Ernie went on to describe the importance of fear by referring to experiences while soloing the Eiger. He explained that the experience of fear indicated that an event needed to be taken seriously and that the event required comprehensive preparation. However, the experience of effective participation despite fear can lead to incredible transformations (Brymer 2012).

A journey of self-discovery and self-construction

Mountaineering has been credited with supporting deep and powerful personal transformations. In this section the voices of mountaineers will be utilized to further investigate the potential of the mountaineering experience to initiate powerful transformations and elicit deep self-awareness. While the outsider might focus on the physicality of the experience and the harshness of the environment the mountaineer would suggest, as is apparent in the experiences documented at the beginning of this chapter, that mountaineering is much more of a mental activity than physical activity:

> when you are climbing in those extreme environments you really have to accept that you have a measure of control but you don't have control. The mountain could fluff you out in a second and to keep going in that environment for days or weeks I don't know whether I think that's about some mental toughness and mental toughness definitely can be learnt.
>
> (Geoff)

In the quote above, Geoff describes two characteristics of high performance mountaineering. First, mountaineering is a mental activity, which requires what he calls 'mental toughness' and second that this mental toughness is not something that he was born with. For Geoff, the mountaineering experience challenges the participant to explore mental capacities not usually challenged in everyday life. For many, the mountaineering experience is so powerful that the mountaineer is required to explore the core of their being and utilize mental capacities usually left untested:

> You are in this incredibly spectacular environment dealing with really, really primal forces. Not only primal forces in the environment but primal forces within yourself! So to go mountaineering is to reinvigorate, re-establish that connection with a really fundamental core part of your being and yourself. You have to go through this to find that core stuff within yourself.

For some participants, mountaineering facilitates the realization of a core component of what it means to be human. That is, the mountaineering experience enables a participant to appreciate human capacities that might otherwise have remained dormant. For example, Jim reflected on the capacity for modern life to emphasize certain aspects of human psychology, to the detriment of others. In particular, Jim spoke about the importance of rekindling experiences that human beings may have appreciated when life was more immediate:

> It comes back to the core of being an animal and that's what I like about it. It's not necessarily that your life is threatened, that's not what I like about it but that's one of the factors that makes it something – that makes it what

it is. That's what attracts me to it; you know to bring out the best of my animal self, which is the best of myself. You know, I'm at my best, I'm at my happiest, my most content, my most satisfied, you know my most me.

Jim goes on to explain that these capacities include the ability to see more clearly and an alertness that is beyond the everyday mundane alertness required for living in a modern society.

For Belinda, high performance mountaineering is also about the capacity to realize her potential in ways not readily available in everyday life. Belinda described the power of the environment and the role of danger in enabling connection with underutilized strengths:

It's all senses and perhaps also intuition, because you are more in touch with yourself as well in those situations, which can be dangerous situations. You tend to be very in tune with your environment and that means that you are going to react very intuitively I suppose to what's around you, once again if you have the experience to deal with whatever is going to be thrown at you.

Belinda continued by reflecting on how the mountaineering experience can often continue beyond the mountain.

Once I was in the water it was click, the mountaineering experience took over and everything was going in slow motion. You have that instant of panic when you are in a dangerous situation and then it's like no if I panic I'm lost, dead, whatever. So the brain works like so well and you have time to think about everything. It's quite amazing really.

In the above quote, Belinda described how the mountaineering experience helped her manage her fear of water. Belinda described how the mountaineering experience 'took over' and that she was able to instil a sense of calm in an unfamiliar environment based on her experiences while mountaineering.

For these participants, mountaineering is more than just the activity of climbing or getting to the top. At its best high performance mountaineering facilitates opportunities for self-discovery not available in everyday life. Mountaineering allows a participant to realize potentials described as core human potentials, where senses become more alive and a participant appreciates what it truly means to be human. Beyond this the mountaineering experience crosses over into other aspects of life. Mountaineering is not considered an isolated or segmented element of life, but something that is core to life. Participants describe how capacities realized in mountaineering help them achieve in other areas of life. That is, high performance mountaineering is not just about being able to get to the top – it is a way of being with life. For these participants at least mountaineering helps them explore their own capacities as human beings. The experiences are not necessarily about drive and performance. Mountaineering is at the very core of their experience and the facilitator of well-being.

Conclusion

It is sometimes tempting to attempt to reduce human experiences, such as mountaineering, to simple cause and effect explanations; however, we do this at a cost. Both the quantitative and qualitative research into mountaineering reveals considerable complexity. Overall, taken together, the personality research literature suggests that mountaineers, as a population, have different personality characteristics when compared to normative and low risk sports participants (Castanier *et al.* 2010; Cronin 1991; Diehm and Armatas 2004; Freixanet 1991; Jack and Ronan 1998; Zuckerman 1983; Fowler *et al.* 1980; Self *et al.* 2007; Monasterio *et al.* 2014). However large variations in the standard deviations across all measures suggests that there isn't a tightly defined mountaineering personality profile (Monasterio *et al.* 2014). Factors other than personality also drive mountaineers. Such factors may include opportunity and access to the natural climbing environment, peer influence, increased popularity, media attention and commercialization of the sport.

At the risk of stating the obvious it is imperative to note that the mountaineering experience is not easily boxed into distinct categories. Mountaineering is multifaceted and involves a fine balance between individual personality biases, the search for meaning and personal development, and environmental and task-related characteristics. For some the drive to succeed might be paramount, for others communion with nature and for others still the realization of enhanced sensory capacities. It is entirely possible that one mountaineer will experience all these motivations at some stage in their career. Ultimately the mountaineering experience provides a tantalizing glimpse into what it means to be human.

References

Alavrez, J., Pustina, A. and Hallgren, M. (2011) 'Escalating commitment in the death zone', *International Journal of Project Management*, 29(8): 971–985.

Brymer, E. (2010) 'Risk and extreme sports: A phenomenological perspective', *Annals of Leisure Research*, 13(1–2): 218–239.

Brymer, E. (2012) 'Transforming adventures: Why extreme sports should be included in adventure programming', in B. Martin and M. Wagstaff (eds) *Controversial issues in adventure programming*, Champaign, IL: Human Kinetics: 165–174.

Brymer, E. and Gray, T. (2010) 'Dancing with nature: Rhythm and harmony in extreme sport participation', *Adventure Education and Outdoor Learning*, 9(2): 135–149.

Brymer, E. and Schweitzer, R. (2013) 'The search for freedom in extreme sports: A phenomenological exploration', *Psychology of Sport and Exercise*, 14(6): 865–873.

Castanier, C., Le Scanff, C. and Woodman, T. (2010) 'Who takes risks in high-risk sports? A typological personality approach', *Research Quarterly for Exercise and Sport*, 81(4): 478–484.

Cloninger, C. R., Przybeck, T. R., Svrakic, D. M. and Wetzel, R. D. (1994) 'Basic description of the personality scales', in R. D. Wetzel and C. R. Cloninger (eds) *The temperament and character inventory (TCI): A guide to its development and use*, St Louis, MO: Center for Psychobiology of Personality, Washington University: 19–29.

Cronin, C. (1991) 'Sensation seeking among mountain climbers', *Personality and Individual Differences*, 12(6): 653–654.

Diehm, R. and Armatas, C. (2004) 'Surfing: An avenue for socially acceptable risk taking, satisfying needs for sensation seeking and experience seeking', *Personality and Individual Differences*, 36(3): 663–677.

Fowler, C. J., Von Knorring, L. and Oreland, L. (1980) 'Platelet monoamine oxidase activity in sensation seekers', *Psychiatry Research*, 3(3): 273–279.

Freixanet, M. G. (1991) 'Personality profile of subjects engaged in high physical risk sports', *Personality and Individual Differences*, 12(10): 1087–1093.

Gunnarsdottir, E. D., Pingitore, R. A., Spring, B. J., Konopka, L. M., Crayton, J. W., Milo, T. and Shirazi, P. (2000) 'Individual differences among cocaine users', *Addictive Behaviors*, 25(5): 641–652.

Jack, S. J. and Ronan, K. R. (1998) 'Sensation seeking among high- and low-risk sports participants', *Personality and Individual Differences*, 25(6): 1063–1083.

Kerr, J. H. and Houge Mackenzie, S. (2012) 'Multiple motives for participating in adventure sports', *Psychology of Sport and Exercise*, 13: 649–657.

Kodas, M. (2008) *High crimes: The fate of Everest in an age of greed*, New York: Hyperion.

Malcolm, M. (2001) 'Mountaineering fatalities in Mt Cook National Park', *New Zealand Medical Journal*, 114(1127): 78–80.

Monasterio, M. E. (2005) 'Accident and fatality characteristics in a population of mountain climbers in New Zealand', *New Zealand Medical Journal*, 118(1208): U1249.

Monasterio, E., Alamri, Y. A. and Mei-Dan, O. (2014) 'Personality characteristics in a population of mountain climbers', *Wilderness and Environmental Medicine*, 25(2): 214–219.

Monasterio, E., Mulder, R., Frampton, C. and Mei-Dan, O. (2012) 'Personality characteristics of BASE jumpers', *Journal of Applied Sport Psychology*, 24(4): 391–400.

Pollard, A. and Clarke, C. (1988) 'Deaths during mountaineering at extreme altitude', *Lancet*, 331(8597): 1277.

Schoffl, V., Morrison, A., Hefti, U., Ullrich, S. and Küpper, T. (2011) 'The UIAA Medical Commission injury classification for mountaineering and climbing sports', *Wilderness and Environmental Medicine*, 22(1): 46–51.

Self, D. R., De Vries Henry, E., Findley, C. S. and Reilly, E. (2007) 'Thrill seeking: The type T personality and extreme sports', *International Journal of Sport Management and Marketing*, 2(1): 175–190.

Wills, T. A., Vaccaro, D. and McNamara, G. (1994) 'Novelty seeking, risk taking, and related constructs as predictors of adolescent substance use: an application of Cloninger's theory', *Journal of Substance Abuse*, 6(1): 1–20.

Zuckerman, M. (1979) *Sensation seeking: Beyond the optimal level of arousal*, Hillsdale, NJ: Erlbaum.

Zuckerman, M. (1983) 'Sensation seeking and sports', *Personality and Individual Differences*, 4(3): 285–294.

Zuckerman, M. and Cloninger, C. R. (1996) 'Relationship between Cloninger's, Zuckerman's and Eysenck's dimensions of personality', *Personality and Individual Differences*, 21(2): 283–285.

Case study 5

Measuring responsible behaviour related to
safety and security and its antecedents
among climbers on Mt Kinabalu, Borneo

Mahdi Esfahani and Selina Khoo

Mt Kinabalu, located in the Malaysian state of Sabah on the island of Borneo, is
the highest mountain in South East Asia. At over 4,000 m above sea level, it is
one of the world's most accessible mountains to climbers. The climb up and
return from Mt Kinabalu is not too arduous but can be extremely spirit lifting
(Salick *et al.* 1999). No unique skills or special equipment are required to scale
the mountain. This fact, along with the designation as a World Heritage site has
made Mt Kinabalu one of the most attractive climbing destinations in the world.
The mountain has attracted an increasing number of climbers. However, despite
its reputation as the one of the easiest mountains to climb, the park records
yearly fatalities and injuries. Therefore, the importance of responsible mountaineering behaviour is vital for the safety and security of climbers.

Responsible behaviour related to safety and security

Responsible behaviour related to safety and security needs to be observed in
dangerous places and high risk destinations (Burnik *et al.* 2009; Maroudas *et al.*
2004). Although many researchers have investigated environmental responsible
behaviour (Bamberg and Möser 2007; Cottrell 2003; Cottrell and Graefe 1997;
De Young 2002; Ong and Musa 2011b; Osbaldiston and Sheldon 2003), limited
research has been conducted on responsible mountaineering behaviour related to
safety and security. Since mountaineering is an adventure sport (Hall and Weiler
1992; Hudson 2003; Pomfret 2006), commonly associated with risk and danger
(Beedie and Hudson 2003; Gyimóthy and Mykletun 2004; Maroudas *et al.*
2004), responsible behaviour is crucial among climbers (Burnik *et al.* 2009) and
plays an essential role in maintaining safety and security. Mountaineering, especially in high altitude destinations (2,500 m and above), entails risk and danger
and climbers need to adopt responsible behaviour to maintain their own health
and safety (Musa *et al.* 2004; Pollard and Murdoch 2003). Esfahani *et al.* (2014)
defined responsible mountaineering behaviour related to safety and security as
specific behaviour that needs to be carried out by the mountaineers to ensure
their safety and security while mountain climbing.

Using the Theory of Planned Behaviour (TPB) (Ajzen 1985, 1991; Ajzen and
Driver 1992) and Expectation Disconfirmation Theory (EDT) (Oliver 1980), this

study examines the relationships between spirituality, personality, satisfaction, attitude towards behaviour, norms and perceived behavioural control (PBC) with responsible behaviour and loyalty intention among climbers on Mt Kinabalu. This study explores the dimensions of responsible mountaineering behaviour, attitude and norms-related health and safety in the mountain. In addition, it develops an integrated model to explain the relationship between spirituality, personality, satisfaction, loyalty intention and components of TPB with responsible mountaineering behaviour using structural equation modelling (SEM).

Respondents are climbers who have just completed the ascent and the descent of Mt Kinabalu. Of the 4,894 climbers who climbed Mt Kinabalu during the month long data collection period (14 March to 14 April in 2013), a total of 916 (61.6 per cent males and 38.4 per cent females) agreed to complete the questionnaires. Preliminary analysis, item-total correlation and Exploratory Factor Analysis (EFA) followed by Confirmatory Factor Analysis (CFA) were performed to test the validity and reliability of the questionnaire. A separate sample of 300 respondents was used to conduct the EFA, while the remaining sample of 616 was used for the CFA and SEM.

Results show that responsible behaviour in the mountain is represented by four dimensions: clothing requirement, food and drink requirement, equipment requirement and obedience requirement. The overall behaviour mean score for responsible mountaineering behaviour is at moderate level with the highest score for clothing requirement followed by food and drink requirement, obedience requirement and equipment requirement. Spirituality is represented by four dimensions: personal (relationship with oneself), communal (relationship with others), environmental (relationship with nature) and transcendental (relationship with God). Climbers have the highest mean score for personal, followed by communal, environmental and transcendental. Personality is represented by five dimensions: agreeableness, extroversion, conscientiousness, neuroticism and openness to experience. The highest score is for agreeableness followed by openness to experience, extroversion, conscientiousness and neuroticism. All personality dimensions positively influence responsible behaviour among climbers with the exception of neuroticism. The results for attitude towards behaviour showed that climbers score higher for awareness than knowledge dimensions. Norms was represented by two dimensions: media norm (websites, social media and books/magazines) and subjective norm (mountaineering partner/group members, other climbers, family members and mountain guides). Climbers have a higher score for subjective norm compared to media norm.

The results from SEM offer support for significant positive effects of spirituality, personality, attitude towards behaviour and norms on responsible mountaineering behaviour but PBC and satisfaction do not have a significant effect on mountaineers' responsible behaviour. Responsible behaviour and satisfaction have significant positive effect on loyalty intention. Consequently, spirituality affects both directly and indirectly on responsible mountaineering behaviour and attitude mediates this relationship. Since both direct and indirect effects are significant, this relationship is considered as partial mediation. The direct effect of spirituality on responsible behaviour is stronger than indirect effect through attitude towards behaviour. Therefore, climbers with a high level of spirituality have a high level of responsible mountaineering behaviour.

We record a high satisfaction among mountaineers on Mt Kinabalu. However, responsible behaviour itself scores only at a moderate level. The insignificant relationship between satisfaction and responsible behaviour may indicate that regardless of the behaviour, mountaineers still achieve high satisfaction.

This study also delineates the different degrees of importance between media and social norms in influencing climbers' behaviour. Despite the current media norms popularity, its mean score is much lower than the subjective norms. This indicates that in safety and security circumstances, or perhaps in most other general matters, mountaineers rely more on the decision and actions of their friends and family members, rather than information from the media.

Theoretical contributions

The current study applies TPB and EDT to understand responsible behaviour and loyalty intention among climbers. Internal factors of personality, spirituality, attitude towards behaviour and norms (subjective norm and media norm) influence responsible mountaineering behaviour. A model which explains the antecedents of responsible behaviour among climbers, which relates to safety and security is shown in Figure CS 5.1.

The current study successfully developed an integrated model of responsible mountaineering behaviour using SEM. It also reveals four distinct responsible behaviour dimensions (clothing, food and drink, equipment and obedience requirements) among climbers, which are related to safety and security.

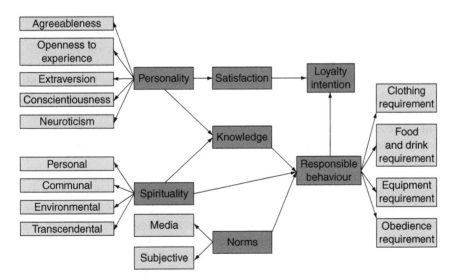

Figure CS 5.1 A model of factors influencing responsible behaviour on Mt Kinabalu.

The core dimensions of mountaineering attitude that relate to responsible mountaineering behaviour are: cognitive (knowledge), affective (awareness) and conative (commitment). However, the conative and affective components are not significant in the full measurement model because of their low factor loadings. The current study reveals that attitude of climbers could be singularly measured by the cognitive (knowledge) dimension. This firmly indicates the importance of the knowledge dimension in the attitude of climbers towards behaviour. Other researchers also confirmed the importance of knowledge in influencing responsible behaviour among tourists (e.g. Cottrell and Graefe 1997; Ong and Musa 2011a; Zanna and Rempel 1988). The study extends the role of personality in influencing the behaviour indirectly through attitude, which also confirms the findings of some other studies (Ong and Musa 2012; Ramanaiah *et al.* 2000) in terms of the personality traits' influence on responsible behaviour.

Managerial contributions

The majority of climbers plan to summit Mt Kinabalu before sunrise. Thus, having the right clothing is important, as the temperature often plunges below 0 °C with pockets of ice commonly to be found along the summit trail. The low score of equipment requirement reflects the ease of the mountain to climb, whereby no technical mountaineering skill and equipment are required. Having adequate warm clothing and comfortable climbing shoes or boots are important for climbers on Mt Kinabalu and the park managers should provide information about such requirements. Water and high energy food are necessary during the climb, thus managers should make sure that climbers bring enough drinking water and high energy food such as chocolate and nuts.

The importance of cognitive (knowledge) dimension and its influence on responsible behaviour is firmly established in this study. Therefore, the Kinabalu National Park should emphasize on promoting responsible mountaineering behaviour through the provision of knowledge and perhaps relevant skills. Mountaineering instructors must provide the necessary information related to rules and regulations, high risk places on the mountain, unique features of Mt Kinabalu, the requirements for climbing and the necessary mountaineering skills. The delivery of preliminary briefing on important mountaineering information will create an excellent opportunity for climbers to increase their knowledge and perhaps relevant skills, which are crucial for them to succeed in climbing Mt Kinabalu.

As stated earlier, all personality dimensions positively influence responsible behaviour among mountaineers with the exception of neuroticism. Managers could enhance educational programmes using both direct and indirect strategies. In indirect strategies, managers could increase the knowledge of guides and instructors so that they could pass this information to the climbers. In direct strategies, managers may need to pay attention to climbers' neuroticism traits, who may appear nervous, worried and insecure. They may need closer supervision and restraint from mountain guides and park authority.

Marketing contributions

The ease of the climb is evident from the statistics of 53,883 successful summiteers in 2012 alone (Januarius 2013). Indeed, this very fact may serve as a marketing message to lure prospective climbers to climb Mt Kinabalu.

Spirituality positively influences responsible behaviour among climbers. This information is useful both for marketing communication and for new product and services development. The spiritual aspect of the mountain could be further enhanced by encouraging the development of related tourism products and services to attract spiritual tourists. Among examples are yoga and meditation retreats. Better tourism interpretation of the spiritual values and traditional religious rituals at Mt Kinabalu could be rejuvenated to enhance further the core value of the mountain, other than it just being regarded as the most accessible mountain to climb among climbers.

Climbers record a high satisfaction score with their experience on Mt Kinabalu in Sabah. The high satisfaction experience was also recorded among divers in Sipadan (Musa 2002) and Layang Layang (Musa *et al.* 2006). This reflects the superior quality tourism products and services offered in all three of Sabah's attractions: Sipadan, Layang Layang and Mt Kinabalu. The high satisfaction score could be highlighted and stressed in marketing communication to attract a constant flow of tourists to Sabah.

References

Ajzen, I. (1985) 'From intentions to actions: A theory of planned behavior', in J. Kuhl and J. Bechmann (eds) *Action control: From cognition to behavior*, New York: Springer Verlag: 11–39.

Ajzen, I. (1991) 'The theory of planned behavior', *Organizational Behavior and Human Decision Process*, 50(2): 179–211.

Ajzen, I. and Driver, B. L. (1992) 'Application of the theory of planned behavior to leisure choice', *Journal of Leisure Research*, 24(3): 207–224.

Bamberg, S. and Möser, G. (2007) 'Twenty years after Hines, Hungerford, and Tomera: A new meta-analysis of psycho-social determinants of pro-environmental behaviour', *Journal of Environmental Psychology*, 27(1): 14–25.

Beedie, P. and Hudson, S. (2003) 'Emergence of mountain-based adventure tourism', *Annals of Tourism Research*, 30(3): 625–643.

Burnik, S., Jug, S., Kajtna, T. and Tušak, M. (2009) 'Differences in personality traits of mountain climbers and non-athletes in Slovenia', *Acta Universitatis Palackianae Olomucensis. Gymnica*, 35(2): 13–18.

Cottrell, S. P. (2003) 'Influence of sociodemographics and environmental attitudes on general responsible environmental behavior among recreational boaters', *Environment and Behavior*, 35(3): 347–375.

Cottrell, S. P. and Graefe, A. R. (1997) 'Testing a conceptual framework of responsible environmental behavior', *Journal of Environmental Education*, 29(1): 17–27.

De Young, R. (2002) 'New ways to promote proenvironmental behavior: Expanding and evaluating motives for environmentally responsible behavior', *Journal of Social Issues*, 56(3): 509–526.

Esfahani, M., Musa, G. and Khoo, S. (2014) 'The influence of spirituality and physical activity level on responsible behaviour and mountaineering satisfaction on Mount Kinabalu, Borneo', *Current Issues in Tourism*, DOI: 10.1080/13683500.2014.987733.

Gyimóthy, S. and Mykletun, R. J. (2004) 'Play in adventure tourism: The case of arctic trekking', *Annals of Tourism Research*, 31(4): 855–878.

Hall, C. M. and Weiler, B. (1992) 'Adventure, sport and health tourism', in B. Weiler and C. M. Hall (eds) *Special interest tourism*, London: Belhaven Press: 141–158.

Hudson, S. (2003) *Sport and adventure tourism*, Binghamton, NY: Haworth Hospitality Press.

Januarius, S. (2013) 'Injured, lost, dead and total number of mountaineers from 2005 to 2012', Statistics Office in Kinabalu National Park, Kota Kinabalu.

Maroudas, L., Kyriakaki, A. and Gouvis, D. (2004) 'A community approach to mountain adventure tourism development', *Anatolia*, 15(1): 5–18.

Musa, G. (2002) 'Sipadan: A SCUBA-diving paradise: An analysis of tourism impact, diver satisfaction and tourism management', *Tourism Geographies*, 4(2): 195–209.

Musa, G., Hall, C. M. and Higham, J. E. S. (2004) 'Tourism sustainability and health impacts in high altitude adventure, cultural and ecotourism destinations: A case study of Nepal's Sagarmatha National Park', *Journal of Sustainable Tourism*, 12(4): 306–331.

Musa, G., Kadir, S. L. S. A. and Lee, L. (2006) 'Layang Layang: An empirical study on SCUBA divers' satisfaction', *Tourism in Marine Environments*, 2(2): 89–102.

Oliver, R. L. (1980) 'A cognitive model of the antecedents and consequences of satisfaction decisions', *Journal of Marketing Research*, 17(November): 460–469.

Ong, T. F. and Musa, G. (2011a) 'An examination of recreational divers' underwater behaviour by attitude–behaviour theories', *Current Issues in Tourism*, 14(8): 779–795.

Ong, T. F. and Musa, G. (2011b) 'SCUBA divers' underwater responsible behaviour: Can environmental concern and divers' attitude make a difference?' *Current Issues in Tourism*, 15(4): 329–351.

Ong, T. F. and Musa, G. (2012) 'Examining the influences of experience, personality and attitude on SCUBA divers' underwater behaviour: A structural equation model', *Tourism Management*, 33(6): 1521–1534.

Osbaldiston, R. and Sheldon, K. M. (2003) 'Promoting internalized motivation for environmentally responsible behavior: A prospective study of environmental goals', *Journal of Environmental Psychology*, 23(4): 349–357.

Pollard, A. J. and Murdoch, D. R. (2003) *The high altitude medicine handbook* (3rd edn), Abingdon: Radcliffe Medical Press Ltd.

Pomfret, G. (2006) 'Mountaineering adventure tourists: A conceptual framework for research', *Tourism Management*, 27(1): 113–123.

Ramanaiah, N. V., Clump, M. and Sharpe, J. P. (2000) 'Personality profiles of environmentally responsible groups', *Psychological Reports*, 87(1): 176–178.

Salick, J., Biun, A., Martin, G., Apin, L. and Beaman, R. (1999) 'Whence useful plants? A direct relationship between biodiversity and useful plants among the Dusun of Mt. Kinabalu', *Biodiversity and Conservation*, 8(6): 797–818.

Zanna, M. P. and Rempel, J. K. (1988) 'Attitudes: A new look at an old concept', In I. D. Bar-Tal and A. W. Kruglanski (eds) *The social psychology of knowledge*, Cambridge: Cambridge University Press: 315–334.

Part III

Place

12 Environmental impacts of mountaineering

Catherine Marina Pickering and Agustina Barros

Introduction

Mountain ecosystems provide key ecological services for local communities including providing fuel, fodder and food, water and soil conservation, reducing the risk of avalanches and landslides, as well as acting as water reservoirs (Messerli *et al.* 2004; Becker *et al.* 2007). They are also important centres of biological diversity due to their high relative relief, diverse topography and geology, and the compression of climatic zones along elevation gradients (Körner 2003; Pickering and Barros 2012). Due to cultural, landscape and topographical factors, mountains are important destinations for a wide range of tourists, including adventure tourists (Buckley 2006; Pomfret 2006). Unfortunately, environmental impacts increase with increasing tourism including impacts on soils, vegetation, wildlife and aquatic systems.

This chapter assesses the environmental impacts of mountaineering and related activities. It starts with a short overview of the ecological significance of mountains then reviews research on the environmental impacts of mountaineering and related activities such as helicopters, rock climbing, hiking, camping and pack animals. This includes discussing factors that influence the severity and types of impacts. Finally, it provides management recommendations for how impacts may be minimized, ameliorated or avoided.

Mountain environments

A characteristic feature of mountains is their vertical zonation as temperatures decrease with increasing elevation (Blyth *et al.* 2002). As a result there are often distinct elevation zones including natural forests in the *montane zone*, a few trees in the *treeline ecotone*, dwarf shrubs, herbs and graminoids in the *low and middle alpine zone*, patchy vegetation in the *upper alpine zone* and open frozen ground in the *nival zone* (Nagy and Grabherr 2009). In some mountains, arid conditions limit tree growth so there is no distinct treeline below the true alpine zone (Körner 2003).

These steep climate gradients result in small-scale habitat differentiation and isolation contributing to the high levels of biodiversity and endemism (Becker *et al.* 2007; Körner *et al.* 2011). For instance, many alpine zones contain around 600 to 650 plant species including the European Alps, New Zealand Alps and the Rocky Mountains (Körner 2003). As a result many alpine regions are considered biodiversity hotspots, including the Tropical Andes which has the highest number of endemic plant species in the world (6.7 per cent of vascular plants globally) (Myers *et al.* 2000). Mountains also provide refuge for a variety of rare and endemic animals, including charismatic threatened species such as snow leopards in the Himalayas, mountain pygmy possums in the Australian Alps and condors in the Andes (Martin 2013).

Mountain ecosystems provide a range of goods and services for local communities (Grêt-Regamey *et al.* 2012). They are the key sources of the world's major rivers, playing a critical role in water cycles by capturing moisture from air masses, storing water in the form of snow and ice, and regulating and providing water for settlements, agriculture and industries downstream (Körner 2003; Grêt-Regamey *et al.* 2012). For example, in semi-arid and arid regions, 50–90 per cent of river flows come from mountains (Messerli *et al.* 2004). Vegetation in mountains increases soil stability, limits flooding and mitigates other natural hazards such as rock falls, landslides and avalanches (Blyth *et al.* 2002; Becker *et al.* 2007).

Mountain environments are subjected to a range of natural and anthropogenic disturbance (Körner and Ohsawa 2005). This includes seismic events and flooding through to global climate change and the loss of vegetation and soils from unsustainable farming (Körner 2003). Increasingly this includes disturbance from tourism and recreation, including skiing, hiking, mountain biking and mountaineering (Pickering and Barros 2012). Mountain environments can be particularly susceptible to anthropogenic disturbance because their biota is often adapted to relatively narrow ranges of temperatures and precipitation, and has limited capacity to recover from some types of disturbance (Becker *et al.* 2007). For alpine vegetation, recovery is often very slow due to the slow growth rates of many alpine plants as a result of short growing seasons and thin poor soils (Bell and Bliss 1973; Körner and Ohsawa 2005).

The following section assesses the environmental impacts of mountaineering and related activities including hiking, rock climbing, back-country skiing, camping, helicopter use, pack animals and campsite services. The environmental impacts of other popular tourism and recreational activities not directly related to mountaineering are not covered here, including those from ski resorts and mountain biking. Further information on their impacts is available in a range of recent literature reviews (e.g. Marion and Wimpey 2007; Pickering *et al.* 2010; Rixen and Rolando 2013; Sato *et al.* 2013).

Environmental impacts

Mountaineering and its associated activities can have a range of impacts including on water, soils, vegetation and wildlife (Monz *et al.* 2010; Pickering *et al.* 2010; Newsome *et al.* 2012) (Table 12.1). Impacts on water sources include changes in drainage patterns due to water extraction at campsites, changes in the physico-chemical properties of water bodies due to waste water discharges and the direct contamination of snow and glaciers by human waste (Hadwen *et al.* 2008; Prideaux *et al.* 2009; Goodwin *et al.* 2012) (Table 12.1). Impacts on native vegetation include those from trampling as a result of hiking, camping, climbing and pack animals, the deliberate and accidental introduction of non-native plants, and plant harvesting for bedding, fuel and fodder (Cole 2004; Monz *et al.* 2010; Pickering *et al.* 2010; Ansong and Pickering 2013; Byers 2014) (Table 12.1). Impacts on soils include erosion and compaction from hiking, camping and pack animals, sediment yield and run off from trail incision and changes in the chemical and microbiological properties of soils from human and pack animal waste (Leung and Marion 1996; Arocena *et al.* 2006; Olive and Marion 2009) (Table 12.1). Impacts on wildlife include changes in species' temporal and spatial distributions, increased food availability including for predators at campsites and huts, damage to nests from trampling and reduced habitat quality associated with the creation of informal trail networks (Arlettaz *et al.* 2007; Thiel *et al.* 2008; Francis and Barber 2013) (Table 12.1).

Impacts of the improper disposal of human waste in mountains can be very problematic, particularly at high altitude where waste takes a long time to breakdown and can contaminate otherwise pristine water sources (Ells and Monz 2011; Goodwin *et al.* 2012) (Figure 12.1). For example, on the climbing route to

Figure 12.1 Human waste left at a high altitude campsite, Aconcagua Provincial Park, Andes, Argentina.

Table 12.1 Environmental impacts of mountaineering and related activities

	Mountaineering-related activities							
	Hike	Rock climbing	Camp	Ski*	Huts	Helicopter	Pack animals	References
Biophysical components								
Water/snow/glaciers	–	–	x	–	x	–	–	1
Modified drainage patterns due to water extraction	–	–	x	–	x	–	–	1
Increased nutrients and associated algal growth due to waste discharge	–	–	x	–	x	–	–	1, 2
Changes in water physico-chemical properties due to waste discharge	–	–	x	x	x	–	–	1
Glacier and snow pollution from human waste	–	–	–	–	–	x	–	3
Oil spills	–	–	–	–	–	–	–	4
Soils and vegetation								
Soil erosion and compaction	x	–	x	–	–	–	x	5, 6, 7
Sediment yield and runoff	x	–	–	–	–	–	x	8
Nutrient addition to soils from manure and human waste	–	–	x	–	x	–	x	9
Changes in the chemical and microbiological properties of soils	–	–	–	–	–	–	–	10
Change to trail width	x	–	–	–	–	–	x	11
Change to trail verge vegetation	x	–	–	–	–	–	x	11
Vegetation clearance from trampling and camping	x	–	x	–	–	–	x	12
Changes in plant composition from trampling and camping disturbance	x	–	–	–	–	–	x	12
Introduction alien species	x	x	x	x	x	x	x	13, 14, 15, 16
Increase of ruderal and alien species	x	x	x	x	x	–	x	17
Alteration of cliff plant communities	–	x	–	–	–	x	–	18, 19
Plant defoliation through grazing	–	–	–	–	x	–	x	20
Fuel wood extraction	–	–	x	–	–	–	x	21

								Sources
Littering	x	x	x	x	x	—	x	22
Wildlife								
Changes in temporal and spatial distribution patterns	x	x	x	x	x	x	x	23
Decrease in foraging	x	x	x	x	x	x	x	23
Increased food availability for general predators	—	—	x	x	x	—	—	24
Alteration of animal behaviour	x	x	x	x	x	x	x	23, 25
Alteration of behaviour and spatial distribution of cliff bird communities	—	x	—	—	—	—	—	18
Increased physiological stress	x	x	x	x	x	x	—	23, 25, 26
Nest predation	x	—	—	—	x	x	x	27
Reduced habitat quality	x	x	x	x	x	x	x	28
Negative effects on bird reproductive success	x	x	x	x	x	x	x	23
Flush birds from snow burrows	—	—	x	—	—	—	—	25

Sources: 1: Hadwen et al. (2008), 2: Prideaux et al. (2009), 3: Goodwin et al. (2012), 4: Barber et al. (2009), 5: Wilson and Seney (1994), 6: Leung and Marion (1996), 7: Olive and Marion (2009), 8: Whinam and Chilcott (2003), 9: Bridle and Kirkpatrick (2003), 10: Arocena et al. (2006), 11: Barros et al. (2013), 12: Cole (2004), 13: Ansong and Pickering (2013), 14: Whinam et al. (2005), 15: Barros and Pickering (2014a); 16: Barros and Pickering (2014b), 17: Monz et al. (2010), 18: Camp and Knight (1998), 19: Vogler and Reisch (2011), 20: Barros et al. (2014), 21: Byers (2009), 22: Kuniyal (2002), 23: Francis and Barber (2013), 24: Storch and Leidenberger (2003), 25: Arlettaz et al. (2007), 26: Thiel et al. (2008), 27: Pakanen et al. (2011), 28: Wimpey and Marion (2011), 29: Heil et al. (2007).

Mt McKinley in Denali National Park in Alaska, faecal bacteria from human waste deposited on snow surfaces or buried in glaciers was still biologically active a year later (Goodwin *et al.* 2012). Near the main base camp for Mt Aconcagua in the Andes the glacier lakes had higher levels of nitrate and higher abundance of algal species tolerant of pollution compared to undisturbed glacier lakes (Barros 2004). Increasing levels of nitrate and phosphorus have also been found contaminating high altitude lakes along the main route to Mt Everest in Sagarmatha National Park in the Himalaya (Ghimire *et al.* 2013).

Solid waste, including steel cans and plastic bottles, can accumulate around huts, lodges and campsites along popular hiking and mountaineering routes, particularly in remote mountains (Ghimire *et al.* 2013; Byers 2014). This is a well-recognized issue in the Nepal Himalayas, with piles of solid waste in some sites and the increasing use of landfill and human waste disposal pits near villages along popular trekking routes (Manfredi *et al.* 2010; Byers 2014). Much of the solid waste is burnt or deposited in landfill close to water sources resulting in water and air pollution (Manfredi *et al.* 2010; Byers 2014). In base camps and high altitude campsites, the accumulation of solid waste is particularly problematic (Basnet 1993). At the Mt Everest base camps in Nepal, clean up campaigns lead by the Sherpa community have removed over 900 kg of human waste and garbage, including oxygen bottles, batteries and food packaging (Sherpa 2008).

Impacts on vegetation include reductions in plant cover due to trampling damage along popular trails, campsites and huts used mountaineers and hikers (Byers 2009, 2014; Barros and Pickering 2014a; Barros *et al.* 2014; Ballantyne *et al.* 2014). This can result in plant composition changes with decreases in trampling sensitive species, e.g. low growing shrubs, and increases in trampling resistant species (Liddle 1997; Cole 2004; Monz *et al.* 2010; Barros and Pickering 2014b).

Damage to vegetation includes the unsustainable harvest of plants, particularly shrubs, for firewood (Byers 2009, 2014) (Figure 12.2). For popular settlements in the Everest region it has been estimated that around 70,000 kg of alpine juniper was harvested annually for cooking and heating as well as for religious ceremonies (Byers 2005). Mountaineering and associated activities can result in the introduction and spread of weeds, particularly along hiking trails (Barros and Pickering 2014b). Pack animals including horses can carry and disperse weed seed in their fur and dung (Mount and Pickering 2009; Ansong and Pickering 2013). Similarly, seeds can be carried on equipment and clothing potentially introducing new weeds into remote environments (Whinam *et al.* 2005; Ansong and Pickering 2014).

Weeds can also colonize mountain cliffs used for alpine rock climbing (McMillan and Larson 2002). Increasing number of weeds have been found on cliffs used for rock climbing, in part due the removal of native vegetation on ledges and other microsites and the accidental introduction of weed seed (McMillan and Larson 2002). These changes in cliff flora are of a particular concern as cliffs often harbour rare and endemic plants (McMillan and Larson 2002; Rusterholz *et al.* 2004; Vogler and Reisch 2011). These plants in the

Figure 12.2 Shrub harvesting in Annapurna region in the Himalayas, Nepal.

cracks and holds on cliffs are particularly at risk when these 'microsites' are used as hand and footholds during climbing (Vogler and Reisch 2011).

Damage to vegetation, soil loss, soil compaction and the proliferation of informal trails are common impacts of hiking into mountaineering peaks and alpine routes (Nepal and Nepal 2004; Barros *et al.* 2013; Ballantyne *et al.* 2014) (Figure 12.3). Some mountains particularly susceptible to trampling impacts such as those in Tasmania, Australia, are characterized by high rainfall, steep slopes, cold temperatures and fragile vegetation. As a result of these conditions vegetation loss and soil erosion occurs after <100 passes by hikers per year (Whinam and Chilcott 2003). Once damaged recovery can be very slow, as found for alpine meadows in tundra ecosystems where recovery from intensive

Figure 12.3 Trail incision by pack animals in an alpine meadow in the Andes, Argentina.

trampling can take several hundred or even thousands of years (Willard and Marr 1970).

The use of pack animals for transporting equipment for mountaineering also damages vegetation. Pack animals can do more damage than hikers due, in part, to the greater pressure exerted on the ground per unit area (e.g. ~4,380 g/cm² for a shod horse with rider), compared to hikers (~410 g/cm² for a hiker) (Liddle 1997; Cole and Spildie 1998; Törn *et al.* 2009). Also, grazing by pack animals removes large amounts of biomass from these ecosystems (McClaran and Cole 1993; Barros *et al.* 2014). Pack animals also contribute to the creation of informal trails particularly on popular routes used by yaks in the Himalayas (Nepal and Nepal 2004) and horses, mules and donkeys in the Andes (Barros *et al.* 2014).

The loss of vegetation can lead to impacts on soils including changes in organic matter affecting soil microbiological activity (Grieve 2001; Lucas-Borja *et al.* 2011). Extensive reductions in soil organic matter, for instance, occur along popular hiking trails in the Cairngorm Mountains in Scotland (Grieve 2001). Camping and associated activities also affect soils, including changing their chemical composition (Arocena *et al.* 2006). At Mt Robson in Canada the disposal of waste water from washing and cooking reduced aluminium and magnesium levels in the soil and increased copper and phosphorus levels due to the decomposition of food wastes (Arocena *et al.* 2006). Pack animals can add nitrogen and phosphorus to soils and waterways with high levels of both elements in horse manure and urine (Pickering *et al.* 2010).

Visitor use of campsites and trails can affect wildlife, including changes in animal behaviour and distribution (Monz *et al.* 2010; Steven *et al.* 2011; Francis and Barber 2013). In the Patagonian Andes in South America, Andean condors leave their roosts when visitors get too close (Herrmann *et al.* 2010). The Andean camelid, the guanaco, abandons its preferred habitat (Malo *et al.* 2011), while grazing by female guanacos is interrupted when visitor use is high and visitors come too close (Fuentes Allende 2011). The rare western capercaillie bird in Germany, is displaced to suboptimal habitats and suffers physiological stress from winter recreational activities including cross-country and downhill skiing (Thiel *et al.* 2008). Similarly, skiing and snowboarding in the Swiss Alps can flush Alpine snow grouse from their burrows, elevating the birds' stress levels (Arlettaz *et al.* 2007).

Activities, infrastructure and transport associated with mountaineering also affect wildlife. Food scraps left in camps and huts can increase the abundance of general predators, such as foxes and corvids, resulting in increased predation on local birds (Rixen and Rolando 2013). Pack animals grazing overnight in campsites can compete for food with native herbivores, potentially displacing native grazers to suboptimal habitats (Puig *et al.* 2001; Borgnia *et al.* 2008). Intensive grazing by pack animals can also increase the risk of egg predation for a range of ground nesting birds by reducing vegetation cover (Roodbergen *et al.* 2012).

Noise pollution from helicopters and snowmobiles affects the behaviour of wildlife in many mountains (Francis and Barber 2013). Studies on noise impacts on wildlife suggest that frequent noise interferes with the animal's capacity to detect critical sounds and that unpredictable noise can be perceived as threats, resulting in wildlife displacement and/or a decrease in foraging efficiency (Francis and Barber 2013). Noise impacts on mountain ungulates include increased heart rate and changes in habitat use by mountain sheep (Maier *et al.* 1998), disruption to feeding patterns in bighorn sheep (Maier *et al.* 1998) and a decrease in food intake by mountain caribou (Stockwell *et al.* 1991). The response of wildlife to helicopter over-flights varies based on factors such as topography and/or noise intensity among others (Frid 2003). Mountain sheep, for instance, are more sensitive to helicopter over-flights when the sheep are in areas where there is a higher risk of predation (Frid 2003). Bighorn sheep were less likely to be affected by helicopter noise when the helicopter was more than 500 m away (Stockwell *et al.* 1991).

Factors affecting environmental impacts

The intensity and extent of mountaineering impacts are influenced by the type of use and behaviour of individual users, the amount and timing of use, the distribution of use and the environmental characteristics of the site (Liddle 1997; Monz *et al.* 2010; Pickering 2010). Information about the relationship between these factors and the severity of impacts can be useful when developing guidelines and policies to minimize the environmental impacts of mountaineering (Monz *et al.* 2010; Pickering 2010). The type and severity of impacts varies among activities (Monz *et al.* 2010; Pickering 2010). As discussed, activities that exert greater ground pressure, such as pack animals and motorized vehicles, do more damage than others such as hiking (Törn *et al.* 2009; Monz *et al.* 2010). For instance, trampling by horses can result in two to three times greater reductions in plant cover and wider and deeper trails compared to trampling by hikers (Cole and Spildie 1998; Törn *et al.* 2009; Barros and Pickering 2014a).

The behaviour of individuals and groups is also important (Cole 2004; Pickering and Hill 2007). Mountaineers following minimum impact codes, such as 'Leave No Trace', are likely to have fewer impacts than those who do not (Daniels and Marion 2005). This includes care in the selection of campsites and routes for hiking and climbing, the appropriate disposal of human and other waste, and the use of fuel stoves instead of firewood for cooking (Marion and Reid 2007; Growcock and Pickering 2011). The type of activities can also influence the behaviour of users (Turner 2001; Park *et al.* 2008) with people undertaking some types of activities apparently less likely to comply with Minimum Impact Codes. It appears that sightseers and picnickers can be more likely to go off trail than people hiking (Walden-Schreiner and Leung 2013). Free ranging pack animals are also more likely to leave trails and take short cuts than those that are better managed increasing the total area damaged (Nepal and Nepal 2004; Barros *et al.* 2014).

The amount of use also affects the severity of impacts. It has generally been assumed that the first users may have more impact per person than later users resulting in a curvilinear relationship between use and impact (Monz *et al.* 2010; Monz *et al.* 2013). As a result, visitor use is often concentrated or confined to specific trails and sites (Monz *et al.* 2013). More recently, different relationships have been found between use and damage including linear, sigmoidal and exponential patterns (Growcock 2005; Monz *et al.* 2013). For sites where there is a sigmoidal or linear relationship, dispersed use may be more appropriate than concentrated use, at least at low levels of use (Monz *et al.* 2013).

The ability of the environment to tolerate impacts depends on the timing of use (Pickering 2010). Trampling when soils are wet can do more damage than when conditions are dry, resulting in more erosion and the formation of ribbon trails (Liddle 1997; Dixon *et al.* 2004). Unfortunately hiking and mountaineering is concentrated during summer which is the peak period of growth and reproduction for many plants and animals (Monz *et al.* 2010; Pickering 2010). For instance, trampling by hikers and pack animals in summer increases the risk of damage to ground nesting birds compared to other times of the year (Barros 2014). Some large mammals, such as native camelids in the Andes, can be displaced by hikers from more optimal habitat when reproducing (Fuentes Allende 2011). Some animals may be more vulnerable at other times of the year, including in winter (Monz *et al.* 2010). Skiing can disturb black grouse, for example, causing them to leave their snow burrows. This affects the birds' fitness and survival, because they need to thermoregulate more intensively when they leave their burrows making them more vulnerable to predation (Arlettaz *et al.* 2007).

The nature and intensity of impacts is affected by the characteristics of the vegetation, soils and topography (Liddle 1997; Monz *et al.* 2010; Pickering 2010). The tolerance of vegetation to trampling is determined by vegetation resistance, which refers to the ability of the vegetation to withstand disturbance before damage occurs, and resilience, which refers to its ability to recover from damage once it happens (Liddle 1997). Alpine plant communities can vary by orders of magnitude in their tolerance to disturbance. Communities dominated by dwarf shrubs and forbs are often less tolerant of trampling than those dominated by grasses (Hill and Pickering 2009; Ballantyne *et al.* 2014). Topographical factors such as slope influences trail degradation (Leung and Marion 1996), with greater soil loss on sloping trails than trails that follow contours (Dixon *et al.* 2004; Nepal and Nepal 2004). Other factors including the amount of organic matter and moisture content of soils influences the severity of impacts (Leung and Marion 1996; Olive and Marion 2009). Trampling on flat surfaces with wet organic soils results in more damage than trampling on durable surfaces because visitors often spread out to avoid muddy sections creating multiple trails (Leung and Marion 1996; Marion and Leung 2004).

The spatial distribution of use also affects impacts (Monz *et al.* 2010; Wimpey and Marion 2011). Campsites and hiking trails are often in areas of high conservation value and/or fragile ecosystems close to water bodies, rather than in sites that are more resistant to damage such as areas naturally free of vegetation and further away from water (Barros 2014). Crowding and unregulated use can also result in the creation of informal trails, which fragment relatively undisturbed habitats and increase the total area damaged (Leung *et al.* 2011; Wimpey and Marion 2011; Barros and Pickering 2012). Similarly, noise impacts from helicopters can affect a wide area, and when flight routes have to change such as during rescues, new areas can be affected (Barros 2014).

Management recommendations

Minimizing and ameliorating impacts from mountaineering and associated activities is challenging, particularly in more remote mountains and when resources are limited (Byers 2000; Nepal 2002; Barros *et al.* 2013). The implementation of educational programmes, including minimum impact codes such as 'Leave No Trace' (https://lnt.org/learn/7-principles), can help minimize impacts. For tour operators, including those providing guiding and campsite services, the use of certified eco-labels can minimize impacts. In addition, protected areas and other land management agencies can provide incentives to tour operators that implement good environmental practices. The following section reviews management strategies for minimizing environmental impacts from mountaineering and associated activities, including examples that have been implemented along popular hiking and climbing routes.

Minimize trails impacts

Better design, development and maintenance of trails can minimize many of their impacts (Marion and Leung 2004; Marion and Wimpey 2009). Selecting the right materials is important with dramatic differences among different trail materials (Hill and Pickering 2006). Avoiding areas of high conservation value and/or vegetation with low tolerance to trampling reduces impacts (Pickering 2010), while the design of trails so they avoid steep slopes, areas of wet soils and areas close to water bodies where erosion is more likely also minimize impacts. For example, on steep slopes side-hill trails are often recommended because they focus the traffic on a narrow tread avoiding trail widening (Marion and Leung 2004). In flat areas, where people and pack animals tend to spread out, the use of borders such as rocks or wood posts can limit trampling to designated trails (Marion and Leung 2004).

Prevent the introduction and dispersal of weeds and pathogens

Reducing the introduction of weeds and pathogens involves ensuring good hygiene practices such as encouraging commercial operators and tourists to clean vehicles, boots and other equipment prior to arrival. For pack animals, the use of weed-free fodder should be encouraged prior to and during expeditions where possible (Pickering and Mount 2010). As disturbance favours weeds, confining traffic to designated trails can also reduce the spread of weed along trails (Pickering and Mount 2010; Newsome *et al.* 2012).

Reduce the use of firewood and promote conservation initiatives

In some mountains the use of firewood for heating and cooking at campsites and huts has been a common practice, including in the Himalayas and the Andes (Byers 2009). Many conservation organizations are increasingly promoting, and often requiring, the use of fuel stoves instead (Byers 2014). This includes conservation initiatives in the Nepal Himalayas which promote the replacement of juniper with kerosene for fuel and the establishment of nurseries for reforestation and restoration (Byers 2014). For base camps in nival zones which have limited vegetation, the use of alternative energy sources such as parabolic solar power, heat retaining boxes and briquettes instead of gas cylinders may be more effective (Sherpa 2008).

Minimize grazing impacts by pack animals

Managing pack animals can be particularly challenging when there is long tradition of their use. Management actions can include reducing the intensity of use of specific campsites, implementing rotational grazing, restrict grazing during certain times of year and requiring the use of weed-free fodder (McClaran and Cole 1993; Moore *et al.* 2000; Cole *et al.* 2004). Some of these practices have been implemented in the United States, including in Sequoia and Kings National Park in the Rocky Mountains (NPS 2014a). In these parks there are areas 'closed to grazing' where pack animals are confined to designated trails and are given substitute feeds, 'day passed through', where pack animals are not allowed to graze or stay overnight and areas 'closed to stock' where no pack animals are permitted.

Manage human and solid waste

Strategies to manage waste including minimum impact codes and innovative technologies are increasingly popular (American Alpine Club 2010). Impact codes often recommend reducing packaging, packing out litter and food wastes, establishing minimum distances between campsites and water sources, and the use of eco-friendly products for cleaning (e.g. biodegradable soaps). Pro-grammes to promote the removal of litter include the payment of environmental deposits. For peaks in the Himalayas, for example, climbers pay a deposit of US$4,000 which is only returned once park rangers have ascertained that all garbage has been carried out by the expedition (Kuniyal 2002).

Human waste practices include the use of cat holes, pack-out systems (e.g. Denali National Park) and surface disposal (Robinson 2010; Ells and Monz 2011). The surface disposal (smearing) is only suggested for very remote, low use alpine and arid settings and only when pack-out systems are not feasible (Ells and Monz 2011). In high use campsites, toilets are recommended. These include pit toilets, composting and dehydration toilets and/or barrel collection toilets (Hill and Henry 2013). The most appropriate type depends on the eco-logical conditions of the site and resources. Some types, such as composting toilets, require constant use and maintenance and hence are not suitable for cold and arid environments (American Alpine Club 2010). Barrel collection toilets, which can involve the use of a helicopter to remove barrels, are expensive and have their own impacts (American Alpine Club 2010; Hill and Henry 2013). To reduce the volume/weight of waste, some park agencies use systems that sepa-rate urine from excreta and that desiccate faecal matter prior to removal (Hill and Henry 2013). Strategies to minimize the impacts of helicopters include restricting the number of flights in total and per day, establishing minimum flight distances from the ground, careful selection of routes to avoid overflying certain areas (e.g. nesting sites, wildlife habitat) and restricting use at certain times of year (e.g. during bird nesting, post calving) (Barber *et al.* 2009; Withers and Adema 2009).

Minimize crowding

Crowding in campsites and on climbing routes is common in some mountain areas (Pettebone *et al.* 2013). To limit numbers, some management agencies implement strategies, such as higher fees for popular times, limiting the number of permits and controlling the direction of travel to avoid congestion. In Denali National Park, for example, climbers ascending Mt McKinley need to book their climb 60 days prior to departure with a cap on the number of climbing parties per day (NPS 2014b).

Minimize rock climbing impacts

Management practices to minimize impacts from this activity include exclusion and zoning areas of high conservation value, restricting use during particular times of year and regulating the types of equipment used (Cater *et al.* 2008). For example, 'climbing-free protection areas' have been established where cliffs are of high conservation value (Müller *et al.* 2004; Vogler and Reisch 2011). Zoning activities allow greater use of more resilient sites (Cater *et al.* 2008), while some sites have seasonal closures or buffer zones to avoid disturbing birds when breeding (NPS 1997). In others, there are restrictions on the type of equipment used for climbing, including restricting the use of fixed bolts for alpine rock climbing (Cater *et al.* 2008).

Conclusion

This chapter demonstrates how mountaineering and its related activities result in a range of environmental impacts including on water, soils vegetation and wildlife, with the severity of impacts varying depending on the environment, the timing and amount of use and the behaviour of users. Given the popularity of mountaineering worldwide, it is important to better manage and monitor these impacts. This review can assist mountaineers, those providing commercial services for mountaineers and managers, so they can minimize impacts on environments that are often of high conservation value and susceptible to damage.

References

American Alpine Club (2010) *Exit strategies: Managing human waste in the wild*, Golden, CO: American Alpine Club.
Ansong, M. and Pickering, C. (2013) 'A global review of weeds that can germinate from horse dung', *Ecological Management and Restoration*, 14(3): 216–223.
Ansong, M. and Pickering, C. (2014) 'Weed seeds on clothing: A global review', *Journal of Environmental Management*, 144(1): 203–211.
Arlettaz, R., Patthey, P., Baltic, M., Leu, T., Schaub, M., Palme, R. and Jenni-Eiermann, S. (2007) 'Spreading free-riding snow sports represent a novel serious threat for wildlife', *Proceedings of the Royal Society B: Biological Sciences*, 274(1614): 1219–1224.
Arocena, J. M., Nepal, S. K. and Rutherford, M. (2006) 'Visitor-induced changes in the chemical composition of soils in backcountry areas of Mt Robson Provincial Park, British Columbia, Canada', *Journal of Environmental Management*, 79(1): 10–19.
Ballantyne, M., Pickering, C. M., McDougall, K. L. and Wright, G. T. (2014) 'Sustained impacts of a hiking trail on changing Windswept Feldmark vegetation in the Australian Alps', *Australian Journal of Botany*, 62(4): 263–275.

Barber, J. R., Fristrup, K. M., Brown, C. L., Hardy, A. R., Angeloni, L. M. and Crooks, K. R. (2009) 'Conserving the wild life therein: Protecting park fauna from anthropogenic noise', *Park Science*, 26(3): 26–31.

Barros, A. (2004) 'Impacto del uso público sobre el suelo, la vegetación y las comunidades acuáticas, quebrada de horcones, Parque Provincial Aconcagua (Mendoza, Argentina)', unpublished masters thesis, Centro de Zoologia Aplicada, Universidad Nacional de Córdoba.

Barros, A. (2014) 'Ecological impacts of visitor use, Aconcagua Provincial Park, Argentina', unpublished doctoral thesis, Griffith School of Environment, Griffith University.

Barros, A. and Pickering, C. M. (2012) 'Informal trails fragment the landscape in a high conservation area in the Andes', in P. Fredman, M. Stenseke, H. Liljendahl, A. Mossing and D. Laven (eds) *Proceedings of the 6th international conference on monitoring and management of visitors in recreational and protected areas*, Stockholm: Mittuniversitet: 360–361.

Barros, A. and Pickering, C. M. (2014a) 'Impacts of experimental trampling by hikers and pack animals on a high altitude alpine sedge meadow in the Andes', *Plant Ecology and Diversity*, 8(2): 265–276.

Barros, A. and Pickering, C. M. (2014b) 'Non-native plant invasion in relation to tourism use of Aconcagua Park, Argentina, the highest protected area in the Southern Hemisphere', *Mountain Research and Development*, 34(1): 13–26.

Barros, A., Gonnet, J. and Pickering, C. (2013) 'Impacts of informal trails on vegetation and soils in the highest protected area in the Southern Hemisphere', *Journal of Environmental Management*, 127(1): 50–60.

Barros, A., Pickering, C. and Renison, D. (2014) 'Short-term effects of pack animal grazing exclusion from Andean alpine meadows', *Arctic, Antarctic, and Alpine Research*, 46(2): 41–51.

Basnet, K. (1993) 'Solid waste pollution versus sustainable development in high mountain environment: A case study of Sagarmatha National Park of Khumbu region, Nepal', *Contributions to Nepalese Studies*, 20(1): 131–139.

Becker, A., Körner, C., Brun, J.-J., Guisan, A. and Tappeiner, U. (2007) 'Ecological and land use studies along elevational gradients', *Mountain Research and Development*, 27(1): 58–65.

Bell, K. L. and Bliss, L. C. (1973) 'Alpine disturbance studies: Olympic national park, USA', *Biological Conservation*, 5(1): 25–32.

Blyth, S., Groombridge, B., Lysenko, I., Miles, L. and Newton, A. (2002) *Mountain watch*, Cambridge: UNEP World Conservation Monitoring Centre.

Borgnia, M., Vilá, B. L. and Cassini, M. H. (2008) 'Interaction between wild camelids and livestock in an Andean semi-desert', *Journal of Arid Environments*, 72(12): 2150–2158.

Bridle, K. L. and Kirkpatrick, J. B. (2003) 'Impacts of nutrient additions and digging for human waste disposal in natural environments, Tasmania, Australia', *Journal of Environmental Management*, 69(3): 299–306.

Buckley, R. (2006) *Adventure tourism*, Cambridge: CABI Publishing.

Byers, A. (2000) 'Contemporary landscape change in the Huascarán National Park and buffer zone, Cordillera Blanca, Peru', *Mountain Research and Development*, 20(1): 52–63.

Byers, A. (2005) 'Contemporary human impacts on Alpine ecosystems in the Sagarmatha (Mt. Everest) National park, Khumbu, Nepal', *Annals of the Association of American Geographers*, 95(1): 112–140.

234   C. M. Pickering and A. Barros

Byers, A. (2009) 'A comparative study of tourism impacts on alpine ecosystems in the Sagarmatha (Mt. Everest) National Park, Nepal and the Huascarán National Park, Peru', in J. Hill and T. Gale (eds) *Ecotourism and environmental sustainability: Principles and practice*, Burlington, VT: Ashgate Publishing: 51–68.

Byers, A. (2014) 'Contemporary human impacts on subalpine and alpine ecosystems of the Hinku Valley, Makalu-Barun National Park and Buffer Zone, Nepal', *Himalaya, the Journal of the Association for Nepal and Himalayan Studies*, 33(1): 25–41.

Camp, R. J. and Knight, R. L. (1998) 'Effects of rock climbing on cliff plant communities at Joshua Tree National Park, California', *Conservation Biology*, 12(6): 1302–1306.

Cater, C., Buckley, R., Hales, R., Newsome, D., Pickering, C. and Smith, A. (2008) *High impact activities in parks: Best management practice and future research*, Gold Coast: Cooperative Research Centre for Sustainable Tourism.

Cole, D. N. (2004) 'Impacts of hiking and camping on soils and vegetation: A review', in R. Buckley (ed.) *Environmental impacts of ecotourism*, Cambridge: CAB International: 41–60.

Cole, D. N. and Spildie, D. R. (1998) 'Hiker, horse and llama trampling effects on native vegetation in Montana, USA', *Journal of Environmental Management*, 53(1): 61–71.

Cole, D. N., Wagtendonk, W. V., Mclaran, M. P., Moore, P. E. and Neil, K. (2004) 'Response of mountain meadows to grazing by recreation packstock', *Journal Range Management*, 57(2): 153–160.

Daniels, M. L. and Marion, J. L. (2005) 'Communicating leave no trace ethics and practices: Efficacy of two-day trainer courses', *Journal of Park and Recreation Administration*, 23(4): 1–19.

Dixon, G., Hawes, M. and McPherson, G. (2004) 'Monitoring and modelling walking track impacts in the Tasmanian Wilderness World Heritage Area, Australia', *Journal of Environmental Management*, 71(4): 305–320.

Ells, M. D. and Monz, C. A. (2011) 'The consequences of backcountry surface disposal of human waste in an alpine, temperate forest and arid environment', *Journal of Environmental Management*, 92(4): 1334–1337.

Francis, C. D. and Barber, J. R. (2013) 'A framework for understanding noise impacts on wildlife: An urgent conservation priority', *Frontiers in Ecology and the Environment*, 11(6): 305–313.

Frid, A. (2003) 'Dall's sheep responses to overflights by helicopter and fixed-wing aircraft', *Biological Conservation*, 110(3): 387–399.

Fuentes Allende, N. E. (2011) 'Efecto del Turismo en la conducta del guanaco en el area del Parque Nacional Torres del Paine', unpublished undergraduate thesis, Facultad de Ciencias Agronómicas, Universidad de Chile.

Ghimire, N. P., Caravellol, G. and Jha, P. K. (2013) 'Bacterial contamination in the surface waterbodies in Sagarmatha National Park and Buffer Zone, Nepal', *Scientific World*, 11(11): 94–96.

Goodwin, K., Loso, M. G. and Braun, M. (2012) 'Glacial transport of human waste and survival of fecal bacteria on Mt. McKinley's Kahiltna Glacier, Denali National Park, Alaska', *Arctic, Antarctic, and Alpine Research*, 44(4): 432–445.

Grêt-Regamey, A., Brunner, S. H. and Kienast, F. (2012) 'Mountain ecosystem services: Who cares?' *Mountain Research and Development*, 32(S1): 23–34.

Grieve, I. C. (2001) 'Human impacts on soil properties and their implications for the sensitivity of soil systems in Scotland', *Catena*, 42(2): 361–374.

Growcock, A. J. W. (2005) 'Impacts of camping and trampling on Australian alpine and subalpine vegetation and soils', unpublished doctoral thesis, Griffith University.

Growcock, A. and Pickering, C. (2011) 'Impacts of small group short term experimental camping on alpine and subalpine vegetation in the Australian Alps', *Journal of Ecotourism*, 10(1): 86–100.

Hadwen, W. L., Arthington, A. H. and Boon, P. I. (2008) *Detecting visitor impacts in and around aquatic ecosystems within protected areas*, Gold Coast: Cooperative Research Centre for Sustainable Tourism.

Heil, L., Fernández-Juricic, E., Renison, D., Cingolani, A. M. and Blumstein, D. T. (2007) 'Avian responses to tourism in the biogeographically isolated high Córdoba Mountains, Argentina', *Biodiversity and Conservation*, 16(4): 1009–1026.

Herrmann, T. M., Costina, M. I. and Costina, A. M. A. (2010) 'Roost sites and communal behaviour of Andean condors in Chile', *Geographical Review*, 100(2): 246–262.

Hill, G. and Henry, G. (2013) 'The application and performance of urine diversion to minimize waste management costs associated with remote wilderness toilets', *Journal of Wilderness*, 19(1): 26–33.

Hill, R. and Pickering, C. (2009) 'Differences in resistance of three subtropical vegetation types to experimental trampling', *Journal of Environmental Management*, 90(2): 1305–1312.

Hill, W. and Pickering, C. M. (2006) 'Vegetation associated with different walking track types in the Kosciuszko alpine area, Australia', *Journal of Environmental Management*, 78(1): 24–34.

Körner, C. (2003) *Alpine plant life: Functional plant ecology of high mountain ecosystems*, Berlin: Springer.

Körner, C. and Ohsawa, M. (2005) 'Mountain systems', in R. Hassan, R. Scholes and N. Ash (eds) *Ecosystems and human well-being: Current state and trends*, Millennium ecosystem assessment series, Washington, DC: Island Press: 681–716.

Körner, C., Paulsen, J. and Spehn, E. M. (2011) 'A definition of mountains and their bioclimatic belts for global comparisons of biodiversity data', *Alpine Botany*, 121(2): 73–78.

Kuniyal, J. C. (2002) 'Mountain expeditions: Minimising the impact', *Environmental Impact Assessment Review*, 22(6): 561–581.

Leung, Y.-F. and Marion, J. L. (1996) 'Trail degradation as influenced by environmental factors: A state of the knowledge review', *Journal of Soil and Water Conservation*, 51(2): 130–136.

Leung, Y.-F., Newburger, T., Jones, M., Kuhn, B. and Woiderski, B. (2011) 'Developing a monitoring protocol for visitor-created informal trails in Yosemite National Park, USA', *Environmental Management*, 47(1): 93–106.

Liddle, M. (1997) *Recreation ecology: The ecological impact of outdoor recreation and ecotourism*, London: Chapman & Hall.

Lucas-Borja, M. E., Bastida, F., Moreno, J. L., Nicolás, C., Andres, M., López, F. R. and Del Cerro, A. (2011) 'The effects of human trampling on the microbiological properties of soil and vegetation in mediterranean mountain areas', *Land Degradation and Development*, 22(4): 383–394.

McClaran, M. P. and Cole, D. N. (1993) *Packstock in wilderness: Use, impacts, monitoring, and management*, Ogden, UT: US Department of Agriculture, Forest Service.

McMillan, M. and Larson, D. W. (2002) 'Effects of rock climbing on the vegetation of the Niagara Escarpment in southern Ontario, Canada', *Conservation Biology*, 16(2): 389–398.

Maier, J. A. K., Murphy, S. M., White, R. G. and Smith, M. D. (1998) 'Responses of caribou to overflights by low-altitude jet aircraft', *Journal of Wildlife Management*, 62(2): 752–766.

Malo, J. E., Acebes, P. and Traba, J. (2011) 'Measuring ungulate tolerance to human with flight distance: A reliable visitor management tool?' *Biodiversity and Conservation*, 20(14): 3477–3488.

Manfredi, E. C., Flury, B., Viviano, G., Thakuri, S., Khanal, S. N., Jha, P. K., Maskey, R. K., Kayastha, R. B., Kafle, K. R. and Bhochhibhoya, S. (2010) 'Solid waste and water quality management models for Sagarmatha National Park and Buffer Zone, Nepal: Implementation of a participatory modeling framework', *International Journal of Climatology*, 30(2): 127–142.

Marion, J. L. and Leung, Y. F. (2004) 'Environmentally sustainable trail management', in R. C. Buckley (ed.) *Environmental impact of tourism*, London: CABI Publishing: 229–244.

Marion, J. L. and Reid, S. E. (2007) 'Minimising visitor impacts to protected areas: The efficacy of low impact education programmes', *Journal of Sustainable Tourism*, 15(1): 5–27.

Marion, J. L. and Wimpey, J. (2007) 'Environmental impacts of mountain biking: Science review and best practices', in IMBA (ed.) *Managing mountain biking: IMBA's guide to providing great riding*. Boulder, CO: International Mountain Bicycling Association: 94–111.

Marion, J. L. and Wimpey, J. (2009) *Monitoring protocols for characterizing trail conditions, understanding degradation, and selecting indicators and standards of quality, Acadia National Park, Mount Desert Island*, Blacksburg, VA: Virginia Tech College of Natural Resources.

Martin, K. (2013) 'The ecological values of mountain environments and wildlife', in C. Rixen and A. Rolando (eds) *The impacts of skiing and related winter activities in mountain environments*, Bussum: Bentham Science Publishers.

Messerli, B., Viviroli, D. and Weingartner, R. (2004) 'Mountains of the world: Vulnerable water towers for the 21st century', *Ambio*, 13(1): 29–34.

Monz, C. A., Cole, D. N., Leung, Y. F. and Marion, J. L. (2010) 'Sustaining visitor use in protected areas: Future opportunities in recreation ecology research based on the USA experience', *Environmental Management*, 45(3): 551–562.

Monz, C. A., Pickering, C. M. and Hadwen, W. L. (2013) 'Recent advances in recreation ecology and the implications of different relationships between recreation use and ecological impacts', *Frontiers in Ecology and the Environment*, 11(8): 441–446.

Moore, P., Cole, D. N., Van Wagtendonk, J., McClaran, M. P. and McDougald, N. (2000) 'Meadow response to pack stock grazing in the Yosemite wilderness: Integrating research and management', *USDA Forest Service Proceedings RMRS-P*, 5(15): 160–163.

Mount, A. and Pickering, C. M. (2009) 'Testing the capacity of clothing to act as a vector for non-native seed in protected areas', *Journal of Environmental Management*, 91(1): 168–179.

Müller, S. W., Rusterholz, H.-P. and Baur, B. (2004) 'Rock climbing alters the vegetation of limestone cliffs in the northern Swiss Jura Mountains', *Canadian Journal of Botany*, 82(6): 862–870.

Myers, N., Mittermeier, R. A., Mittermeier, C. G., da Fonseca, G. A. B. and Kent, J. (2000) 'Biodiversity hotspots for conservation priorities', *Nature*, 403(24): 853–858.

Nagy, L. and Grabherr, G. (2009) *The biology of alpine habitats*, Oxford: Oxford University Press.

National Park Service (NPS) (1997) 'Climbing management plan'. Online, available at: www.nps.gov/acad/planyourvisit/climbmgtplan.htm (accessed 3 July 2014).

National Park Service (NPS) (2014a) 'Stock users guide to the wilderness of Sequoia and Kings Canyon National Parks'. Online, available at: www.nps.gov/seki/planyourvisit/stockuse.htm (accessed 3 July 2014).

National Park Service (NPS) (2014b) 'Denali National Park, mountaineering'. Online, available at: www.nps.gov/dena/planyourvisit/mountaineering.htm (accessed 3 July 2014).

Nepal, S. K. (2002) 'Mountain ecotourism and sustainable development: Ecology, economics, and ethics', *Mountain Research and Development*, 22(2): 104–109.

Nepal, S. K. and Nepal, S. A. (2004) 'Visitor impacts on trails in the Sagarmatha (Mt. Everest) National Park, Nepal', *Ambio*, 33(6): 334–340.

Newsome, D., Moore, S. A. and Dowling, R. K. (2012) *Natural area tourism: Ecology, impacts and management*, New York: Channel View Publications.

Olive, N. D. and Marion, J. L. (2009) 'The influence of use-related, environmental, and managerial factors on soil loss from recreational trails', *Journal of Environmental Management*, 90(3): 1483–1493.

Pakanen, V.-M., Luukkonen, A. and Koivula, K. (2011) 'Nest predation and trampling as management risks in grazed coastal meadows', *Biodiversity and Conservation*, 20(9): 2057–2073.

Park, L. O., Manning, R. E., Marion, J. L., Lawson, S. R. and Jacobi, C. (2008) 'Managing visitor impacts in parks: A multi-method study of the effectiveness of alternative management practices', *Journal Park and Recreation Administration*, 26(1): 97–121.

Pettebone, D., Meldrum, B., Leslie, C., Lawson, S. R., Newman, P., Reigner, N. and Gibson, A. (2013) 'A visitor use monitoring approach on the Half Dome cables to reduce crowding and inform park planning decisions in Yosemite National Park', *Landscape and Urban Planning*, 118(10): 1–9.

Pickering, C. and Barros, A. (2012) 'Mountain environments and tourism', in A. Holden and D. Fennell (eds) *Handbook of tourism and the environment*, London: Routledge: 183–191.

Pickering, C. M. (2010) 'Ten factors that affect the severity of environmental impacts of visitors in protected areas', *Ambio*, 39(1): 70–77.

Pickering, C. and Mount, A. (2010) 'Do tourists disperse weed seed? A global review of unintentional human-mediated terrestrial seed dispersal on clothing, vehicles and horses', *Journal of Sustainable Tourism*, 18(2): 239–256.

Pickering, C. M. and Hill, W. (2007) 'Impacts of recreation and tourism on plant biodiversity and vegetation in protected areas in Australia', *Journal of Environmental Management*, 85(4): 791–800.

Pickering, C. M., Hill, W., Newsome, D. and Leung, Y.-F. (2010) 'Comparing hiking, mountain biking and horse riding impacts on vegetation and soils in Australia and the United States of America', *Journal of Environmental Management*, 91(3): 551–562.

Pomfret, G. (2006) 'Mountaineering adventure tourists: A conceptual framework for research', *Tourism Management*, 27(1): 113–123.

Prideaux, B., Timothy, D. and Cooper, M. (2009) 'Introducing river tourism: Physical, ecological and human aspects', in P. Prideaux and M. Cooper (eds) *River tourism*, Cambridge: CABI Publishing: 1–22.

Puig, S., Videla, F., Cona, M. I. and Monge, S. A. (2001) 'Use of food availability by guanacos (Lama guanicoe) and livestock in Northern Patagonia (Mendoza, Argentina)', *Journal of Arid Environments*, 47(3): 291–308.

Rixen, C. and Rolando, A. (2013) *The impacts of skiing and related winter activities in mountain environments*, Bussum: Bentham Science Publishers.

Robinson, R. (2010) 'Leave no waste: The evolution of clean climbing practices in Denali National Park', Proceedings of 'Exit strategies: Managing human waste in the wild', American Alpine Club, Golden, CO, 30–31 July and August. Online, available at: www.americanalpineclub.org/p/exit-strategies-supplement (accessed 3 March 2015).

Roodbergen, M., Werf, B. and Hötker, H. (2012) 'Revealing the contributions of reproduction and survival to the Europe-wide decline in meadow birds: Review and meta-analysis', *Journal of Ornithology*, 153(1): 53–74.

Rusterholz, H.-P., Miller, S. W. and Baur, B. (2004) 'Effects of rock climbing on plant communities on exposed limestone cliffs in the Swiss Jura mountains', *Applied Vegetation Science*, 7(1): 35–40.

Sato, C. F., Wood, J. T. and Lindenmayer, D. B. (2013) 'The effects of winter recreation on alpine and subalpine fauna: A systematic review and meta-analysis', *PLoS ONE*, 8(5): e64282.

Sherpa, D. W. (2008) 'Eco everest expedition 2008'. Online, available at: www.alanarnette.com/downloads/ecoeverest.pdf (accessed 3 July 2014).

Steven, R., Pickering, C. and Guy Castley, J. (2011) 'A review of the impacts of nature based recreation on birds', *Journal of Environmental Management*, 92(10): 2287–2294.

Stockwell, C. A., Bateman, G. C. and Berger, J. (1991) 'Conflicts in national parks: A case study of helicopters and bighorn sheep time budgets at the Grand Canyon', *Biological Conservation*, 56(3): 317–328.

Storch, I. and Leidenberger, C. (2003) 'Tourism, mountain huts and distribution of corvids in the Bavarian Alps, Germany', *Wildlife Biology*, 9(4): 301–308.

Thiel, D., Jenni-Eiermann, S., Braunisch, V., Palme, R. and Jenni, L. (2008) 'Ski tourism affects habitat use and evokes a physiological stress response in capercaillie Tetrao urogallus: A new methodological approach', *Journal of Applied Ecology*, 45(3): 845–853.

Törn, A., Tolvanen, A., Norokorpi, Y., Tervo, R. and Siikamäki, P. (2009) 'Comparing the impacts of hiking, skiing and horse riding on trail and vegetation in different types of forest', *Journal of Environmental Management*, 90(3): 1427–1434.

Turner, R. (2001) 'Visitor behaviors and resource impacts at Cadillac Mountain, Acadia National Park', unpublished doctoral thesis, University of Maine.

Vogler, F. and Reisch, C. (2011) 'Genetic variation on the rocks: The impact of climbing on the population ecology of a typical cliff plant', *Journal of Applied Ecology*, 48(4): 899–905.

Walden-Schreiner, C. and Leung, Y.-F. (2013) 'Spatially characterizing visitor use and its association with informal trails in Yosemite valley meadows', *Environmental Management*, 52(1): 163–178.

Whinam, J. and Chilcott, N. (2003) 'Impacts after four years of experimental trampling on alpine/subalpine environments in western Tasmania', *Journal of Environmental Management*, 67: 339–351.

Whinam, J., Chilcott, N. and Bergstrom, D. (2005) 'Subantarctic hitchhikers: Expeditioners as vectors for the introduction of alien organisms', *Biological Conservation*, 121(3): 207–219.

Willard, B. E. and Marr, J. W. (1970) 'Effects of human activities on alpine tundra ecosystems in Rocky Mountain National Park, Colorado', *Biological Conservation*, 2(4): 257–265.

Wilson, J. P. and Seney, J. P. (1994). 'Erosional impact of hikers, horses, motorcycles, and off-road bicycles on mountain trails in Montana', *Mountain Research and Development*, 14(1): 77–88.

Wimpey, J. and Marion, J. L. (2011) 'A spatial exploration of informal trail networks within Great Falls Park, VA', *Journal of Environmental Management*, 92(3): 1012–1022.

Withers, J. and Adema, G. (2009) 'Soundscapes monitoring and an overflights advisory council: Informing real time management decisions at Denali National Park and Preserve', *Park Science*, 26(3): 42–45.

Case study 6

Mountaineering and climate change

C. Michael Hall

Climate change is one of the most significant aspects of global and regional environmental change. According to the 2013 Intergovernmental Panel on Climate Change (IPCC) report on the physical science basis for climate change 'Warming of the climate system is unequivocal, and since the 1950s, many of the observed changes are unprecedented over decades to millennia' (p. 2). The IPCC concludes 'It is extremely likely that human influence has been the dominant cause of the observed warming since the mid-20th century' (p. 15). It also notes, with a high degree of confidence, that 'Glacier retreat could also impact activities in high mountainous ecosystems such as alpine tourism, mountaineering and adventure tourism' (Magrin *et al.* 2014: 1522).

Given the potential implications of climate change at first glance to focus on the effects of climate change on mountaineering or indeed on mountain tourism overall may seem trite. However, there are many areas for which mountaineering is economically significant, and therefore also relevant to the environmental and social well-being of alpine communities. For example, in the case of one of the most internationally recognized mountaineering locations, Sagamartha National Park in Nepal, about 65 per cent of households within the boundaries of the National Park are dependent to some degree on the trekking/climbing economy (Byers 2005). Furthermore, in a wider context the profound political, economic and social repercussions of the impacts of global climate change will also impact the attractiveness and security of mountain regions (Khoday 2007; Ritter *et al.* 2012).

Much of the focus on the relationship between climate change and mountain tourism has been in relation to skiing, snow reliability and the viability of winter resort destinations (Scott *et al.* 2012). Indeed, Beniston (2003) suggested that alpine mountaineering and hiking may be a form of adaptation for some locations and provide compensation for reduced skiing, and help maintain the attractiveness of some mountain region destinations. However, the capacity of mountaineering to adapt to climate change is perhaps not as straightforward as Beniston (2003) appears to suggest. Apart from the obvious issue of the capacity to change tourist behaviour and grow the mountaineering market for specific products and locations (see Muhar *et al.* 2006; Gössling *et al.* 2012), there are a number of direct and indirect effects of climate change on outdoor climbing and mountaineering. Perhaps most significantly the temperature, humidity and precipitation shifts associated with climate change can substantially affect the capacity for certain types of climbing in particular locations. For example, in the case of the Scottish Highlands. Harrison *et al.* (2005) report that respondents in their study had, on the whole, come to the conclusion that snow and ice climbing had become unreliable as a result of climate change, and that there had been a shift towards mixed buttress climbing and a more general diversification of mountain 'experiences', including winter mountain leader training and assessment (see also Scottish Natural Heritage 2009).

Another important effect of climate change is the increased frequency of high magnitude weather events. Harrison *et al.* (2005) also found that the changing nature of the winter weather in the Scottish Highlands had created a number of safety problems. The heavy snows and rapid thaws had increased the avalanche risk in some areas while the absence of snow had tempted many less experienced hill walkers into the mountains. 'Walkers had occasionally been overtaken by sudden snowstorms and there was the ever-present risk of hypothermia in cold, wet and windy conditions' (Harrison *et al.* 2005: 148). The implications of such weather extremes go beyond activities and also have implications for infrastructure. For example, Scottish Natural Heritage (2009) reported that higher specifications in path and other infrastructure may be needed to cope with more visitors or extreme rain events, coastal and inland flooding, more frequent and extreme fluctuations in freeze/thaw, and less snowfall. Although, more positively, they also noted that longer growing seasons could help in revegetating and reinstating ground damaged through recreational use.

The issues of climbing safety and infrastructure impacts of climate change are extremely important for areas in which rock faces are affected by permafrost, which may thaw under warmer conditions or thaw for longer therefore creating rock instability. In the case of the Swiss Alps, Matasci (2012) identifies permafrost thaw as an issue for two significant destinations, Pontresina – St Moritz and Zermatt. In the case of the latter a member of the local tourism office commented

> Zermatt is a climbing destination, and we note more accidents with rock falls ... because often permafrost freezing is not there anymore.... You can see an increase of accidents in this way.... And also, going back to the cable car company, all these stations in the mountains with the posts holding the cables, they have to be examined more now because all the anchors are in the frozen rocks and they have to see if this is still OK.
>
> (quoted in Matasci 2012: 88)

At a larger scale regional climate-related environmental change may also be significant. Even if climbing routes and access are unaffected by shifts in climatic factors, changes in the relative attractiveness of mountaineering locations, as with any tourism and recreations destination under climate change, can occur via shifts in overall average temperatures and relative humidity. For example, humidity levels can affect climbing tactics and route selection as well as choice of clothing. Furthermore, new disease vectors may be introduced into areas where they previously did not exist also affecting attractiveness and health and safety considerations (Hall 2015). The provision of accurate meteorological data for mountaineering will become even more important.

Little is known of the adaptive capacity of mountaineering locations with specific respect to being able to continue as activity destinations. Some places may be able to continue to offer attractive climbing routes; however, the degree of potential substitution of either activities or location is unknown. One possibility being a growth in Via Ferrata climbing, as has occurred in some locations in Austria, Slovenia and Italy already (Muhar *et al.* 2006). However, given the limited size of the mountaineering market it is likely that some existing destinations, for example those that specialize in glacier and ice climbs, will not be able to continue as before. Further, loss of permafrost, shorter periods of significant sub-zero temperatures and more extreme weather events will affect the stability of many rock faces potentially leading to briefer climbing seasons, the selection of new routes and, in some cases, the abandonment of some routes and locations altogether.

References

Beniston, M. (2003) 'Climatic change in mountain regions: A review of possible impacts', *Climatic Change*, 59(1–2): 5–31.

Byers, A. (2005) 'Contemporary human impacts on Alpine ecosystems in the Sagarmatha (Mt. Everest) national park, Khumbu, Nepal', *Annals of the Association of American Geographers*, 95(1): 112–140.

Gössling, S., Scott, D., Hall, C. M., Ceron, J.-P. and Dubois, G. (2012) 'Consumer behaviour and demand response of tourists to climate change', *Annals of Tourism Research*, 39(1): 36–58.

Hall, C. M. (2015) 'Tourism and biological exchange and invasions: A missing dimension in sustainable tourism?' *Tourism Recreation Research*, 40(1), 81–94.

Harrison, S. J., Winterbottom, S. J. and Johnson, R. C. (2005) 'Changing snow cover and winter tourism and recreation in the Scottish Highlands', in C. M. Hall and J. Higham (eds) *Tourism, recreation and climate change*, Clevedon: Channel View: 143–154.

IPCC (2013) 'Summary for policymakers', in T. F. Stocker, D. Qin, G.-K. Plattner, M. Tignor, S. Allen, J. Boschung, A. Nauels, Y. Xia, V. Bex and P. Midgley (eds) *Climate change 2013: The physical science basis. Contribution of working group I to the fifth assessment report of the intergovernmental panel on climate change*, Cambridge: Cambridge University Press.

Khoday, K. (2007) 'Climate change and the right to development: Himalayan glacial melting and the future of development on the Tibetan Plateau', Background Paper for 2007 UNDP Global Human Development Report, Geneva, 7 May.

Magrin, G., Marengo, J., Boulanger, J.-P., Buckeridge, M. S., Castellanos, E., Poveda, G., Scarano, F. R. and Vicuña, S. (2014) 'Central and South America', in *Climate change 2014: Impacts, adaptation, and vulnerability, contribution of working Group II to the fifth assessment report of the intergovernmental panel for climate change*, Cambridge: Cambridge University Press.

Matasci, C. (2012) 'Swiss tourism in the age of climate change: Vulnerability, adaptive capacity, and barriers to adaptation', unpublished doctoral thesis, École Polytechnique Fédérale de Lausanne.

Muhar, A., Schauppenlehner, T. and Brandenburg, C. (2006) 'Trends in alpine tourism: The mountaineers' perspective and consequences for tourism strategies', in D. Siegrist, C. Clivaz, M. Hunziker and S. Iten (eds) *Exploring the nature of management: Proceedings of the third international conference on monitoring and management of visitor flows in recreational and protected areas*, Rapperswil: University of Applied Sciences, 13–17 September: 23–27.

Ritter, F., Fiebig, M. and Muhar, A. (2012) 'Impacts of global warming on mountaineering: A classification of phenomena affecting the alpine trail network', *Mountain Research and Development*, 32(1): 4–15.

Scott, D., Gössling, S. and Hall, C. M. (2012) *Tourism and climate change: Impacts, adaptation and mitigation*, Abingdon: Routledge.

Scottish Natural Heritage (2009) *Climate change and the natural heritage: SNH's approach and action plan*, Battleby: Scottish Natural Heritage.

Case study 7

Managing human waste on Aconcagua

Agustina Barros and Catherine Marina Pickering

Context

Environmental impacts and risks to human health arise from the improper disposal of human waste in mountainous areas. The challenges in dealing with this issue are explored here by focusing on how human waste from hikers and mountaineers is dealt with around the highest mountain in the Southern Hemisphere, Mt Aconcagua (6,962 m) in the Argentinean Andes. Mt Aconcagua and its surrounded protected area, Aconcagua Provincial Park (710 km², 69°56'W, 32°39'S), is a popular destination for mountaineering and hiking. It was declared a Category II IUCN protected area in 1983 to conserve glaciers, rivers and glacier lakes, alpine ecosystems and archaeological sites (Barros *et al.* 2013). Aconcagua is also the main water catchment for the Mendoza river which provides water for the direct use of over one million people and for irrigating important agricultural areas.

The Park is in the tundra climatic zone, characterized by a cold and dry climate with snow cover for more than four months each year (Barros 2014). Due to the harsh conditions, only 30 per cent of the Park is covered by vegetation, with nearly all vegetation restricted to the low and intermediate alpine zones between 2,400 and 3,800 m. Above this altitude, in the high alpine zone, there is very limited vegetation and there are permafrost soils. The nival/glacial zone above 4,400 m is dominated by permafrost soils, glaciers and snow with no vegetation (Barros 2014).

Prior to its declaration as a Park, there was limited human use of the area. More recently it has become a popular destination for commercial mountaineering which mainly occurs during the warmer months from November to March. Around 2,500 hikers use campsites located between 3,200 and 4,300 m and around 3,500 mountaineers attempt the summit each year. In addition, the Park receives around 27,000 day visitors per year in its low altitude areas (Barros 2014).

Due to high levels of visitor use and the subsequent production of large amounts of human waste, the Park Agency is increasingly allocating resources to manage human waste including funding, personnel and helicopter services. For example, based on an average 15 day round trip for mountaineers and three to five day trip for hikers, approximately 12,000 kg of human faeces is generated during the mountaineering season (based on an average of 0.156 g of faeces, per person, per day) (Barros and Rossi 2010).

Human waste management

There is limited road access within the Park, with 114 km of hiking trails and 19 remote campsites used by visitors. In the low and intermediate alpine zones, trails and campsites are restricted to the valley floors in close proximity to creeks and springs. In the high alpine and nival/glacial zones, campsites are located close to glacier lakes, rivers, snow covered and glaciated areas which provide water for visitors.

Historically, the management of human waste in campsites involved pit latrines in the alpine zones with no official management system for human waste in the nival zone. All human waste in pit latrines was left on site with the solid waste covered with soil and rocks once the pit was full. This accumulation of human waste had the potential to contaminate water bodies and threaten human health. The climbing community, recognizing this problem, organized the removal of solid human waste and garbage from high altitude campsites in the nival zones in 1993. Since then, several clean up campaigns have been conducted in the high altitude campsites. In 2002, the Park agency started implementing different human waste management practices in the Park ranging from flush toilets in lower altitudes sites, barrel collection toilets in the high alpine zone and pack-out systems for human faeces in the nival zone (see Figures CS 7.1, CS 7.2 and CS 7.3 below).

Campsites in the low and intermediate alpine zones receive around 63,000 person nights per season. The flush toilet system in these campsites consists of a set of toilets each connected to a septic tank to reduce the solid waste load (Figure CS 7.1). Each septic tank is connected through a pipe to a pit to discharge liquid effluent. Also, grey water from showers is deposited in the septic tanks. Although an obvious improvement on past practices, the system has problems including limited decomposition of solid waste in the septic tanks due to the cold and dry conditions. As a result, pollution of soils and water bodies may occur from untreated waste water from the pits. Also, the capacity of many of the septic tanks is exceeded due to high use with over 10,000 person nights per season in one of the popular campsites resulting in around 170,000 litres of waste water.

Campsites in the high alpine zone are mainly used by mountaineers along with commercial operators and Park staff who provide base camp facilities. As a result there are around 31,000 person nights each season in total for these campsites. The barrel collection toilets consist of a set of latrines attached to a removable barrel where human solid waste collects. These barrels are removed manually by Park staff and flown out of the Park attached below helicopters (Figure CS 7.2). To reduce weight, the bottoms of the barrels have holes in them to allow liquid waste to drain away. The solid waste in the barrels is disposed in a sewage treatment

Figure CS 7.1 Flush toilet systems in low altitude campsite.

plant located in Mendoza city. Currently, over 120 barrels are flown out by heli-copter each season, which equates to around 22,500 kg, requiring around 60 flights just to remove solid human waste at an approximate cost of US$36,000 per year. Current problems with this system include the high usage of helicopters and asso-ciated costs, and the potential pollution of glaciated areas and water bodies from urine and human faeces leaking from the holes in the barrels.

The high altitude basecamps in the nival zones (>4,400 m) are used by moun-taineers overnight before attempting and returning from the summit. Due to the high altitude, strong winds and occasional snow storms, it is not possible to use a fly out barrel system for human faeces in these campsites. Instead, a range of pack-out systems are used (Figure CS 7.3). At basecamps, park rangers provide

Figure CS 7.2 Barrel collection toilets (flyout) in the high alpine.

Figure CS 7.3 Pack-out systems for the nival zones.

each climber with a plastic bag with a unique registration number for depositing faeces. These bags are returned to the Park rangers at base camps after the climb, and later transported by helicopter outside the Park. Some tour operators use alternative pack-out systems including plastic containers or biodegradable bags, which are carried to base camps by porters or guides. Also, some tour operators provide 'toilet tents' for commercial expeditions to provide shelter for users. Due to the difficulties in controlling compliance in these remote locations, >10 per cent of faeces is estimated to be left in high altitude campsites, resulting in the direct contamination of snow and other water sources. Also, there are no regulations for urine, with all urine left in campsites, including close to water sources.

Conclusions and management recommendations

Human waste management has improved in the last ten years, with around 90 per cent of the human faeces produced by people in the high alpine and nival zones removed from the Park. However, some of the practices are not environmentally sustainable with potential impacts on aquatic ecosystems and to human health. For example, the improper disposal of waste water in the low altitude campsites could be polluting otherwise pristine creeks close to campsites. In the high alpine zone, nutrient addition to glacial lakes from human urine and faeces and grey water discharges can change these sensitive aquatic ecosystems (Clitherow *et al.* 2013). In the nival zones, the transmission of water-borne diseases can be common as coliform bacteria from faeces can persist on snow for extended periods (Goodwin *et al.* 2012). For instance, in the popular base camp, Plaza de Mulas (4,300 m), one to two people are diagnosed with water-borne diseases each week during the mountaineering season (Carr *et al.* 2002).

Human waste management on Aconcagua could be further improved by adapting techniques used in some other popular mountaineering destinations. For example, solar dehydration toilets could be used in the lower altitude areas as they are effective in dry and cold conditions (Hill and Henry 2013). At higher altitudes, the capacity of barrel collection toilets could be increased by implementing solid/liquid separation, thereby reducing the number of helicopter flights needed to remove human waste. Separation systems could involve the diversion of urine to a septic field where it is then evaporated while faecal matter is dehydrated in trays (Hill and Henry 2013). At higher altitudes, better controls on pack-out systems can include weighing human faeces pack-out containers when people return to base camps and the application of fines for non-compliance. In addition, the implementation of environmental education programmes is likely to increase awareness and minimize the improper disposal of human waste in the Park. Regular monitoring of water quality is also important both to assess the effectiveness of management actions, and to minimize impacts on human health.

References

Barros, A. (2014) 'Ecological impacts of visitor use, Aconcagua Provincial Park, Argentina', unpublished doctoral thesis, Griffith University.

Barros, A. and Rossi, S. D. (2010) 'Human waste management in Aconcagua Provincial Park: descriptions and main limitations', Paper presented at Exit Strategies Conference: Management Human Waste in the Wild, Golden Colorado, July.

Barros, A., Gonnet, J. and Pickering, C. M. (2013) 'Impacts of informal trails on vegetation and soils in the highest protected area in the Southern Hemisphere', *Journal of Environmental Management*, 127(1): 50–60.

Carr, C., Berris, M. J., Hilstad, M. O. and Allen, P. B. (2002) 'Water quality and fecal contamination on Mt. Aconcagua: Implications for human health and high altitude', Massachusetts Institute of Technology, Cambridge, MA.

Clitherow, L. R., Carrivick, J. L. and Brown, L. E. (2013) 'Food web structure in a harsh glacier-fed river', *PLoS ONE*, 8(4): e60899.

Goodwin, K., Loso, M. G. and Braun, M. (2012) 'Glacial transport of human waste and survival of fecal bacteria on Mt. McKinley's Kahiltna Glacier, Denali National Park, Alaska', *Arctic, Antarctic, and Alpine Research*, 44(4): 432–445.

Hill, G. and Henry, G. (2013) 'The application and performance of urine diversion to minimize waste management costs in remote wilderness environments', *International Journal of Wilderness*, 19(1): 26–33.

13 Mountaineering, commodification and risk perceptions in Nepal's Mt Everest region

Sanjay K. Nepal and Yang (Sunny) Mu

Introduction

On 15 October 2014, the Canadian Broadcasting Corporation (CBC) reported the deaths of four Canadian and one Indian hiker due to avalanche in Phu, a village in northwestern region of Nepal. The snow blizzard in northwest Nepal killed 39 people while dozens were reported missing (www.ekantipur.com). Earlier this year, a deadly high-altitude avalanche hit on 18 April 2014, just above Everest Base Camp and Camp I at more than 5,800m above sea level. A group of about 50 people, mostly Nepali Sherpa guides, were in the area near the Khumbu Icefall setting ropes and preparing the climbing routes for the busiest climbing season in the following weeks, when they were swept away in snow slide. The avalanche killed 13 people while three remain missing and are presumed dead. The accident became the most deadly in Mt Everest's climbing history.

Perhaps one of the most disturbing influences, particularly of mountaineering expeditions in the region, is the high frequency of deaths of Khumbu Sherpa who work as high altitude porters and guides in Mt Everest mountaineering (Ortner 1999). In recent years, the overcrowding of trekkers and climbers in the Everest region has been described as 'a five-lane motorway during bank holiday weekend' (Kelly 2013). A striking photo by German mountaineer Ralf Dujmovits showed a long queue of climbers waiting on their way up to summit during 2012. Many professional climbers (or Mt Everest veterans) are worried about the congestion, which they believe is primarily a result of the recent influx of inexperienced climbers. The potential impact of the congestion on the safety of climbers and guides has become a major concern. However, the number of trekkers and climbing permits has not been controlled by the Nepalese government because it is very likely to impact on many local people's livelihoods, and revenues for the Ministry of Tourism and Civil Aviation (MoTCA).

Avalanche and similar other natural disasters triggered deaths of foreign trekkers and their Nepalese support staff continue to paint a bleak picture of high risks associated with mountain adventure in Nepal, but the industry is hardly slowing down. What justifies the risks? Is there a correlation between commodification of mountaineering and associated injuries and deaths? What are the consequences of commodification? What are local perspectives on commodification of mountaineering and associated risks? This chapter addresses these issues in the context of Mt Everest climbing expeditions.

Mountaineering risks and deaths on Mt Everest

The Nepalese Himalaya has been a mecca for high mountain adventure sports like trekking and mountaineering. However, more recently, the Nepalese Himalaya has also attracted the attention of the international media for all the wrong reasons – frequent fatal natural disasters like avalanches. This raises the question whether mountaineering in the Nepalese Himalaya is prone to repeat disasters and therefore vulnerable to market forces as more and more people try to avoid the region altogether. Evidence, however, suggests otherwise. While 2014 has been a highly volatile period for international mountaineering expeditions in Nepal, if the events unfolding after the 1996 disaster on Mt Everest is taken as a lesson (Krakauer 1999), mountaineering and high mountain trekking in Nepal will continue to attract international visitors in record numbers. However, one key question remains unanswered, that is, whether increases in high mountain adventure activities are contributing to the deaths and disasters in the Nepalese Himalaya.

Adventure tourism, including mountaineering and high altitude trekking is sometimes described as 'individualized protest' against modernity, and an expression of their wishes to transcend the limits of self, as well as the limits of a controlled, normalized life (Bott 2009). Climbers seek for a set of meanings towards life and death in high altitude mountaineering and view risks and deaths as the payoff of this individualized self-discovery. High altitude mountaineering is widely recognized as an extremely risky outdoor activity, with a remarkably high incidence of injury and death. The most frequent kinds of death on Mt Everest, include: 'a slip or a drop off a sheer face, or a fall into a crevice, the biggest killer in terms of numbers – burial in an avalanche or a slow death from altitude sickness' (Ortner 1999: 6). According to the data compiled from government reports (MoTCA 2010, 2013) and other sources including *American Alpine Journal*, the Himalayan Database, 8000er.com (www.8000ers.com), everest-summiteersassociation.org and adventurestats.com, more than 4,350 people have successfully summited Mt Everest from the Nepalese side. Of the total, 2,112 were foreign climbers. Climbers from the United States accounted for nearly 11.4 per cent of all the summiteers, followed by the United Kingdom (5.4 per cent). Nepali climbers represented more than 50 per cent of all summiteers, the vast majority of whom were Sherpa guides and porters hired by expedition teams to provide vital support for foreign climbers. In 2013 alone, 272 (or 89.2 per cent) out of 305 Nepali summiteers were identified as Sherpa.

Since 1922, Mt Everest has been the domain of professional climbers and expeditions with strong support in finance and supplies. Climbers took years to prepare for their expeditions and had trained extensively before attempting even the most straightforward routes. This domination of professional climbers started to change in the 1990s when increased commercialization of mountaineering started to occur. For the first time in 1993, there were more than 100 successful summits during a single season (Figure 13.1). In 2013, a total of 538 people had successfully reached the summited in one season. According to Jenkins from *National Geographic* (2013), only 18 per cent of attempts to summit Mt Everest were successful in 1990. This figure jumped to 56 per cent in 2012. Our data shows a similar trend; in 2012, a record 169 climbers reached the top on a single day from the Nepalese side (Figure 13.2). By contrast, as recently as the year 2000, the most successful ascent on a single day was 18, and five years later the number stood at 75.

Likewise, since the 1953 British expedition, 259 mountaineers (including their support staff) have paid with their lives trying to reach to the top. In the

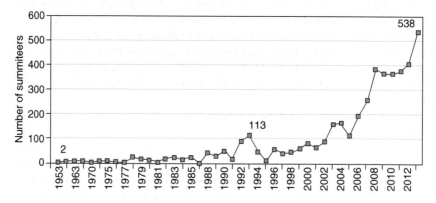

Figure 13.1 Successful summits of Mt Everest per year, 1953–2013.

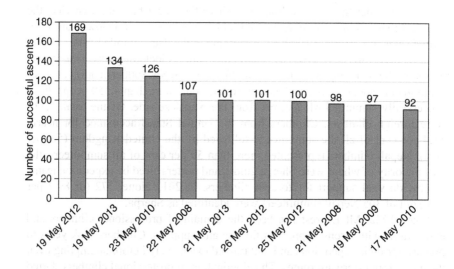

Figure 13.2 Ten highest numbers of ascents on Everest on a single day (Nepal).

history of Mt Everest, there have been five years when the annual death toll has been ten or over; 11 in 1982, ten in 1988, 15 in 1996, 11 in 2006 and ten in 2012. The avalanche on 18 April 2014 made it the deadliest accident in its history. Of the 259 fatalities, 151 had died on the southeast route in Nepal (Figure 13.3). Foreign climbers represented 51.7 per cent of the fatalities and Nepalese Sherpa accounted for 48.3 per cent. The most frequently reported causes of death, for years when data are available, include fall and avalanche (Figure 13.4). The primary causes of deaths between Sherpa and foreign climbers differ somewhat; more Sherpa than foreign climbers have died due to avalanche.

It is reasonable to assume increases in the number and rate of fatalities in recent years as there are more expeditions now than before, but data show that the overall death to summit ratio has been declining in recent years (Table 13.1).

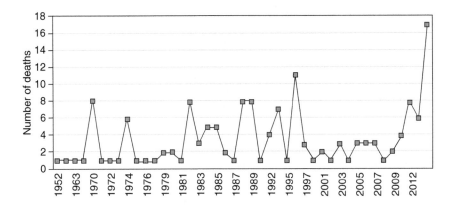

Figure 13.3 Fatalities from Nepal side, 1952–2014.

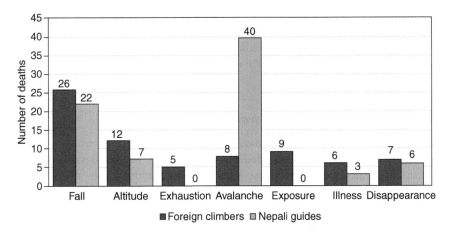

Figure 13.4 Reported cause of death (1990–2014) comparing Sherpa guides and foreign climbers.

Table 13.1 Death to summit ratio on Mt Everest*

Period	Summits	Deaths	Death/summit (%)
1952–2013	4,350	134	3.1
1980–1989	161	43	26.7
1990–1999	529	28	5.3
2000–2013	3,571	37	1.0

Notes

* This excludes the most recent reported deaths of 16 Sherpa, of which three are presumed dead as their bodies have not been found yet.

Many factors can be attributed to this which include better climbing equipment and safety gear, more awareness of mountain hazards and better organized expeditions. Climbing Mt Everest is actually safer than before, as the death per summit ratio has dropped from 26.7 per cent in the 1980s to 5.3 per cent in the 1990s and further to 1.0 per cent in the 2000s. Table 13.1 shows that compared to the 1990s, the number of successful ascents after 2,000 is almost seven times higher but the death to summit ratio is five times lower. When fatalities are compared between Sherpa and foreign climbers, while historically more Sherpa than their foreign counterparts have died on Everest, since 1990 the death to summit ratio for both have been similar; for example, it is around 1 per cent for both groups since the year 2000.

Commodification and consequences

While the data in Table 13.1 cannot establish a direct correlation between increased frequencies of climbing Mt Everest and the total number of deaths, it is reasonable to assume that increased frequency of human presence in such a confined and hazardous territory contributes to potential increases in human injuries and deaths. There are other consequences too. Four types of consequences are summarized here, which include increase in the number of inexperienced climbers, increased congestion on climbing routes, persistent garbage management problems and increased safety concerns among the local Sherpa support team.

Increase in the number of inexperienced mountaineers

According to Cohen (1988), commodification is the process by which objects and activities come to be evaluated in terms of their exchange value in the context of trade, in addition to use value that such commodities might have (Beedie and Hudson 2003). In that sense, the regulation and control of permits, the payment of fees required to climb Mt Everest, as well as the associated logistical arrangements (guides, etc.) could be viewed by some as commodification of the mountaineering experience. However, our use of the term here relates to the increased mountaineering activity performed by amateur climbers, many of whom do it simply because they think their Sherpa guide can lead them to the top of Mt Everest, and that they have the money to engage in this rather expensive adventure. This seems to be the general narrative amongst professional mountaineers who bemoan the fact that Mt Everest has been crowded to the extent that it no longer offers mountaineering opportunities in its classic sense of adventure, exploration and discovery (Jenkins 2013).

As commercialization of mountaineering switched to a higher gear in the 1990s, Mt Everest witnessed an influx of more inexperienced, non-professional climbers on its steep snowy ridges during April and May. Today, the extreme experience of Everest is sold to a very unique group of people. This group consists primarily of 'executive adventurers' as Palmer (2002) identified it, predominantly men with high profile, white collar professions, who spend their weekends and holidays mountaineering (p. 330). Online searches of key phrases like 'cost of climbing Everest', 'Everest expedition companies' and 'costs of Sherpa guides on Everest' produce hundreds of websites on Google with detailed list of expenses and preparation guides for climbing the highest mountain in the world. The Everest experience has become easy to purchase, and the prospects of being on its top presented as an attainable goal even without years of professional training. There are numerous studies on the motivations for attempting such a potentially deadly endeavour on high mountains, for example, Elstrud (1999 cited in Bott 2009: 289) explored the deliberate risk-taking behaviour of backpacking travellers, and argued their participation in high risk activities as a process of identity construction which hinge on individualized narratives of risks. High altitude mountaineering climbers disassociate themselves from established definition of tourists. To them, danger and risk are central to the aesthetics of high altitude mountaineering (Palmer 2002). The extreme hardship above 8,000 m challenges climbers' physical and mental capabilities and this sets climbers apart from others, who are set within normalized and controlled, non-risky leisure activities (Bott 2009).

Since the 1990s, guided expeditions have become the norm for climbing high mountains in the Everest region. The majority of climbers of commercial expeditions are summarized as 'executive adventurers' or 'elite adventurers' who pay on average US$30,000–65,000 to be guided to the top of the world. Sometimes the cost can be as high as $100,000 depending on the number of people they hire for themselves. While past mountaineers have described their motivations in spiritual, psychological and socio-cultural terms (Johnston and Edwards 1994), many mountaineers today are less likely to consider spiritual reason as the main motivation, and are more driven by economic interests and personal glory.

However, the transition in climbers' background and experience didn't cause the death rate to soar. To the opposite, the data showed that Everest is actually becoming safer as the death per summit ratio dropped to 1.0 per cent in the 2000s. The linkage between mountaineering experience and survival rate on Everest has been examined by Westhoff *et al.* (2012). Their research indicated that an experienced climber was, on average, no more or no less likely to die on a climb than a first timer who climbs the same mountain. What such studies do not reveal, however, is that local Sherpa high altitude porters now spend more time above the Everest Base Camp (EBC) due to increases in mountaineering traffic, and thus are vulnerable to high risks of injury and death. The combined effect of high mountaineering activity, and unstable weather conditions such as the one reported this year that caused unprecedented number of casualties in the Annapurna region will not be a one-off event.

Increased congestion on climbing routes

The rapidly increasing number of summits on a single day still raises wide concerns among mountaineering circles and the media. Many professional mountaineers and Sherpa guides are worried that the congestion and huge influx of inexperienced climbers are bound to cause tragic consequences (Kelly 2013; Connolly 2012). Experienced climbers are frustrated that long queues of amateur climbers using fixed ropes are slowing them down which may lead to disastrous consequences such as the sudden blizzard in 1996 which killed eight climbers and stranded several others near the summit, or the widely reported brawl between Sherpa guides and foreign climbers in April 2013 (www.ekantipur. com). The high traffic causes many climbers to slow down and wait for the right of way to move higher up on the route. The extended time on the upper reaches of the ascent route also wastes precious oxygen required by a climber. The lack of oxygen affects mental judgement when making sensible life and death decision such as whether or not to abort the climb (Figueroa 2013).

Added to the extremities of the Mt Everest region is the desire by increasing number of trekkers to the EBC to develop interests in climbing the mountain. During our fieldwork in April 2014, one of our Sherpa guides indicated that many climbers come to Everest first as trekkers, 'and they are just determined to challenge themselves and start training for climbing Everest the next time'. The guide was concerned about the lack of professional and consistent training among these 'trekkers turned climbers', and was sceptical of their success in reaching the summit.

While some mountaineers are quick in placing blame of deaths on overcrowding, this is rarely the major cause for death on Everest. With the exception of 1996, large commercial operators appear to have the safest record for climbing Mt Everest, measuring by number of deaths per summit. Our data also revealed the death per summit ratio for both foreign climbers and Nepalese Sherpa guides decreased even after the increase in number of expedition teams on Mt Everest. But there have been some changes in the causes of death over the years. The number of high altitude-related deaths (pulmonary oedema, cerebral oedema, cerebral apoplexy etc.) and other illnesses have increased since 2000. This might imply that climbers with less experience may have been the primary victims of such illnesses as they spend less time to acclimatize. It is not uncommon to see many inexperienced climbers pushing themselves into exhaustion, climbing in poor weather, refusing to turn around when knowing their oxygen will run out or weather suddenly changes. Many experienced climbers are aware of the altitude-related illnesses and know that critical decisions to whether continue climbing or retreat are life and death decisions. But the same cannot be said about less experienced climbers who are likely to be less willing to give up any chance and often push themselves too hard, especially when they have paid a fortune for a 'promised' summit. This notoriously bad judgement associated with summiting at any cost was defined as 'summit fever' (Westhoff *et al.* 2012).

Persistent problems of garbage management at higher altitudes

One of the consequences of increasing number of climbers on Mt Everest is the accumulation of tons of waste that are left on Mt Everest by expedition teams. Commercial expedition teams have been blamed by Nepali officials for leaving crumpled food wrappers, broken tents, shredded clothes, empty oxygen bottles and even human excrement on the highest peak in the world. While the Sagarmatha Pollution Control Committee (SPCC), a local NGO responsible for various environmental programmes in the region has made significant efforts through their annual clean up campaigns (SPCC 2011), these efforts are not sustainable given that the NGO's activities are based on funding support from various other partners. The enormity of the problems is evident when one considers that during the fiscal year 2010/2011 (Nepali calendar year 2067/2068) SPCC received 53.2 tons of burnable garbage from expedition teams. This does not include 32.7 tons of human waste and 9.8 tons of kitchen waste buried in the pits in Lobuche area, a few hours south of the EBC. In addition, the expedition teams also returned 5,561 empty camping gas containers and 4,297 empty oxygen cylinders to Kathmandu. Occasionally, expedition teams organizing clean up campaigns also help with garbage removal. Last year, MoTCA implemented a policy of requiring each Everest climber to return with 8 kg garbage, in addition to their own. Penalties apply to those who don't, including a ban on future expedition on Everest. The question remains if this will be monitored regularly and if any penalty will be imposed on the violators. As the volume of climbers increases so does the amount of garbage and human waste. More liberal use of supplemental oxygen (usually weighted around 17 lbs each) and clients' increasing demands for high quality food, commercial goods and high tech products has resulted in much heavier loads to be taken on higher camps, all done by Sherpa guides and porters. Many of these products have been discarded on the slopes after being used.

Safety implications for high altitude Sherpa guides and porters

As depicted in the documentary *Sherpas: The true heroes of Mount Everest*, Sherpa guides and porters have to carry heavy loads many times through the most dangerous part of the ascent – the Khumbu Icefall. Many Sherpa guides and porters believe that the more they can carry on their backs, the more positive feedback and possibly extra cash bonus they are going to receive from their clients at the end of the expedition. Feedback and recommendation from clients will give them more job opportunities in next season's expeditions. While commercial expeditions on Mt Everest have indeed become safer for both climbers and Nepalese Sherpa guides and porters, guides and porters in expedition teams bear more pressure and burdens than their clients. The unprecedented dependency on Sherpa support in high altitude mountaineering aggravates their potential risks.

There are five reasons why climbing Mt Everest is a lot safer nowadays compared to the expeditions in the 1950s and 1960s. First, the routes up to the summit are very well known and have been almost unchanged for 60 years. According to the statistical record published by the Nepalese government, over 95 per cent of expeditions take one of the two major routes: southeast ridge in Nepal or northeast ridge in Tibet. These established routes have been attempted by thousands of climbers and Sherpa guides over the years. Potential risks are mitigated by avoiding dangerous and unstable terrain as much as possible. Experienced Sherpa guides and porters have installed bolts and fixed ropes along the routes which significantly reduce the time climbers spend on some dangerous steep slopes. Second, the mountaineering equipment and gear have improved considerably. As long as a climber can afford them, even a climber with limited mountaineering experience can armour him/her-self with lighter, warmer gear which protects them from extreme weather. Advanced orientation devices help accurately locating climbers up in the mountains from base camps. Better understanding and forecasting of weather has contributed in lowering the death rate as well.

Furthermore, the use of supplemental oxygen has helped alleviate altitude sickness. Advanced oxygen bottles are not only lighter they are also more comfortable and easier to wear and change, and with fewer leaks (www.alanarnette. com). More liberal use of oxygen, along with several prescribed medicines such as dexamethasone also help cope with problems caused by lack of air at high altitudes. However, perhaps the most important reason for a safer climbing experience on Mt Everest is due to the excellent support of Nepalese Sherpa guides and porters. Commercial expedition teams provide their clients an unprecedented ratio of Sherpa guides and porters: on average, for every western climber there are three to five Sherpa staff. Therefore, most summiteer's success is inseparable from the efforts of Sherpa guides and porters, who do most of the heavy and specialized work such as fixing ropes and ladders, setting up camps, preparing food and making critical suggestions such as when to ascent and retreat. The higher the number of commercial expedition teams, the greater is the dependency on Sherpa guides and porters. In other words, mountaineering business practices have encouraged many Sherpa people to venture beyond the EBC and on to the hazardous territory of Mt Everest. This higher ratio of western climber and Sherpa staff is naturally the leading cause of higher exposure to death among the latter.

Data show that the major causes of death of Sherpa guides and porters in Mt Everest expeditions are avalanche and fall. Like the avalanche in 2014, many Sherpa guides have lost their lives when preparing routes, fixing ropes and carrying supplies to higher camps for their clients. Foreign climbers spend less time in the Khumbu Icefall section, which is the most challenging and strenuous part of the climb. Most climbers make only a single round trip through the Khumbu Icefall, whereas the Sherpa guides and porters supporting them have to pass through this most hazardous terrain numerous times during the course of a climb. One of our guides told us that some Sherpa guides need to carry 20 kg or more when they travel across the Khumbu Icefall. Even more difficult work is demanded when the expedition teams encounter bad weather and when congestion occurs at high altitudes (Krakauer 2014). When disorganized crowds move at different speeds and climbers become stalled on steep slopes, the job of a Sherpa carrying a heavy load suddenly becomes very dangerous. In the documentary mentioned earlier, several high altitude porters expressed that they often have to risk their own lives to support inexperienced climbers in very challenging situations. Our guide, who had worked for several high altitude expeditions, stated that many Sherpa tend to hide their anxiety and negative emotions in front of their clients because it might appear unprofessional, affect their reputation and possibly undermine future opportunities. Many new climbers are not aware, or do not pay attention to the fact that even Sherpa guides cannot perform well at very high altitudes (Brutsaert 2008).

Narratives of risks and deaths

Death as attraction

A strong serenity and calmness towards deaths on Everest has been identified in many climbers' personal narratives. Climbers have described the 'inescapable lure of Everest' with passion and are prepared for the dangers, even death on Everest (Adler 1999). Most climbers think highly of the meaning behind climbing Everest and generally reflect their deep spiritual approach to mountaineering and Everest, as illustrated in this quote attributed to a climber interviewed at EBC in 1996:

> there's a passion and closeness when you face your mortality with your close friends … climbers are people who hold onto life more than people who don't climb, and what we learn up there we also bring home to our loved ones.
>
> (Adler 1999)

Climbers are fully aware of the dangers of dying on the mountains and that in case of death their body may not be recovered for years. In fact, it is reported that some Everest expedition companies ask their clients to sign a form asking them if they wish to choose to remain on the mountain in the event of a fatal accident, and whether or not they want to have their bodies removed for an additional cost (Weidinger 2013). Climbers encounter death more directly when they pass through the 'rainbow valley' near the summit of Mt Everest, a section of the climbing route where several bodies of former climbers dressed in various colourful climbing gear litter around. Their bodies have even become part of Everest's landmarks. The most 'famous' one is 'green boots' on the northeast ridge route, commonly believed to be the body of Indian climber Tsewang Palijor (Nuwer 2012). Climbers have to experience such ghastly encounters on their way to the summit, as reminders of the real possibility of death in their pursuits of high mountain adventure.

Risks versus gains

Mountaineering has been a significant component of the tourism industry in the Everest region. The popularity of films such as *Everest* (www.imdb.com/title/tt0120661) and books such as *Into thin air* by Krakauer (1999) have fuelled the fascination with Everest and its high altitude Sherpa inhabitants. Local Sherpa have become increasingly dependent upon tourism-related occupations, shifting from an economy based on agro-pastoralism and trade, to an economy based on tourism services, supplemented by agro-pastoralism and trade (Stevens 1993). Today, Sherpa are so entwined with mountaineering work that their name, Sherpa, has come to represent the occupation of mountaineering, portering and trekking guide (Nepal et al. 2002). For many Sherpa from poor households, working for climbing expeditions has become their passport to prosperity. Sherpa are not only employed by mountaineering expedition teams, they work as porters and trekking guides in the Lower Khumbu (i.e. Pharak and below) region too. According to recent research, over 95 per cent of porters in the Everest region earn between US$5 and US$7 daily; 45 per cent showed dissatisfaction with their wages considering the hardships (Panzeri et al. 2013). Trekking guides usually get paid higher than porters but their income is highly unstable. The volatile nature of the tourism industry in Everest has caused many Sherpa guides and porters at lower regions to consider joining the high altitude mountaineering expedition teams so as to earn a good wage within a very short period of time. Local guides and porters in high altitude expedition teams are almost exclusively Sherpa. They can earn up to US$5,500 during a single expedition, higher than a teacher's annual income in Kathmandu. But that level of earning comes with a significant amount of risk of death and other life altering injuries, as depicted in a recent documentary entitled the *Disposable man* (http://vimeo.com/69673509).

Literature on Sherpa's perception towards mountaineering-related risks and deaths is very limited. Vincanne Adams argues in her book *Tigers of the snow and other virtual sherpas* (1996) that the Sherpa have been portrayed by westerners as fearless, courageous and possessing impressive physical qualities beyond normal human capabilities. That misperception of Sherpa's physical strength has been denounced by several medical research papers, which show that even Sherpa guides with years of experience on the mountains can suffer from altitude sickness and injuries during expeditions, and even indigenous high altitude natives indeed have higher limits of work performance in hypoxia (Droma et al. 2006; Newcomb et al. 2011). Despite the lower incidence of acute mountain sickness, many Sherpa guides and porters feel that they are at greater risk than visitors. Sherpa's access to diagnostics and medication are more limited than those of visitors. More importantly, Sherpa do not have control over ascent plans and are reluctant to report physical discomforts because it may affect their earnings. Besides sickness and injuries, many Sherpa guides and porters have also lost their lives during the preparatory phases of the expedition in the Khumbu Icefall area, which is one of the most unstable and dangerous landscapes on Everest.

Bjonness (1986), Ortner (1999) and Bott (2009) have argued that risks and death are perceived and understood differently in the climbing careers of Sherpa and their foreign clients. Ortner (1999) has repeatedly emphasized that the primary incentive for Sherpa to risk their lives in mountaineering has always been the need for money – greater the risk, higher the wage. The occurrence of dangers and harm from nature are considered both accidental and intentional. The control of danger in the environment is assumed to be not in the hands of human but invisible forces (Bjonness 1986), and they are more uncontrollable, inevitable and involuntary, which reflect Sherpa's Buddhist religious values. But incidence like the April 2014 avalanche fuel strong negative reactions among high altitude porters and their families which often lead them to quit after a few years working for expedition teams. Resistance from family members was the strongest motivation for a Sherpa to refuse the 'opportunity' of becoming an expedition guide.

Strong Tibetan Buddhism beliefs encourage the Sherpa to relate mountain hazard with the anger of respective spirits and deities who possess that particular mountain or region (Bjonness 1986). However, there is also a prevailing attitude among many local Sherpa that tragedy like the one in April 2014 was brought upon by the high altitude porters themselves, especially younger Sherpa who are not as religious as their forefathers were (based on our interview with some lodge owners and guides in Namche). They argue that as mountaineering is becoming more commercial, increasing number of western climbers come to Everest to enhance their ego and personal achievement who often overlook basic rules of mountaineering safety for themselves as well as their Sherpa guides and porters. Lack of adequate insurance coverage is not uncommon among expedition Sherpa, especially porters who are on the lowest rung of mountaineering hierarchy. Our own trekking guide provided the spiritual side of interpretation of these mountain tragedies. He thought that the younger generation of expedition porters and guides are oblivious to spiritual connection and respect that elder Sherpa have had with the mountains. Traditionally, religious ceremonies (*puja*) are performed repeatedly at the base camp during expeditions; offerings are given to the gods on mountains before pushing to the summit. Tragedies in the mountains, including both natural and human caused disasters, have led the Sherpa to take religious precautions such as carving mantra on stones, hanging up prayer flags in order to please the gods and prevent future risks. However, the younger generation of Sherpa is less concerned with the spiritual side of the mountain and many are lured by money hoping to make a quick ascent at the mountain and never return to face its wrath next year. They are lured again when the money runs out.

Conclusion

Much of mountaineering literature is focused on pursuits of adventure, risk-taking, flow experience, search for meanings of self or affirmation of identity. A significant part of this literature dwells on motivations, rationality and expressions of human freedom. While these emotive experiences are critical to understand why mountaineers engage in what others view as risky activities, the literature on mountain disasters and their influences on perception of risk and behavioural actions among those involved in the tourist trade is somewhat limited.

This study covered three themes: success and deaths on Mt Everest, commodification of mountaineering and its consequences, and narratives of mountaineering risks. The study shows that the sports of mountaineering and high mountain adventure have expanded beyond the limited number of professionals to include amateurs and others who think of climbing Mt Everest simply as a 'bucket list' item to be checked off. High mountain guiding businesses in Nepal are increasingly responding to the latter type of clientele. The result is increased level of activity on Mt Everest and record number of people making their attempts to reach the top. The consequence of such a high level of activities is that fatalities continue to occur, but the mountain itself has proven to be safer (i.e. lower death rate) than ever. Congestion along the main ascent routes has created a chaotic situation for all parties involved in mountaineering leading to human errors, conflicts between guides and climbers, and exposure to uncertain and unstable physical conditions. Congestion has become a primary factor for increased amount of garbage on higher slopes.

There is not a single solution to the complex problem of making mountaineering on Everest sustainable. Increases in permit fees, fewer climbers on each team, establishing a local search and rescue team, recruiting local (Sherpa) environmental liaison officers, investing more in environmental clean ups that include international and local expedition teams are suggested. Those who do not follow established rules and adopt higher environmental standards could also be denied permits for a few years. How many more deaths should the local community endure till they spring into action? The saga of death and despair on Mt Everest unfolds anew and seems to reach new proportions every year, as more and more people flock to the mountain. It is time stricter limits are introduced to the mountain and safety of those conducting expeditions put above all else. The Nepalese government, international climbers and guides, and the local Sherpa all must work together to develop sound policies and action plans to address issues of risk, safety, adequate life insurance and financial compensation. Above all, they must ensure that the mountains are treated with respect and fear. Only by making the Everest climbing experience exclusive and targeted to climbing professionals, who've shown the mettle required to scale this deadly summit, can safety be improved and tragedies prevented.

References

Adams, V. (1996) *Tigers of the snow and other virtual sherpas: An ethnography of Himalayan encounters*, Princeton, NJ: Princeton University Press.

Adler, J. (1999) 'Ghost of Everest', *Newsweek*. Online, available at: www.newsweek.com/ghost-everest-167062 (accessed 2 September 2014).

Beedie, P. and Hudson, S. (2003) 'Emergence of mountain-based adventure tourism', *Annals of Tourism Research*, 30(3): 625–643.

Bjonness, I. M. (1986) 'Mountain hazard perception and risk avoiding strategies among the Sherpas of Khumbu Himal, Nepal', *Mountain Research and Development*, 6(4): 277–292.

Bott, E. (2009) 'Big mountain, big name: Globalized relations of risk in Himalayan mountaineering', *Journal of Tourism and Cultural Change*, 7(4): 287–230.

Brutsaert, T. D. (2008) 'Do high-altitude natives have an enhanced exercise performance at high altitude?' *Applied Physiology, Nutrition, and Metabolism*, 33(3): 582–592.

Cohen, E. (1988) 'Authenticity and commoditization in tourism', *Annals of Tourism Research*, 15(3): 371–386.

Connolly, K. (2012) 'Everest mountaineers say crowding by "hobby climbers" is path to tragedy'. Online, available at: www.theguardian.com/world/2012/may/30/everest-mountaineer-crowding-hobby-tragedy (accessed 2 August 2014).

Disposable man (2013) *Outside* magazine. Online, available at: http://vimeo.com/69673509 (accessed 16 October 2014).

Droma, Y., Hanaoka, M., Basnyat, B., Arjyal, A., Neupane, P., Pandit, A., Sharma, D. and Kubo, K. (2006) 'Symptoms of acute mountain sickness in Sherpas exposed to extremely high altitude', *High Altitude Medicine and Biology*, 7(4): 312–314.

Elstrud, T. (1999) 'Risk creation in travelling: Risk-taking as narrative and practise in backpacker culture', Paper presented at the 1st International Conference on Consumption and Representation, University of Plymouth, September.

Figueroa, P. (2013) 'Vanity, pollution and death on Mt. Everest', *Our World Web Magazine by United Nation University*. Online, available at: http://ourworld.unu.edu/en/vanity-pollution-and-death-on-mt-everest (accessed 18 August 2014).

Himalayan Database (2014) Online, available at: www.himalayandatabase.com/ (accessed 22 May 2014).

Jenkins, M. (2013) 'Maxed out on Everest: How to fix the mess at the top of the world', *National Geographic*, June. Online, available at: http://ngm.nationalgeographic.com/2013/06/125-everest-maxed-out/jenkins-text (accessed 23 July 2014).

Johnston, B. R. and Edwards, T. (1994) 'The commodification of mountaineering', *Annals of Tourism Research*, 21(3): 459–478.

Kelly, J. (2013) 'Everest crowds: The world's highest traffic jam', *BBC News Magazine*. Online, available at: www.bbc.com/news/magazine-22680192 (accessed 12 August 2014).

Krakauer, J. (1999) *Into thin air: A personal account of the Mt. Everest disaster*, New York: Anchor Books/Doubleday (paperback edn).

Krakauer, J. (2014) 'Death and anger on Everest', *New Yorker*, 21 April. Online, available at: www.newyorker.com/news/news-desk/death-and-anger-on-everest (accessed 12 August 2014).

Ministry of Culture, Tourism and Civil Aviation (2010) *Mountaineering in Nepal: Facts and figures*, Kathmandu: MOTCA.

Ministry of Culture, Tourism and Civil Aviation (2013) *Nepal tourism statistics 2012*, Kathmandu: MoTCA.

Nepal, S. K., Kohler, T. and Banzhaf, B. (2002) *Great Himalaya: Tourism and the dynamics of change in Nepal*, Berne: Swiss Foundation for Alpine Research.

Newcomb, L., Sherpa, C., Nickol, A. and Windsor, J. (2011) 'CME available: A comparison of the incidence and understanding of altitude illness between porters and trekkers in the Solu Khumbu Region of Nepal', *Wilderness and Environmental Medicine*, 22(3): 197–201.

Nuwer, R. (2012) 'There are over 200 bodies on Mount Everest, and they're used as landmarks', *Smithsonian Magazine*, November. Online, available at: www.smithsonianmag.com/smart-news/there-are-over-200-bodies-on-mount-everest-and-theyre-used-as-landmarks-146904416/?no-ist (accessed 2 September 2014).

Ortner, S. (1999) *Life and death on Mount Everest: Sherpas and Himalayan mountaineering*, Princeton, NJ: Princeton University Press.

Palmer, C. (2002) ' "Shit happens": The selling of risk in extreme sport (Interlaken and Everest tourist tragedies)', *Australian Journal of Anthropology*, 13(3): 323–336.

Panzeri, D., Caroli, P. and Haack, B. (2013) 'Sagarmatha Park (Mt. Everest) porter survey and analysis', *Tourism Management*, 36: 26–34.

Sagarmatha Pollution Control Committee (SPCC) (2011) *Annual progress report, 2011*, Namche Bazaar: SPCC.

Sherpas: The true heroes of Mount Everest (2009) Full length documentary, directed by Frank Senn, Hari Thapa and Otto C. Honegger: 95 minutes.

Stevens, S. F. (1993) 'Tourism, change, and continuity in the Mount Everest region, Nepal', *Geographical Review*, 83(4): 410–427.

Weidinger, P. (2013) '10 harrowing stories of life and death on Mount Everest', *Listverse*. Online, available at: http://listverse.com/2013/06/13/10-harrowing-stories-of-life-and-death-on-mount-everest/ (accessed 22 August 2014).

Westhoff, J. L., Koepsell, T. D. and Littell, C. T. (2012) 'Effects of experience and commercialization on survival in Himalayan mountaineering: retrospective cohort study', *BMJ: British Medical Journal*, 344(e3782): 1–17.

Websites

everestsummiteersassociation.org (accessed 9 October 2014).

www.8000ers.com Online, available at: www.8000ers.com/cms/en/lists-of-ascents-mainmenu-226.html (accessed 18 May 2014).

www.adventurestats.com (accessed 24 May 2014).

www.alanarnette.com 'Blogsite maintained by Alan Arnette'. Online, available at: www.alanarnette.com/blog/everest-2013-coverage/ (accessed 18 August 2014).

www.ekantipur.com Online, available at: www.ekantipur.com/the-kathmandu-post/2013/04/29/nation/not-listening-to-sherpas-caused-everest-brawl/248158.html (accessed 22 October 2014).

www.imdb.com/title/tt0120661/ (accessed 4 September 2014).

Case study 8

Mountaineering on Mt Everest: evolution, economy, ecology and ethics

Gyan P. Nyaupane

Introduction

There is no place on Earth where mountain climbing, a form of adventure tourism, is more popular than in Nepal. Nepal is home to ten of the 14 world's highest peaks over 8,000 m, including Mt Everest, at 8,848 m, the world's tallest peak. This chapter discusses the evolution of climbing on Mt Everest, its economic contributions and associated issues, particularly ecological and ethical.

Evolution

Mt Everest was unknown to the world until the Great Trigonometric Survey of India under the British Empire identified it as the world's highest mountain in 1852 (Brunner 2014). The mountain was named after George Everest, who was India's surveyor general under the British Empire from 1830 through 1843, but he did not survey it. In Nepal, Mt Everest is known as Sagarmatha, 'Head of the Earth Touching the Heaven', and in Tibet as Chomulungma, 'Goddess Mother of the World'. The history of Mt Everest climbing started in 1921 when the kingdom of Tibet opened its borders to foreigners (Brunner 2014). The most prominent was a British expedition led by George Mallory and Andrew Irvine in 1924. Both of them disappeared, and no evidence of where and how they vanished or whether they made it to the top was found. Over the next three decades, ten more expedition teams attempted, but failed to reach the summit. Thirteen more climbers lost their lives. Finally, on 29 May 1953, Tenzing Norgay Sherpa and Edmund Hillary first summited Mt Everest through the South Col route, on the Nepal side. Since then, more than 5,000 climbers from more than 80 countries have reached the summit. As a result of better equipment and guides, the success has increased significantly, from six reaching the top in 1963 to more than 500 in the spring of 2012 (Jenkins 2013). A record number of 135 summited Mt Everest on a single on 22 May 2008 (Ministry of Culture, Tourism and Civil Aviation 2013).

Economy

Mt Everest climbing has been a golden goose for Nepal's government. The government collects about Rs 270 million (US$3.33 million) in annual revenue from Mt Everest climbing permits. There are two different rates for different climbing routes: (1) southeast ridge and (2) other routes. The permit fees for the southeast route are listed in Table CS 8.1. The permit fee for other routes is US$50,000 for up to seven members.

Although the government collects fees to climb other peaks, the revenue from Mt Everest represent more than 75 per cent of the total revenue from expeditions (Nepal Tourism Statistics 2012). In addition, mountain climbing has helped stimulate the economy through employment and helped the region's infrastructure development. In 2012 alone, 353 climbers from 35 expedition teams summited Mt Everest (Nepal Tourism Statistics 2012). Most of the expeditions take place within a very small window of a few weeks in the spring, when the weather is better.

The Khumbu region, a valley below Mt Everest, and once a largely inaccessible region, has now become a popular destination for trekking and the main artery for Mt Everest expeditions (Fisher 1990). It has changed the economic, cultural and physical landscape of the region through mountaineering and trekking tourism. In addition to expeditions, each year, 36,000 visitors hike to view and experience the majesty of the world's tallest mountains. Mountaineering and trekking have brought employment and income opportunities to the communities along the trekking routes and to the Khumbu valley (Nyaupane et al. 2014). As a result, the economic condition of the Khumbu region is much better than other regions of Nepal. Along with economic prosperity, mountain climbing and trekking have brought social-ecological challenges.

Table CS 8.1 Mt Everest climbing royalty

Member of expedition team*	Climbing fee (US$)
1	25,000
2	40,000
3	48,000
4	56,000
5	60,000
6	66,000
7	70,000

Source: Mountaineering Regulations (2002: 2059 BS).

Note
* Up to five members can be added to the team for an additional $10,000 for each member.

Ecological issues

Ecological issues that the Khumbu region has faced include deforestation caused by the increasing consumption of firewood and demand for timber, increased litter and waste, the trampling of vegetation and increased soil erosion in trekking areas (Byers 2005; Nyaupane *et al.* 2014; Stevens 2003). The issues of litter and waste are different at higher elevations from the valleys on the foothills. Many climbers have died on the mountain because of the extremely harsh environment. Their bodies were often left where they died. Many climbers leave items, such as abandoned tents, equipment, empty oxygen canisters, batteries, cans, food wraps and many other items, while ascending. More importantly, because of the cold weather and icy conditions, the litter and bodies do not decompose, and they are clearly visible from far away when the snow melts. To deal with the issue of litter, the government has initiated a deposit of US$4,000 per expedition team for trash management (Mountaineering Regulations 2002). Although the issue of litter is often seen as a paramount issue, it can be potentially managed in two ways. First, by educating locals, trekkers, expedition members and their porters, guides and support staff about the environment and their responsibility of keeping the area clean and ecologically intact. Second, Sagarmatha National Park, in collaboration with Sagarmatha Pollution Control Committee, a local NGO, and other NGOs, can play an important role in effectively managing the waste. Some efforts have also been made by the national park and NGOs to reduce or replace the dependency on the forests as a fuel source. Examples include efficient wood-burning stoves, back-boiler water heaters, kerosene depot, micro-hydroelectricity and low-wattage cookers. Although Sagarmatha National Park was established to protect the Khumbu region and the alpine ecosystem, its role is more limited to forest and wildlife protection at lower elevations. However, the high alpine ecosystems have been significantly impacted by the expedition teams (Byers 2005; Stevens 1993).

The Sherpa and mountain climbing ethics

The Sherpa, an ethnic group now known as professional mountain guides, are synonymous with mountaineering in the Himalayas. Their traditional home is the Khumbu valley and other foothills of the highest peaks in Nepal. More than 70,000 Sherpa live in Nepal, and only 5,000 live in the Khumbu region as many of them migrated to lower elevations and cities, including Kathmandu, Nepal's capital city. Khumbu Sherpa are the most adaptive humans for living in harsh and low-oxygen conditions. Traditionally, they were shepherds, farmers and traders. As the most adaptive mountainous people who have survived in the environs of high mountains for millennia, they have provided climbing support for Himalayan expeditions since the start of the twentieth century. They are usually involved in carrying supplies, cutting routes, fixing ropes, cooking, setting up camps and rescuing climbers (Ortner 1997). They serve as not only mountain guides and high-altitude porters, but also operate family-owned lodges and hotels in the Khumbu region and own and run trekking companies in Kathmandu.

Climbing on Mt Everest is challenging and dangerous because of avalanches, crevasses, ferocious winds of up to 125 mph, unexpected storms, extremely cold temperatures of 40 °F below zero, and oxygen deprivation. The 'death zone', above 25,000 ft, particularly, is very risky as the chances of hypothermia, frost-bite, high-altitude pulmonary oedema and high-altitude cerebral oedema are very high (Brunner 2014). An analysis of cause of death on over 6,000 m peaks between 1950 and 2009 indicates that avalanches and falling were the leading causes of deaths, followed by acute mountain sickness (AMS) (Salisbury and Hawley 2011).

In the most recent tragic accident, on 18 April 2014, an avalanche took the lives of 16 Sherpa as they were clearing the route through the Khumbu Icefall. Every year, the Sagarmatha Pollution Control Committee, coordination with the expedition companies, hires a group of Sherpa, also known as the Icefall Doctors, to perform one of the most dangerous jobs: making a passable route for climbers through the icefall stringing ropes and placing aluminium ladders over the crevasses and up the cliffs (Schaffer 2014). The Sherpa submitted a petition with 13 demands, including an additional US$10,000 in disability coverage for workers who were permanently injured, US$1,000 for funeral, a permanent mountaineering relief fund from 30 per cent of the government's permit royal-ties, guaranteed pay for the season even if the season is cancelled, a plot of land in Kathmandu to build a memorial to the 16 dead and official recognition of the catastrophic season by making 18 April a national holiday (Schaffer 2014). The government of Nepal met some of their demands. However the government did not meet the demand for guaranteed pay for all Sherpa even if the season was going to cancel, which was not accepted by the surviving Sherpa (Jenkins 2014; Schaffer 2014). Since the government failed to meet their demands and the Sherpa were devastated by the loss of their fellow Sherpa, they decided not to climb for the entire season. There have been some efforts by Mountain Spirit a local NGO by bringing wider Sherpa communities and guides to resolve the issue. Although the government of Nepal should have played an important role in resolving the labour issue, it is also the expedition companies' responsibility to provide better insurance, compensation and benefits to their employees, the Sherpa guides.

This accident is the most significant event that led to closing Mt Everest expe-ditions for the whole season. This clearly is a reflection of growing division between expedition members, who pay hefty amounts to reach the world's highest peak, and their highly skilled guides who are often taken for granted, underpaid and under/uninsured (Norgay 2014). This incident also illustrates the acute problems of the relationships between western mountain climbers and the Sherpa. First, they have different intentions and motivations for climbing. For western climbers, climbing is a form of 'deep play' or 'serious leisure', whereas for the Sherpa, the primary motivation for climbing has been livelihood (Ortner 1997). The risks, particularly accidents and death, have different meanings for these two groups. Since western climbers climb to fulfil their inner self and obtain fame, the risk of accident and death is worthwhile. The Sherpa's involve-ment in climbing historically is to make a living, although the motives for some Sherpa have recently begun to change as a result of exposure to western culture, values and influences. Therefore the risks of death and accidents are perceived differently by the Sherpa and western climbers (Ortner 1997). Approximately one in eight climbers does not return from a Mt Everest expedition, which is much higher than other mountain climbing, and there is one death for every five successful summits (Orther 1997). Second, although the ratio has been significantly improved, the risks and challenges are disproportionate between Sherpa and their expedition members. Norgay (2014), son of Tenzing Norgay Sherpa, mentioned that while foreign climbers are sipping coffee at base camp, Sherpa work in the most treacherous conditions. Avalanches cause 46.4 per cent of deaths of hired Sherpa, and 28.8 per cent for members because the Sherpa spend more time and energy establishing and supplying camps in avalanche-prone zones (Salisbury and Hawley 2011). The risk of death, therefore, is much higher for Sherpa than their western clients.

Mountain climbing has been a blessing for Sherpa, and, because of this, they have been silent for many years. They make more than their fellow countrymen, but their pay is nothing compared to professional western climbers and guides. There is a pyramid of profit in mountain climbing. Most money is made by foreign expedition companies, which narrows down the ladder as it goes to western guides, Sherpa and low-altitude porters. Western literature and media often portray Sherpa as loyal servants of western climbers whose living conditions have significantly improved over the last six decades as Everest expeditions became popular. However, young Sherpa have begun to challenge the relationship of 'saheb' and 'servant' and demand fair treatment.

Conclusion

Mountaineering is a complex social phenomenon, which is impacted by the modern time crunch as climbers want to pursue their dreams within the limited time they have, which instigates a new set of challenges as they have less time to learn the host society, their culture and the environment. Mountaineering is a business and there is also huge competition among the outfitters, from local to international, and small to large companies, and a trip to Mt Everest can be purchased at as low as US$30,000. At the same time, climbers' expectations from the Sherpa guides, expedition teams and the government for service are on the rise. This puts pressure on everyone who is involved in climbing Mt Everest.

Climbing Mt Everest is an example of demand-based mountaineering tourism, where the government of Nepal is unable to manage this complex mountaineering with its limited resources, and, more importantly, for the lack of transparency and accountability in managing the resources. There is a need for a wider and meaningful coordination and cooperation among the stakeholders, including the Nepal Mountaineering Association (NMA), an NGO established to promote and manage mountain tourism, climbing sports, protect mountain environments, Sagarmatha Pollution Control Committee and other NGOs, government agencies, including Sagarmatha National Nark, the Ministry of Tourism, Culture and Civil Aviation, independent climbing outfitters and guides, expedition companies, the Sherpa and climbers. The government should be able to deal with safety hazards, compensation and benefits, permits and pollution with policies that are just, timely, transparent, accountable and beneficial to all stakeholders without compromising the ecological and social integrity of the Mt Everest region and the Sherpa.

Climbers, large expedition companies and small outfitters, and their guides should promote more ethical practices and, more importantly, unfair, unethical and deceptive treatment of Sherpa and porters must end. Norgay (2014) suggests that Sherpa climbers need to establish a sensible 'code of operation' and stand behind it, which may include gaining better training and be competitive, and at the same time, foreign expeditions and their leaders must see their role as more than 'providing jobs' – a morally dubious outlook at best, and practice more socially responsible acts, like Sir Edmund Hillary did to improve the living conditions of the Sherpa. Therefore, there is a need for dialogue among the stakeholders to rethink and reform the ethics and practices of mountain climbing.

References

Brunner, B. (2014) 'Mortals of Mount Olympus: A history of climbing Mount Everest'. Online, available at: www.factmonster.com/spot/everest2.html (accessed 15 July 2014).

Byers, A. C. (2005) 'Contemporary human impacts on alpine ecosystems in the Sagarmatha (Mt. Everest) National Park, Khumbu, Nepal', *Annals of the Association of American Geographers*, 95(1): 112–140.

Fisher, J. (1990) *Sherpas: Reflection on change in Himalayan Nepal*, Berkeley, CA: University of California Press.

Jenkins, M. (2013) 'Maxed out on Everest', *National Geographic*, 223(6): 84–88. Online, available at: http://ngm.nationalgeographic.com/2013/06/125-everest-maxed-out/jenkins-text (accessed 10 October 2014).

Jenkins, M. (2014) 'Everest's Sherpas issue list of demands with climbing season in question: Sherpas want changes in working conditions', *National Geographic*. Online, available at: http://news.nationalgeographic.com/news/2014/04/140422-everest-sherpa-manifesto-avalanche-nepal-himalaya-base-camp-khumbu-icefall/ (accessed 30 October 2014).

Ministry of Culture, Tourism and Civil Aviation (2013) 'Mountaineering in Nepal: Facts and figures (2013)', Kathmandu, Nepal.

Mountaineering Regulations (2002) Ministry of Tourism, Kathmandu, Nepal.

Nepal Tourism Statistics (2012) *Annual statistical report 2012*, Kathmandu, Nepal: Ministry of Culture, Tourism and Civil Aviation.

Norgay, D. T. (2014) 'The Sherpas' guide to ethical behavior. Project syndicate: The world's opinion', 26 April. Online, available at: www.project-syndicate.org/commentary/curtis-s-chin-and-dhamey-t-norgay-consider-the-responsibility-of-rich-country-consumers-toward-poor-country-workers (accessed 26 October 2014).

Nyaupane, G. P., Lew, A. and Tatsugawa, K. (2014) 'Perceptions of trekking tourism and social and environmental change in Nepal's Himalayas', *Tourism Geographies*, 16(3): 415–437.

Ortner, S. B. (1997) 'Thick resistance: Death and the cultural construction of agency in Himalayan Mountaineering', *Representations*, 59(1): 135–162.

Salisbury, R. and Hawley, E. (2011) *The Himalaya by the numbers: A statistical analysis of mountaineering*, Kathmandu, Nepal: Vajra Publications. Online, available at: www. himalayandatabase.com/index.html (accessed 15 October 2014).

Schaffer, G. (2014) 'Black year: Everest's deadliest season', *Outside Magazine*, August. Online, available at: www.outsideonline.com/outdoor-adventure/climbing/mountaineering/ Sherpas-Death-business-Everest-Darkest-Year.html (accessed 25 October 2014).

Stevens, S. F. (1993) 'Tourism, change and continuity in the Mount Everest region, Nepal', *Geographical Review*, 83(4): 410–427.

Stevens, S. F. (2003) 'Tourism and deforestation in the Mt Everest regional of Nepal', *Geographical Journal*, 169(3): 255–277.

14 Climbing Kili

Ethical mountain guides on the roof of Africa

Brent Lovelock

Introduction

I sit in a hotel in Moshi, Tanzania, the 'gateway to Mt Kilimanjaro', sipping my Kilimanjaro beer and pleasantly (but a little apprehensively) contemplating my ascent of Kilimanjaro, due to start the next day. And while I cannot see Kiliman-jaro from the hotel restaurant because of clouds, there is a huge mural of the mountain painted on the wall of the restaurant. Elephants and giraffes adorn its flanks while its snow-capped summit glistens alluringly. A middle aged, fair, American has just walked in accompanied by a slim young Tanzanian man. They settle down for cokes and soon a map is pulled out and spread on the table and the guide traces the route that he will be taking with his client the next day as they tackle the 5,895 m (19,341 ft) 'roof of Africa'. I find myself wondering how this American gentleman came to want to climb 'Kili', and how he chose his climbing company? What does he know about the company, their standards, environmental behaviours, how much they pay their porters, their cooks and guides, and how they 'do business' in general? Then I came to consider how I, soon to tackle Kili too, accompanied by my son, decided upon our provider, but also on more profound questions such as whether or not I should be climbing Kili at all? And whether or not the US$3,000 I am paying for the two of us to get to the top of Kili could be spent better elsewhere. Perhaps, for example, to help in some small way to relieve the incredible poverty so evident in this part of the world? Or, more selfishly, to help pay for my son's university education? Or, more prosaically, to help pay for the roof repairs so urgently needed for our old house back in New Zealand? In short, my pleasant mental meanderings soon led me into a dark and menacing moral maze, from within which I began to question and re-question the ethics of our climb.

Of course some of these personal questions are not of interest to this book's reader – what I hope to explore is the importance of the mountain tourism guide in moderating our mountain 'moral encounters' (Mostefanezhad and Hannam 2014), and ensuring an ethical climb. I ask how we go about selecting an ethical provider, and consider some of the barriers that we may face. I draw upon my climb of Mt Kilimanjaro in the auto-ethnographic manner (e.g. Coffey 2002; Ellis and Bochner 2000) to inform the discussion, noting that 'the climb', physically and ethically, really begins at home when planning our trip. This chapter also builds naturally on the contribution by my colleague Kokel Melubo (in this volume), which provides a thorough and thought provoking coverage of the issues faced by porters on Mt Kilimanjaro.

Mountain tourism impacts and ethics

Not long before my son and I left New Zealand to travel to Tanzania, there had been an avalanche on Mt Everest killing 16 Nepalese Sherpa porters. This tragedy, and the consequent decision by the Sherpa to suspend climbing for the 2014 season as a mark of respect for their fallen colleagues, brought to international attention the conditions that mountain guides and porters work under and the risks that they faced. The conditions for porters on other mountains, such as Kilimanjaro did not escape such attention either (e.g. Caulderwood 2014). The 'arduous and dangerous' conditions on Kilimanjaro, where up to 20 guides and porters die every year on the mountain from altitude sickness, hypothermia and pneumonia (Christie *et al.* 2013) raise questions about how climbers can contribute to better lives for those working on the mountain (Caulderwood 2014).

With lives and livelihoods at stake, 'to climb or not climb?' is indeed the question, but *how* to climb is as equally pertinent. The sustainability of mountain tourism has increasingly come into question, with a range of issues – environmental, economic, social and cultural – identified by researchers and commentators in the field (e.g. Godde *et al.* 2000; Kuniyal 2002; Nepal 2000, 2002; Nyaupane *et al.* 2006), many of which are addressed by other contributors in this volume. The sustainability framework is increasingly being complemented by other alternative tourism frameworks that variously lend weight to, or sometimes challenge, aspects of the broad-brush sustainability paradigm. Among these is the ethical tourism approach, championed by a number of researchers in recent years (e.g. Fennell 2006; Smith and Duffy 2003; Lovelock and Lovelock 2013). An ethical tourism approach is defined as tourism in which all stakeholders involved apply principles of good behaviour (justice, fairness and equality), to their interactions with one another, with society and with the environment and other life forms (Lovelock and Lovelock 2013: 12).

Although an ethical approach is sought for all tourism interactions (e.g. Macbeth (2005) argues for it as the 'sixth platform' for tourism) arguably certain tourism environments call for a more intense and careful application. Undoubtedly, the mountain tourism environment is one such environment. Indeed, Stettner (1993) refers to the role of ethics as being critical to sustainable mountain tourism development. Why? Because of conflicting values, multiple stakeholders and the potential for mountain tourists to create harm. Mountains are spaces that are often ecologically sensitive; they are harsh environments that are dangerous for tourists and tourism providers; they are often culturally and spiritually significant, not only for local people, but having wider, even global significance. They are also places of commerce, providing livelihoods for a range of stakeholders for which the remuneration may range from being barely above subsistence level (e.g. for local guides and porters, accommodation and food providers) to thousands of dollars (e.g. for international guides); they are places therefore of inequity and struggle, yet the tourist activities that occur there can contribute to poverty alleviation.

Mountains as moral spaces

Mountain tourism is therefore an activity that is rife with what Norton (1988) would call 'moral situations' or what Mostefanezhad and Hannam (2014) term 'moral encounters'. Fittingly, the simile of 'climbing a mountain' is often used in meta-ethical discussion (e.g. Chappell 2012), while environmental philosopher Aldo Leopold (1949) in his proposal for a land ethic suggested that we 'think like a mountain'. McCoy's (1983) 'Parable of the Sadhu', set on a snowy Himalayan mountain pass is often used in ethics classes, and aptly captures some of the moral issues faced on mountains, but with broader application to many aspects of our lives.

Mountains as spaces possess certain special characteristics. As such they offer extreme experiences that challenge the spirit, the mind and the body, and also our relationships with others. Certainly many cultures have assigned great value to mountains (e.g. Mt Kailash, India, abode of Shiva; Mt Olympus, Greece, home of the Greek Pantheon; Mt Sinai, where Moses received the ten commandments; Uluru, Australia, sacred to the Anangu people). And these centuries of pre-existing symbolism mediate our personal experience of climbing a mountain (Wheeler 2013), and the mountain top 'stands for all kinds of excellence; the high point, the acme, the peak of perfection and the sublime' (2013: 553). Writing on 'Why climbing matters', McArthy (2008) asserts that the strenuous bodily work of climbing leads to greater environmental consciousness and spiritual transcendence (see also Evola's (1998) *Mountain climbing as metaphor for the spiritual quest*). Thus being on mountains is associated with opportunities for an enhanced spirituality, and, by association, enhanced morality (see Walker and Reimer (2006) and Giacalone and Jurkiewicz (2003) who write about the association between enhanced spirituality and morality). But mountains as well as being spaces of moral improvement are often also spaces of commerce. These multiple and sometimes divergent values associated with mountains can lead to tensions between stakeholders, and, potentially, ethical dilemmas. The question arises as to whether mountain tourists can reach this peak of spirituality without addressing some key ethical aspects, the most important of which is the choice of an ethical mountain tourism provider, and an ethical relationship with the provider and its staff – the guides, porters, cooks and others essential to many mountain tourism experiences.

Mountain morality – the literature

Despite the importance of mountains for tourism and other uses, and the potential ethical challenges thereof, there is a limited literature addressing the ethics of mountain tourism. To date such discussion has largely been focused on the ethics of climbing, in terms of how this manifests physically on the mountain and the physical or aesthetic experience of the climb. Waterman and Waterman (1993: 7) note that since the sport of climbing began over a century ago, climbers have argued over 'the meaning and content of ethics and style' of climbing. Much of this debate has been fixated on the impacts of climbing technology (e.g. the so called 'Bolt Wars' over the use of permanent anchor points on climbing routes), or the moral legitimacy of participation in such a dangerous activity, that may result in harm to individuals and cost to others (family, rescue workers, society) (Olivier 2006). The size and style of mountaineering expeditions has also received some coverage, with Cullen (1987) identifying a link between 'mountaineering ethics' and size of the expedition party and associated environmental impacts.

More specifically, the issue of mountain guiding operations (particularly the conditions for guides, porters and other employees or providers of goods and services) has received very little coverage from tourism researchers to date. Arguably there has been more detailed coverage of the conditions for pack animals (e.g. Cousquer and Allison 2012) than for their human counterparts, the mountain porters. Indeed, the companion case study by Kokel Melubo in this book is one of the first to give in-depth coverage of these aspects of mountain guiding within a tourism-focused volume.

Guides and mediated mountain moral encounters

The stages or components of the mountain tourism experience through which moral encounters may occur, include:

- the selection of tourism service/experience providers;
- interaction between tourists and workers providing portering and other services;
- interaction of the tourist with the physical environment;
- consumption of products and services on the mountain;
- interaction with other tourists on the mountain;
- interaction with local and/or indigenous people on the mountain;
- post-trip actions (in relation to the mountain environment, communities, providers, other tourists).

Looking at the list above, we can see that most moral encounters are personally managed but that some may be mediated through a third party provider, i.e. the mountain guide or the mountain guiding company. And for mountain tourism contexts where regulations *require* that visitors engage a guiding company for reasons of safety or logistics, as a cultural requirement, or to manage environmental impacts (Mt Kilimanjaro is in this category, as are many others), this third party may play a highly significant role. Such a provider will, to varying degrees, mediate the multiple moral encounters that visitors may have on the mountain: in relation to the environment; with local and indigenous people; with employees; with other users of the mountain, touristic and non-touristic; and with providers of goods and services to the expedition. They may also provide appropriate cultural and spiritual advice and interpretation. The limited research on mountain guides and ethics, suggests that guides acknowledge that they have such a moral role (Long *et al.* 2012). However there is some tension between this and their business responsibilities.

Being an ethical mountain tourist is about considering a multitude of often micro-ethical choices that we make before, on, around and after being on the mountain, and involves a range of issues and interests. And while obviously this involves more than just the choice of an ethical mountain guide, ultimately, because of the power of the guiding provider, choosing a mountain guiding company may be the greatest moral decision made by the mountain tourist.

But how do we go about selecting an ethical provider? Interestingly, while there is a substantial literature addressed towards the supply side about how to go about being an ethical tourism business/provider (e.g. addressing codes of practice, conduct and certification, accreditation programmes), and although there is a growing literature on the *theory* of touristic ethical consumption, with motivation and behaviours increasingly being studied, there is a relative dearth of literature addressing either descriptively or prescriptively how tourists may choose an ethical provider. We are, however, able to take direction from the wider popularist material that informs the general consumer about the proper steps to take. Some publications will even take that responsibility off the consumers' hands and assess the ethical nature of specific service and goods providers for you (e.g. Tourism Concern's *Ethical travel guide* (Patullo and Minelli 2009). But for most of us, and for most tourism situations, we are on our own.

Selection of an ethical guiding company

As noted above, our moral encounter with the mountains really begins at home. For me it began when choosing our mountain guiding company – compulsory for a Kilimanjaro climb. My search for an ethical provider began with a web search, where entering 'Kilimanjaro climb' retrieves many sites of companies offering climbs. So I am faced with dozens of operators offering the climb. What next? I had wanted to choose a company that met three broad criteria: they were 'reliable', 'good' (ethical) and within my budget. I apply the criteria to help narrow my choice of providers. Cost unfortunately, assumes some prominence for me in this process. Most companies provide details of their climbs – routes, times, equipment needed, etc. – and many also provide up-front prices. This is when I had to reach for my heart pills, as the prices offered were, in my view, astoundingly high, ranging from a rock bottom bargain bin price of around US$1,000, up to and beyond US$4,000. How can simply climbing a mountain, and one located in a less developed country, where presumably labour and other inputs would be relatively low cost, be so expensive? I am in a state of shock. Of course, this would be my first ever guided, commercial trek, after experiencing a lifetime of free hiking and climbing, and access to the outdoors in New Zealand.

However, I accepted that I needed to employ a guide, due to the Tanzanian government's regulations requiring us to do so, but, also, there are other very good reasons to have a guide on Kili. Climbing Kili involves exposure to a high altitude environment (5,895 m/19,341 ft asl), with associated risks from weather and acute mountain sickness. Every year approximately 1,000 people are evacuated from the mountain, and approximately ten deaths are reported (Ultimate Kilimanjaro 2014). So employing a guide was important for managing the safety aspect of our climb.

However, it is reassuring to learn that I am not alone in letting my skinflint habits impact upon my choice of ethical tourism provider. Research into the sustainable tourism behaviour (or not!) of tourists identifies a range of personal barriers to good behaviour, with internal and external barriers noted (Budeanu 2007). Among these are lack of knowledge, the financial situation of the tourist, time, habits, convenience and personal preferences. This gap between intention and actual purchasing behaviour has led researchers to discuss the 'myth of the ethical consumer', questioning whether consumers really care about corporate responsibility (a.k.a. ethics), implicating the role of affordability, among other factors in ethical (or non-ethical) consumption behaviour (e.g. Boulstridge and Carrigan 2000; Carrigan and Attala 2000).

So, my parsimoniousness approach immediately reduces my 'choice set' of mountain guiding companies to a manageable number, as I limit the price of the trek to around US$1,500 for each of us, based on our travel budget. This process unfortunately removed from my list a number of appealing companies, many of which were the larger, sometimes foreign-owned businesses, with well-established social or environmental programmes. The smaller independent companies, locally owned, were less likely to claim such responsible behaviour, perhaps lacking the financial aptitude (or marketing savvy?) to do so. This posed an ethical dilemma for me, as I wanted my trekking fees to contribute in some small way to either helping local social or environmental causes, but also to support a small-scale, locally owned and operated company. But overarching this need to do good, were the above financial realities: as there would be two of us travelling, and the likely cost would be over US$1,500 each, this would be the single most expensive tourist activity that I had ever purchased.

So although my new set of companies were those that met my budget criterion many 'good' candidates were eliminated. An example of one of these good companies is 'Zara Tours'. This company was started by a Tanzanian woman (brownie points for that!). It is a member of Sustainable Tourism International and it undertakes twice-yearly 'Clean-up Kilimanjaro' trips (some other companies also participate in this). It includes 'charity' climbs in its range of climbs: these involving a visit (at an extra cost to the client) to a Kilimanjaro orphanage with a contribution made to the orphanage. It also has its own charity, which plays 'a vital role to enhance community economic development especially by supporting vulnerable groups in the community such as orphans, a Maasai women's group, and poor people such as porters who climb Mt Kilimanjaro' (Zara Tours 2014). The company set up the Kilimanjaro Porters Society in

2004 to improve the working conditions of porters, and has won an international humanitarian award. But it was too expensive...

Also too expensive was Private Expeditions who ticked a lot of boxes as being a 'Good' operator. To support the local communities, there are three things that it does:

> first we pay all our employees the best rates of pay and that all goes back to local families. Second we only use local Tanzanians on our climbs. Thirdly for every climber who comes with us we make a donation to the Amani Children's home.
>
> (Private Expeditions 2014)

This company also operates to 'leave no trace guidelines' carrying out all rubbish from the park and disposing of it properly – very impressive.

To help progress my choice of ethical provider, I resorted to searching for advice from the Internet. The first site that I found was 'How to pick the best safari guide' (Wogan and Trubowitz 2013) which I thought vaguely appropriate since it was Africa focused and because many Kilimanjaro operators also offer safaris. But the site was not in the least helpful, referring only to guide licensing, costs and tipping, with no reference at all to ethical issues. The next site, 'Choosing the right tour company' (Nomadic Matt 2014) while not addressing mountain climbing or Africa per se, was encouraging in that it did mention environmental impact and the use of local providers. So, yes, my intuition that choosing a local provider may be the ethical way to go was confirmed. However, the next site I visited 'How to choose a tour operator to climb Mt Kilimanjaro' advised me *not* to use a local provider! Zephyr Adventures discusses whether or not to choose a local operator, noting the lower price associated with doing so. However it strongly implies that there is a strong risk of my money 'disappearing' between the time that I pay and when I arrive in Tanzania. It even suggests that I would be 'rolling the dice' on guide quality if I chose a local company. However...

> If you book with an international operator, you can generally be assured that company has done the research to make sure they are using excellent local guides.... The truth is, an American tour guide will understand the needs and desires of American travelers better than will a Tanzanian guide.
>
> (Zephyr Adventures 2014)

I was becoming confused. And then I realized that the above advice was not exactly impartial, but was actually offered by an American company operating climbs. Just as another traveller 'Sarah' noted in her quest on a travel discussion site, 'How to find and choose a tour guide?', many sites that purport to offer independent advice 'are just new kind of travel agencies (taking their revenue by commissions basis)' ('Sarah' in Fodors 2014) and promote either their own tours or those who pay a commission to be recommended. '*Lonely Planet*?' I hear you ask? Well yes I did refer to its Tanzania guide and while it does recommend a few companies these were primarily a cross-section and based on cost and word of mouth recommendation, with no transparent criteria applied.

I found another website in this category which 'helps' you to choose a company and identifies four categories based on criteria that include porter welfare (or lack thereof). Being aware of the plight of the Sherpa on Everest, and porters in general, it was heartening to see someone taking this issue seriously. The site groups companies as those where the 'Crew is commonly underpaid; the Crew is paid minimum or below; Crew is paid minimum or above' (Amani Afrika 2014). Based upon the latter as being the only acceptable situation, plus other criteria such as guide qualifications, camping equipment and pricing, it recommends itself as the best company to go with!

Similarly, the website 'Choosing Kilimanjaro guides – porter welfare' highlights the issue of porter welfare, noting that there are:

> independent organizations who look out for the porters on Kilimanjaro. The Kilimanjaro Porter Assistance Project (KPAP) and the International Mountain Explorer Connection's (IMEC) Partnership for Responsible Travel are organizations that monitor companies on Kilimanjaro to ensure that staff are treated properly – in terms of pay, food, clothing and shelter.
>
> (Kilimanjaro Guides 2014)

They note that to be recognized by KPAP and IMEC as a partner company is quite a statement, considering the 'several hundred' companies on the mountain, and that only a few dozen comply with IMEC's Guidelines for Proper Porter Treatment. Kilimanjaro Guides is, of course, such a partner company. This 'accreditation' looked like a good basis to choose a 'good' (ethical) company, but then I had a nagging thought (based upon experiences in other countries) that perhaps many companies, especially small locally owned Tanzanian companies, may not be able to afford the price of accreditation with the above organizations, or have the necessary connections to enable this. So I decided that this may not necessarily point to the most ethical companies.

To help narrow the field, I applied a further criterion, considering 'logistics' and emailed my now limited number of trekking companies to see that climbs were available on our chosen dates, and for the route that I had identified as the most suitable for us (based on our levels of fitness, the scenery and habitats that we would encounter, and our desire to be on a 'quieter' and less used route). Once all the email replies had been received, I narrowed my choice down to two companies. One was Team Maasai. I had a vague idea of Maasai as being a proud and noble people, eking a living from the harsh and unforgiving lands of the Serengeti. It seemed somehow appropriate to consider giving my hard earned cash to these enterprising and resilient people.

> Team Maasai is a hard-working team of Maasai porters who have been hand-drawn and selected by our traditional leaders and elders from the

Ngorongoro Crater area ... Our Arusha-based sponsor ... work[s] with the Nanapai foundation to promote the development of our people without compromise to our traditional culture.

(Team Maasai 2014)

Their website describes how the Maasai guides maintain their families and bomas on their traditional homelands, and spurn urban living, contrasting their situation with guides from other tribes. The Team Maasai guides climb because they enjoy it.

This company seemed 'good', *and* they were one of the cheapest providers, coming in at around US$1,000. It explained that it could offer climbs at this price, because of compromises around using good but second hand equipment, more basic but filling meals and junior guides. It, in the spirit of complete transparency, identify the fixed costs per climber of Kilimanjaro Park Fees payable to the Tanzanian tourism ministry (US$748 for a six-day climb). Interestingly it notes that it is not a member of any porters' associations, but that it was 'trusting their own elders and village leaders to represent any concerns or requests that they may have to their operation managers' (Team Maasai 2014). Perfect! I had almost hit the 'Pay Now' button on my browser, when I decided to make enquiries through a Tanzanian contact, who happens to be Maasai. Sadly, Team Maasai was not on his personal list of recommended providers, so I denied my own ethical desire to 'do good' by choosing it, and rather opted instead for another company that on the surface appeared to be less 'ethical', and to cost more – Popote Africa Adventures.

So why did I choose Popote (who, by the way, provided fantastic service)? It is a small start-up company that did not claim any charity work, no environmental responsibility and does not belong to any tourism organization (the owner later told me that he would join once he could afford to, but the cost was currently prohibitive for him). This was a company that did not purport to do any social or environmental good, yet I felt from my personal communication with it, from the level of information that it provided, that it was a good and ethical company. Well at least ethical in terms of its primary ethical responsibility: that is to provide its client with honest information about the product, and to provide a good service – which in this case was to safely get us to the top of Kilimanjaro and back. But perhaps the clincher was that it offered a 15 per cent discount for my 16 year old son. While this may have been a cold-hearted business move, I felt not. I felt that the owner of the company had a genuine love of young people and was offering the discount as a way of helping to get my son up Kili. It turned out that upon meeting the company owner, Sabino, that he did indeed really enjoy my son's company, going out of his way to make him feel welcome and special. Indeed, this attitude applied to all his and his staff's interactions with my son (and with me) before, during and after the climb. So, while the company may not espouse any grand ethical principles, or profess any investment into the local environment or society, or support any charities, it does the one thing that any company should do, and that is manage the relationship with its clients in a thoroughly clear, honest and ethical way.

While to some readers this may appear to be an ethical cop-out, I believe that I still ended up employing an ethical company. Chatzidakis *et al.* (2007) argue that consumers use neutralization techniques to justify pursuing their more selfish goals instead of purchasing more ethical products. I think that this was the case for me, where my need to meet a budget 'neutralized' my desire to employ a guiding company that may have walked a more ethical walk. However, I still felt that Popote was an ethical company. One way it demonstrated this was around the issue of conditions for porters. Popote provided very clear information about its porters, their conditions and appropriate tipping rates etc. Our experience on the mountain was that our team of 11 porters and one cook, were not overloaded, they had good tents and equipment, appeared to have a very good relationship with the two guides and with the company owner, and to be genuinely satisfied with their work conditions. In a sense, we had a serendipitous ethical experience: we were lucky that our company treated its staff well. And while many trekking companies such as Popote may not have any overt CSR activities, the simple fact that it employs a large team of people on each trek, and that these porters and cooks get remunerated fairly (to the extent that being a porter on Kili is a sought after job) is a simple ethical act of social responsibility in itself.

Conclusion

We need to understand better the moral implications associated with consumption practices and processes (Caruana 2007), and this especially applies to mountain tourism environments with their complex of interacting ethical issues. Wheale and Hinton (2007) suggest that amongst the population of green consumers there is a hierarchy of importance of ethical drivers in the purchase decision-making process, with the environment rated as the most important ethical driver during purchasing decisions followed by human rights then animal rights/welfare issues. For some mountain tourism environments, however, human rights issues, especially those of porters and associated workers and providers needs to assume greater prominence. This can happen through, as Budeanu (2007) suggests, providing more information to ensure an informed decision is made: in the case of mountain tourism, this means ensuring that consumers are informed about conditions of workers within the industry. The Ethical Consumer refers to this in its 'A beginners guide to ethical consumer' (2014), as a 'fully screened approach'.

This begs the question of how such an approach may be implemented in a complete and effective way, especially as employers may be reluctant to provide information, and workers may be fearful that 'spilling the beans' will make them vulnerable. Here, the likes of porters' associations can play a role, as can tourism industry umbrella organizations, although there may also be some reluctance on the part of those organizations to tarnish the image of their region's/nation's tourism product. Third party media and watchdog organizations can play a role too. The next step, and what is lacking now, at least in an impartial way, are guidelines for potential mountain tourists, about how to go about selecting their provider. To date much of the prescriptive work on ethical consumption has focused on consumer goods rather than the services that we may consume in tourism. While the complexity of the moral encounters in mountain tourism may mean that developing such an approach is challenging, the ongoing issues faced by workers and communities associated with mountain tourism provide an urgent imperative for this to happen.

References

Amani Afrika (2014) 'How to choose the best Kilimanjaro tour operator?'. Online, available at: www.amaniafrika.com/best-kilimanjaro-tour-operator-vs-right-kilimanjaro-climb-company (accessed 25 August 2014).

Boulstridge, E. and Carrigan, M. (2000) 'Do consumers really care about corporate responsibility? Highlighting the attitude–behaviour gap', *Journal of Communiation Management*, 4(4): 355–368.

Budeanu, A. (2007) 'Sustainable tourist behaviour: A discussion of opportunities for change', *International Journal of Consumer Studies*, 31(5): 499–508.

Carrigan, M. and Attala, A. (2001) 'The myth of the ethical consumer: Do ethics matter in purchase behaviour?' *Journal of Consumer Marketing*, 18(7): 560–578.

Caruana, R. (2007) 'Morality and consumption: Towards a multidisciplinary perspective', *Journal of Marketing Management*, 23(3–4): 207–225.

Caulderwood, K. (2014) 'As Everest Sherpas boycott climbing season, the porters on Kilimanjaro work for less', *International Business Times*, 30 April. Online, available at: www.ibtimes.com/everest-sherpas-boycott-climbing-season-porters-kilimanjaro-work-less-1577402 (accessed 29 August 2014).

Chappell, T. (2012) 'Climbing which mountain? A critical study of Derek Parfit, *On what matters* (OUP 2011)', *Philosophical Investigations*, 35(2): 167–181.

Chatzidakis, A., Hibbert, S. and Smith, A. P. (2007) 'Why people don't take their concerns about fair trade to the supermarket: The role of neutralisation', *Journal of Business Ethics*, 74: 89–100.

Christie, I., Fernandes, E., Messerli, H. and Twining-Ward, L. (2013) *Tourism in Africa: Harnessing tourism for growth and improved livelihoods*, Washington, DC: World Bank. Online, available at: http://documents.worldbank.org/curated/en/2013/01/ 18320011/ tourism-africa-harnessing-tourism-growth-improved-livelihoods (accessed 1 September 2014).

Coffey, A. (2002) 'Ethnography and self: Reflections and representations', in T. May (ed.) *Qualitative research in action*, London: Sage: 313–331.

Cousquer, G. and Allison, P. (2012) 'Ethical responsibilities towards expedition pack animals: The mountain guide's and expedition leader's ethical responsibilities towards pack animals on expedition', *Annals of Tourism Research*, 39(4): 1839–1858.

Cullen, R. (1987) 'Expeditions, efficiency, ethics and the environment', *Leisure Studies*, 6(1): 41–53.

Ellis, C. and Bochner, A. (2000) 'Autoethnography, personal narrative, reflexivity: Researcher as subject', in N. K. Denzin and Y. S. Lincoln (eds) *Handbook of qualitative research*, London: Sage: 733–768.

Ethical Consumer (2014) 'A beginners guide to ethical consumer'. Online, available at: www.ethicalconsumer.org (accessed 3 September 2014).

Evola, J. (1998) *Meditations on the peaks: Mountain climbing as metaphor for the spiritual quest*, Rochester, VT: Inner Traditions.

Fennell, D. (2006) *Tourism ethic*, Clevedon: Channel View.

Fodors (2014) 'Travel tips and trips ideas forums: How to find and choose a tour guide'. Online, available at: www.fodors.com/community/travel-tips-trip-ideas/how-to-find-and-choose-a-tour-guide.cfm (accessed 25 August 2014).

Giacalone, R. A. and Jurkiewicz, C. L. (2003) 'Right from wrong: The influence of spirituality on perceptions of unethical business activities', *Journal of Business Ethics*, 46: 85–97.

Godde, P. M., Price, M. F. and Zimmermann, F. M. (2000) *Tourism and development in mountain regions*, Wallingford: CABI Publishing.

Kilimanjaro Guides (2014) 'Porter welfare: Why you should care'. Online, available at:www.kilimanjaroguides.com/choosing-kilimanjaro-guides-porter-welfare (accessed 25 August 2014).

Kuniyal, J. C. (2002) 'Mountain expeditions: Minimising the impact', *Environmental Impact Assessment Review*, 22(6): 561–581.

Leopold, A. (1949) *A sand county Almanac*, New York: Oxford University Press.

Long, T., Bazin, D. and Massiéra, B. (2012) 'Mountain guides: Between ethics and socio-economic trends', *Journal of Moral Education*, 41(3): 369–388.

Lovelock, B. and Lovelock, K. M. (2013) *The ethics of tourism: Critical and applied perspectives*, London: Routledge.

McArthy, J. M. (2008) 'Why climbing matters', *Interdisciplinary Studies in Literature and Environment*, 15(2): 157–174.

Macbeth, J. (2005) 'Towards an ethics platform for tourism', *Annals of Tourism Research*, 32(4): 962–984.

McCoy, B. H. (1983) 'The parable of the Sadhu', *Harvard Business Review*, 3(September/October): 103–108.

Mostefanezhad, M. and Hannam, K. (2014) *Moral encounters in tourism*, Farnham: Ashgate.

Nepal, S. K. (2000) 'Tourism in protected areas: The Nepalese Himalaya', *Annals of Tourism Research*, 27(3): 661–681.

Nepal, S. K. (2002) 'Mountain ecotourism and sustainable development: Ecology, economics, and ethics', *Mountain Research and Development*, 22(2): 104–109.

Nomadic Matt (2014) 'Choosing the right tour company'. Online, available at: www.nomadic-matt.com/travel-tips/choosing-the-right-tour-company/ (accessed 25 August 2014).

Norton, D. L. (1988) 'Moral minimalism and the development of moral character', *Midwest Studies in Philosophy*, XIII(1): 180–195.

Nyaupane, G. P., Morais, D. B. and Dowler, L. (2006) 'The role of community involvement and number/type of visitors on tourism impacts: A controlled comparison of Annapurna, Nepal and Northwest Yunnan, China', *Tourism Management*, 27(6): 1373–1385.

Olivier, S. (2006) 'Moral dilemmas of participation in dangerous leisure activities', *Leisure Studies*, 25(1): 95–109.

Pattullo, P. and Minelli, I. (2009) *The ethical travel guide*, London: Earthscan.

Private Expeditions (2014) 'Climb Kilimanjaro: Private expeditions'. Online, available at: www.privateexpeditions.com/climb-kilimanjaro/ (accessed 1 September 2014).

Smith, M. and Duffy, R. (2003) *The ethics of tourism development*, London: Routledge.

Stettner, A. C. (1993) 'Community or commodity? Sustainable development in mountain resorts', *Tourism Recreation Research*, 18(1): 3–10.

Team Maasai (2014) 'team-maasai.com: About us'. Online, available at: http://climb-kilimanjaro.co/about-us/ (accessed 3 September 2014).

Ultimate Kilimanjaro (2014) 'Altitude acclimatization'. Online, available at: www.ultimatekilimanjaro.com/acclimatization.htm (accessed 25 August 2014).

Walker, L. J. and Reimer, K. S. (2006) 'The relationship between moral and spiritual development', in P. Benson, P. King, L. Wagener and E. Roehlkepartain (eds) *The handbook of spiritual development in childhood and adolescence*, Newbury Park, CA: Sage: 265–301.

Waterman, L. and Waterman, G. (1993) *Yankee rock and ice: A history of climbing in the northeastern United States*, Harrisburg, PA: Stackpole Books.

Wheale, P. and Hinton, D. (2007) 'Ethical consumers in search of markets', *Business Strategy and the Environment*, 16(4): 302–315.

Wheeler, E. A. (2013) 'Don't climb every mountain', *Interdisciplinary Studies in Literature and Environment*, 20(3): 553–573.

Wogan, J. and Trubowitz, L. (2013) 'How to pick the best safari guide'. Online, available at: www.cntraveler.com/stories/2013-12-03/how-to-pick-the-best-safari-guide (accessed 25 August 2014).

Zara Tours (2014) 'Trekking Kilimanjaro with Zara Tours'. Online, available at: www.zaratours.com/kilimanjaro (accessed 25 August 2014).

Zephyr Adventures (2014) 'How to choose a tour operator to climb Mount Kilimanjaro'. Online, available at: www.zephyradventures.com/blog/how-to-choose-a-tour-operator-to-climb-mount-kilimanjaro/ (accessed 25 August 2014).

Case study 9

The working conditions of *Wagumu* (high altitude porters) on Mt Kilimanjaro

Kokel Melubo

Introduction

While considerable research has been conducted on Mt Kilimanjaro from the fields of conservation biology (e.g. Newmark 1991) and climatology (e.g. Thompson *et al.* 2009), the same cannot be said of the thriving Kilimanjaro climbing industry in the aspect of the welfare of porters, colloquially known as *Wagumu* (the tougher) or *Wapiganaji* (the fighters). Yet the importance of porters serving on Mt Kilimanjaro tourism cannot be overestimated. Porters, like Sherpa in Nepal, play a pivotal role in the development of tourism in Mt Kilimanjaro. They are the heart and soul of the trekkers on the mountain. This study highlights the welfare of these salient partners to climbers as a means to understand better how mountain tourism in the Tanzanian context operates.

Mt Kilimanjaro in Tanzania – 5,895 m – is Africa's highest mountain. Mt Kili, the mountain's name by local Chagga people, has two dominant volcanoes, Kibo (5,895 m) and Mawenzi (5,149 m), and Shira (3,962 m). It is a habitat for rare endemic and endangered flora and fauna. In terms of size, Mt Kilimanjaro covers an area of about 756 km² with elevation from 2,800 m to its summit. Mt Kili is located about 41 km from Moshi Municipality. Despite the high altitude, climbing Mt Kilimanjaro requires no technical climbing skills or equipment. There are six designated routes (Marangu, Machame, Rongai, Umbwe, Shira and Mweka) to the peak. The Marangu route, colloquially known as the 'Coca-Cola Route', is the easiest to trek and most preferred by tourists and takes six days to climb (including descending). Mt Kilimanjaro is Tanzanian national parks' top earner (Christie *et al.* 2013) yielding the revenue of US$51 million (around 55 billion Tanzania shillings) in 2013 alone. Every year, around 40,000 tourists attempt to climb Kilimanjaro (Mitchell *et al.* 2009). In 2013, according to the Kilimanjaro National Park (KINAPA), 55,553 tourists, largely foreigners predominantly from the USA and Europe, visited the area, and half of them attempted to climb to the summit. However, it is not only the tourists who make the journey to the mountain. In fact the number of tourists is outnumbered by local Tanzanians. For every one tourist (foreigner in particular) who climbs the mountain there are at least three porters, a cook as well as a guide. It is estimated that there are 10,000 porters, 500 cooks and 400 guides who labour beside climbers on Mt Kilimanjaro (Mitchell *et al.* 2009).

In this sense, the mountain offers the most intensive employment for locals in Tanzania's national park system.

Porters are an essential and crucial component in Mt Kilimajaro tourism. In this study, porters are individuals, employed temporarily or permanently to carry the luggage of the tourists up and down the mountain, set up and re-pack sleeping gear, bring down trash and sometimes prepare food. Porters are the sole means of 'transport' of tourists' luggage and supply to the mountain as other beasts of burden are not utilized. Simply put, the absence of porters could stall further tourism on Mt Kilimanjaro. Unlike their counterparts, for example in Nepal, information on the general welfare of Tanzanian locals' supporters to mountain climbers is limited. As a step towards bridging this gap, this study examines the working conditions of porters. To understand better the working conditions of porters on Mt Kilimanjaro, the following issues are examined: transport to the entrance gates, wages, head-shoulder load, meals, shelters and health and safety. I shall begin with the profile characteristics of porters including age, gender, background and education.

Porters' profiles on Mt Kilimanjaro

There are no actual figures available for the number of porters working on Mt Kilimanjaro. However, it is estimated that as many as 10,000 individuals work as porters on the mountain. The majority of them come from the local farming community of the Chagga people. Some porters are from the neighbouring regions of Arusha, Tanga and Manyara. Aside from being a hub for climbers, Kilimanjaro, which has reliable rainfall and fertile volcanic soils, is also a coffee growing region (Campbell *et al.* 2004). However, in comparison with agriculture, tourism is perceived to be the most profitable activity in the area. A porter on the mountain can earn more than US$2 a day, which is a typical daily wage for a farmer in Tanzania (Spenceley 2010).

There is no restriction on gender in portage on Kilimanjaro. However, the majority of porters are male, as most of the women are at home, working on the farm, taking care of the children, going to the market and fetching water (Monah 2011). In addition, female porters feel a sense of discomfort in the camps or huts as there are no special provisions for them (Mitchell *et al.* 2009). Despite these socio-cultural and health barriers, there are some female porters; several of whom, through the Kilimanjaro Porters Assistance Project (or KPAP) training support, have subsequently become mountain guides. KPAP is one of the associations that strives to improve the working conditions of porters, which includes offering classes in English, organizing HIV/AIDS awareness and first aid management, and lending porters mountain equipment. KPAP encourages climbing companies to follow ethical guidelines for the treatment of porters. Other associations include the Kilimanjaro Guides and Porters Union, Kilimanjaro Porters Assistance and Tanzania Porters Organization.

A porter's age may indicate the fitness to climb and the ability to carry the heavy weights of tourists' belongings and other supplies. Porters working on

Kilimanjaro are relatively young, ranging from 18 to 40 years old (Climb Mt Kilimanjaro 2014). On rare occasions, older porters, above the age of 50, have been found carrying tourists' luggage on the mountain.

Education (which in this context means an ability to speak English) is an essential ingredient in portage as it facilitates the ability to interact with tourists and obtain better employment. Although in Tanzania, Swahili is used in primary school education and English is the medium of instruction at the primary and post-secondary levels, the majority of local people have poor command of English (Sa 2007). Porters with good English proficiency are likely to work as mountain guides which yield better pay. It is estimated that the vast majority of porters working on Mt Kilimanjaro have seventh grade education (Ndekirwa *et al.* 2011). Inability to speak English reduces the opportunity for porters to advance in their career for better paying jobs such as mountain guiding.

Working conditions of the porter

Back-head luggage

Among tourists, the ascent on Mt Kilimanjaro is considered not difficult for its gradual terrain and sufficient time taken for acclimatization. But this is not true among porters who have to carry some water in one hand, cooker in another, rucksack on the back and picnic table on the head (Climb Mount Kilimanjaro 2014) (Figure CS 9.1). Excessive loads threaten the health of porters causing injuries and general body fatigue. According to KINAPA, the official limit for porter back-head load is 25 kg/55 lbs, 20 kg/44 lbs being for the tourist and 5 kg/11 lbs for own necessities. Each company porter is expected to comply with that amount of weight. For proper adherence of this, each ascending porter is required to weigh the luggage at park gate entrances. The non-compliance to the recommended amount of luggage has been a major concern amongst porters and porters associations. It has been established that the vast majority of porters are overweighed. In a surprise reweighing, Mafuru *et al.* (2009) observed an additional 2 kg on top of the 25 kg limit. Excessive back-head loads are common in July to August, and November to December when tourism on the mountain is at the peak. KPAP's (Ndekirwa *et al.* 2011) survey on 2,285 porters indicated that porters who work with climbing companies that partner to KPAP carry the recommended 25 kg or less luggage load and more luggage for porters who works with non-KPAP members. There are three reasons for the overweight loading. First, the inaccurate measurements by the KINAPA scale (Ndekirwa *et al.* 2011). Second, results from the nature of porters' recruitment. Because of the sheer number of porters, obtaining portage is becoming challenging. The head guide, who has been assigned by the climbing company to hire porters, sometimes distributes baggage that could have been carried by three porters amongst two. This is to reduce the expenditure on staff (the head guide then pockets the money for him/herself). On hiring, porters are conditioned to accept the offer and because they are in need of jobs, they left with limited options and power of

Figure CS 9.1 Porters carrying heavy luggage on Mt Kilimanjaro.

negotiation. There have been instances of porters paying head guides as a bribe to get the job (Monah 2011). The third reason is corruption at the weighing stations. KINAPA employees who are required to weigh the load of the porters at each camping site, have been accused of accepting payment from trekking companies or head guides to allow more than the 25 kg weight to be carried by the porters (Peaty 2012). The heavy packs carried by porters on their heads and backs can negatively impact their health.

Health and safety

Health and safety is another critical concern of porters on Kilimanjaro. Similar to tourists, porters suffer from heavy rains, strong winds, cold, altitude sickness and medical symptoms such as pneumonia, hypothermia, frostbite, stomach ailments and high altitude cerebral and pulmonary oedema (Karinen *et al.* 2008). Unlike tourists, guides do not receive the standard care and treatment. Porters rarely have proper and adequate clothing, footwear, sleeping bags or backpacks (Ndekirwa *et al.* 2011). In addition, porters do not carry much of their belongings to the mountain, to allow more space for tourists' luggage. With harsh environmental conditions, it is estimated that up to 20 porters die each year as they attempt to ascend or descend the mountain with inadequate equipment and the relentless pressure to keep working (Reid 2008). For example, in September 2002, three porters died due to harsh weather conditions on the mountain (Keats 2002)

Furthermore, some of the techniques to climb Mt Kilimanjaro successfully such as *walk slowly* and *climb high sleep low* seem not practical with porters, because they are required to move ahead to pitch tents and cook food for tourists. To achieve this better, porters are obliged to move quickly to the next campsite to set up what is required and cook. In the quest for money, on the descending day, porters rush downhill to surrender the luggage and then be on standby in case of any tender to return to the mountain. Moreover, porters' health and safety concerns occupy a back seat in KINAPA. Since the early 2000s KINAPA began first aid training for tourists' supporters. The training equips individuals with safety and rescue evacuation skills but only targets mountain guides and excludes porters. They argue that, unlike porters, mountain guides are the closest to tourists and KINAPA's helping hands and therefore should receive hands-on training. This assumption is untrue. According to KPAP (Ndekirwa *et al.* 2011), it is often the porters who help the KINAPA rescue team to transport sick tourists off the mountain to meet the rescue vehicles.

Porters on Mt Kilimanjaro also have no health assistance. When a porter gets a health problem that may require medication, she/he is often responsible for the expenses. The costs of medication at the nearby health centres such as Kilimanjaro Medical Centre (Mwanza) are expensive. Instead, the impoverished porter opts to purchase drugs from the local pharmacies, which are a relatively cheaper cost, and without a proper diagnosis. The worst case scenario is when a porter gets injured or ill on the mountain. They are likely to be sent down on their own and sometimes denied pay. With the fear of losing jobs, porters hardly ever admit their injuries or health ailments (Peaty 2012).

Remuneration concern

Wage inequality is another serious concern to the porters on Mt Kilimanjaro. Although KINAPA has a guideline on wages for porters, their payment is the responsibility of the hiring climbing company. Since 2010, the minimum daily wage for porters working on Kilimanjaro was agreed to be US$10 (10,000 Tanzania shilling). Though there is no formalized method of payment, on many occasions porters receive part of their wages before climbing the mountain to buy personal items and leave some for their families. They receive the rest of their wages at the end of the trip (Ndekirwa *et al.* 2011).

Despite the recommended amount of wage to each porter per trip, disparity exists on the amount of payment. In this case, there are two distinct types of the porters: standby porters and porters on permanent contracts. The former refers to porters who hang around the park gate entrance, waiting for the 'opportunity'. They are flexible to climb the mountain with any group at any time. This group, which is by far the largest, is highly disadvantaged; they get fewer payments (US$5–6) and are often ill equipped with climbing gear such as sleeping bags or backpacks (Ndekirwa *et al.* 2011). The latter involves porters who are employed on a short/long-term basis by a climbing company. Depending on the company, this group has the potential of getting trained and getting a good and reliable salary (US$8–10 per day) and sometimes good climbing gear such as sleeping bags (Peaty 2012). Some companies which are partners to KPAP, do pay extra bonuses for collecting and removing waste generated and left out by other companies (Thomson Safaris 2014). This is done to keep the mountain clean. Littering in the form of tin cans, plastic bottles and organic matter, paper and textiles metals is one of the critical challenges associated with climbing parties facing the mountain (Kaseva and Moirana 2010).

Although the subject of tipping, colloquially called 'mboneka', may sound improper in some countries, it is an expectation on Mt Kilimanjaro. It constitutes a significant proportion of the most underpaid mountain crew's (guides, porters and cooks) wages. There are no guidelines on the amount of tipping. However, some companies such as Team Kilimanjaro and Climb Mt Kilimanjaro have suggested to clients the amount and how to approach tipping. Unfortunately the approach has not been well practised. One approach of payment is at the end of the trip – climbers give the tips to the head guide who in turn distributes to porters and cooks. Lack of transparency on the transfer of tips from the head guide to the porters is a major concern. Head guides have been accused of stealing some of the money intended for porters. In fear that the head guide may be paying porters less than the full tipping amounts, climbers are encouraged to pay them directly at the end of the trek (Ndekirwa *et al.* 2011).

Food

Food provides energy to the human body (Wardlaw *et al.* 2004). Physical activity such as mountain climbing increases energy expenditure beyond that typically experienced while at rest. Eating the right amount of food with a balanced complex of carbohydrates, protein and fat is essential for all mountain climbers irrespective of their status. Lack of sufficient food appropriate to the high altitude and harsh cold weather remains a concern for porters on Mt Kilimanjaro. The majority of hiring climbing companies do not provide meals to porters. With the current state of meagre wages, the majority of porters are unable to purchase sufficient nutritious food. It is understood that on average a porter receives one light meal a day (D. Francis, personal communication, 15 July 2014). *Ugali* (stiff porridge made from corn meal), or popcorn/chapatti with a steaming hot cup of tea is the staple food for many porters. Porters who are on a short-term contract with climbing companies eat two meals a day. In order to keep themselves fuelled to carry the load to the mountain, porters have come up with a packed meal known as *Makomeo. Makomeo* which literary means 'wrap up' or 'eat once for all', is a mixture of groundnuts, slice of bread and chapatti. With a *Makomeo* many porters are able to carry on with portage. The making of *Makomeo* is not understood by the novice porters.

Transport

While transport to Mt Kilimanjaro for porters is relatively easy and affordable, unreliability and expense become a concern during the return from the mountain. It has been established that the standby porters experience transport problems on descending from the mountain. This is because the company which employs porters on short contract does not cater for porters' transport. On many occasions the company collects the tourists and leaves the porters to exist in the misery of cold. With the pressure to save their little earnings many porters opt to wait for public transport, which often is unreliable. The minibuses, locally known as *daladala* are the main mode of public transport for porters to the gates of the mountain. Transport with *daladala* sometimes becomes a mess during the rainy season when roads are muddy, slippery and at times impassable. In this case fatigue and sometimes shivering porters are obliged to wait at the gate for hours or walk down to the nearest bus station. Transport from the gate entrances after the hike is not a concern of a porter who works for climbing members of KPAP. Members of KPAP are conditioned to offer fair treatment to porters in all aspects of welfare, including guaranteed transport to and from the mountain. They do this by sending vehicles to collect the mountain crew (guides, porters and cooks) and their equipment or pay for their transport.

Accommodation

The availability of sleeping gear on the mountain is another concern for porters. Most porters reside in lower elevation areas, for example Moshi town, 950–700 m above sea level, thus do not adapt well when working on the mountain. Yet they do not have sufficient money to purchase sleeping gear. In addition, porters have less space in the KINAPA's campsites or huts, such as Marangu, Horombo and Kibo, built along the mountain trekking route. KINAPA accommodation facilities are meant for tourists but, when space is available, the other supporting crew can be accommodated. In many occasions it is the guides, bosses of porters, who get the bedding at KINAPA huts. In this case porters are left with few options in accommodation but to sleep outside covering themselves with the ragged canvas of tents or plastics. Porters who work with climbing companies that are members of KPAP receive tents that are warmer and waterproof (Ndekirwa *et al.* 2011). Sleeping gear for mountain crews means added weight to porters. In resolving this, companies that are partners of KPAP add extra porters to carry the luggage of the visitor supporting crew.

Conclusion

While the 2010 and 2011 KPAP survey reports (Ndekirwa *et al.* 2011) contribute significantly to the content of this case study, it should be pointed out that the reports may not be accurate. In light of the above, this study sets out to explore the working conditions of porters on Mt Kilimanjaro. It uncovers issues faced by porters in terms of remuneration fairness, transport to and from the mountain, quality of accommodation, quality of food and health and safety. The findings, however, are limited as the analysis is based on the researcher's personal communication from a long association with porters on Mt Kilimanjaro.

The dominant theme emerging from this report is that the working conditions of porters accompanying climbers on Mt Kilimanjaro are unsatisfactory and could be improved. From the human rights perspective, it appears that mountain tourism on Mt Kilimanjaro may have transgressed the rights of porters. Fair pay, proper climbing gear such as clothing and footwear, and proper medical care to porters remain inadequate and unsatisfactory. Many lose their lives in their effort to earn a meagre income to support their families. Many may also have been exploited by the irresponsible trekking companies who put the welfare of the porters secondary to their own desire to make more money.

The tourism industry, including climbers and climbing companies, has a responsibility in helping to address the unsatisfactory working conditions of porters on the mountain. In particular, KINAPA, a government agency in charge of tourism operations on the mountain, could reaffirm its commitment on tourism supporting staff issues by adopting and enforcing appropriate regulations that support good working conditions for porters. Adequate and gender sensitive facilities for the female porters should be considered. Climbing companies should adopt codes of conduct and standards that will raise the level of compliance to all employees, porters in particular. Tourists, through their preference for engaging with socially irresponsible climbing companies, should be part of the movement to ensure fairer treatment to the porters. If responsible mountain tourism is a mantra, the climbing industry must incorporate human rights standards within their core business.

References

Campbell, D. J., Misana, S. B. and Olson, J. M. (2004) 'Comparing the Kenyan and Tanzanian slopes of Mt. Kilimanjaro: Why are the neighbouring land uses so different?' The land use change, impacts and dynamics project, Working Paper No. 44. Online, available at: www.lucideastafrica.org/publications/Campbell_LUCID_WP_44.pdf (accessed 17 July 2014).

Christie, I., Fernandes, E., Messerli, H. and Twining-Ward, L. (2013) *Tourism in Africa: Harnessing tourism for growth and improved livelihoods*, Washington, DC: World Bank.

Climb Mountain Kilimanjaro (2014) 'Your crew: Kilimanjaro porters'. Online, available at: www.climbmountkilimanjaro.com/on-the-mountain/porters/ (accessed 17 July 2014).

Karinen, H., Peltonen, J. and Tikkanen, H. (2008) 'Prevalence of acute mountain sickness among Finnish trekkers on Mount Kilimanjaro, Tanzania: An observational study', *High Altitude Medicine and Biology*, 9(4): 301–306.

Kaseva, M. and Moirana, J. (2010) 'Problems of solid waste management on Mount Kilimanjaro: A challenge to tourism', *Waste Management and Research*, 28(8): 695–704.

Keats, S. (2002) 'Deaths on Kilimanjaro raise concern about porters safety', *National Geographic News*, 15 November.

Mafuru, N., Wakibara, J. and Ndesari, K. (2009) 'Tourism-related impacts on Mount Kilimanjaro, Tanzania: Implications for tourism management on mountain ecosystems', *Journal of Tourism Challenges and Trends*, 2(1): 111–123.

Mitchell, J., Keane, J. and Laidlaw, J. (2009) 'Making success work for the poor: Package tourism in Northern Tanzania', Oversees Development Institute, London.

Monah, W. (2011) 'The welfare of porters on Mount Kilimanjaro', unpublished diploma research paper, College of African Wildlife Management, Mweka, Moshi.

Ndekirwa, P., Mtuy, D., Bernard, J., Valenti, K. and Forrest, R. (2011) *Porters surveys 2010*, Moshi, Tanzania: Kilimanjaro Porters Assistance Project.

Newmark, W. D. (ed.) (1991) *The conservation of Mount Kilimanjaro* (Vol. 16), Gland, Switzerland: IUCN.

Peaty, D. (2012) 'Kilimanjaro tourism and what it means for local porters and for the local environment', *Journal of Ritsumeikan Social Sciences and Humanities*, 4: 1–11.

Reid, M. (2008) 'Scandal of the Kilimanjaro Sherpas', *Times Online*, 26 May. Online, available at: www.thetimes.co.uk/tto/opinion/columnists/melaniereid/article1891827.ece (accessed 17 July 2014).

Sa, E. (2007) 'Language policy for education and development in Tanzania'. Online, available at: http://hdl.handle.net/10066/10203 (accessed 1 July 2014).

Spenceley, A. (2010) 'Tourism product development interventions and best practices in sub-Saharan Africa: Part 1: Synthesis', unpublished report for the World Bank, Washington, DC.

Team Kilimanjaro (2014) 'Tipping on Kilimanjaro'. Online, available at: www.teamkilimanjaro.com/tipping.html (accessed 17 July 2014).

Thompson, L. G., Brecher, H. H., Mosley-Thompson, E., Hardy, D. R. and Mark, B. G. (2009) 'Glacier loss on Kilimanjaro continues unabated', *Proceedings of the National Academy of Sciences*, 106(47): 19770–19775.

Thomson Safaris (2014) 'Porters ethics'. Online, available at: www.thomsontreks.com/mount-kilimanjaro-porter-ethics/ (accessed 17 July 2014).

Wardlaw, G. M., Hampl, J. S. and DiSilvestro, R. (2004) *Perspectives in nutrition*, New York: McGraw Hill.

15 Health and safety issues in mountaineering tourism

Ghazali Musa and Thinaranjeney Thirumoorthi

Introduction

Mountains constitute 24 per cent of the Earth's surface (UNESCO 2014). Over the years, activities of mountaineering, skiing, via ferrata and hiking are becoming popular (Pomfret 2006; Kruk *et al.* 2007), all of which form the development of mountaineering tourism. In Nepal, trekking and mountaineering tourists increased from 86,260 in 2011 to 105,015 in 2012 (Manadhar 2013), and about ten million people visited Austria's Alps every year (*Austrian Times* 2008). A total of 6,854 people have climbed Mt Everest successfully from the year 1953 to 2013 (Travel Doctor 2014b). Gardner (2007) and Burtscher and Ponchia (2010) highlighted that mountaineering is commonly linked to danger of personal injury and even death. Participants in these activities should be aware of and accept these risks and be responsible for their own actions.

Mountaineering is characterized by the 'deliberate seeking of risk and the uncertainty of outcome' (Ewert 1989: 8). It carries risks – financial (Sirakaya and Woodside 2005), physical (e.g. injury or death) (Sönmez and Graefe 1998a, 1998b), social (e.g. humiliation) (Carter 1998), emotional (e.g. fear, anxiety) (Mackenzie and Kerr 2012) and also health (Clift and Grabowski 1997; Larsen *et al.* 2007). While the physical and health risks inherent in adventure tourism are presumably managed by responsible adventure providers, other risks (e.g. psychological and emotional) may be mismanaged, or overlooked entirely, by adventure tourism operators (Mackenzie and Kerr 2012: 128). Ironically, the tourism operators are selling the risk linked with the activities while simultaneously minimizing the adverse impact by taking safety measures into account (Bartkus and Davis 2010; Buckley 2006). This is to circumvent issues such as medical and legal costs, negative image of the operator and injury and fatalities (Bartkus and Davis 2010).

There is accumulating evidence of adverse experiences in mountaineering (Bentley *et al.* 2001b). Groucher and Horrace (2012) recorded the death rate among Everest climbers as 0.87 per cent. In New Zealand, based on hospital discharge and mortality data, mountaineering/tramping are the biggest contributor (50 per cent) of adventure tourism-related mortality (Bentley *et al.* 2001b). Despite the adverse impact of injury and death, the number of people engaging in mountaineering continues to grow (Travel Doctor 2014b). Researchers have identified areas of risk associated with the activity such as mountaineers, environments and organizations that contribute to mountaineering injuries (Bentley *et al.* 2001b, 2001c, 2007). This chapter discusses issues on health and safety in mountaineering. It consists of mountaineering safety and security framework, health ailments and common injuries, general susceptibility and pre-existing medical condition, first aid kit, travel insurance and health education communication.

Mountaineering safety and security framework

The safety aspect plays an important role in destination selection (Bentley and Page 2001). It is defined as:

> concerns for the well-being, welfare, and wider safety of the tourist not only while traveling from the origin area to the destination, but particularly, the way in which personal safety is affected by activity patterns in their own action space.
>
> (Bentley and Page 2001: 706)

Safety management revolves around managing the risk and the ability of participants to perform related activities (Bentley *et al.* 2006). Injuries and accidents (Bentley *et al.* 2008) are commonly under-reported, thus travellers should be vigilant about their safety and security.

Page *et al.* (2005) proposed three factors which influence health and injuries among adventure tourists. These are clients (mountaineers), equipment and uncontrollable factors. Mountaineer elements are determined by physical fitness, present medical conditions, skill possessed, the ability to handle own emergency and the presence of others. Equipment are all the objects required to facilitate the success of mountaineering such as ropes, crampons, pitons, ice axes etc. The uncontrollable elements in mountaineering are weather, mountain terrains/routes, snow, avalanches etc. With the growing popularity of guided mountaineering (refer Chapter 5), we argue that there is the fourth element which can play an increasing role to safeguard mountaineering health and safety, which is mountaineering operators (refer Figure 15.1). The operators are the companies with staff employed to assist mountaineers' goal to reach the summit in climbing expeditions. They may include mountain guides, porters, cook etc. All the four elements will influence mountaineers' susceptibility to health ailments and injuries in the mountains.

Most common ailments and injuries in the mountains are trauma, musculoskeletal and soft tissue injuries, infections such as upper respiratory infection and diarrhoea, and high altitude sickness (HAS) (Musa *et al.* 2004), all of which will be discussed in detail in the next section. Once health ailments and injuries occur, dealing with them depends on the presence of medical expertise (individual and group), the availability of medical first aid kit, adequate insurance coverage and the presence of emergency deployment in the area. The availability

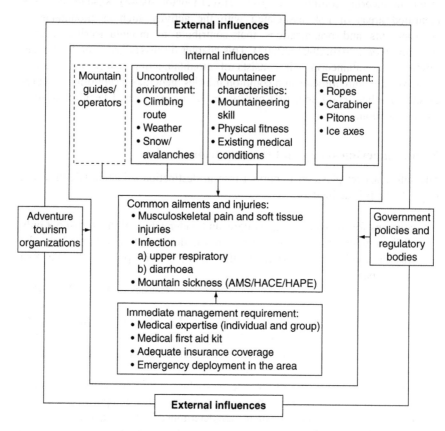

Figure 15.1 Mountaineering health and safety framework.

of the stated elements will depend on the policy and regulation of the adventure tourism industry and government policy of both destination and tourist generating region.

Adventure tourism-related accidents and fatalities mainly occur among unguided skiing and mountaineering (Bentley *et al.* 2001a, 2001b). Mountaineers must be aware of the potential risk and expertise required before engaging in the activity (Bentley *et al.* 2001b). Mountaineers are to be mindful of environmental factors especially weather (Bentley *et al.* 2008). There is need for a careful match of individual capabilities with selected mountain terrains and the right choice of climbing partners. Novice climbers should climb with mountain guides to minimize the accident rates. Mountaineers preferably should ensure physical fitness (Burtscher and Ponchia 2010) by having adequate pre-climbing physical training to endure the demanding task of mountaineering. Preferably they should engage in their expedition under the supervision of experienced guides together with sufficient medical support (Boulware 2006).

Apart from the mountaineers, the adventure operators are also responsible for the safety aspects as many of them employ guide services. The operators must focus on both physical and psychological risks (Mackenzie and Kerr 2012) associated with mountaineering, to minimize accidents and fatalities. Numerous efforts can be taken to manage the risks such as improving cross-cultural communication skills, gaining a better understanding of clients' diverse abilities, backgrounds and expectations prior to the trip, providing sufficient skills training and safety information throughout the trip, demonstrating genuine concern and caring for clients, improving logistical organization, providing quality equipment and ensuring challenges can be met, or exceeded, by clients' skill levels (Mackenzie and Kerr 2012).

Proper planning is essential to ensure safe trips. The operators should manage the logistic and itinerary in advance so that they can focus on the safety aspects during the trip. The mountaineers must be informed about skill- and safety-related information to build the protective frame (Mackenzie and Kerr 2012). The guides must receive adequate training particularly in psychological aspects and emotional management. They must be able to handle fear and anxiety during accidents (Carnicelli-Filho 2013) as well as guide the mountaineers.

The operators must strictly follow the safety instructions and ensure that all mountaineers have adequate knowledge, understanding of potential hazards, fitness levels and experience (Bentley *et al.* 2001b). Both verbal and non-verbal communications between the guides and travellers (Holyfield 1999; Sharpe 2005) are necessary to form desirable behaviour. Problems may arise due to dissimilarities in terms of experience and attitude to risk (Buckley 2010). Guides must be able to identify the clients who are in danger and calm them down to reduce their anxiety. They are expected to display both bravery and calm character (Holyfield 1999) in handling critical situations.

Apart from the personal factor, the environmental conditions also affect the safety aspects. For instance global warming causes the permafrost to melt in European Alps (Beaumont 2012) which can be dangerous to the climbers. Among other risks are frostbite (Boulware 2006), high altitude (Bauer 2012; Buroker *et al.* 2012; *New York Times* 2013; Travel Doctor 2014a), crevasses (Boulware 2006) and avalanches (Boulware 2006). The operators can take additional measures such as carefully choosing the terrain, weather conditions and clothing and footwear to minimize the risk (Bentley *et al.* 2001a).

Over the years, various advances have taken place such as the improvement in alpine techniques and the availability of mobile phones which enable mountaineers to inform the rescue services and helicopter evacuation. Despite the ease of mountain rescue deployment, mountaineering remains a high risk activity (Lischke *et al.* 2001). The activity is hazardous among mountaineers with lack of exercise (Burtscher *et al.* 2007). The exposure to extreme weather (Beedie and Hudson 2003) may lead to adverse cardiovascular effects (Burtscher *et al.* 2007; Ponchia *et al.* 2006). The American Alpine Club (2011) reported among the common mishaps in North America: mountaineering off route, inability to self-arrest, falls on snow, climbing unroped, poor position, misjudged pendulum, climbing alone, lack of protection, inability to ascend rope, inadequate self-rescue skills and communication problems. Lischke *et al.* (2001) pointed out that lack of training, insufficient information, overestimation of one's abilities and underestimation of the forces of nature are among the causes of accidents in mountains.

Injury is largely preventable. On a bigger scale, the operators must be aided by the relevant authorities to develop safety management and it should be monitored (Bentley *et al.* 2008) so that all of them will be managing risks well. It requires both individual responsibility and governmental help. Governmental bodies can assist with improved data collection and analysis, set regulatory statutes, laws and incentives, and carry out prevention research. The next section discusses the major ailments and injuries in mountaineering.

Health ailments and common injuries

Trauma, musculoskeletal and soft tissue injuries

Mountaineering is more dangerous than rock climbing or trekking, and the risk increases with the presence of snow or ice (Spira 2006). While the rate of mountaineering accidents is increasing worldwide, the death rate is not (most likely due to advanced evacuation with helicopters). Spira (2006) stated that at Mont Blanc (France), there were 5,200 rescue operations between 1988 and 1997, of which 7 per cent of people were dead upon arrival, 12 per cent had skull or spine injuries and the overall mortality rate was 12 per cent. In the Himalayas, the mountaineering death rate is 2,100/100,000. The incidence of mountaineering and rock climbing accidents in the Grand Teton National Park is 2.5/1,000 climbers/year. In the Alps, traumatic deaths are four times more common among mountaineers than skiers (Spira 2006).

Heggie (2008) conducted a retrospective review of all search and rescue incident reports filed by the National Park Service units in Alaska during 2002. There were 25 reported search and rescue incidents involving 38 individuals. The majority of incidents (19 of 25) occurred at Denali National Park and Preserve. Thirteen fatalities were reported in six incidents, nine incidents involved traumatic injuries, eight involved illnesses and two involved both injuries and an illness. Mountain climbing (20) and hiking (eight) were the most common subject activities at the time search and rescue assistance was required. Climbing solo (four), uneven and wet terrain (four), falls into crevasses (three) and a lack of experience or ability (three) were the factors most commonly contributing to search and rescue incidents. Males accounted for 33 of the 38 individuals involved in all search and rescue incidents.

McDermott and Munir (2012) who interviewed 20 mountaineering instructors in the UK reported that the majority of participants experienced musculoskeletal pain as a result of their work. Such pain was reported in the knees, hips and back. Key factors identified as preventing effective rehabilitation are a 'macho' attitude among young instructors, self-imposed extended working hours/days and mismanagement of injuries. Self-employed instructors reported that sick leave after a minor injury or illness is not financially viable.

Hillebrandt (2007) discovered that among international mountain guides, 86 per cent (72) of respondents reported a chronic musculoskeletal problem with the majority (40) reporting musculoskeletal pain in the knees. The prevalence of musculoskeletal pain reported in this study is higher than some other occupations. They also reported on poor management of some injuries. Despite this, the majority of participants demonstrated high motivation, job satisfaction and commitment to their work.

Musa *et al.* (2004) who studied the health consequences of high altitude trekking and mountaineering in Sagarmatha National Park discovered that muscle strain/pain (42.3 per cent), joint pain (21.7 per cent), backache (15.5 per cent), blisters (14.6 per cent) and cuts/bruises (7.0 per cent) are common symptoms of injuries and musculoskeletal pain reported among 448 tourists

Spira (2006) stated that causes of trauma include slips on snow or ice, rock climbing falls, falling rocks, rappel failure, becoming stranded and panic. Most injuries are associated with poor judgement, overconfidence, inexperience, being off-route or being lost, inadequate equipment, equipment failure or inadequate clothing or foot-gear. In one study, the lower extremities were injured more commonly than the upper extremities, and fractures were surprisingly more common than contusions or abrasions or ligament injury, although those suffering sprains and strains may have self-excluded themselves by not seeking medical care.

Infections

Among trekkers in the Mt Everest Region, Murdoch (1995) found 87 per cent have some form of infection. Musa *et al.* (2004) in their study among 448 high altitude trekkers in the same region reported the infection symptoms of diarrhoea (37.2 per cent), stomach discomfort (31.5 per cent), vomiting (14.9 per cent), cough (37.4 per cent), sore throat (24.5 per cent) and respiratory infection (10.8 per cent). Common infection symptoms are coryza, cough, sore throat and diarrhoea. Dry air in high-altitude irritates respiratory mucosa linings, causing cough and respiratory-tract infection (Murdoch 1995). Those with infection symptoms are more likely to develop acute mountain sickness (AMS).

Diarrhoea is common among high altitude trekkers (Basnyat *et al.* 2000a; Musa 2008) particularly those travelling from developed countries to developing countries. This results from unhygienic conditions and aetiological agents such as bacteria, viruses, amoebas and cyclospora (Basnyat *et al.* 2000a). Even though it is a self-limiting problem, it may cause unpleasant experience and affects the travelling plan (Dietz 2000). The common mode of diarrhoea transmission is contaminated food and water. Mountaineers need to emphasize more on dietary hygiene by avoiding drinking untreated water, raw vegetables, uncooked food etc. Bacterial diarrhoea can be treated with norfloxacin, ciprofloxacin and ofloxacin antibiotics (Dietz 2000). Anecdote 1 highlights that in less developed countries, perhaps the preferred management of diarrhoea is to immediately treat with a broad spectrum antibiotic. This will markedly improve the quality of holiday or mountaineering.

> In 1999, I was trekking in the Everest Region with a companion. When we reached Namche Bazaar (3400 m), he suddenly experienced violent diarrhoea and vomiting. A standard treatment for this ailment is hydration salts, to replace the water and minerals that have been lost. That was what I gave to him. The diarrhoea and vomiting continued for two days. On the second day he rushed to the toilet every 30 minutes, and could not sleep all night. I could feel his suffering, and quickly explored the other treatment options in my medical first aid kit. What else could I give him? I dosed him with Cyclofloxacine, a broad spectrum antibiotic. Within one hour the diarrhoea stopped and he went into a long deep sleep. When he woke up few hours later, he whispered, 'Man … why didn't you give that medicine from the beginning?'
>
> (Anecdote 1 by first author)

High altitude sickness

Murdoch (1995) recorded 57 per cent symptoms of AMS among trekkers in the Everest region. AMS symptoms are the result of tissue hypoxia, which is the decrease in oxygen pressure with increasing altitude gain among mountaineers in high altitude. Numerous factors influence hypoxic stress including rate of ascent, duration of exposure and also altitude itself. The degree of stress can be reduced by returning or descending to low altitude instead of sleeping in high altitude (Hackett and Shlim 2013).

AMS occurs in high altitude environments (Bauer 2012; Buroker et al. 2012; New York Times 2013; Travel Doctor 2014a), regardless of age, gender and previous experience (Bauer 2012). It occurs above 2,600 m (Hackett and Roach 2001) and normally 6–12 hours after being in high altitude (Buroker et al. 2012). The main AMS symptoms are headache, anorexia, nausea, vomiting, fatigue, dizziness and sleep disturbance (Basnyat et al. 2000b; Hackett and Roach 2001; Silber et al. 2003). Among high altitude sickness symptoms recorded by Musa et al. (2004) from 448 high altitude trekkers/mountaineers in Sagarmatha National Park are headache (61.0 per cent), shortness of breath on exertion (49.1 per cent), insomnia (36.7 per cent), loss of appetite (33.8 per cent), dizziness (15.3 per cent), shortness of breath at rest (9.2 per cent), loss of balance (6.1 per cent) and confusion (2.5 per cent). AMS can be treated by descending to a lower altitude or ceasing from ascending to a higher altitude (Buroker et al. 2012). Anecdote 2 illustrates the danger of ascending too quickly and not getting enough rest while climbing in high altitude.

> At Kibo Hut (4,700 m) on Mt Kilimanjaro, the air was thin and rarefied. That morning, I climbed quickly and hardly took any rest. At around 5 am I

reached the lower rim of Mt Kilimanjaro (5,700 m). From here, the trek would take another 90 minutes to reach the summit. Climbing up too quickly without enough rest in between, altitude began to take toll on me. My energy was drained but I continued dragging my legs ahead with a dwindling pace. When I reached the summit at 7 am, I was all spent. There was little energy left. Probably I only spent one minute on the summit. I could not enjoy the beautiful view from the peak of Kilimanjaro. I told my guide 'I don't feel well; and I must go down now'. I rushed down the mountain, followed by my guide. About 100 m below the summit, I discarded my own climbing stick and began to talk nonsense. Observing my confusion and difficulty, my mountain guide walked closely by my side. At about 5,600 m, I felt sleepy and went down on my knees on the mountain scree slope. I remembered uttering 'please let me rest; I feel very sleepy.' My guide held my shoulders and whispered into my ears, 'No, you cannot sleep my friend. If you do, you might not be able to wake up.' My guide took me on his back, and I curled my arms around his neck, to cooperate with his sacrifice transporting me down the mountain. He carried me all the way down to Kibo Hut. From Kibo Hut I was rushed further down the mountain as quickly as possible with the help of porters. After descending about 1,000 m from the summit, I was back to my normal self. However my excessive desire to attain the summit of Kilimanjaro continues to haunt me for the rest of my life. Not only had I caused trouble to myself, but also to my guides and porters.

(Anecdote 2 by the first author)

Kayser (1991) reported that AMS is higher among women and this is further supported by other studies (Basnyat *et al.* 2000b; Murdoch and Curry 1998; Santantonio *et al.* 2014). Children and adults are more likely to suffer AMS than those who are older (>50 years) (Honigman *et al.* 1993; Pollard *et al.* 2001). Similarly, in their study at Putre (Chile) Moraga *et al.* (2008) found that children exposed acutely to high altitude are more sensitive to hypobaric hypoxia than their parents, as manifested by symptoms of AMS. Mountaineers with acute respiratory illness are three times more likely to develop AMS (Basnyat *et al.* 2000b). Roach *et al.* (2000) also discovered that exercise induces AMS at high altitude.

If untreated, AMS may progress to HAPE (high altitude pulmonary oedema) and HACE (high altitude cerebral oedema) (Basnyat *et al.* 2000b). HAPE is a 'non-cardiogenic pulmonary oedema characterized by exaggerated pulmonary hypertension leading to vascular leakage through over-perfusion, stress failure, or both' (Basnyat and Murdoch 2003: 1970). Those with HAPE will experience cough, nausea, headache and chest congestion (Hultgren *et al.* 1996). Similar to AMS, females are five times more likely to develop HAPE than males (Basnyat *et al.* 2000b). Individuals at above 3,000 m are more likely to develop HAPE (Bärtsch *et al.* 2005). Various factors such as rate of ascent, altitude and susceptibility influence the incidence of HAPE (Bärtsch *et al.* 2005).

HACE is a dangerous complication and the final stage of AMS (Basnyat and Murdoch 2003). Individuals with AMS and ataxia may develop HACE which can progress into coma and death. Some studies reported that the symptoms of AMS and HACE are similar – dehydration, exhaustion, migraine, hypothermia and viral infection – and must be carefully differentiated and diagnosed (Hackett and Roach 2001; Luks *et al.* 2010). However, the cardinal signs of HACE include ataxia and confusion (Luks *et al.* 2010). The symptoms demand immediate descent to avoid fatality (Hackett and Shlim 2013). Similar to AMS and HAPE, women are more likely to develop HACE than men (Buroker *et al.* 2012).

The treatment for severe AMS, HAPE and HACE is to descend at least 500 to 1,000 m (Kasic *et al.* 1991). One can prevent high altitude sickness from occurring by climbing at a slow rate (Basnyat and Murdoch 2003; Murdoch 1999). The sleeping altitude should not be more than 300 to 400 m from previous night (Basnyat *et al.* 2000b; Forgey 2006; Hackett 1980; Hackett and Shlim 2013; Murdoch 1999). Descending by 400–500 m will relieve the altitude sickness symptoms or, if the condition is not severe, mountaineers must avoid further ascent or simply rest sufficiently (Basnyat and Murdoch 2003). Oxygen supplement alleviates AMS symptoms (Basnyat and Murdoch 2003).

Acetazolamide is commonly used to reduce AMS symptoms (Donegani *et al.* 2014; Hackett and Shlim 2013; Luks *et al.* 2010; *New York Times* 2013) as it increases respiration which aids travellers to adapt to the altitude (Hackett and Shlim 2013). Dexamethasone can be used to treat all AMS, HAPE and HACE (Hackett and Shlim 2013; Luks *et al.* 2010; *New York Times* 2013). It is important to note that dexamethasone should not be used to prevent altitude sickness due to the side effects (Hackett and Shlim 2013). Nifedipine, tadalafil, sildenafil and salmeterol are drugs used to prevent HAPE (Donegani *et al.* 2014; Hackett and Shlim 2013; Luks *et al.* 2010; *New York Times* 2013). Ibuprofen can also be used to treat headache (*New York Times* 2013).

Other alternative medication such as gingko biloba has anti-oxidant properties which also reduce the AMS symptoms (Hackett and Shlim 2013; Ho and Siu 2010; Luks *et al.* 2010; Moraga *et al.* 2007). Some Chinese herbs – rhodiola rosea – (Ho and Siu 2010) and coca leaves (Luks *et al.* 2010) are widely used to prevent and treat mountain sickness. Luk *et al.* (2010) stated that the chewing of coca leaves, coca tea and other coca-derived products are commonly recommended for travellers in the Andes for prophylaxis, and anecdotal reports suggest they are now being used by trekkers in Asia and Africa for similar purposes. Referring to Anecdote 3 (below), the first author explained how even Tibetan butter tea could be beneficial in treating AMS. However, other than gingko biloba, the utility of other alternative medicines described here in preventing altitude illness has never been systematically studied. Thus they should not be substituted for other established preventive measures described in this chapter.

Two years after my ordeal on Mt Kilimanjaro, I flew to Nepal, to embark on the greatest adventure in my life: cycling from Lhasa to Kathmandu. The distance is 1,000 km, with average elevation of 4,600 m and there are six passes which are over 5,000 m. In Lhasa I met Andreas, a German medical student who happened to share the same ambition. After one week of acclimatization in Lhasa (3,700 m), we commenced our expedition, with the target of completion within 30 days. On the second day of cycling, Andreas who used to cycle Tour De France, came out with the motivation to cycle the first high pass (4,790 m) and sleep on the other side by Nyamrok Lake at the elevation of 4,400 m (about the height of the Matterhorn). This is over 1,000 m of elevation to be accomplished in a single day. I knew from the beginning this would not be physically possible without serious consequences. But who was I to stop him. He said, 'if you cannot climb the pass, I will see you tomorrow on the other side.' Andreas cycled quickly and soon we were tackling the endless zigzag corners of the mountain leading to Kamba Pass. The highest point looked unreachable at least to me, and the sun was disappearing quickly over the pass. After about two hours climbing, Andreas vanished from my view, left me struggling to tackle my own fate and survival. After five hours climbing on the bicycle, my power was diminishing quickly. I felt breathless and experienced headache and dizziness. I stopped beside the road and searched for a clearing, to pitch a tent and settle for the night. Suddenly, I saw a Tibetan man waving his hand from about 50 m above, indicating that I should push my bicycle up and follow him. He took me to a worker quarter built by the Chinese government for the labourers assigned for the endless work of maintaining the Friendship Highway. Inside his house, the fire was on, and his wife quickly prepared butter tea for all of us, especially me. Butter tea is a mixture of tea, yak butter and a bit of salt. They instructed me to be close to the fire, and pressured me to drink butter tea every ten minutes. I must have drunk about 20 cups of butter tea that night. By mid-night my head completely cleared of headache and dizziness; and I was ready to sleep. However, suddenly I heard the knock on the door. When my Tibetan host opened the door, 'it was Andreas'. He looked very sick and was delivered by a Chinese truck driver who found him on the highway exhausted, in the dark. It was my turn now, to look after Andreas, by encouraging him to drink butter tea. Andreas was less keen to drink salty buttery tea. While I completely recovered from mountain sickness symptoms, Andreas continued to suffer for the next two days. I still cannot stop thinking how foolish it was, to gain elevation of over 1,000 m in one day from an already high elevation. I also think perhaps Andreas could have drunk more butter tea that night.

Numerous studies acknowledge the relationship between AMS and dehydration (Basnyat *et al.* 2000b; Cumbo *et al.* 2002). Both ailments may also display the same symptoms. However a study by Nerin *et al.* (2006) concluded that fluid intake is not significantly correlated with the incidence and degree of AMS. In fact, 'forced' or 'over'-hydration has also never been shown to prevent altitude illness and may even increase the risk of hyponatremia. However, researchers all agree that the maintenance of adequate hydration while mountaineering is important because symptoms of dehydration can mimic those of AMS.

Sudden cardiac death

In high altitude, climbers may suffer medical conditions such as cardiac arrest (Albert *et al.* 2000; Kawamura 2005). Burtscher (2007) stated that sudden cardiac death (SCD) is higher for those who are older. Hikers and skiers above 35 years old particularly male constitute 90 per cent of all SCDs.

Extreme weather such as cold may lead to heart problems (Woods *et al.* 2008). Sudden physical effort and dehydration may trigger cardiac arrest, resulting from sudden changes in heart rate and blood pressure (Albert *et al.* 2000; Kawamura 2005). Physical exertion may affect the sympathetic nervous system, leading to ventricular fibrillation (Albert *et al.* 2000). Therefore prior physical training is vital to avoid mountaineers' SCD (Burtscher and Ponchia 2010).

Individuals with myocardial infarction history are recommended to engage in prior physical activity and behavioural responses therapy, in preparation for high altitude environment (Burtscher and Ponchia 2010). SCD may be prevented by adequate rest at altitude, ascending gradually and adequate fluid and food intake to avoid hypoglycaemia and dehydration. Early detection of those with myocardial infarction or those who are not physically fit to engage in mountaineering activities must be obtained, to minimize the risk of SCD (Burtscher and Ponchia 2010).

Medical and management interventions

General susceptibility and pre-existing medical conditions

The individual climber's differences such as age, gender, concurrent illness, level of fitness, may influence one's ability to tolerate weather and other conditions. Mountaineering requires physical exertion and those with medical issues maybe more affected by the altitude. It is recommended for mountaineers to check with physicians (Hackett and Shlim 2013) to avoid serious injuries or fatalities. Individuals with diabetes are less likely to face problems. However they need to be physically fit and be cautious of blood glucose. Glucose meters may not be accurate at high altitude. Thus the climbers particularly those who are diagnosed with Type 1 diabetes need to monitor their symptoms as altitude illness may trigger diabetic ketoacidosis (Hackett and Shlim 2013). Mountaineers are advised to have a dental check-up as those with caries and broken fillings may experience pain at high altitude. People with radial keratotomy may face acute farsightedness due to high altitude and may not be able to climb the mountain. LASIK (Laser-Assisted in situ Keratomileusis) may be performed to correct their vision (Hackett and Shlim 2013). The *European Heart Journal* (2014) reported that blood pressure is higher at high altitude compared to lower altitude.

Travel insurance

Even though the potential risk drives the tourists to pay for and engage in certain activities (Lipscombe 2007), health and safety aspects are often covered in adventure tourism packages (Carnicelli-Filho 2013). It is a necessity for extreme or adventure travellers to purchase travel insurance (Boulware 2006). Mountaineers may fail to anticipate high altitude sickness and physical injury (JS Insurance 2014). Leggat and Fischer (2006) stated that travel insurance is the most important safety net for travellers in the event of misadventure, and the purchase of travel insurance should be reinforced by travel health advisers. About 60 per cent of GPs in New Zealand, 39 per cent of GPs in Australia and 39 per cent of travel clinics worldwide give advice on travel insurance to tourists. Nonetheless, it is not known what proportion of travel agents or airlines give advice routinely on travel insurance. And, it is not clear that all travel insurance is adequate for the emergency needs that travellers might face. Mountaineers may consult their household insurer for any adventure expeditions and check whether it covers mountaineering activities. The policy offered by household insurers is cheaper than travel agents (Project Himalaya 2014).

Mountaineers should be fully aware of the policy and terms of the insurance provided particularly on the cover, limits and exclusions (Boulware 2006). This is to avoid a 'false sense of security'. Different insurance may provide different ranges of coverage. Some insurance policies cover up to 7,000 m (Project Himalaya 2014) while others provide air ambulance (JS Insurance 2014) and mountain rescue (JS Insurance 2014; Travel Doctor 2014a). The British Mountaineering Council (2014)'s insurance coverage includes cancellation, medical and additional expense abroad, search and rescue expenses abroad, travel delay, personal property, loss of passport/driving licence abroad, money, personal accident, curtailment, personal liability, overseas legal advice and expenses, missed departure, hospital benefit abroad, hijack and catastrophe. Adventures Travel Insurance (2014) offers coverage for medical and emergency, personal accident, personal liability, activity equipment, legal expenses, possessions, personal effects, money and documents personal possessions, cancellation, loss of deposit or curtailment, unexpected events travel disruption and optional independent traveller.

For mountaineers, it is crucial that travel insurance covers emergency evacuation or repatriation especially if mountaineering activities are in remote areas and difficult to access. Mountaineers should take note of the magnitude of expenses one may incur if it is not covered by the insurance. In Nepal, it costs between US$5,000 and US$10,000 to rescue a trekker or climber from the Himalayas, where medical facilities are extremely limited (Spira 2006). Further evacuation and additional expense may be incurred with additional transport to other medical facilities (e.g. in Singapore, Bangkok or New Delhi).

Medical first aid kit

Leggat and Fischer (2006) recommended travellers to routinely carry a travel medical (or 'first aid') kit, which should be customized to their anticipated itinerary and activities. The first aid kit should have basic health information (name, birth date, vaccination history, current medication use – with dosages noted, known medical allergies, blood type and chronic health conditions). For common soft tissue injuries, antiseptics solutions and lotions, bandaging supplies and perhaps splinting material are mandatory. Adventurous travellers engaging in strenuous physical activity should have more extensive first aid supplies. They should also have common health care products such as sunscreen and insect repellent. Routinely used over-the-counter medications (antipyretics, analgesics, topical anti-inflammatory and anti-pruritic skin creams, and antihistamines) may also be included. Routine prescription medications should be included, with a second supply of important or unusual medicines in another part of the luggage in case the traveller is separated from some bags en route. Some presumptive use medications should also be placed in the medical kit, including items such as anti-malarial, anti-diarrhoeal and oral rehydration salts.

There are specific requirements that will reflect a particular expedition, and clearly extra drugs and equipment may be needed to deal with problems in particular areas. Nevertheless, it is often difficult to judge how much, and what sort of, medical equipment to take. This will depend upon such factors as the medical knowledge of the expedition medical officer, the size and organization of the party, whether or not each individual will require a personal medical kit, duration of the trip, the remoteness of the location and the likelihood of having to treat local staff and villagers (Leggat and Fischer 2006). As stated earlier, common diseases to be encountered on the trip are non-traumatic disease, gastrointestinal problems, respiratory disease and skin problems. Minor accidents and trauma are not uncommon. Each case must be assessed according to the severity of the condition and the remoteness of the expedition. Take specialist advice if necessary, particularly from other expedition doctors who may have the relevant experience to make an informed decision.

Communication and intervention

With regards to high altitude sickness, despite its prevalence, the awareness among travellers remains low. Hatzenbuehler *et al.* (2009) surveyed 130 skiers in Big Sky Ski Resort, Montana, and found that only 55 per cent of respondents had some knowledge of AMS, and only 30 per cent had knowledge of AMS symptoms. Similarly, Merritt *et al.* (2007) who surveyed 100 foreign travellers in Cuzco found that over half of the respondents (51 per cent) rated their knowledge of AMS as 'low' or 'none'. Very few respondents knew about acetazolamide (Diamox) as prophylaxis for (9 per cent) or treatment of AMS (5 per cent). While AMS knowledge was poor, the majority of travellers (90 per cent) indicated compliance with recommended pre-travel vaccinations.

Intervention to minimize injuries and fatalities lies on the travellers, management of adventure operations, adventure tourism industry and government regulatory authorities (Bentley *et al.* 2001b). Health and safety communication is a crucial aspect of adventure tourism (Buckley 2010). On an individual scale, safety communications should be targeted to independent travellers or those who engage in solo climbing (Bentley *et al.* 2001a) as they face higher risk compared to those with guides (American Alpine Club 2011).

Bentley *et al.* (2001b) reported that injury is common among young male tourists (20–30 years), therefore safety communication should be specially targeted to this group. Information on safety should be disseminated through various modes such as at country of origin medical centres, destination visitor centres, at airports, travel offices, in in-flight entertainment and accommodation to reduce the rate of injuries (Bentley *et al.* 2001a).

Heggie (2008) conducted a retrospective review of all search and rescue incident reports filed by National Park Service units in Alaska during 2002. It was proposed that preventive education efforts should be carried out at park visitor centres and at the lower and upper base camps on Mt McKinley. In addition, pre-departure travel education efforts via the Internet should be expanded for all park units and match the detail provided on the Denali National Park and Preserve website.

Hatzenbuehler *et al.* (2009) stated that the Internet is the most attractive source of information. According to Merritt *et al.* (2007) who surveyed 100 foreign travellers in Cuzco, the two potential avenues for improved dispersal of information are (1) guidebooks for countries of concern and (2) national health agency websites linked to information on pre-travel vaccinations

Shaw (2006) stated that all travellers need to be aware of potential health problems and consequences of their travel, and they need up to date authoritative advice. Travel health clinics should provide this advice in a structured, practical and authoritative format. Such a format should be discussed, and applied with the skills of medical, nursing and management practitioners. The four steps for giving travellers the foundation for healthy journeys are to assess pre-health, to analyse itineraries, to select appropriate vaccines and to provide education about the prevention and self-treatment of travel-related diseases. Clinics that specialize in travel health advice need to provide authoritative and current health information for those travelling overseas, pre- and post-travel clinical assistance in the prevention of disease and have sources that provide up-to date health information.

Conclusion

Mountaineering is a high risk adventure-based activity. The numbers of mountaineers are increasing year by year despite the reports on injuries and fatalities. Since it is a high risk activity due to hazardous environment and skill requirements, mountaineers should be aware of and anticipate the potential morbidity and mortality before commencing the activity as there is no room for error. They preferably need to undergo strenuous exercise to be physically fit. Mountaineers' medical conditions need to be checked with physicians and also ensured that pre-existing medical conditions allow them to climb mountains in high altitude (depending on location). Besides that, they need to be aware of potential hazards such high altitude sickness as its prolonged condition may result in death. Other common health ailments are musculoskeletal and soft tissue injuries and infection such as upper respiratory tract infection and diarrhoea. It is mandatory to have sufficient insurance coverage, to carry first aid kits and to preferably join mountaineering expeditions with full medical support. The safety aspect is not only the concern of mountaineers due to self-reliance, but also the operators of adventure activities, who play a vital role in dealing with hazards. They need to have a proper risk management system to sustain their business. The operators need to focus on educating and creating awareness about health and safety issues to the mountaineers besides providing proper training to the guides on skills such as navigating, communication, emotion management etc. With the involvement of the local authorities, regulations can be formulated to protect mountaineers and also to create safety standards, along with accurate recording and monitoring of accidents, injuries and fatalities.

References

Adventures Travel Insurance (2014) 'What's covered'. Online, available at: www.adventures-insurance.co.uk/whats-covered.aspx (accessed 14 October 2014).

Albert, C. M., Mittleman, M. A., Chae, C. U., Lee, I.-M., Hennekens, C. H. and Manson, J. E. (2000) 'Triggering of sudden death from cardiac causes by vigorous exertion', *New England Journal of Medicine*, 343(19): 1355–1361.

American Alpine Club (2011) 'Accidents in North American mountaineering', *American Alpine Club Golden Co.* Online, available at: www.rockandice.com/aac-accident-report-flip-books/aac-report-1 (accessed 14 October 2014).

Austrian Times (2008) 'Alpine fatalities soaring', 28 August. Online, available at: http://austriantimes.at/news/General_News/2008-08-27/8309/Alpine_fatalities_soaring-newentry (accessed 30 September 2014).

Bartkus, V. O. and Davis, J. H. (2010) *Social capital: Reaching out, reaching in*, Cheltenham: Edward Elgar Publishing.

Bärtsch, P., Mairbäurl, H., Maggiorini, M. and Swenson, E. R. (2005) 'Physiological aspects of high-altitude pulmonary edema', *Journal of Applied Physiology*, 98(3): 1101–1110.

Basnyat, B. and Murdoch, D. R. (2003) 'High-altitude illness', *Lancet*, 361(9373): 1967–1974.

Basnyat, B., Cumbo, T. A. and Edelman, R. (2000a) 'Acute medical problems in the Himalayas outside the setting of altitude sickness', *High Altitude Medicine and Biology*, 1(3): 167–174.

Basnyat, B., Subedi, D., Sleggs, J., Lemaster, J., Bhasyal, G., Aryal, B. and Subedi, N. (2000b) 'Disoriented and ataxic pilgrims: An epidemiological study of acute mountain sickness and high-altitude cerebral edema at a sacred lake at 4300 m in the Nepal Himalayas', *Wilderness and Environmental Medicine*, 11(2): 89–93.

Bauer, I. (2012) 'Australian senior adventure travellers to Peru: Maximising older tourists' travel health experience', *Travel Medicine and Infectious Disease*, 10(2): 59–68.

Beaumont, P. (2012). "Mont Blanc avalanche: Why the Alps are deceptively dangerous for climbers', *Guardian*, 13 July. Online, available at: www.theguardian.com/world/2012/jul/12/european-alps-dangerous-mont-blanc (accessed 30 September 2014).

Beedie, P. and Hudson, S. (2003) 'Emergence of mountain-based adventure tourism', *Annals of Tourism Research*, 30(3): 625–643.

Bentley, T., Macky, K. and Edwards, J. (2006) 'Injuries to New Zealanders participating in adventure tourism and adventure sports: An analysis of Accident Compensation Corporation (ACC) claims' *NZ Medical Journal*, 119(1247): 1–9.

Bentley, T., Meyer, D., Page, S. and Chalmers, D. (2001a) 'Recreational tourism injuries among visitors to New Zealand: An exploratory analysis using hospital discharge data', *Tourism Management*, 22(4): 373–381.

Bentley, T., Page, S., Meyer, D., Chalmers, D. and Laird, I. (2001b) 'How safe is adventure tourism in New Zealand? An exploratory analysis' *Applied Ergonomics*, 32(4): 327–338.

Bentley, T. A. and Page, S. J. (2001) 'Scoping the extent of adventure tourism accidents', *Annals of Tourism Research*, 28(3): 705–726.

Bentley, T. A., Page, S. and Edwards, J. (2008) 'Monitoring injury in the New Zealand adventure tourism sector: An operator survey', *Journal of Travel Medicine*, 15(6): 395–403.

Bentley, T. A., Page, S. J. and Laird, I. (2001c) 'Accidents in the New Zealand adventure tourism industry', *Safety Science*, 38(1): 31–48.

Bentley, T. A., Page, S. J. and Macky, K. A. (2007) 'Adventure tourism and adventure sports injury: The New Zealand experience', *Applied Ergonomics*, 38(6): 791–796.

Boulware, D. R. (2006). 'Travel medicine for the extreme traveler', *Disease-a-Month*, 52(8): 309–325.

British Mountaineering Council (2014) 'BMC travel insurance: What's covered?' Online, available at: www.thebmc.co.uk/modules/insurance/WhatsCovered.aspx (accessed 10 October 2014).

Buckley, R. (2006) *Adventure tourism*, Wallingford: CAB International.

Buckley, R. (2010) 'Communications in adventure tour products: Health and safety in rafting and kayaking', *Annals of Tourism Research*, 37(2): 315–332.

Buroker, N. E., Ning, X.-H., Zhou, Z.-N., Li, K., Cen, W.-J., Wu, X.-F., Zhu, W.-Z., Scott, C. R. and Chen, S.-H. (2012) 'EPAS1 and EGLN1 associations with high altitude sickness in Han and Tibetan Chinese at the Qinghai–Tibetan Plateau', *Blood Cells, Molecules, and Diseases*, 49(2): 67–73.

Burtscher, M. (2007) 'Risk of cardiovascular events during mountain activities', in R. C. Roach, P. D. Wagner and P. H. Hackett (eds) *Hypoxia and the circulation*, New York: Springer: 1–11.

Burtscher, M. and Ponchia, A. (2010) 'The risk of cardiovascular events during leisure time activities at altitude', *Progress in Cardiovascular Diseases*, 52(6): 507–511.

Burtscher, M., Pachinger, O., Schocke, M. and Ulmer, H. (2007) 'Risk factor profile for sudden cardiac death during mountain hiking', *International Journal of Sports Medicine*, 28(7): 621–624.

Carnicelli-Filho, S. (2013) 'The emotional life of adventure guides', *Annals of Tourism Research*, 43: 192–209.

Carter, S. (1998) 'Tourists' and travellers' social construction of Africa and Asia as risky locations', *Tourism Management*, 19(4): 349–358.

Clift, S. and Grabowski, P. (1997) *Tourism and health: Risks, research, and responses*, London: Pinter.

Cumbo, T., Basnyat, B., Graham, J., Lescano, A. and Gambert, S. (2002) 'Acute mountain sickness, dehydration, and bicarbonate clearance: Preliminary field data from the Nepal Himalaya', *Aviation, Space, and Environmental Medicine*, 73(9): 898–901.

Dietz, T. E. (2000) 'Dietary hygiene in the prevention of travellers' diarrhea'. Online, available at: www.high-altitude-medicine.com/diarrhea.html (accessed 14 October 2014).

Donegani, E., Hillebrandt, D., Windsor, J., Gieseler, U., Rodway, G., Schöffl, V. and Küpper, T. (2014) 'Pre-existing cardiovascular conditions and high altitude travel', *Travel Medicine and Infectious Disease*, 12(3): 237–252.

European Heart Journal (2014) 'Everest study finds high altitude affects blood pressure'. Online, available at: www.wardspharmacy.com/article.php?id=691089 (accessed 14 October 2014).

Ewert, A. (1989) *Outdoor adventure pursuits: Foundations, models, and theories*, Scottsdale, AZ: Publishing Horizons, Inc.

Forgey, W. W. (2006) *Wilderness medical society practice guidelines for wilderness emergency care*, Guilford, CT: Globe Pequot.

Gardner, T. (2007) 'Risk and safety', British Mountaineering Council (BMC), 29 March. Online, available at: www.thebmc.co.uk/risk-and-safety (accessed 30 September 2014).

Goucher, J. and Horrace, W. C. (2012) 'The value of life: Real risks and safety-related productivity in the Himalaya', *Labour Economics*, 19(1): 27–32.

Hackett, P. (1980) *Mountain sickness: Prevention, recognition and treatment*, New York: American Alpine Club.

Hackett, P. H. and Roach, R. C. (2001) 'High-altitude illness', *New England Journal of Medicine*, 345(2): 107–114.

Hackett, P. H. and Shlim, D. R. (2013) 'Altitude illness, Centers for Disease Control and Prevention', 1 August. Online, available at: wwwnc.cdc.gov/travel/yellowbook/2014/chapter-2-the-pre-travel-consultation/altitude-illness (accessed 1 October 2014).

Hatzenbuehler, J., Glazer, J. and Kuhn, C. (2009) 'Awareness of altitude sickness among visitors to a North American Ski Resort', *Wilderness and Environmental Medicine*, 20(3): 257–260.

Heggie, T. W. (2008) 'Search and rescue in Alaska's National Parks', *Travel Medicine and Infectious Disease*, 6(6): 355–361.

Hillebrandt, D. (2007) 'Occupational health problems of British mountain guides operating internationally', *Journal of the British Travel Health Association*, 10(29): 43–47.

Ho, M.-K. and Siu, A. Y.-C. (2010) 'High altitude medicine', *Hong Kong Medical Diary*, 15(6): 32–34.

Holyfield, L. (1999) 'Manufacturing adventure the buying and selling of emotions', *Journal of Contemporary Ethnography*, 28(1): 3–32.

Honigman, B., Theis, M. K., Koziol-Mclain, J., Roach, R., Yip, R., Houston, C. and Moore, L. G. (1993) 'Acute mountain sickness in a general tourist population at moderate altitudes', *Annals of Internal Medicine*, 118(8): 587–592.

Hultgren, H., Honigman, B., Theis, K. and Nicholas, D. (1996) 'High-altitude pulmonary edema at a ski resort', *Western Journal of Medicine*, 164(3): 222.

JS Insurance (2014) 'Trekking (between 4,000 and 6,000 metres) travel insurance'. Online, available at: www.jsinsurance.co.uk/travel_insurance/trekking-4000-6000-metres-travel-insurance.html#calculator (accessed 14 October 2014).

Kasic, J. F., Yaron, M., Nicholas, R. A., Lickteig, J. A. and Roach, R. (1991) 'Treatment of acute mountain sickness: Hyperbaric versus oxygen therapy', *Annals of Emergency Medicine*, 20(10): 1109–1112.

Kawamura, T. (2005) 'Sudden cardiac death during exercise in the elder persons', *Nihon rinsho. Japanese Journal of Clinical Medicine*, 63(7): 1243–1248.

Kayser, B. (1991) 'Acute mountain sickness in western tourists around the Thorong pass (5400 m) in Nepal', *Journal of Wilderness Medicine*, 2(2): 110–117.

Kruk, E., Hummel, J. and Banskota, K. (2007) *Facilitating sustainable mountain tourism:*

Volume 1, resource book, Nepal: International Centre for Integrated Mountain Development (ICIMOD).

Larsen, S., Brun, W., Øgaard, T. and Selstad, L (2007) 'Subjective food-risk judgements in tourists', *Tourism Management*, 28(6): 1555–1559.

Leggat, P. A. and Fischer, P. R. (2006) 'Accidents and repatriation', *Travel Medicine and Infectious Disease*, 4(3–4): 135–146.

Lipscombe, N. (2007) 'The risk management paradox for urban recreation and park managers: Providing high risk recreation within a risk management context', *Annals of Leisure Research*, 10(1): 3–25.

Lischke, V., Byhahn, C., Westphal, K. and Kessler, P. (2001) 'Mountaineering accidents in the European Alps: Have the numbers increased in recent years?' *Wilderness and Environmental Medicine*, 12(2): 74–80.

Luks, A. M., Mcintosh, S. E., Grissom, C. K., Auerbach, P. S., Rodway, G. W., Schoene, R. B., Zafren, K. and Hackett, P. H. (2010) 'Wilderness medical society consensus guidelines for the prevention and treatment of acute altitude illness', *Wilderness and Environmental Medicine*, 21(2): 146–155.

McDermott, H. and Munir, F. (2012) 'Work-related injury and ill-health among mountain instructors in the UK', *Safety Science*, 50(4): 1104–1111.

Mackenzie, S. H. and Kerr, J. H. (2012) 'A (mis)guided adventure tourism experience: An autoethnographic analysis of mountaineering in Bolivia', *Journal of Sport and Tourism*, 17(2): 125–144.

Manadhar, E. (2013) 'Adventure tourism gains popularity', *Himalayan Time*, 31 August. Online, available at: www.thehimalayantimes.com/fullNews.php?headline=Adventure+tourism+gains+popularity&NewsID=389311 (accessed 30 September 2014).

Merritt, A. L., Camerlengo, A., Meyer, C. and Mull, J. D. (2007) 'Mountain sickness knowledge among foreign travelers in Cuzco, Peru', *Wilderness and Environmental Medicine*, 18(1): 26–29.

Moraga, F. A., Flores, A., Serra, J., Esnaola, C. and Barriento, C. (2007) Ginkgo biloba decreases acute mountain sickness in people ascending to high altitude at Ollagüe in Northern Chile', *Wilderness and Environmental Medicine*, 18(1): 251–257.

Moraga, F. A., Pedreros, C. P. and Rodríguez, C. E. (2008) 'Acute mountain sickness in children and their parents after rapid ascent to 3500 m (Putre, Chile)', *Wilderness and Environmental Medicine*, 19(4): 287–292.

Murdoch, D. (1999) 'How fast is too fast? Attempts to define a recommended ascent rate to prevent acute mountain sickness', *International Society for Mountain Medicine Newsletter*, 9(1): 3–6.

Murdoch, D. and Curry, C. (1998) 'Acute mountain sickness in the Southern Alps of New Zealand', *New Zealand Medical Journal*, 111(1065): 168–169.

Murdoch, D. R. (1995) 'Symptoms of infection and altitude illness among hikers in the Mount Everest region of Nepal', *Aviation, Space, and Environmental Medicine*, 66(2): 148–151.

Musa, G. (2008) *Travel health experience in high altitude destination: Case studies of Sagarmatha National Park (Nepal) and Tibet (China)*, Berlin: VDM Verlag.

Musa, G., Hall, M. and Higham, J. (2004) 'Tourism sustainability and health impacts in high altitude adventure, cultural and ecotourism destinations: A case study of Nepal's Sagarmatha National Park', *Journal of Sustainable Tourism*, 12(4): 306–331.

Nerín, M. A., Palop, J., Montaño, J. A., Morandeira, J. R. and Vázquez, M. (2006) 'Acute mountain sickness: Influence of fluid intake', *Wilderness and Environmental Medicine*, 17(4): 215–220.

New York Times (2013) 'Traveler's diarrhea diet'. Online, available at: www.nytimes.com/health/guides/nutrition/travelers-diarrhea-diet/travel-precautions.html (accessed 10 October 2014).

Page, S. J., Bentley, T. A. and Walker, L. (2005) 'Scoping the nature and extent of adventure tourism operations in Scotland: How safe are they?' *Tourism Management*, 26(3): 381–397.

Pollard, A. J., Niermeyer, S., Barry, P., Bärtsch, P., Berghold, F., Bishop, R. A., Clarke, C., Dhillon, S., Dietz, T. E. and Durmowicz, A. (2001) 'Children at high altitude: An international consensus statement by an ad hoc committee of the International Society for Mountain Medicine', *High Altitude Medicine and Biology*, 2(3): 389–403.

Pomfret, G. (2006) 'Mountaineering adventure tourists: A conceptual framework for research', *Tourism Management*, 27(1): 113–123.

Ponchia, A., Biasin, R., Tempesta, T., Thiene, M. and Dalla Volta, S. (2006) 'Cardiovascular risk during physical activity in the mountains', *Journal of Cardiovascular Medicine*, 7(2): 129–135.

Project Himalaya (2014) Online, available at: www.project-himalaya.com/c-insurance.html (accessed 14 October 2014).

Roach, R., Maes, D., Sandoval, D., Robergs, R., Icenogle, M., Hinghofer-Szalkay, H., Lium, D. and Loeppky, J. (2000) 'Exercise exacerbates acute mountain sickness at simulated high altitude', *Journal of Applied Physiology*, 88(2): 581–585.

Santantonio, M., Chapplain, J.-M., Tattevin, P., Leroy, H., Mener, E., Gangneux, J.-P., Michelet, C. and Revest, M. (2014) 'Prevalence of and risk factors for acute mountain sickness among a cohort of high-altitude travellers who received pre-travel counselling', *Travel Medicine and Infectious Disease*, 12(5): 534–540.

Sharpe, E. K. (2005) 'Going above and beyond: The emotional labor of adventure guides', *Journal of Leisure Research*, 37(1): 29–50.

Shaw, M. (2006) 'Running a travel clinic', *Travel Medicine and Infectious Disease*, 4(3–4): 109–126.

Silber, E., Sonnenberg, P., Collier, D., Pollard, A., Murdoch, D. and Goadsby, P. (2003) 'Clinical features of headache at altitude: A prospective study', *Neurology*, 60(7): 1167–1171.

Sirakaya, E. and Woodside, A. G. (2005) 'Building and testing theories of decision making by travellers', *Tourism Management*, 26(6): 815–832.

Sönmez, S. F. and Graefe, A. R. (1998a) 'Determining future travel behavior from past travel experience and perceptions of risk and safety', *Journal of Travel Research*, 37(2): 171–177.

Sönmez, S. F. and Graefe, A. R. (1998b) 'Influence of terrorism risk on foreign tourism decisions', *Annals of Tourism Research*, 25(1): 112–144.

Spira, A. M. (2006) 'Preventive guidance for travel: Trauma avoidance and medical evacuation', *Disease-a-Month*, 52(7): 261–288.

Travel Doctor (2014a) 'Altitude or mountain sickness'. Online, available at: www.travel-doctor.co.uk/altitude.htm (accessed 14 October 2014).

Travel Doctor (2014b) 'Drugs used to prevent and treat mountain sickness'. Online, available at: www.traveldoctor.co.uk/diamox.htm (accessed 14 October 2014).

UNESCO (2014) 'Exhibition "climate change impacts on mountain regions of the world"'. Online, available at: www.unesco.org/new/en/natural-sciences/resources/communication-materials/exhibitions/climate-change-impacts-on-mountain-regions-of-the-world/ (accessed 30 September 2014).

Woods, D., Allen, S., Betts, T., Gardiner, D., Montgomery, H., Morgan, J. and Roberts, P. (2008) 'High altitude arrhythmias', *Cardiology*, 111(4): 239–246.

16 Management perspectives of mountaineering tourism

Carl Cater

As this book has shown, past decades have seen a change in mountaineering tourism from individual recreation to more commercialized opportunities, in parallel to an underlying trend of vastly increased numbers of people seeking to experience mountains. This volume fills the gap identified by Pomfret who suggested 'previous studies on mountaineers have focused on mountaineering as a form of adventure recreation rather than adventure tourism' (2006: 113), with limited prior research on the tourism elements of mountaineering recreation. It is impossible to separate mountaineering from mountain tourism more generally because the increasing convergence in the industry has increased commercialization. Indeed, authors such as Varley (2006) have documented the existence of the spectrum of adventure pursuits called the Adventure Commodification Continuum, which is applicable to mountaineering tourism, and can be classified as soft tourism or hard tourism (Hill 1995). Soft mountaineering activities might include undertaking less challenging mountain routes independently, taking part in activities led by experienced guides, or participating in a mountaineering course to develop technical skills and enable progression to greater goals. These usually entail low levels of risk, minimum commitment and beginner level skills. Hard mountaineering activities include rock climbing, mountaineering expeditions and strenuous treks (Millington *et al.* 2001). These activities have been dubbed SCARRA (Skilled Commercial Adventure Recreation in Remote Areas) by Buckley (2006), and are commonly motivated by risk, challenge and exploration. While competent mountaineers may undertake these activities unaided, for example in the UK mountains, logistical support and guiding is often required for higher peaks in the Greater Ranges. Thus mountaineering provides plenty of scope for participation at different levels and is growing in popularity.

However, it is somewhat unhelpful to divide these ends of the spectrum as many new and existing mountain tourism practices rely on the same supporting infrastructure. For example, mountain tourists to the Himalaya all use the same airstrips, trekking routes, teahouses and base camps, whether they are casual trekkers or committed mountaineers. Whilst the former are partly inspired by the latter, they are all part of a commodification of mountain environments that began with the expeditions of the twentieth century, and has intensified since the 1960s. Clearly mountain-based tourism can bring economic benefits to areas with few other economic opportunities and can have a significant impact on the host community. Mountaineering can provide opportunities for local people including guiding and logistical support, retailing equipment and hospitality. It can also result in development benefits, for example in the Khumbu area of Nepal, which Hillary first passed through on his way to summit Everest in 1953, reporting high levels of poverty amongst the indigenous mountain Sherpa. Today, mountain tourism has brought not only many shops and lodges but also schools, sewerage treatment, healthcare, electricity and street lighting to places such as Namche Bazaar, the main settlement of the region.

Johnston and Edwards were perhaps the earliest commentators to foretell how the activity of mountaineering has become progressively commodified over past decades:

> Corporate sponsorship has shaped mountain experiences and even the fantasy of a mountain experience in order to sell commodities to a consuming culture ... many more well-equipped, stylishly dressed holiday consumers are travelling to mountain regions ... sent by an ever-growing legion of adventure travel companies who advertise their services in Adventure Travel magazines and guides. They arrive carrying clothing and equipment purchased at outdoor shops staffed by adventure enthusiasts; and they are guided through their mountain adventure by mountaineers turned tour guides.
>
> (1994: 468)

This commercialism has been led by both technological and organizational changes, as suggested by Pomfret (2011: 502) who contends that 'numerous factors have facilitated an increase in people doing mountaineering, including gear improvements, high-tech support systems, improved tourist infrastructure, easier accessibility and diminished risk levels'. Whilst 'mountains (still) represent escape locations that offer excitement, stimulation, and potential adventure' (Beedie and Hudson 2003: 625), that adventure is often the source of a business opportunity.

Thus, as with leisure and tourism, the 'boundaries between mountaineering and tourism have become blurred' (Beedie and Hudson 2003: 626). A particular example of this has been the increased development of mountain trekking, often including the ascent of 'trekking peaks', which may involve the use of safety ropes and basic equipment, but do not require the more developed climbing skills required by other ascents. Trekking is normally a multi-day journey, undertaken on foot in areas where other means of transport are generally not available. Mowforth and Munt (2009) explain that, 'trekking is the visiting of off-the-beaten-track locations and involves walking, often but not always in organized parties accompanied a number of porters' (p. 216). Many treks take place in tough mountainous environments at high altitudes, for example in the Himalayas or Andes and can include high mountain passes and peaks. Pobocik and Butalla (1998) found that the majority of those trekking for leisure in the

Himalayas were from Europe and North America and were mostly older male trekkers trekking in groups. Motivation for trekking can be wide ranging. Participants trek for leisure and adventure, to experience local culture, view wildlife or go on pilgrimages to sacred sites. A key part of the appeal is the challenge. Mountain trekking has also begun to become more popular in Asian markets, as detailed in Case Study 2 examining mountain hiking in Taiwan. Mountain hikers in China have recently been dubbed 'donkey friends', because they walk along trails carrying provisions on their back. In Yunnan there are plans to develop historical silk road trails such as the *Ancient Tea Horse Road* as China's first long distance trail. In Korea the 735 km Baekdu-daegan long-distance hiking trail is being developed to cross the peninsula (Mason 2009). This trail combines religious elements of temple visits with hiking activity and is being promoted as a sustainable form of mountain recreation.

However, mountains are still dangerous places, particularly as 'weather conditions undergo dramatic changes over relatively short periods of time in mountain regions, and this directly affects mountaineering successes' (Pomfret 2006: 118). They are also 'wild rugged places that contain objective dangers, such as exposure to extreme elemental conditions and loose rock, which make mountain recreation activities inherently risky and hazardous' (Beedie and Hudson 2003: 627). Ironically, two tourists died in 2010 whilst visiting the recently erupted Eyjafjallajökull volcano in Iceland, not from extreme heat, but from hypothermia caused by extreme cold (Heikkinen 2011). Many climbers, skiers and hikers are injured whilst performing their recreational pursuits in these environments every year, and as more and more people voyage there, the numbers will only further increase. Several hundred climbers now attempt to climb Mt Everest every year for example (Hales 2007).

Despite greater technology and knowledge of this environment, 'an analysis of the death rate on Mt Everest between 1980 and 2002 found it had not changed over the years, with about one death for every 10 successful ascents' (Sutherland 2006: 452). Although most deaths are put down to injury or exhaustion, Sutherland (2006) suggests that the environment itself is a major contributory factor. A significant number of deaths, and a major reason for admission to base camp medical facilities, are caused by high altitude cerebral oedema (HACE) and high altitude pulmonary oedema (HAPE) (commonly lumped together as altitude sickness), which is why these high altitude areas are often called the 'death zone'. However, tourists do not have to be this extreme to suffer the ill effects of the mountain environment, as 77 per cent of trekkers climbing Kilimanjaro in Tanzania suffered from acute mountain sickness (AMS) during their trek, in extreme cases leading to 16 altitude-related tourist deaths between 1996 and 2003 (Davies *et al.* 2009).

While mountaineering can be a low-impact activity, in areas such as the Khumbu which attracts large numbers of mountaineers on multi-day commercial expeditions, it can have a negative impact on the mountain environment, particularly littering and human waste. In recent years, action has been taken to address these problems and the situation has somewhat improved. For example, there are organized clean-ups on major peaks retrieving rubbish from past expeditions, expeditions are now fined if they do not carry out their rubbish and local environmental non-governmental organizations are campaigning for the installation of toilets at Everest Base Camp. In recognition of the impacts that mountain-based tourism can have on mountain environments and communities there are global campaigns for improved management of mountain areas. One example is the International Mountaineering and Climbing Federation's (UIAA) 'Mountain Protection Award'. The award recognizes best practice in mountain tourism in ways that offer long-term benefits to the global mountain tourism industry as well as to the local mountain people and their environment particularly in less-developed countries (Huang and Talbot 2015).

These risks to mountain tourists, mountain communities and mountain environments, clearly require active management. Responses to these are many, and we can examine some of these through various management strategies. First, mountain awareness includes the provision of adequate training and guiding of mountaineering tourists. This includes building indigenous mountaineering skills in mountain areas. Second, attention needs to be paid to livelihoods of the communities that host mountain tourism, to ensure that opportunities augment existing options available and impacts are minimized. Last, it is important that mountain environments are protected through effective management regimes.

Mountain awareness

Guides are clearly very important in mountain areas, and can be central to the safe completion of the experience. In her study of package mountaineering tourists, Pomfret notes

> Guides are an essential element of the package mountaineering holiday … they are renowned for their expertise in the mountains and have substantial knowledge and experience in mountaineering … essentially, guides know how to cope in the mountains and how to look after their clients.
>
> (2011: 508)

Despite the obvious economic opportunity, increased guiding has not been without controversy. For example Everest has remained both the pinnacle of mountaineering experience and attendant commodification, with guided trips for wealthy, although not necessarily able, clients being the norm. On 19 May 2012 a record 234 people summited the mountain in one day, and images of huge queues on the slopes circulated in the world's media (BBC 2013). In 2013 there was controversy as two talented western climbers clashed with Sherpas laying ropes for the season's paying clients. This high altitude mountaineering tourism industry has become dominated by a handful of very successful high end operators, such as IMG (International Mountain Guides) or Jagged Globe. The latter, originally set up in 1988, conducted the first UK commercial trip to Everest in 1993. The company has approximately 1,000 clients a year and includes adventure skiing in its portfolio which is focused on exclusive mountain experiences. The delivery and marketing of the trips has emphasis on an expedition approach, and whilst staff are highly trained, clients are not 'guided' in a traditional package format.

However, one problem in guiding is the continued dominance of western guides over locally trained personnel. Many developing countries have a limited mountaineering skills base with which to support the development of indigenous mountaineering tourism. However, in some cases international mountaineering tourists can be used to support skills development. One positive example of this is in Azerbaijan, where a small facility was set up by western individuals to teach climbing skills. Azerbaijan Mountain Adventures runs a small climbing wall in the town of Sheki, nestled at the base of the greater Caucasian range. This was in response to two independent trends, the first of which was an increasing interest from western tourists to explore the Caucasian peaks. The second was a recognition that Azerbaijan had a large number of IDP (internally displaced persons) following the conflict in the southern region of Nagorno Karabakh. This put pressure on many northern towns such as Sheki which had limited community and sports facilities to provide for these migrants. Thus a climbing centre was set up in 2011 to fulfil both the need for a community centre and to build climbing skills, and to provide guiding services to western clients (Figure 16.1). Arguably the former has been most successful to date, with the centre being used as a multifunctional space for community-based meetings and other sports including table tennis and dancing and classes on debating, English and computing. However, it has also nurtured home-grown climbing talent and supported the development of a National Climbing Federation. Specific female only climbing sessions have allowed women and girls to develop their climbing skills in a traditionally patriarchal society, and allowed them to compete in national competitions.

Nevertheless, it is not just local skills that are important, but also skills of the tourists, particularly as the trend has been towards lower skilled individuals being commercially guided through mountain environments. One issue of particular importance in mountainous areas is avalanche awareness and preparation. In 2012–2013, there was a number of fatal avalanche incidents in the Scottish mountains, including three individuals who were killed in a multiple burial incident. These individuals were part of a mountain skills training group from Glenmore Lodge, Scotland's National Mountain Training Centre. A subsequent review and investigation led to the centre deciding to implement mandatory avalanche safety equipment and training for all students and staff engaged in their winter mountain courses. Personal avalanche safety equipment includes a transceiver, shovel and probe (or TSP), which can be used to quickly locate and dig out any avalanche victims. Use of avalanche safety equipment in mountaineering contexts has been the subject of debate, since it complicates the alpine approach to mountaineering prevalent in mountain culture (Varley *et al.* 2012).

Figure 16.1 Mountaineering skills development, Azeri Mountain Adventures, Sheki, Azerbaijan.

Mountain livelihoods

One of the principal concerns of the management of mountaineering tourism is how to ensure that the industry contributes sustainably to the livelihoods of mountain communities. It is clear that activities such as mountaineering and trekking do have the potential to bring benefits to local communities. For example in Nepal, in the past two decades, the numbers trekking and mountaineering grew from 42,308 in 1991 to 86,260 in 2011 (Visit Nepal 2013). The impact of this is that the trekking industry of Nepal provides nearly 24,000 full-time jobs, and approximately 70,000 people are employed as porters on a freelance basis (Mowforth and Munt 2009), providing incomes in areas where there are limited other economic opportunities. However, trekking can also bring negative impacts as large numbers descend on fragile mountain environments which normally sustain only small populations. Key impacts on the environment include littering, human waste disposal and excessive fuelwood consumption. Despite the benefits brought, lowland porters carry extreme loads and are often ill equipped to deal with extreme weather conditions at higher altitudes. In worst cases they may suffer frost bite and injury jeopardizing their ability to make a living from tourism in the future, which has prompted action by Tourism Concern under the *Trekking Wrongs: Porters' Rights* campaign.

This campaign has been developed to improve working conditions for mountain porters in trekking destinations. In contrast to their well-heeled clients, porters often face lack of shelter, inadequate clothing and food, and low pay. Nepalese porters, who are often poor farmers from lowland areas, and are unused to high altitudes and harsh mountain conditions, are four times more likely to suffer accidents and illnesses than western trekkers, facing frostbite, altitude sickness and even death (Tourism Concern 2011). There are many reports of porters being abandoned by tour groups when they fall ill or being abandoned in life-threatening blizzards while trekkers get rescued by helicopter. In April 2014 16 Nepalese guides were killed in an avalanche on Everest whilst preparing the route for commercial clients. Many porters and guides feel that the highly physical nature of the job and the menial task makes operators and tourists treat them as 'beasts of burden', with limited rights. Tourism Concern sought to address this issue by working with the trekking industry and tour operators to address porters' rights and working conditions. This included developing a code of practice with minimum standards of working conditions that could be used as a basis for policies on porters' rights. They also campaigned publicly on this issue to raise awareness amongst trekkers and mobilize their support for improved industry practice and, by 2009, 49 out of 79 UK operators had policies on porters. In Tanzania, the code of conduct has been used by the Kilimanjaro Porters Assistance Project (KPAP) to develop its own guidelines for proper porter treatment. In addition KPAP has provided proper mountain climbing gear for 4,782 porters and has sponsored classes in first aid and HIV/AIDS awareness (Tourism Concern 2011). In Peru there is now a US$8 a day minimum wage for porters and tighter control over agencies that fail to comply with the regulations.

Tourism contributions to mountain livelihoods can be assessed using the Sustainable Livelihoods Framework. This framework enables us to 'understand and analyze the complex livelihoods of rural people' (Lee 2005: 216), through assessing the context, livelihood resources, livelihood strategies and institutional processes inherent in a development situation (Scoones 1998). The Sustainable Livelihoods Approach (SLA) has been particularly applied in sub-Saharan settings, particularly by the UK Department for International Development (DfID), especially those deemed to have a high degree of vulnerability, but can be equally applied to montane communities. At the core of the framework are community resources or 'the basic material and social, tangible and intangible assets that people have in their possession ... such livelihood assets may be seen as the "capital" base from which different productive streams are derived, from which livelihoods are constructed' (Scoones 1998: 7). These were placed broadly into categories of natural, economic, human and social assets, with later refinement in DfID models of physical and financial descriptors in place of economic capital. Although not specifically focused on tourism, the model has proved useful in evaluating baselines and changes to community assets caused by tourism development (Lee 2005; Tao and Wall 2009), adding to other conceptual models of fractions of capital in tourism studies such as that by Hampton and Christensen (2007). However, there has been some further degree of refinement; for example in the context of coastal tourism, cultural capital was added to the SLA framework due to 'the cultural resources (heritage, customs, traditions) [being] very much a feature of local livelihoods' (Cater and Cater 2007: 114), as well as being seen as central to the tourism product. Further, Wang and Cater (2014) identified the importance of political capital in a mountain community in Taiwan seeking to use ecotourism as a recovery tool following a major earthquake.

The vulnerability of mountain communities in western Nepal led to the establishment of the Annapurna Conservation Area Project (ACAP) to address environmental problems and promote sustainable community development in the Annapurna area of Nepal. Livelihood protection has been a foundation of their management approach over nearly three decades (Figure 16.2). The ACA was established in 1986 in response to deforestation that was generally attributed to tourism development and was integrated within the ACAP, run by the non-governmental organization, the King Mahendra Trust for Nature Conservation now re-named the National Trust for Nature Conservation (NTNC). Aiming to integrate sustainable development, emphasis is placed upon the participation of village peoples in development decision making and capacity building to realize self-directed opportunities and eventual self-management of ACA. Partnerships between ACAP and village representatives have subsequently been established, for example with village development committees (VDCs), lodge management committees (LMCs) and women's development committees (WDCs). Alongside sustainable tourism management, ACAP's activities include forest and wildlife management, the promotion of alternative energy sources to relieve the pressure on the forests (for example solar power and backboilers), strategies to minimize littering (for example encouraging tourists to use re-fillable water bottles and village clean-up

Figure 16.2 Mountain livelihood options in the Annapurna Conservation Area Project.

campaigns), conservation education and training for trekking lodge operators (Visit Nepal 2013). One of the most successful of the alternative energy sources has been the introduction of backboilers which has increased energy efficiency and was subsidized 50 per cent by ACAP. Instead of using a separate fireplace for heating water, this fuelwood-saving device feeds water pipes connected to a tank (frequently a disused oil drum) into the cooking hearth. The water, thus heated, returns through convection to this backboiler. This simple, appropriate technology fix means that during cooking, water can be simultaneously heated for showers and other purposes. Its introduction resulted in a 675 kg reduction per month per lodge of fuelwood consumption during the tourist season. Mountain Tourism has a specific economic role in contributing to the financing of these programmes such as these, raising monies from entry permits into ACA (see below) and through direct tourist expenditure in the area. The ACA has been acknowledged from different sources (including winning the British Airways 'Tourism for Tomorrow Award' in 1991 and the World Wide Fund for Nature (WWF) Conservation Merit Award in 2000), as an exemplar of how tourism can be used for nature conservation and community development in mountain regions. The principles of the ACAP have been applied to other trekking destinations throughout the world, for example the Rinjani ecotrek programme (Cater 2012). Respecting local communities and being environmentally friendly benefits trekkers, local residents and the environment. This is a win–win situation for humans and ecosystems and makes trekking activity more sustainable in the long term.

Mountain protection

A further mechanism to ensure the sustainability of increasing mountaineering tourism is to develop effective protection regimes through protected area management. Mountain areas are a vitally important ecosystem, often influencing more populated lowland areas in significant ways, for example in vital water and sediment transport. For example 3,700 m Mt Rinjani, a popular mountain trekking destination on the Indonesian island of Lombok, provides approximately 70 per cent of the island's population (approximately three million people) with water for drinking and agriculture, especially rice cultivation. Therefore the vast majority of mountain regions popular for mountaineering tourism are located within protected areas. Ensuring protection may involve working with a wide range of stakeholders, for example in the UK, the British Mountaineering Council (BMC) works with stakeholders such as landowners and conservationists to address climbing-related issues. The BMC works with the Royal Society for the Protection of Birds (RSPB) to impose climbing bans during nesting periods on rock faces where rare birds breed. Management agencies and protected area authorities are often responsible for enforcing such management.

Table 16.1 lists the protected area authority, number of ascents and the permit costs for the 'Seven Summits', or the highest peaks on each of the seven continents. This has become an increasingly popular bucket list for dedicated mountaineers, echoing the enduring popularity of lesser heights (but perhaps equal feats) of the Munros of Scotland or the 100 mountains of Taiwan described in Case Study 2. Over 350 people had completed the list of the Seven Summits by 2012. The allure of completing this list has led to the emergence of specialist tourism operators catering specifically for achieving all of the peaks, often in a given time frame. All of the peaks in the list bar Mt Vinson in Antarctica are contained within a protected area. The latter is undeniably unusual as it is not located within a territorial entity. However, all tourism activities in Antarctica are governed by the International Association of Antarctic Tourism Operators (IAATO), which has noted the increase in adventure tourism (including mountaineering) on the continent in recent years. All of those peaks within protected areas fall into the IUCN category II of national park, except for the huge areas of Denali national park and Qomolangma National Nature Preserve (QNNP). Denali is listed as category VI which is a protected area with sustainable use of natural resources. QNNP is a vast area of the Tibetan plateau which has a mosaic of various levels of protection. QNNP is distinctive because no warden force protects its natural and cultural resources. Management is instead enforced by local communities, especially the governments of the four counties that comprise

Table 16.1 Protected areas, fees and ascents of the Seven Summits

Mountain	Height	Protected area, date established and size	IUCN category	High season climbing fee	2013 attempts (and successful summits)
Mt Everest, Nepal/Tibet	8,848 m	Sagarmatha National Park (1976) 1,148 km² Qomolangma National Nature Preserve (1989) 36,000 km²	II	Fee $11,000 (reduced from $25,000 in 2014)	800 (658)
Aconcagua, Argentina	6,980 m 22,902 ft	Aconcagua Provincial Park (1983) 710 km²	II	$5,500 ($6,500 without a guide)	3,500 (1,000)
Denali Alaska, North America	6,194 m 20,320 ft	Denali National Park and Preserve (1917) 24,500 km²	VI	$365	1,151 (783)
Kilimanjaro, Tanzania, Africa	5,896 m 19,340 ft	Mt Kilimanjaro National Park 753.5 km²	II	$70/day + huts Approx $525/trip	Approx 30,000
Elbrus, Russia	5,642 m 18,513 ft	Prielbrusie National Park (1986) 1,014 km²	II	€25	n.a., but up to 100 climbers/day in peak season
Mt Vinson, Antarctica	4,897 m 16,067 ft	n.a.	n.a.	n.a.	640 total climbing activities in Antarctica in 2012/2013
Carstensz Pyramid, West Papua, New Guinea	4,884 m 16,023 ft	Lorentz Nature Monument (1919) Lorentz National Park (1997) 25,056 km²	II	Multiple permits required from different levels of government: total expedition cost about $18,500	Very low due to inaccessibility, estimated <500 total

the preserve (Tingri, Dinjie, Nyalam and Kyirong) with a Management Bureau in Shigatse, the prefecture headquarters. However this leads to exploitation of the lax tourism management by operators who often recirculate permits with different groups of mountain tourists, as was our experience in 2007.

Permits are the principal method for managing mountaineering access and are widely used, particularly in less developed countries to maximize revenue from their mountain resources. It is not known how much of this revenue goes towards mountain protection, although this is often used as a justification for charging mountaineering tourists. Nepal for example earns some $3.3 million annually from climbing permits (Coldwell 2014). Interestingly Argentinian authorities charge more for a permit to climb Aconcagua should climbers be climbing without a locally certified guide. This is to disincentivize independent climbers due to the higher incidence of accidents and consequent costs of rescue for these climbers. As the easiest of the peaks, Kilimanjaro permits are much lower, with many more tourists ascending the peak than the others. However, here permits are charged by the day, which some commentators believe has contributed to rushing the easiest of the Seven Summits, leading to an estimated ten deaths a year on the mountain. Given the potential revenue, permitting is usually heavily policed, with Cartenz Pyramid being notorious for the difficulty of collecting the plethora of permits required to climb the mountain. In Tibet, Chinese authorities threaten a fine of US$200 should tourists venture beyond the limits of the base camp for Everest on the north side (Figure 16.3).

Figure 16.3 Warning of fines at Mt Everest/Qomolangma base camp, Tibet.

Mountain management or managing mountains?

This chapter has built on the previous contributions in illustrating the growing importance of mountain regions for tourism, but emphasizing that management of this activity takes at least three forms; mountain awareness, in the form of guiding and training; mountain livelihoods, for recognizing and supporting mountain communities; and mountain protection for managing these fragile environments. Although the latter often predates the two earlier themes, experience has shown that protection and management cannot be successful without attention to the needs both of tourists and of host communities. It is undeniable that mountains will only further cement their allure for tourism and recreation, as the commercialization and access described in this volume accelerates. Indeed, one only needs to examine the 'virtual' popularity of mountains in adventure film making. Mountain film festivals are becoming increasingly popular with a wide audience, and one of the longest established, the Banff Mountain Film Festival, now embarks on an annual world tour with stops in around 285 communities and 30 countries. Despite such drivers, the attitudes of mountaineering tourists will inevitably have to change, particularly in regard to the previous trend towards first ascents. In common with polar tourism, mountains are places that, once conquered, no longer meet the wilderness criteria of 'treading where no human has done so before' (Stonehouse and Crosbie 1995). Of course this concept, which has dominated some sectors of mountaineering tourism to date, is a false and inherently unsustainable one promoted by western attitudes towards these regions.

The greatest threat to mountain environments is, however, not the tourism that takes place within them, but our unsustainable practices below them. It is widely recognized that climate change will bring dramatic changes to high altitude regions, with retreating glaciers, reduced snow cover and a host of attendant ecosystem changes. The International Year of the Mountains in 2002 was an initiative to increase international awareness of the global importance of mountain ecosystems (UNSA 2002). Indeed the IYM was partially a response to the Intergovernmental Panel on Climate Change study on the threat posed by global warming to alpine glaciers. As 'water towers' of the world, mountains are essential to life on Earth. Yet, globalization, urbanization and tourism (both mass and mountain based) pose a threat to mountain communities and their natural resources that many rely upon in order to sustain livelihoods both there and in the lowlands (UNEP 2012).

References

BBC News (2013) 'Everest crowds: The world's highest traffic jam', 28 May. Online, available at: www.bbc.co.uk/news/magazine-22680192 (accessed 29 May 2014).

Beedie, P. and Hudson, S. (2003) 'Emergence of mountain-based adventure tourism', *Annals of Tourism Research*, 30(3): 625–643.

Buckley, R. C. (2006) *Adventure tourism*, Wallingford: CABI.

Cater, C. (2012) 'Community involvement in trekking tourism: The Rinjani Trek Ecotourism Programme, Lombok, Indonesia', in B. Garrod and A. Fyall (eds) *Contemporary Cases in Tourism, Vol. 1*, Oxford: Goodfellow: 191–212.

Cater, C. and Cater, E. (2007) *Marine ecotourism*, Oxford: CABI.

Coldwell, W. (2014) 'Nepal slashes cost of climbing Everest', *Guardian*, 14 February.

Davies, A. J., Kalson, N. S., Stokes, S., Earl, M. D., Whitehead, A. G., Frost, H., Tyrell-Marsh, I. and Naylor J. (2009) 'Determinants of summiting success and acute mountain sickness on Mt Kilimanjaro (5,895 m)', *Wilderness and Environmental Medicine*, 20(4): 311–317.

Hales, R. (2007) 'Mountaineering', in R. Buckley (ed.) *Adventure tourism*, Wallingford: CABI: 260–285.

Hampton, M. P. and Christensen, J. (2007) 'Competing industries in islands: A new tourism approach', *Annals of Tourism Research*, 34(4): 998–1020.

Heikkinen, J. (2011) 'The impact of the Eyjafjallajökull-eruption on the in-bound tourism in Iceland', unpublished thesis, Kajaani University of Applied Sciences School of Business.

Hill, B. J. (1995) 'A guide to adventure travel', *Parks and Recreation*, 30(9): 56–65.

Huang, M. F. and Talbot, A. J. (2015) 'Mountaineering', in C. Cater, B. Garrod and T. Low (eds) *The encyclopaedia of sustainable tourism*, Oxford: CABI, forthcoming.

Johnston, B. R. and Edwards, T. (1994) 'The commodification of mountaineering', *Annals of Tourism Research*, 21(3): 459–478.

Lee, M. H. (2005) 'Networks, partnership and community support: Farm tourism cooperation in Taiwan', in D. Hall, I. Kirkpatrick and M. Mitchell (eds) *Rural tourism and sustainable business*, Clevedon: Channel View: 201–226.

Mason, D. A. (2009) 'Mountain-adventure tourism combined with religious tourism: A fresh paradigm for sustainable-green destination-development in Korea', 한국관광학회학술대회발표논문집, 66th Korea Tourism Association Symposium and Research Papers Competition, 2009(7): 85–99.

Millington, K., Locke, T. and Locke, A. (2001) 'Adventure travel', *Travel and Tourism Analyst*, 4(1): 65–97.

Mowforth, M. M. and Munt, I. (2009) *Tourism and sustainability: Development, globalisation and new tourism in the third world* (3rd edn), London and New York: Routledge.

Pobocik, M. and Butalla, C. (1998) 'Development in Nepal: The Annapurna conservation area project', in C. M. Hall and A. A. Lew (eds) *Sustainable tourism: A geographical perspective*, Harlow: Pearson Education: 159–172.

Pomfret, G. (2006) 'Mountaineering adventure tourists: A conceptual framework for research', *Tourism Management*, 27(1): 113–123.

Pomfret, G. (2011) 'Package mountaineer tourist holidaying in the French Alps: An evaluation of key influences encouraging their participation', *Tourism Management*, 32: 501–510.

Scoones, I. (1998) 'Sustainable rural livelihoods: A framework for analysis', Discussion Paper 296, Institute of Development Studies, University of Sussex.

Stonehouse, B. and Crosbie, K. (1995) 'Tourist impacts and management in the Antarctic peninsula area', in C. M. Hall and M. E. Johnston (eds) *Polar tourism: Tourism in the arctic and antarctic regions*, Chichester: Wiley: 217–233.

Sutherland, A. I. (2006) 'Personal views: Why are so many people dying on Everest?' *British Medical Journal*, 333(7565): 452.

Tao, T. C. H. and Wall, G. (2009) 'A livelihood approach to sustainability', *Asia Pacific Journal of Tourism Research*, 14(2): 137–152.

Tourism Concern (2011) *Why the tourism industry needs to take the human rights approach: The business case*, London: Tourism Concern.

UNSA (2002) 'International year of the mountains'. Online, available at: www.unspecial.org/UNS607/UNS-607_T16.html (accessed 29 May 2014).

UNEP (2012) 'UNEP and the international year of the mountains'. Online, available at: www.unep.org/Documents.Multilingual/Default.asp?DocumentID=239&ArticleID=3019 (accessed 29 May 2014).

Varley, P., Taylor, S. and Johnston, T. (eds) (2012) *Adventure tourism: Meaning, experience and education*, Oxford: Routledge.

Varley, P. J. (2006) 'Confecting adventure and playing with meaning: The adventure commodification continuum', *Journal of Sport and Tourism*, 11(2): 173–194.

Visit Nepal (2013) ACAP. Online, available at: www.visitnepal.com/acap/ (accessed 16 February 2013).

Wang, C. and Cater, C. (2014) 'Ecotourism as a sustainable recovery tool after an earthquake', in B. W. Ritchie and K. Campiranon (eds) *Tourism crisis and disaster management in the Asia-Pacific*, Wallingford: CABI Publishing: 209–226.

17 Mountaineering tourism

Looking to the horizon

Ghazali Musa, Anna Thompson-Carr and James Higham

In many respects the commercialization of mountaineering and mountaineering tourism resembles similarities to developments in sport tourism (Chapter 1). In this volume we adopt the sport model by Weed and Bull (2004) and Weed (2005) who conceptualize sport and tourism as a complex interplay of activity, people and place. 'Activity' relates to the geographical, historical and social development of mountaineering. 'People' focuses on those who (directly or indirectly) engage in the activity of mountaineering, which includes the motivation, personality, experience, satisfaction and behaviour of mountaineer tourists. 'Place' addresses unique destination contexts relating to the hosting of mountaineers to facilitate their climb, impacts on environment and host community, together with management practices. Thus, for the purpose of this book, we define mountaineering tourism as the activities of mountaineering tourists, their interplay with members of the climbing community and all associated stakeholders, together with associated impacts and management at the environmental and local community level. The final concluding chapter discusses mountaineering tourism based on the three main components of activity, people and place. Before making the concluding remarks we will highlight future considerations for mountaineering tourism and its research.

Activity

The United Nations Environmental Programme (UNEP) provides various categorizations of mountains (Blyth *et al.* 2002), to capture the wide diversity of mountain environments in terms of ecology and biomass, latitude and longitude (Chapter 1). It also proposes seven mountain terrain categories which include any land area over 2,500 m (high mountains) and topographic prominence of over 300 m within a 7 km radius (low mountains). Using the UNEP definition, mountains comprise 27.5 per cent of the total land area of the Earth (see Chapter 2). Mountains are a source of ecosystem services by providing resources of freshwater, energy, mining and genetic diversity (Næss 1989). In Chapter 4, Hall and Page (2002) summarize the wilderness values of mountains which include experiential values that support recreation and tourism, mental and restorative values for enhancing individuals, scientific values of wilderness (e.g. genetic resources, ecological research), and economic values that accrue from the commodification of wilderness, mountain resources and activities.

The significance of mountain regions for mountaineering tourism is influenced by three factors; the geographic location including accessibility, the opinions of professional and amateur mountain hikers and climbers, and the popular media images of mountain destinations (Chapter 2). Iconic international mountaineering destinations are in Asia (the Himalaya), South America (the Andes) and Europe (the Alps); whilst iconic specific mountain sites include the Tour du Mont Blanc (France, Italy and Switzerland), the Everest Base Camp Trek (Nepal), Mt Kilimanjaro (Tanzania) and the Inca Trail (Peru).

Chapter 3 observes that in many cultures, mountains are the source of religious significance, homes of gods and destinations for spiritual pilgrims (Benbaum 2006). During the Industrial Revolution of the nineteenth century, modern technologies increasingly exploited nature for utilitarian and economic goals, resulting in environmental and urban pollution in Europe (Williams and Lew 2014). In response, the Romantic Movement arose, during which mountains and wilderness landscapes were idealized in art and literature.

The wilderness concept has evolved from a place to be feared to a place of the sublime, a place to be explored and utilized, a place to be preserved and most recently a place for recreation and tourism, where wilderness is commoditized for tourism experiences (Chapter 4). European Romantics were the first recreational mountain trekkers and climbers (Davidson 2002). Romanticism has recalibrated people's perceptions of mountains as previously inhospitable places to objects of the sublime and attractions or places of escape from urban life and mass tourism (Macfarlane 2003: 15). With increasing comfort of urban living, many now yearn to experience thrills, excitement and otherness (Giddens 1990). In response, a progressive commodification in many parts of the world has transformed wilderness and mountains to tourism products (Mowforth and Munt 2008; Neves 2004, 2010).

In the mountaineering tourism literature the symbolic capital of the activity is accumulated and translated into social or cultural capital, to create individual status and distinctiveness (Chapter 4). The social construction of mountain landscapes continues retaining the essential attractions through a set of carefully projected images, words and ideas. Better risk management in mitigating negative outcomes result in the surge of commercialized adventure tourism activities. There are two social worlds in mountaineering: dedicated professional climbers who have experience, knowledge and technical skills to operate independently in the mountains; and adventure tourists who are often guided. The former may value escapism and the search for authenticity, while the later focus on the accumulation of social capital.

Whymper's expedition success and tragedy on the Matterhorn in 1865, resulted in re-assessment of how risk is managed (Chapter 3). The tragedy did not diminish the general public attraction towards the mountains but, instead, mountaineering associations responded by seeking to make the activity safer. The event also ignited increasing interest in mountain guiding in the Alps, whereby locals with intimate knowledge of the mountains were hired to facilitate the success of climbing expeditions. Risk management in mountaineering adventure allows the activity to be commodified as tourism products and services (Varley 2006).

Chapter 5 states that guided mountaineering has a history dating back to the early nineteenth century where the activity was necessary to alleviate negative risks in the European Alps (Johnston 1989, 1992; Boekholt 1983). This was the beginning of mountaineering commodification and guided experience as examined by several researchers (Carr 2001; Beedie 2003, 2010, 2013; Beedie and Hudson 2003; Houge Mackenzie and Kerr 2013; Johnston and Edwards 1994; Martinoia 2013 and Pomfret 2011). Professional guides facilitate the adventure experience, judge appropriate challenge, facilitate safe(r) routes, help in navigation and assist in responding to weather and alpine conditions. They also help mountaineers to build skills and experience (Beedie 2013).

Referring to Chapter 5, the International Federation of Mountain Guides' Associations (IFMGA) was formed in Italy in 1965, and provides an internationally recognized training and certification scheme for mountain guiding. Individual country's national mountain guides' associations may apply for IFMGA membership for their country's guides to have IFMGA qualifications. Fully qualified IFMGA guides may work internationally as climbing and ski guides. The New Zealand Mountain Guides' Association (NZMGA) was formed in 1975, and in 1981 was admitted as the eighth member of the IFMGA. New Zealand guiding professionals have had an international impact through providing services overseas as individual guides who are IFMGA qualified.

In New Zealand (see Case Study 1), climbers have developed a climbing subculture largely modelled on the British approach, reflecting the broader international diffusion of sports and the cultural foundation of climbing through a subculture of science and exploration (Johnston 1993). The New Zealand Alpine Club was initiated in 1891 and published the *New Zealand Alpine Journal*, paying tribute to the formative influence of the Alpine Club in England (Johnston 1993). Initially membership was only open to experienced climbers, the club embraced change to provide climbing instruction, and to inculcate values of safety-first training through a club camp. There has been an ongoing clash in approaches to safety between the 'old guard' and the new enthusiasts (Johnston 1993). Early mountaineering journal writings by the Alpine Club in England addressed the struggle for attention and recognition between escapism mountaineers and those motivated by exploration and discovery (Chapter 6).

From an eastern perspective (Case Study 2), interest in Taiwan's mountains started with tea plantation (Ling 2008). Japanese climbers explored the mountains for measurement and academic activities, surveying the country for mapping, uncovering new species and engaging with local indigenous communities. In 1915, they started to encourage civilians to be involved in sports, during which mountain hiking was considered as teaching activities throughout primary school to university (Ling 2008). This led to the establishment of the Taiwanese Mountaineering Association in 1926, which was later renamed as the

Chinese Taipei Alpine Association (CTAA). It started the concepts of the 'Five Mountain Club' and '100 Mountain Club' to lure people to climb specific mountains, parallel to the establishment of the Munros which list all peaks over 3,000 ft in Scotland or the Nuttalls in Wales and England which are those mountains over 2,000 ft.

In contrast to the UNEP mountain classification, the Taiwanese mountain classification takes emotive and historical aspects into their consideration, other than absolute height (Case Study 2). Mountains were classified based on the availability of the mountain's name and triangulation point, the historical perspective from records and ancestors' oral histories, the shape of the mountain and the emotive characteristic which evokes the hikers' emotion during their walk. Taiwanese mountain hikers/mountaineers are motivated by the 'pocket peak' in alpine mountaineering, rather than improving mountaineering skills or knowledge. The Sports Affairs Council (2003) recorded that over five million Taiwanese take part in mountain hiking yearly (one in four Taiwanese), who climb mainly for aesthetic and health reasons.

People (mountaineers)

Historically, mountaineering experience and identity was based on self-reliance and the desire to experience nature 'on nature's terms' (Chapter 7). Lacking opportunities for 'self-realizing action' or to express individualism in modern western society (Taylor 1989) results in an increasing need to engage in activities that offer elements of risk. Through the activity, mountaineers have the illusion of controlling the uncontrollable, deriving a sense of competence and compensating for boredom and the lack of authenticity in ordinary life (Vester 1987: 238). Mountaineering allows mountaineers to explore their capabilities and limitations through self-reliance and action in an environment which does not forgive inaccurate assessments of the self. They expand their sense of self by progressing through a series of ever-increasing challenges. Their climbing style becomes the expression of their individuality. However, these experiences are increasingly threatened by the tourism industry with its commercialism and new technologies (Davidson 2011). Sports become too rationalized and institutionalized (Mitchell 1983) where participants' actions and abilities have little impact on the outcome. The rationalization encroaches the world of mountaineering through forms of regulation, commercialization and commodification (Kiewa 2002; Heywood 1994).

Chapter 9 details the motivation and satisfaction of mountaineers. Among mountaineers the traditional motivation theories implicated are instinctual drive (Klausner 1968; Noyce 1958), arousal seeking (Berlyne 1960), attributional constructs (Heider 1958), the peak experience (Maslow 1968) and expectancy valence theory (Atkinson 1964). More contemporary mountaineering motivation perspectives are normative influences (Celsi *et al.* 1993), flow (Csikszentmihalyi and Csikszentmihalyi 1990) and edgework (Lyng 1990). Emotions are vital to adventure tourism experiences (Carnicelli-Filho *et al.* 2009). Pomfret (2006) proposes joy and fear as two core emotions evoked by mountaineering, and their existence was empirically confirmed by Faullant *et al.* (2011). In mountaineering experience, joy increases satisfaction, while fear results in dissatisfaction. Extraversion personality traits positively relate to joy, while neuroticism traits relate to fear.

Chapter 11 states that amongst serious mountaineers, fear is not considered something to hide away from, but rather to be embraced. The experience of effective participation despite fear can lead to incredible self-transformations (Brymer 2012) when mountaineers elicit deep self-awareness that eventually supports that powerful personal transformation. Mountaineers have the ability to see more clearly with an alertness beyond the everyday mundane alertness required for living in a modern society. This enables connection with the inner underutilized strengths. Similarly, Lockwood (2011) pointed out even though risk is an important element in mountaineering, it is not a powerful motivating factor. Risk is a bridge to becoming positively transformed (Allman *et al.* 2009) which is essential to their life's quality. Mountaineering offers the individual opportunities to exert considerable influence over the outcome through their skills, strategies and perseverance (Mitchell 1983). Rather than seeking the risk (danger), they seek the challenge to diminish it, which results in satisfaction (Pomfret 2006). Obtaining a positive perception of overcoming the challenges and fears is a primary emotion and important to gaining a sense of satisfaction from the experience.

Over the years, mountaineering motivations have changed from extrinsic motives being concerned about religion, science or nationalism, to more intrinsic and contemporary motives such as personal fulfilment and adventure-seeking (Chapter 9). Less experienced mountaineers may place higher levels of importance on motivations related to technical skill development, while more experienced mountaineers tend to place greater importance on motives related to personal and aesthetic factors. Based on the Adventure Recreation Model (Ewert and Hollenhorst 1989; Todd *et al.* 2002), as the level of engagement increases, so too does skill, frequency of participation, internalized locus of control and preferred level of risk. Additionally, their motivations for participation will become more aligned with internal motivations such as challenge, achievement, control and risk-taking, as opposed to external motivations such as feeling pressured by friends or family to participate (Buckley 2012; Ewert and Hollenhorst 1989).

Case Study 4 enlightens us as to the flow experiences that can be achieved in serious mountaineering (Stebbins 2007). To achieve this, Csikszentmihalyi (1990: 48–67) set out eight elements which must be present simultaneously in mountaineering activity. These are (1) sense of competence, (2) requirement of concentration, (3) clarity of goals, (4) immediate feedback, (5) sense of deep and focused involvement, (6) sense of control, (7) loss of self-consciousness, and (8) sense of time is truncated. Element 1 and 6 are intricately intertwined: feeling competent in doing an activity generates a sense of being able to exercise control, especially in difficult situations. Element 1 necessitates the participant to be capable to performing at least a moderately challenging activity. Flow fails to develop when the activity is either too easy or too difficult. Element 6 refers to the perceived degree of control the participant has over execution of the activity. During peak experience, 'the climber feels at one with the mountain, the clouds, the rays of the sun, and the tiny bugs moving in and out of the shadow of the fingers holding to the rock' (Csikszentmihalyi 1988: 33).

Chapter 11 identifies and explores the personality traits of mountaineers. Monasterio *et al.* (2014) observe variations in standard deviations across all personality measures which suggests that mountaineering personality profiles cannot be tightly defined. However, some studies are conclusive in explaining the personality traits of mountaineers. Sensation-seeking is the most commonly studied personality factor in the literature (Castanier *et al.* 2010; Cronin 1991; Diehm and Armatas 2004; Freixanet 1991; Jack and Ronan 1998; Zuckerman 1983). The factor explains the need for varied, novel and complex sensations and experiences and the willingness to take physical and social risks for the sake of such experience (Zuckerman 1979: 10). Mountaineers tend to score higher on Zuckerman's Sensation Seeking (SS) Scale compared to low risk sports participants and control groups (Cronin 1991; Freixanet 1991; Jack and Ronan 1998; Zuckerman 1983; Fowler *et al.* 1980). Among high risk climbers, Freixanet (1991) found that extraversion personality traits are positively correlated, while neuroticism is negatively correlated with the activity participation. Using the Temperament and Character Inventory (TCI) Monasterio *et al.* (2012) and Monasterio *et al.* (2014) found that mountaineers are higher in novelty seeking and self-directness and lower on harm avoidance and self-transcendence compared to an age matched normative population.

Mountaineers' personality influences their behaviour on the mountains in relation to environment, local community and safety and security. Esfahani *et al.* (2014) define responsible mountaineering behaviour related to safety and security as specific behaviour that needs to be carried out by the mountaineers to ensure their safety and security while mountain climbing. Referring to Case Study 5, mountaineers on Mt Kinabalu (Borneo), which is frequently climbed by novice mountain trekkers, displayed four responsible behaviour dimensions. These are clothing requirement, food and drink requirement, equipment requirement and obedience requirement. Mountaineers have high awareness of responsible behaviour but behave only moderately responsibly on the mountain. Knowledge is the only attitude dimension which influences responsible behaviour. Climbers with a high level of spirituality have a high level of responsible mountaineering behaviour. Mountaineers place a greater trust on the information obtained via word of mouth (from family and relatives) than compared with media information on issues related to responsible behaviour.

While adventure tourists are motivated by fear and thrills (Cater 2006) and the ability to overcome the challenge which matched their skill (e.g. Ewert and Hollenhorst 1989), mountaineering tourists seek a 'protective frame' to enjoy challenges safely (Chapter 10). They do not seek risk, but rather a 'secure' environment in which to successfully complete an activity beyond personal skill levels. A 'protective frame' provides feelings of protection from risk or danger and is generally operationalized as confidence in oneself, others and/or equipment (Apter 1993). Through auto-ethnographic research, Chapter 10 confirmed four key elements of a protective frame which are the guides, the equipment, other participants and the environment; of which interpersonal interactions with the guides emerged as the single most influential factor in determining overall experience quality and satisfaction.

Perhaps one of the least explored aspects of mountaineering activities relates to research about the influence of gender (Chapter 8). Masculinity is reflected in many published mountaineers' personal narratives, media representations and records of people's experiences of mountaineering. Early narratives convey hegemonic masculine features, such as bravery and risk-taking (Frohlick 1999; Logan 2006; Moraldo 2013), while feminine features such as cooking, the camaraderie and friendship developed during expeditions are largely obscured in mountain narratives (Frohlick 1999). Women are frequently regarded as consumers of soft adventure and play only a supportive role in mountaineering expeditions. However, in rock climbing and commercially guided mountaineering, female mountaineers transcend the gender stereotype. Rock climbing possesses both masculine (high risk and strength) and feminine (good technique, balance and grace) characteristics. Having all the logistics and arrangements taken care of, commercial guided mountaineering offers women a more gender-neutral landscape, allowing distinct mountaineering identities to be forged, skills to be developed and specific ambitions to be realized. Gender studies offer much further scope of fascinating insights into the human dimensions of mountaineering tourism.

Place

Case Study 6 addresses global warming impacts on activities in high mountainous ecosystems such as alpine tourism, mountaineering and adventure tourism (Magrin *et al.* 2014). In Scotland, Harrison *et al.* (2005) reported that snow and ice climbing have become unreliable. Global warming results in increase frequency of high magnitude weather events, raising concern on the safety and security of mountain trekkers, who occasionally ventured on to higher elevation and faced with hostile and unpredictable weather. Rock faces are affected by permafrost, causing potential instability which put climbers in danger (Matasci 2012). New disease vectors may be introduced into areas where they previously did not exist, affecting destination attractiveness and health and safety considerations (Hall 2015). Fluctuating weather necessitates higher specification in the development of mountain paths and other related infrastructure.

Chapter 12 details that mountaineering and its related activities result in a range of environmental impacts on water, soils, vegetation and wildlife; and its intensity and extent are influenced by the type of use and behaviour of individual users, the amount and timing of use, the distribution of use and the environmental characteristics of the site (Liddle 1997; Monz *et al.* 2010; Pickering

2010). Environmental impacts arise from mountaineering and related activities that include hiking, rock climbing, back-country skiing, camping, helicopter use, pack animals and campsite services. Solid waste, such as steel cans and plastic bottles, can accumulate around huts, lodges and campsites along popular hiking and mountaineering routes, particularly in remote mountains (Ghimire *et al.* 2013; Byers 2014). The improper disposal of waste water in low altitude camp-sites pollutes pristine creeks; while urine, faeces and grey water discharges add nutrients to glacial lakes, changing the sensitive aquatic ecosystems (Clitherow *et al.* 2013). In high altitudes the transmission of water-borne diseases (e.g. col-iform bacteria) from faeces can persist on snow for extended periods (Goodwin *et al.* 2012). On Aconcagua, the management of human waste in campsites involved pit latrines in the alpine zones, and no official management system for human waste in the nival zone (Case Study 7). All human waste in pit latrines was left on site with the solid waste covered with soil and rocks once the pit was full.

In Nepal's Everest region, mountaineering and trekking have brought employ-ment and income opportunities to the communities along the trekking routes and to the region (Nyaupane *et al.* 2014) (refer Chapter 13 and Case Study 8). Together with economic prosperity, the activities also have brought social-ecological challenges, such as increase in number of inexperienced climbers, congestion on climbing routes, garbage management problems and safety con-cerns among the local Sherpa support team. Mt Everest has been crowded to the extent that it no longer offers mountaineering opportunities in its classic sense of adventure, exploration and discovery (Jenkins 2013). The number of trekkers and climbing permits has not been controlled by the Nepalese government because it is very likely to impact on many local people's livelihoods, and rev-enues for the country.

Ecological issues arising in the Khumbu region include deforestation, litter and waste, the trampling of vegetation and increased soil erosion in trekking areas (Byers 2005; Nyaupane *et al.* 2014; Stevens 2003). Many climbers have succumbed on Mt Everest and their bodies have remained on the mountain. Climbers have also left tents, equipment, empty oxygen canisters, batteries, cans, food wraps and many other items in the area. On 18 April 2014, 16 Sherpa died from an avalanche while fixing ropes for commercial guided climbers on the Khumbu icefall. Feeling insufficiently compensated by the government and expedition teams, Sherpa guides decided to abandon the entire climbing season. They demanded the government and expedition companies provide better insur-ance and compensation to Sherpa guides and their families. Many highly skilled Sherpa guides are taken for granted, underpaid and under/uninsured by some expeditions (Norgay 2014). Motivation, risk and death are perceived differently between western climbers and Sherpa (Ortner 1997). As western climbers, climbing for serious leisure, motivated to fulfil their inner self, the risk of acci-dent and death is worthwhile. Most Sherpa's primary motivation has always been for making a living (Ortner 1997), and any death will be tragic to the family members and Sherpa community.

With regards to health and safety issues, Chapter 15 and Case Study 9 highlight health ailments relevant to mountaineers as well as guides and porters. Chapter 15 proposes four factors which influence health and injuries among mountaineers. These are clients (mountaineers), equipment, uncontrollable factors and mountaineering operators. Mountaineer elements are determined by physical fitness, the present medical conditions, skill possessed, the ability to handle their own emergency and the presence of others. Equipment (e.g. ropes, crampons, pitons, ice axes) are all the objects required to facilitate the success of mountaineering. The uncontrollable elements in mountaineering include weather, mountain terrains/routes, snow and avalanches. The operators are the companies with staff employed to assist guided and non-guided mountaineers to reach the summit in climbing expeditions. They may include mountain guides, porters and base camp staff such as cooks. All four elements will influence mountaineers' susceptibility to health ailments and injuries in the mountains.

The most common ailments and injuries in the mountains are trauma, musculo-skeletal and soft tissue injuries, infections such as upper respiratory infection and diarrhoea, and high altitude sickness (Musa *et al.* 2004). In the Everest region, a significant number of deaths, and a major reason for admission to base camp medical facilities, are caused by high altitude cerebral oedema and high altitude pulmonary oedema. Once health ailments and injuries occur, dealing with them depends on the presence of medical expertise (individual and group), the availability of medical first aid kits, adequate insurance coverage and the presence of emergency deployment in the area. The availability of the stated elements will depend on the policy and regulation of the adventure tourism industry by governments of both destination and tourist generating regions. Chapter 13 highlights that climbing Mt Everest is actually safer now than in previous decades, if measured using the death per summit ratio which has dropped from 26.7 per cent in the 1980s to only 1 per cent in the 2000s. Factors attributed to this are better climbing equipment and safety gear, increased awareness of mountain hazards and better organized expeditions. Pomfret (2011) stated that, increasingly, numerous factors have facilitated an increase in people engaging in mountaineering, including gear improvements, high-tech support systems, improved tourist infrastructure, easier accessibility and diminished risk levels. With the exception of 1996, large commercial operators appear to have the safest record for climbing Mt Everest, measuring by number of deaths per climber summiting.

Case Study 8 and Case Study 9 highlight that guides and porters in the Everest region and Kilimanjaro have received considerable attention by the media, reflecting the increasing concern on ethical climbing around the world, raising questions about how climbers can contribute to better living standards for those working on mountains (Caulderwood 2014). The 'arduous and dangerous' conditions on Kilimanjaro recorded 20 guides and porters die every year on the mountain from altitude sickness, hypothermia and pneumonia (Christie *et al.* 2013). Porters in Kilimanjaro are often pressured to carry heavier weight, appear not to look sick and are deprived of fair remuneration, transport, medical care and food. Economic pressure, the need for continuous employment, the need for positive references for future tenure and extra tips result in porters hiding the realities of their own health conditions while working as porters on the mountains.

Management perspectives

Proper management of mountaineering tourism ensures mountaineers' satisfaction, mitigates misadventure and minimizes detrimental impacts on the environment and local community's welfare. For management considerations we maintain the discussion on the proposed issues using the three dimensions of the mountaineering tourism model which are the management of activity, people (mountaineers) and place.

Management of activity

Mountain awareness includes the provision of adequate training and guiding of mountaineering tourists through various certifications and accreditation schemes as well as the standard of equipment used. Training and certification schemes, and support from international and national mountain guides associations (Chapter 5), are crucial to professional safe guiding practices. There should be a plan for capacity building among local people (such as teaching them mountaineering skills) to ensure greater economic participation by residents in mountaineering tourism regions.

The International Union for the Conservation of Nature (IUCN)'s report stresses the complex nature of mountaineering tourism requiring site specific approaches, often with solutions that may seem to be paradoxical. For instance there are diverse opinions and numerous dilemmas surrounding the magnitude and diversity of infrastructure, in particular the practice of incorporating 'ladders, chains, abseil posts or other anchors, fixed bolts and pitons' (IUCN 2004: 56). The IUCN advocates cautious use of such devices unless visitor safety issues are paramount.

Another professional organization, the International Mountaineering and Climbing Federation (UIAA), also provides alternative support to mountaineering tourism. The organization accredits and certifies equipment such as alpine ropes and carabineers, advising on health and safety and promoting and regulating general ethics and codes relevant to alpinism (UIAA 2014b). The UIAA has led discussions on the pros (increased safety) and cons (harmful to natural terrain) of certain infrastructure aiming to provide balanced compromises in the management of mountain tourism activities (for instance bolting rock routes, see UIAA 2014a). Other mountaineering landscape setting features requiring consideration by mountain destination managers are huts, transportation networks, communication and base camp equipment.

Management of people (mountaineers)

There are two types of mountaineers who need to be managed accordingly to ensure mountaineering satisfaction. Serious mountaineers who mainly climb with internal motivations require pristine and uncrowded environments with a continuous challenge to maintain their ideal and expansion self (see Chapter 7). On the other hand for organized and commercially guided mountaineers, guides and mountaineering operators need to be mindful to guard the mountaineers' protective frame (Chapter 10). Mountaineers in this category, perform the activity within safety limits and comfort zones that are largely influenced by the guides, equipment, other climbers and the state of environment. Thus, for these mountaineers, providing a detailed and logistically well-organized itinerary may be highly desirable.

Case Study 5 reveals that on Mt Kinabalu knowledge is the only attitude dimension which influences responsible behaviour among mountaineers. Thus mountaineers should take opportunities to improve knowledge and necessary skills that are available in the mountain region. Knowledge could be conveyed either directly to the mountaineers or indirectly through their mountain guides and porters. Climbers need to be mindful of all aspects of responsible behaviour in the mountain towards the environment, local community and for their safety and security. Any climbing expedition or activity should be supported by easy medical access, a medical first aid kit, adequate insurance coverage and an emergency deployment system.

Management of place

Academic texts have suggested general management frameworks encompassing the environmental and social aspects of mountaineering tourism (Godde *et al.* 2000; Hales 2006). For instance, Godde *et al.* advocate that environmental stewardship and socio-cultural understanding between local communities, managers and visitors is essential for sustainable mountain tourism, preferably through the empowerment of local communities. Of the two crucial elements to be managed (environment and social culture), Wheale and Hinton (2007) suggested that amongst green consumers, two ethical drivers in the purchase decision-making process are related to the environment, followed by human and animal rights/welfare issues. Therefore we divide our 'place' management into environmental protection and local livelihoods.

Environmental protection

Generally alpine area managers use systems of peak permits or concessions to manage mountaineering tourism activities. Another management approach is to educate locals, trekkers, expedition members and their porters, guides and support staff about the environment and their responsibility of keeping the area clean and ecologically intact. The implementation of educational programmes, including minimum impact codes such as 'Leave No Trace' (https://lnt.org/learn/7-principles), the use of certified eco-labels, incentives to tour operators that implement good environmental practices should be stressed. Impact codes often recommend reducing packaging, packing out litter and food wastes, establishing minimum distances between campsites and water sources, and the use of eco-friendly products for cleaning (e.g. biodegradable soaps). Programmes to promote the removal of human waste practices include the use of cat holes, pack-out systems (refer Case Study 7) and surface disposal (Robinson 2010; Ells and Monz 2011). Other possible management approaches are solar dehydration toilets (Hill and Henry 2013), solid/liquid separation, better controls on pack-out systems, the implementation of environmental education programmes and regular monitoring of water quality.

Better design, development and maintenance of trails can minimize many of the physical (environmental) impacts of mountaineering (Marion and Leung 2004; Marion and Wimpey 2009). Selecting the right materials is important with dramatic differences among different trail materials used (Hill and Pickering 2006). Pack animals should be fed weed-free fodder to prevent the invasion of alien weed species in mountain regions. Reducing the introduction of weeds and pathogens involves ensuring good hygiene practices such as encouraging commercial operators and tourists to clean vehicles, boots and other equipment prior to arrival (Case Study 6). Stakeholders' collaboration in mountain regions can play an important role in effectively managing waste, and to reduce and replace the dependency on the forests to fuel source (Chapter 13 and Case Study 8). A commitment to environmental stewardship by land managers and sustainable environmental or socio-cultural behaviours amongst members of mountaineering expeditions or climbing parties is essential to ensure the ongoing attractiveness and sustainability of mountaineering destinations.

Local livelihoods

Mountaineering tourism needs to pay close attention to the livelihoods of the communities in mountain regions, to allow better economic and social opportunities and minimize socio-cultural impacts. Mountaineering provides local people with opportunities to participate in guiding and managing logistical support, retailing equipment and hospitality. Unlike in Nepal (e.g. Annapurna Conservation Area) where mountain tourism management incorporates decisions from local people (see Chapter 16), in Taiwan, mountain management often conflicts with the need of indigenous population (Case Study 2). In Yushan National Park (Taiwan), the government imposed its values and interest upon indigenous minorities (Chi and Wang 1996), resulting in continuing conflicts between the park service and the indigenous residents (Lai *et al.* 2013: 41).

Government organizations should be able to use a variety of management approaches to address safety hazards, compensation and benefits, permits and pollution with policies that are just, timely, transparent, accountable and beneficial to all stakeholders without compromising the ecological and social integrity of the local people (Chapter 16 and Case Study 8). Climbers, large expedition companies and small outfitters, and their guides already promote more ethical practices amongst commercial operations; however, such approaches can be more widespread. For Sherpa guides in the Everest region, Norgay (2014) proposes the need to establish a sensible 'code of operation' and stand behind it, which may include gaining better training and being competitive, and, at the same time, foreign expeditions and their leaders must see their role as more than providing a job and practise more socially responsible acts.

The International Union for the Conservation of Nature (IUCN) points out the benefits of accommodation (often huts) being located where local communities can benefit through remuneration as hut providers or suppliers; and the need to ensure mountain huts are accessible in emergency situations. The importance of up to date management approaches, and visitor information on alpine hazards, weather, route advice and health issues (and the presence of experienced search and rescue personnel) are also advocated by the IUCN (IUCN 2004: 59). Budeanu (2007) states that more information with regards to conditions of workers should be provided to facilitate informed ethical decision making. Climbing operators should ensure fair remuneration, proper climbing gear such as clothing and footwear, proper medical care, insurance coverage, transport and food for the guides and porters (Case Study 9).

Mountaineers should have the opportunity to select ethical operators, among whom are guiding companies with International Federation Mountain Guides' Associations (IFMGA/UIAGM) accreditation, membership of environmental certification schemes such as 'Leave No Trace' and voluntary adoption of code of ethics/codes of conduct. The role of managers or governing bodies of mountaineering tourism destinations, and that of international organizations, such as the IFMGA and not for profit groups, such as Tourism Concern, are essential in providing options for mountaineers in selecting ethical operators and promoting the rights of mountain workers. Ensuring guides are qualified to an international standard, and local porters equipped, cared for and paid fairly is one way mountain managers can promote a level of certainty about the risk managing capabilities and ethical approaches to operating mountaineering tourism services. Chapters 5 and 16 note the interactions with local communities by guides and clients are an increasingly important consideration. Also, geopolitical borders have challenges, not just at the start of expeditions where concessions or permits enable the commercial activities associated with mountaineering to take place, but throughout the duration of mountaineering trips.

The future of mountaineering tourism and research

Contemplating future mountaineering tourism raises a range of fascinating questions. Participation in mountaineering tourism has grown, and continues to grow, rapidly (Chapter 8). Climate change (Case Study 6) is unlikely to decrease the demand for mountaineering tourism experiences. Its resilience will witness innovative business diversification, or necessary adaptations utilizing infrastructure to access the environments within which visiting climbers, guides and support workers interact. In Scotland, there has been a shift towards mixed buttress climbing and a more general diversification of mountain experiences (Harrison *et al.* 2005). Alpine rock climbing and glacier hiking may be a form of adaptation for some locations (Beniston 2003).

The availability of guiding operators, the motivational forces of literature, film and other forms of media, technology assisted access, increasing leisure time available for recreation throughout the world, not to mention the commercialism of mountaineering through media and retail equipment stores, have seen high numbers of novices through to expert climbers engaging in mountaineering tourism. The movie industry has fuelled the demand for 'armchair experiences' and perhaps there is a conversion to actual participation in mountaineering, with film productions such as *K2* (1991), *Vertical Limit* (2000) and *Touching the Void* (2003), and the ever popular Banff Film Festival. Climbing and trekking retail stores, improved access and commercial guiding operations have also engaged participants who would not normally be tempted above the snowline.

On the mountain routes themselves, there will be more adaptation which results in permanent infrastructure, via ferrata and permanent ropes and bolts, for example, to facilitate greater access of inexperienced guided mountaineering tourists. Technological improvements are increasingly allowing inexperienced mountaineers to explore and venture further into high altitudes despite the rarified air and extreme cold temperatures and winds.

The future will also see the continuous monitoring of environmental impacts for the benefit of both operators and mountain area managers, to facilitate appropriate and effective management approaches to businesses and settings. The impact of climate change and changing biodiversity in alpine areas are also relevant to the field of mountaineering tourism. Place-based management approaches and comparative studies that cross geographical boundaries and provide international data for benchmarking and standards setting will continue to be shared through networks facilitated by organizations such as the UIAA, IFMGA and IUCN (not to mention national tourism organizations and land management agencies in countries with a high level of mountain tourism activities).

From a theoretical perspective, the philosophies, changing values, attitudes and other psychological aspects of the mountaineering tourism experience deserve ongoing attention. Histories of mountain tourism destinations, including development, but also cultural, spiritual and religious aspects, need to be researched and written. Research exploring social issues including community development, workers' rights and aged or gendered influences would further illustrate the human dimensions of mountaineering tourism. Other research issues that need to be attended to with some urgency include managing impacts from crowding and commodification of mountains with spiritual significance of cultural values to local peoples. Sensitive and authentic cultural interpretation about intangible and tangible cultural heritage can ensure local values for spiritually or traditionally significant mountain areas are an outcome of such research (Carr 2004; Pfister 2000).

Research into the development of mountaineering businesses can inform the academic disciplines of marketing, management, entrepreneurship and leisure studies. The impact of literature, film and media (media induced factors related to mountaineering tourism) and the role of social media influencing mountaineers' motivations, their decision making and social networking can inform marketing strategies and social relationships. More importantly content analysis exploring the real time reporting of mountaineers' satisfaction levels with the activity (e.g. via blogs and social media) deserves further critique.

The influence of technology that may be used during climbing or on expeditions, including computers, personal locator beacons, GPS, smart phones and APPs; and how the adoption of such technology in the mountains transforms the mountaineers' experiences both socially but also from the perspective of risk management and safety are also worthy of attention.

Finally, further research exploring the psychological and physiological dimensions of those engaging in mountaineering activities – both the mountaineers and the local workers – would have a real impact on health and safety, and risk management perspectives.

Concluding remarks

This book details perspectives of mountaineering tourism within a theoretical framework that holistically explores activity, people and place. Contributors' chapters discuss the history and development of mountaineering (guided and non-guided), the development of guiding as a profession, gender and equity issues, personal experiences of mountaineers and mountaineering tourists and psychological aspects of mountaineering as an extreme sport. The ethical issues surrounding mountaineers' decision making, involvement of local communities and the working conditions of porters and guides are examined. The roles of clubs, companies, governments and international organizations including the IFMGA, UIAA and IUCN are explained through relevant examples. Business and management approaches from international, national and regional perspectives provide insight into best practice and future challenges facing mountain tourism entrepreneurs and managers. Environmental issues affecting mountaineering tourism such as climate change, and the need to manage the negative environmental impacts arising from mountaineering tourism activities are addressed. Examples and case studies from a range of mountaineering tourism destinations, spanning most continents add insights into the diversity of experiences and management approaches.

'Mountain adventure tourism will continue to grow, and the risks inherent in the activities are likely to appear to diminish as knowledge, experience, and technical capacity increases' (Beedie and Hudson 2003: 640). Although a decade has elapsed since Beedie and Hudson wrote about the future of mountaineering adventure tourism, and despite the challenges facing the mountaineering tourism as influenced by external forces such as climate change and socio-political turmoil, their words are still valid. Whether mountaineering tourism can evolve in a manner that is beneficial to the environment, tourists, guiding companies and local communities will largely depend on such factors as ethical decision making, experienced risk management, appropriate infrastructure, enhancement of workers' rights, entrepreneurial adaptations and environmentally sustainable behaviours that counteract such challenges. Informed management at local levels that must be led and resourced with prudent governance by national and international organizations, will be essential for the future of mountaineering tourism. This book critically explores a selection of contemporary issues arising from and challenging the development of mountaineering tourism. There is little doubt, given the dynamic nature of this subject of enquiry, that mountaineering tourism offers fertile ground for critical tourism studies both now and in the future.

References

Allman, T. L., Mittelstaedt, R. D., Martin, B. and Goldenberg, M. (2009) 'Exploring the motivations of BASE jumpers: Extreme sport enthusiast', *Journal of Sport and Tourism*, 14(4): 229–247.

Apter, M. J. (1993) 'Phenomenological frames and the paradoxes of experience', in J. H. Kerr, S. J. Murgatroyd and M. J. Apter (eds) *Advances in reversal theory*, Amsterdam: Swets & Zeitlinger: 27–39.

Atkinson, J. W. (1964) *An introduction to motivation*, New York: Van Nostrand.

Beedie, P. (2003) 'Mountain guiding and adventure tourism: Reflections on the choreography of the experience', *Leisure Studies*, 22(2): 147–167.

Beedie, P. (2010) *Mountain based adventure tourism*, Saarbrucken: Lambert Academic Publishing.

Beedie, P. (2013) 'The adventure enigma: An analysis of mountain based adventure tourism in Britain', in S. Taylor, P. Varley and T. Johnston (eds) *Adventure tourism: Meanings, experience and learning, contemporary geographies of leisure tourism and mobility series*, London: Routledge: 22–33.

Beedie, P. and Hudson, S. (2003) 'Emergence of mountain-based adventure tourism', *Annals of Tourism Research*, 30(3): 625–643.

Benbaum, E. (2006) 'Sacred mountains: Themes and teachings', *Mountain Research and Development*, 26(4): 304–309.

Beniston, M. (2003) 'Climatic change in mountain regions: A review of possible impacts', *Climatic Change*, 59(1–2): 5–31.

Berlyne, D. E. (1960) *Conflict, arousal and curiosity*, New York: McGraw-Hill.

Blyth, S., Groombridge, B., Lysenko, I., Miles, L. and Newton, A. (2002) *Mountain watch: Environmental change and sustainable developmental in mountains*, Cambridge: UNEP World Conservation Monitoring Centre.

Boekholt, K. (1983) 'The Copland track', unpublished diploma dissertation, Parks and Recreation, Lincoln College, Christchurch.

Brymer, E. (2012) 'Transforming adventures: Why extreme sports should be included in adventure programming', in B. Martin and M. Wagstaff (eds) *Controversial issues in adventure programming*, Champaign, IL: Human Kinetics: 165–174.

Buckley, R. (2012) 'Rush as a key motivation in skilled adventure tourism: Resolving the risk recreation paradox', *Tourism Management*, 33(4): 961–970.

Budeanu, A. (2007) 'Sustainable tourist behaviour: A discussion of opportunities for change', *International Journal of Consumer Studies*, 31(5): 499–508.

Byers, A. (2014) 'Contemporary human impacts on subalpine and alpine ecosystems of the Hinku Valley, Makalu-Barun National Park and Buffer Zone, Nepal', *Himalaya, the Journal of the Association for Nepal and Himalayan Studies*, 33(1): 25–41.

Byers, A. C. (2005) 'Contemporary human impacts on alpine ecosystems in the Sagarmatha (Mt. Everest) National Park, Khumbu, Nepal', *Annals of the Association of American Geographers*, 95(1): 112–140.

Carnicelli-Filho, S., Schwartz, G. M. and Tahara, A. K. (2009) 'Fear and adventure tourism in Brazil', *Tourism Management*, 31(6): 953–956.

Carr, A. (2001) 'Alpine adventurers in the Pacific Rim', *Pacific Tourism Review*, 4(4): 161–170.

Carr, A. (2004) 'Mountain places, cultural spaces: Interpretation and sustainable visitor management of culturally significant landscapes, a case study of Aoraki/Mount Cook National Park', *Journal of Sustainable Tourism*, 12(5): 432–459.

Castanier, C., Le Scanff, C. and Woodman, T. (2010) 'Who takes risks in high-risk sports? A typological personality approach', *Research Quarterly for Exercise and Sport*, 81(4): 478–484.

Cater, C. I. (2006) 'Playing with risk? Participant perceptions of risk and management implications in adventure tourism', *Tourism Management*, 27(2): 317–325.

Caulderwood, K. (2014) 'As Everest Sherpas boycott climbing season, the porters on Kilimanjaro work for less', *International Business Times*, 30 April. Online, available at: www.ibtimes.com/everest-sherpas-boycott-climbing-season-porters-kilimanjaro-work-less-1577402 (accessed 29 August 2014).

Celsi, R. L., Rose, R. L. and Leigh, T. W. (1993) 'Exploration of high-risk leisure consumption through skydiving', *Journal of Consumer Research*, 20(1): 1–21.

Chi, C.-C. and Wang, J. C. S. (1996) 'Environmental justice: An analysis of the conflicts between aboriginal peoples and national parks in Taiwan'. Online, available at: http://wildmic.npust.edu.tw/sasala (accessed 18 February 2014).

Christie, I., Fernandes, E., Messerli, H. and Twining-Ward, L. (2013) *Tourism in Africa: Harnessing tourism for growth and improved livelihoods*, Washington DC: World Bank. Online, available at: http://documents.worldbank.org/curated/en/2013/01/18320011/tourism-africa-harnessing-tourism-growth-improved-livelihoods (accessed 1 September 2014).

Clitherow, L. R., Carrivick, J. L. and Brown, L. E. (2013) 'Food web structure in a harsh glacier-fed river', *PLoS ONE*, 8(4): e60899.

Cronin, C. (1991) 'Sensation seeking among mountain climbers', *Personality and Individual Differences*, 12(6): 653–654.

Csikszentmihalyi, M. (1988) 'The flow experience and its significance for human psychology', in M. Csikszentmihalyi and I. S. Csikszentmihalyi (eds) *Optimal experience: Psychological studies of flow in consciousness*, New York: Cambridge University Press: 15–35.

Csikszentmihalyi, M. (1990) *Flow: The psychology of optimal experience*, New York: Harper & Row.

Csikszentmihalyi, M. and Csikszentmihalyi, I. S. (1990) 'Adventure and the flow experience', in J. C. Miles and S. Priest (eds) *Adventure education*, State College, PA: Venture: 149–156.

Davidson, L. (2002) 'The "spirit of the hills": Mountaineering in northwest Otago, New Zealand 1882–1940', *Tourism Geographies*, 4(1), 44–61.

Davidson, L. (2011) 'On nature's terms: Preserving the practice of traditional backcountry recreation in New Zealand's national parks', in E. Dorfman (ed.) *Intangible natural heritage: New perspectives on natural objects*, New York: Routledge: 105–124.

Diehm, R. and Armatas, C. (2004) 'Surfing: An avenue for socially acceptable risk taking, satisfying needs for sensation seeking and experience seeking', *Personality and Individual Differences*, 36(3): 663–677.

Ells, M. D. and Monz, C. A. (2011) 'The consequences of backcountry surface disposal of human waste in an alpine, temperate forest and arid environment', *Journal of Environmental Management*, 92(4): 1334–1337.

Esfahani, M., Musa, G. and Khoo, S. (2014) 'The influence of spirituality and physical activity level on responsible behaviour and mountaineering satisfaction on Mount Kinabalu, Borneo', *Current Issues in Tourism*, DOI: 10.1080/13683500.2014.987733.

Ewert, A. and Hollenhorst, S. (1989) 'Testing the adventure model: Empirical support for a model of risk recreation participation', *Journal of Leisure Research*, 21(2): 124–139.

Faullant, R., Matzler, K. and Mooradian, T. A. (2011) 'Personality, basic emotions, and satisfaction: Primary emotions in the mountaineering experience', *Tourism Management*, 32(6): 1423–1430.

Fowler, C. J., Von Knorring, L. and Oreland, L. (1980) 'Platelet monoamine oxidase activity in sensation seekers', *Psychiatry Research*, 3(3): 273–279.

Freixanet, M. G. (1991) 'Personality profile of subjects engaged in high physical risk sports', *Personality and Individual Differences*, 12(10): 1087–1093.

Frohlick, S. (1999) 'The "hypermasculine" landscape of high-altitude mountaineering', *Michigan Feminist Studies*, 14(1999–2000): 83–106.

Ghimire, N. P., Caravellol, G. and Jha, P. K. (2013) 'Bacterial contamination in the surface waterbodies in Sagarmatha National Park and Buffer Zone, Nepal', *Scientific World*, 11(11): 94–96.

Giddens, A. (1990) *The consequences of modernity*, Cambridge: Polity Press.

Godde, P. M., Price, M. F. and Zimmermann, F. M. (2000) *Tourism and development in mountain regions*, Wallingford: CABI Publishing.

Goodwin, K., Loso, M. G. and Braun, M. (2012) 'Glacial transport of human waste and survival of fecal bacteria on Mt. McKinley's Kahiltna Glacier, Denali National Park, Alaska', *Arctic, Antarctic, and Alpine Research*, 44(4): 432–445.

Hales, R. (2006) 'Mountaineering', in R. Buckley (ed.) *Adventure tourism*, Wallingford: CAB International: 260–281.

Hall, C. M. (2015) 'Tourism and biological exchange and invasions: A missing dimension in sustainable tourism?' *Tourism Recreation Research*, 40(1), in press.

Hall, C. M. and Page, S. J. (2002) 'Tourism and recreation in the pleasure periphery', in C. M. Hall and S. J. Page (eds) *The geography of tourism and recreation* (2nd edn), London: Routledge: 249–282.

Harrison, S. J., Winterbottom, S. J. and Johnson, R. C. (2005) 'Changing snow cover and winter tourism and recreation in the Scottish Highlands', in C. M. Hall and J. Higham (eds) *Tourism, recreation and climate change*, Clevedon: Channel View: 143–154.

Heider, F. (1958) *The psychology of interpersonal relations*, New York: Wiley.

Heywood, I. (1994) 'Urgent dreams: Climbing, rationalization and ambivalence', *Leisure Studies*, 13(3), 179–194.

Hill, G. and Henry, G. (2013) 'The application and performance of urine diversion to minimize waste management costs associated with remote wilderness toilets', *Journal of Wilderness*, 19(1): 26–33.

Hill, W. and Pickering, C. M. (2006) 'Vegetation associated with different walking track types in the Kosciuszko alpine area, Australia', *Journal of Environmental Management*, 78(1): 24–34.

Houge Mackenzie, S. and Kerr, J. (2013) 'Stress and emotions at work: Adventure tourism guiding experiences in South America', *Tourism Management*, 36(June): 3–14.

IUCN (2004) 'Guidelines for planning and managing mountain protected areas', (synthesized and edited by L. Hamilton and L. McMillan), IUCN, Gland, Switzerland, and IUCN World Commission on Protected Area, Cambridge.

Jack, S. J. and Ronan, K. R. (1998) 'Sensation seeking among high- and low-risk sports participants', *Personality and Individual Differences*, 25(6): 1063–1083.

Jenkins, M. (2013) 'Maxed out on Everest', *National Geographic*, 223(6): 84–88. Online, available at: http://ngm.nationalgeographic.com/2013/06/125-everest-maxed-out/jenkins-text (accessed 10 October 2014).

Johnston, B. and Edwards, T. (1994) 'The commodification of mountaineering', *Annals of Tourism Research*, 21(3): 459–478.

Johnston, M. (1989) 'Peak experiences: Challenge and danger in mountain recreation in New Zealand', unpublished doctoral dissertation, University of Canterbury, Christchurch.

Johnston, M. (1992) 'Facing the challenges: Adventure in the mountains of New Zealand', in B. Weiler and C. Hall (eds) *Special interest tourism*, London: Belhaven Press: 159–169.

Johnston, M. (1993) 'Diffusion and difference: The subcultural framework for mountain climbing in New Zealand', *Tourism Recreation Research*, 18(1): 38–44.

Kiewa, J. (2002) 'Traditional climbing: Metaphor of resistance or metanarrative of oppression?' *Leisure Studies*, 21: 145–161.

Klausner, S. (ed.) (1968) *Why man takes chances: Studies in stress-seeking*, New York: Anchor Books.

Lai, P.-H., Hsu, Y.-C. and Nepal, S. K. (2013) 'Representing the landscape of Yushan national park', *Annals of Tourism Research*, 43: 37–57.

Liddle, M. (1997) *Recreation ecology: The Ecological impact of outdoor recreation and ecotourism*, London: Chapman & Hall.

Ling, M. J. (2008) *Centenary history of Taiwan mountaineering*, Taipei: Taiwan Interminds.

Lockwood, N. C. (2011) 'Motivations for mountain climbing: The role of risk', unpublished doctoral thesis, University of Sussex.

Logan, J. (2006) 'Crampons and cook pots: The democratization and feminisation of adventure on Aconcagua', in L. A. Vivanco and R. J. Gordon (eds) *Tarzan was an eco-tourist … and other tales in the anthropology of adventure*, Oxford: Berghahn Books: 161–178.

Lyng, S. (1990) 'Edgework: A social psychological analysis of voluntary risk taking', *American Journal of Sociology*, 95(4): 851–886.

Macfarlane, R. (2003) *Mountains of the mind: A history of a fascination*, London: Granta.

Magrin, G., Marengo, J., Boulanger, J.-P., Buckeridge, M. S., Castellanos, E., Poveda, G., Scarano, F. R. and Vicuña, S. (2014) 'Central and South America', in *Climate change 2014: Impacts, adaptation, and vulnerability, contribution of working group II to the fifth assessment report of the intergovernmental panel for climate change*, Cambridge: Cambridge University Press.

Marion, J. L. and Leung, Y. F. (2004) 'Environmentally sustainable trail management', in R. C. Buckley (ed.) *Environmental impact of tourism*, London: CABI Publishing: 229–244.

Marion, J. L. and Wimpey, J. (2009) *Monitoring protocols for characterizing trail conditions, understanding degradation, and selecting indicators and standards of quality, Acadia National Park, Mount Desert Island*, Blacksburg, VA: Virginia Tech College of Natural Resources.

Martinoia, R. (2013) 'Women's mountaineering and dissonances within the mountain guide profession: "Don't go thinking he was a guide for the ladies"', *Journal of Alpine Research*, 101–110.

Maslow, A. (1968) *Toward a psychology of being*, Princeton, NJ: D. Van Nostrand Company Inc.

Matasci, C. (2012) 'Swiss tourism in the age of climate change: Vulnerability, adaptive capacity, and barriers to adaptation', unpublished doctoral thesis, École Polytechnique Fédérale de Lausanne.

Mitchell, R. G. (1983) *Mountain experience: The psychology and sociology of adventure*, Chicago, IL: University of Chicago Press.

Monasterio, E., Mulder, R., Frampton, C. and Mei-Dan, O. (2012) 'Personality characteristics of BASE jumpers', *Journal of Applied Sport Psychology*, 24(4): 391–400.

Monasterio, E., Alamri, Y. A. and Mei-Dan, O. (2014) 'Personality characteristics in a population of mountain climbers', *Wilderness and Environmental Medicine*, 25(2): 214–219.

Monz, C. A., Cole, D. N., Leung, Y. F. and Marion, J. L. (2010) 'Sustaining visitor use in protected areas: Future opportunities in recreation ecology research based on the USA experience', *Environmental Management*, 45(3): 551–562.

Moraldo, D. (2013) 'Gender relations in French and British mountaineering: A lens of autobiographies of female mountaineers, from d'Angeville (1794–1871) to Destivelle (1960)', *Journal of Alpine Research*, 101-1: 2–12.

Mowforth, M. and Munt, I. (2008) *Tourism and sustainability: New tourism in the third world* (3rd edn), London: Routledge.

Musa, G., Hall, M. and Higham, J. (2004) 'Tourism sustainability and health impacts in high altitude adventure, cultural and ecotourism destinations: A case study of Nepal's Sagarmatha National Park', *Journal of Sustainable Tourism*, 12(4): 306–331.

Næss, A. (1989) *Ecology, community and lifestyle: Outline of an ecosophy*, Cambridge: Cambridge University Press.

Neves, K. (2004) 'Revisiting the tragedy of the commons: Whale watching in the Azores and its ecological dilemmas', *Human Organization*, 63(3): 289–300.

Neves, K. (2010) 'Critical business uncritical conservation: The invisibility of dissent in the world of marine ecotourism', *Current Conservation*, January(2010): 18–21.

Norgay, D. T. (2014) 'The Sherpas' guide to ethical behavior. Project syndicate: The world's opinion', 26 April. Online, available at: www.project-syndicate.org/commentary/curtis-s-chin-and-dhamey-t-norgay-consider-the-responsibility-of-rich-country-consumers-toward-poor-country-workers (accessed 26 October 2014).

Noyce, W. (1958) *The springs of adventure*, New York: World Publishing Company.

Nyaupane, G. P., Lew, A. and Tatsugawa, K. (2014) 'Perceptions of trekking tourism and social and environmental change in Nepal's Himalayas', *Tourism Geographies*, 16(3): 415–437.

Ortner, S. B. (1997) 'Thick resistance: Death and the cultural construction of agency in Himalayan mountaineering', *Representations*, 59(1): 135–162.

Pfister, R. (2000) 'Mountain culture as a tourism resource: Aboriginal views on the privileges of storytelling', in P. Godde, M. Price and F. Zimmerman (eds) *Tourism and development in mountain regions*, Wallingford: CABI Publishing: 115–136.

Pickering, C. M. (2010) 'Ten factors that affect the severity of environmental impacts of visitors in protected areas', *Ambio*, 39(1): 70–77.

Pomfret, G. (2006) 'Mountaineering adventure tourists: A conceptual framework for research', *Tourism Management*, 27(1): 113–123.

Pomfret, G. (2011) 'Package mountaineer tourist holidaying in the French Alps: An evaluation of key influences encouraging their participation', *Tourism Management*, 32(3): 501–510.

Robinson, R. (2010) 'Leave no waste: The evolution of clean climbing practices in Denali National Park', Proceedings of 'Exit strategies: Managing human waste in the wild', American Alpine Club, Golden, CO, 30–31 July and August. Online, available at: www.americanalpineclub.org/p/exit-strategies-supplement (accessed 3 March 2015).

Sports Affairs Council ROC (Taiwan) (2003) '2002 annual report'. Online, available at: www.sac.gov.tw/WebData/WebData.aspx?WDID=69&wmid=500 (accessed 2 March 2010).

Stebbins, R. A. (2007) *Serious leisure: A perspective for our time*, New Brunswick, NJ: Transaction.

Stevens, S. F. (2003) 'Tourism and deforestation in the Mt Everest regional of Nepal', *Geographical Journal*, 169(3): 255–277.

Taylor, C. (1989) *Sources of the self: The making of modern identity*. Cambridge, MA: Harvard University Press.

Todd, S. L., Anderson, L., Young, A. and Anderson, D. (2002) 'The relationship of motivation factors to level of development in outdoor adventure recreationists', *Research in Outdoor Education*, 6: 124–138.

UIAA (2014a) Online, available at: http://theuiaa.org/to-bolt-or-not-to-be.html (accessed 14 November 2014).

UIAA (2014b) Online, available at: www.theuiaa.org/news-161-Advice-sheet-on-risks-of-drug-use-in-the-mountains-developed-by-UIAA-Medical-Commission.html (accessed 14 November 2014).

Varley, P. (2006) 'Confecting adventure and playing with meaning: The adventure commodification continuum', *Journal of Sport and Tourism*, 11(2): 173–194.

Vester, H.-G. (1987) 'Adventure as a form of leisure', *Leisure Studies*, 6: 237–249.

Weed, M. (2005) 'Sports tourism theory and method: Concepts, issues and epistemologies', *Sport Management Quarterly*, 5(3): 229–242.

Weed, M. E. and Bull, C. J. (2004) *Sport tourism: Participants, policy and providers*, Oxford: Butterworth Heinemann.

Wheale, P. and Hinton, D. (2007) 'Ethical consumers in search of markets', *Business Strategy and the Environment*, 16(4): 4302–4315.

Williams, S. and Lew, A. A. (2014) *Tourism geography* (3rd edn), Oxford: Routledge.

Zuckerman, M. (1979) *Sensation seeking: Beyond the optimal level of arousal*, Hillsdale, NJ: Erlbaum.

Zuckerman, M. (1983) 'Sensation seeking and sports', *Personality and Individual Differences*, 4(3): 285–294.

Index

For Product Safety Concerns and Information please contact our
EU representative GPSR@taylorandfrancis.com Taylor & Francis
Verlag GmbH, Kaufingerstraße 24, 80331 München, Germany